Numbers in Motion

A Balanced Approach to Measurement and Evaluation in Physical Education

Library of Congress Catalog Card Number: 79-91835
International Standard Book Number: 0-87484-503-3

Manufactured in the United States of America
Mayfield Publishing Company
285 Hamilton Avenue, Palo Alto, California 94301

This book was set in Bookman and Helvetica by Chapman's
Phototypesetting; the cover was printed by Autoscreen Lehigh
and the text was printed and bound by Von Hoffmann Press.
Sponsoring editor was C. Lansing Hays, Maggie Cutler
supervised editing, and Cheryl Smith was manuscript editor.
Book design by Nancy Sears and cover design by Russ Leong.
Technical art prepared by Pat Rogondino. Photo editor was
Roberta Spieckerman and textual photographs by Sara Bess
Wood. Michelle Hogan supervised production.

Credit for Chapter Opening Photographs

Chapter 1 / Courtesy, University of California Archives, The
Bancroft Library   *Chapter 2* / Tom Gillespie/Camera South
Chapter 3 / Lorraine Rorke   *Chapter 4* / Janet Fries/Icon
Chapter 5 / H. S. Chapman/Icon   *Chapter 6* / Gordon Clark/
Icon   *Chapter 7* / Tom Gillespie/Camera South   *Chapter 8* /
L. D. Dwinell   *Chapter 9* / H. S. Chapman/Icon   *Chapter 10* /
Elizabeth Crews/Icon   *Chapter 11* / Elizabeth Crews/Icon
Chapter 12 / L. D. Dwinell   *Chapter 13* / Cheryl A. Traendly/
Icon   *Chapter 14* / Elizabeth Crews/Icon   *Chapter 15* /
Michelle Vignes/Icon   *Chapter 16* / Suzanne Arms/Jeroboam
Chapter 17 / Lorraine Rorke   *Chapter 18* / Gordon Clark/Icon
Chapter 19 / Janet Fries/Icon   *Chapter 20* / L. D. Dwinell
Chapter 21 / Jim Engle

Contents

v

Dedication

All the world's a stage
And all the men and women
merely players
They have their exits and their
entrances

Shakespeare
As You Like it

To Jamie Bryan Mood (May 14, 1969– May 2, 1971)
whose curtain call came before his
part was established.

Preface

Until approximately fifteen years ago there were only a few textbooks available in the area of measurement in physical education. In general, those initially published prior to 1965 consist mainly of descriptions and procedures for administering and scoring a great number of relevant tests constructed since the beginnings of measurement within physical education. These books continue to serve a valuable function as resource banks of tests.

In the early 1970s a change began in the subject matter emphasized in physical education measurement textbooks. The content began dealing less with previously constructed tests and more with a detailed description of the methods for constructing one's own tests. Probably two factors are most responsible for this shift in themes.

First, the list of constructed tests has grown so that it is increasingly difficult to incorporate all tests into one book. (A consequence of this is the appearance of measurement books concentrating in one area—exercise science, for example.) Second, and more important, testing conditions have become so specific—due to differences in philosophy, needs, facilities, equipment, and the like—that the "catalog of tests" approach is no longer adequate.

Given the important knowledges concerning construction techniques, the physical education teacher should be capable of building the best test for his or her specific situation. That is the basis of this book. Techniques and suggestions for testing mental, social, and physical performance objectives of physical education, from planning to analysis, are presented in this book. Armed with this information, some practical experience, and a great deal of common sense, a physical educator should be able to implement a sound and meaningful measurement program.

Two criteria were applied when examining the myriad of tests for possible inclusion in this book. Both were based on usefulness. First, the tests had to be useful to a physical education teacher rather than a physical education researcher. Second, most tests presented are practical (in terms of time, equipment, and expense).

Some of the tests presented might be adopted without change by the physical educator, but because great differences occur in objectives, students, and facilities throughout the country, most of these tests will require modification to fit a particular situation. The ability to modify existing tests is becoming increasingly important due to recent legislation (Title IX, P.L. 94 – 142) putting the physical educator in contact with a wider variety of students than in the past. The major purpose of the descriptions and lists of tests is to provide a source for ideas around which each physical educator may develop measuring devices to fit his or her own circumstances.

The author wishes to express sincere gratitude for help received in preparing this book. Thanks to my teachers who started me on this path. Thanks to my students who served as subjects during the experimental stages for many of the suggestions that appear (and some that do not) in this book. Thanks to authors of tests for permission to present the tests they devised. And finally a special thanks to my wife Maureen, for typing the manuscript, and to all of my family for the sacrifices they made in order that this book could be written.

SECTION 1

INTRODUCTION

Chapter 1

Measurement in Physical Education

A PHILOSOPHY OF EDUCATION

The fundamental purpose of education is to prepare youth to cope with their surroundings. No matter how primitive or advanced a society, the task of its educators is to teach the knowledges and skills necessary for survival. The more complex the society, the more complex this educational process. For example, in a primitive setting the emphasis of "education" is on physical survival and rituals. In our complex society the process of education involves virtually every knowledge and skill from tying shoes to landing on the moon.

The number of different situations for which youth in a primitive society must be prepared is limited in comparison to the infinite situations for which youth in a complex society must be prepared. Since it is impossible to prepare for each specific life situation, basic knowledges and skills must be taught and the ability to utilize these fundamentals in new situations fostered. To accomplish this, education in modern society has become general rather than specific. Subject areas such as reading education, science education, physical education, and the like have evolved.

OBJECTIVES OF PHYSICAL EDUCATION

Lists of the general aims and objectives of physical education as expressed by leaders in the field can be found in the professional literature. Most of these contain basically similar information. Generally the following four headings are recognized: (1) physical development, (2) motor development, (3) mental development, and (4) social development.

When the physical educator teaches a particular unit, he or she should have in mind specific objectives that describe the way in which the unit promotes the general physical education objectives. For example, in a high school weight training unit, one of the specific objectives might be the development of upper arm strength. This is one of many possible specifics that might be listed under the general objective of physical development mentioned above. The important fact to realize at this point is not what the specific objectives of physical education are but rather that they exist.

MEASUREMENT IN TEACHING

E. L. Thorndike once stated, "Whatever exists at all exists in some amount."[1] William A. McCall later expanded this notion by stating that "Anything that exists in amount can be measured."[2] Not only *can* the objectives of physical education be measured but it is imperative that they *are* measured, for otherwise it is not possible to know whether the important goals of physical education are being accomplished.

This measurement, to be effective, requires that the physical educator know how and what to measure and how to organize the resulting data into meaningful information. This in turn requires constructing or selecting the proper test and knowing the techniques of administering and evaluating measuring devices.

Proper measurement practices are necessary in each of the four steps of teaching:

1. Determining the objectives of instruction.
2. Selecting the methods and materials to be used during instruction.
3. Executing the teaching plan using the selected materials.
4. Evaluating to see if the objectives were met.

Determining reasonable objectives for a particular group of students implies knowledge about these students' needs, interests, and abilities. These

are frequently assessed through a variety of subjective and objective measuring devices.

Selecting methods and materials for instruction also suggests an evaluative process. The establishment of criteria as the basis for this selection, for example, is a measurement procedure, as is the testing of possible methods and materials against these criteria.

During the teaching process itself the physical educator should continually be measuring to determine what is working effectively and what is not. Again, techniques that apply to subjective and objective measurement should be utilized.

Certainly the most obvious step for the application of measurement procedures is the fourth. If this step is omitted, little improvement in teaching is possible. Application of all manners of measuring devices and techniques is called for in this step.

It is important to notice that the four steps presented above actually form a complete circle because step one follows step four to begin the process over again. In addition, if the decision at step four is that objectives have not been met, all steps must be examined to determine possible modification. Perhaps the original objectives were too difficult, or the approach and materials used were not selected properly. The teacher's actual delivery of the concept may require change or the evaluation of the success or lack of it in meeting the objectives might have been faulty.

The processes of measurement are based for the most part on common sense and proper application of various tools and procedures. Over time these instruments and methods have undergone some changes. Since present practices are often derived from previous experiences, it is often valuable to examine the past.

A BRIEF HISTORY OF MEASUREMENT IN PHYSICAL EDUCATION

1776–1860

The United States was predominantly an agrarian society until the industrial revolution, which had its beginnings around the turn of the century. From 1776–1830, education in the United States was mostly provided by and for the aristocratic segments of the population. This was the era of the Latin grammar school with educational emphasis on classical studies. Beginning in the 1830s a trend toward more useful education developed, and the population of the United States began to realize the necessity of universal education supported by taxes.

Physical education was very unstructured throughout this period. The basic influences on physical activity during the later stages were Pestalozzi and his disciple Joseph Neff, the German Turners, and the establishment of various religious organizations such as the YMCA. In general the philosophy of these individuals and organizations was that physical activity (mostly in the form of gymnastic movements) should be engaged in for healthful reasons and to serve as a diversion from other aspects of life. Measurement in physical education was virtually nonexistent during this time.

1860–1900

Some historians cite the early part of this period as the beginning of formal physical education in the United States. In 1861 Dr. Edward Hitchcock was appointed director of the department of hygiene and physical education at Amherst College. The establishment of such a department by William Stearns, the president of Amherst, gave academic status to the discipline of physical education for the first time. Like Dr. Hitchcock, many of the physical education leaders of this period had medical degrees and as youths had become interested in gymnastics. Dr. Dudley Sargent, professor of physical education at Harvard, Dr. Edward M. Hartwell, director of physical education at Johns Hopkins, and Dr. William G. Anderson, associate director of the gymnasium of Yale University, are examples of such men.

The medical backgrounds of many of the physical education leaders of this period probably explains their interest in anthropometric measurements. Students at Amherst College were periodically given a series of tests centered around anthropometric and strength measures. Cromwell investigated the growth patterns of boys and girls between the ages of eight and eighteen. Statues of the typical male and female, constructed on the basis of a vast number of anthropometric measurements taken and recorded by Sargent, were displayed at the 1893 World's Fair in Chicago.

The most common form of organized physical activity during this period was gymnastics. Individuals advocated use of the German or Swedish systems or systems they themselves had developed. The German system involved apparatus work and free exercise; the Swedish system was more scientifically and medically oriented. Dio Lewis and Francois Delsarte are two who advocated use of their own gymnastics systems.

Although the schools of the time were heavily influenced by the proponents of these various gymnastics systems, the beginnings of two other forms of physical activity—strength development and athletics—can be traced to this period. The exercise regimes of George Winship and William Blackie are examples of programs devised during this period for the purpose of developing and maintaining strength. As previously mentioned, Hitchcock's periodic testing at Amherst involved strength measures. Sargent also expressed an interest in the measurement of strength. In fact, he devised a battery of tests that included items intended to measure the strength of the legs, back, grip, arms, and respiratory muscles. This test battery became known as the Intercollegiate Strength Test and was used as a basis for intercollegiate competition. It was later revised by Rogers and later still by McCloy. Thus the development and consequently the measurement of various strength parameters gradually became integrated with the existing anthropometric measurement programs in this period.

Athletic programs, both intramural and intercollegiate, were common at many of the educational institutions during this period. However, athletics were primarily considered to be of recreational value, with gymnastics and physical training programs serving as the basis for physical education classes. Many events — the establishment of the United States Lawn Tennis Association in 1881, the invention of basketball in 1891, the formation of the United States Golf Association in 1894, and the participation of some athletes from the United States in the revived Olympic Games in 1896, to name a few — depict the growing interest in athletic activities. It was during the latter portion of this period that the application of measurement techniques to athletics was begun. For example, in 1890 Luther H. Gulick devised a pentathlon consisting of a rope climb and four track events including the 100-yard dash, hop-skip-jump, running high jump, and shot put.

1900–1940

Measurement in the beginning of this period continued in the trend of anthropometrics. However, several seemingly isolated events were beginning to have a cumulative effect on the educators of the time: the implications in Darwin's theories; the early development of the science of psychology as a study of the relationships between the mind and the body; and the educational theories of E. L. Thorndike, John Dewey, and G. Stanley Hall in which transfer of training, learning by doing, and identification of stages of development were integral parts.

Thomas D. Wood and Clark W. Hetherington are often cited by historians as two physical education leaders who, in the early 1900s, did much to influence the philosophy of physical education. Generally their contention, influenced by the changing educational philosophies of the day, was that physical education should not only be education of the physical, but also education through the physical. Hetherington proposed that social and intellectual, as well as organic and neuromuscular, objectives could be met through physical education programs.

The dramatic shift in educational philosophy during the early part of this period resulted in sweeping changes in the curricula of the schools and the methods of instruction. Along with these changes came a realization of the importance of measurement in education. The initial emphasis was the development, refinement, and administration of intelligence tests. James K. Catell, Lewis M. Terman, and Henry H. Goddard are names of some of the most prominent workers in this area.

In physical education it became important to measure many parameters besides body structure and strength. In 1902 Sargent's Universal Test for Speed, Strength, and Endurance was introduced. An interest arose in the circulatory system, as shown by Crampton's Blood Ptosis Test presented in 1905 and by the norms for blood pressure and heart rate developed by J. H. McCurdy in 1910. In 1913 the Athletic Badge Tests in baseball, basketball, tennis, and volleyball were devised. These are a few examples of the diverse areas into which the physical educators of the period were expanding.

By the middle of the period initial tests had been developed for most of the parameters that are measured in physical education classes today. Many of these initial attempts were crude, subjective, and inexact, but they were refined as time passed. Precision, objectiveness, and test construction methods improved. Most importantly, advances made in the areas of mathematics and statistics made possible better measurement techniques. Measurement equipment, used in some cases, improved with the increase of technological skills.

1940–1945

World War II generated a great increase in concern for physical fitness. The main emphasis of physical education in the United States swung away from the expanded and varied program to physical training.

The elementary schools retained physical education programs in the sense that the curricula generally involved games, folk dancing, basic sports skills, and gymnastics. The secondary school physical education programs, however, were influenced more strongly by the war effort. The High School Victory Corps was organized nationally, partially to emphasize physical fitness and military drill in high school physical education classes. In colleges and universities the physical fitness emphasis was manifested by a revival of self-defense and survival activities such as weight-lifting, combatives, and swimming. Although several physical educators of the time questioned the switch in objectives by pointing out that physical education should be considered more than education of the physical, the stress on physical fitness prevailed.

Measurement in physical education, of course, followed the national trend, and measurement of physical fitness parameters became dominant. The military services established physical fitness tests during this period. Unfortunately, because of the extreme interest in and emphasis on physical fitness measurement during this time, physical education measurement has become synonymous with physical fitness testing to a great segment of the population of the United States.

1945–1950

There are abundant examples throughout history of the pendulum effect, in which emphasis swings gradually from one extreme to another. One of these examples is provided by the fluctuation of the major thrust of physical education during and after World War II.

After the war the people of the United States, tired from the strains of maintaining the war effort, became interested in peaceful pursuits. Educators began returning to the consideration of social objectives that had been becoming prevalent before the war. Physical educators shared in the movement by once again stressing the social and recreational objectives of physical education.

1950–1960

Unfortunately, peace did not last long. The early 1950s brought the Korean conflict and the beginning of the cold war between the United States and Russia. The Minimum Muscular Fitness Test of Hans Kraus and Sonya Weber indicated a significant difference in favor of European children over American children. These and other events once again stirred up a great interest in physical fitness. The return to concern for physical fitness was reflected in many events: the organization of the President's Council on Youth Fitness, development of the AAHPER Youth Fitness Test, and President John F. Kennedy's article in *Sports Illustrated*, "The Soft American," to name only a few. The social, intellectual, and recreational objectives of physical education, although certainly not completely ignored, were once again considered of secondary importance.

1960–1970

The period shortly after the launching of Sputnik 1 in 1957 is often cited as the beginning of the tremendous emphasis placed on sciences in American schools during the 1960s. This shift in educational philosophy resulted in critical examination of the "nonscientific" segments of school curricula and consequently a defensive attitude on the part of many physical educators.

Although generalizations can be misleading, if only one word could be used to describe the greatest single concern of physical education in this decade, that word would be "research." Certainly research was done in physical education throughout the twentieth century, but during this period the volume of research quite possibly equaled all that done previously. Three related factors led to this occurrence.

After World War II, physical educators in the United States stressed the social and recreational objectives of physical education

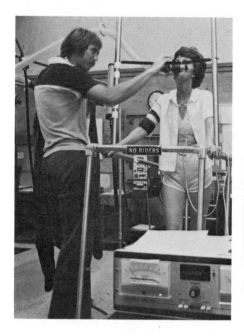
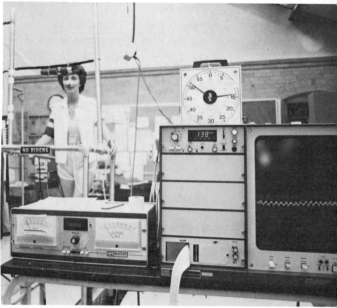

First, the number of institutions offering undergraduate and graduate degrees in physical education had increased sharply. The ability to do research is considered important for students in these programs, so the amount of physical education research being done increased. Second, with the emphasis on sciences, federal funding for research and research facilities was available. Third, again due to the emphasis on sciences, nonscientific segments of the curricula were being pared, and physical educators had to have research available to argue for their retention in the curriculum.

Obviously the increased efforts in physical education research had a tremendous impact on physical education tests and measurements. During this time a great proportion of the measurement techniques and tools now in use were developed, studied, revised, and described in the literature.

1970–1979

Certainly the most difficult time period to examine in a historical manner is the present. It is difficult to determine whether an event is a relatively isolated occurrence or part of a developing trend. With this in mind, an examination of important recent events reveals possible directions for physical education and consequently physical education measurement.

One of the most important single events in this period was the Vietnam war. The sustained effort in this conflict had two major effects on physical education. The concern for physical fitness remained a dominant influence throughout the United States. (This fact is still reflected in several current trends including the increase in articles and books dealing primarily with physical fitness, and the inclusion of physical fitness units in most physical education curricula.) And the national economic problems started during the Vietnam era have eliminated or reduced many sources of monies for research projects in many fields, including physical education.

In accordance with the pendulum effect mentioned earlier, physical educators may be swinging away from the extreme emphasis on physical education research seen in the sixties. A valid and difficult question is, if this is so, toward what emphasis is the pendulum now swinging? Greater concern for improving the quality of physical education teaching is a possible answer.

Physical education research will not disappear, but it will change. It appears that the type of research being done in the seventies is becoming wider in scope. Some researchers are branching into more theoretical types of study, while others are concentrating on what might be called applied research.

In any case it is clear that there is a great amount of work to be done in the area of physical education measurement for it is one aspect of physical education that is crucial to both research and teaching. For research to be meaningful and teaching to be effective, evaluations must be made, and the basis of evaluating anything is the ability to measure it accurately.

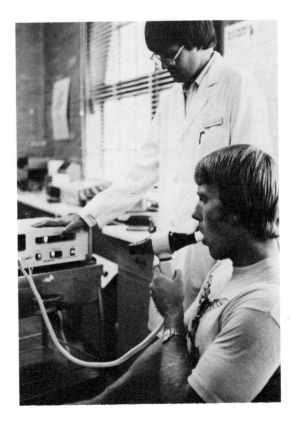

Many of the physical education measurement techniques and tools now in use were developed in the sixties, a decade that saw increased efforts in physical education research

CRITICISMS OF MEASUREMENT

Every so often an article is published in which the author condemns the practice of administering tests and making measurements during the educational process. Some common criticisms are: test scores are not exact measures of achievement but are often used as though they are; too much weight is given test results in making important decisions; students become pigeon-holed into certain categories because of their test results; and testing causes unnecessary stress and anxiety among students. Very often many of the remarks made in these articles are justified. Frequently it is not the use of measurement that is at fault, but the misuse of measurement. The purpose of this book is to demonstrate how tests can be used for the improvement of the educational process.

REFERENCES CITED

[1] E.L. Thorndike, *The Seventeenth Yearbook of the National Society for the Study of Education,* Part II (Bloomington, Ill.: Public School Publishing Company, 1958), p.16.

[2] William A. McCall, *Measurement* (New York: The MacMillan Company, 1939), p. 15.

Chapter 2

Fundamentals of Measurement

DEFINITIONS OF COMMON MEASUREMENT VOCABULARY

Words are used differently in various disciplines, and thus it becomes important to define some basic terms. This procedure helps assure better communication and more complete understanding than if words that actually differ in meaning are used interchangeably.

For example, the words measurement and evaluation are often incorrectly used interchangeably. *Measurement* refers to the procedure of assigning a number to each member of a group of individuals or objects based on some characteristic. The degree to which each individual or object possesses the characteristic being measured determines the number assigned. *Evaluation*, on the other hand, is a subjective judgment, usually based in part on measurements about the quality of the characteristic possessed by each individual or object. Ebel presents an analogy that helps differentiate the meaning of these two words: "If the scale shows that a man weighs 210 pounds it is reporting a measurement. This fact may be unpleasant, but there is nothing personal about it and no good cause for anger at the scale. But if a tactless acquaintance suggests that he is getting too fat, the acquaintance is making an evaluation."[1]

Three other words used interchangeably are *quiz, test,* and *examination*. These words are similar in the sense that all refer to some type of an instrument or process for measuring an attribute of an individual or object. The difference among the meaning of these words involves the completeness with which the measurement is made. When measuring mental processes, a quiz is usually thought to be rather short and informal, whereas a test is a carefully prepared set of questions, and an examination most often refers to a very complete and comprehensive measuring process. For measuring physical attributes the word *quiz* does not apply and the word *examination* has little application except in the medical sense. However, the word *test* is applicable and refers to a process, sometimes involving equipment, for measuring some particular physical trait such as height, leg power, or arm strength.

Two other words often used in conjunction with those already defined are *data* and *research*. The word *data* refers to a collection of facts, usually measurements. Data is plural and the singular form, datum, is used to indicate one measurement in the collection. Research is a careful investigation, usually done to confirm or contradict a particular hypothesis.

To aid in understanding the meaning of these words, consider the following situation. A physical education teacher believes that the students in his or her school are below the city average in leg strength. Consequently he or she would like to request additional equipment to remedy the situation. Rather than go to the principal armed only with personal judgment, the

teacher decides to undertake some research in an effort to confirm this belief. The intricacies of the research design need not be of concern at this time, except to realize that the physical educator would have to collect data relative to the leg strength of the students at the school and the leg strength of the group of students to which he or she desires a comparison. Measurements might be obtained through a leg strength test utilizing cable tensiometer techniques. Through the use of other tests further measures might be obtained and, using some inferential statistical procedures, the physical educator could finally arrive at an evaluation of the leg strength of his or her students as compared to the leg strength of other students in the city.

Three other words that are used in discussions about the accuracy and value of measurements are *reliability, validity,* and *objectivity.* The validity of a measurement is the degree to which it measures what it is intended to measure. Reliability refers to the degree of consistency exhibited by a measurement. Objectivity is reflected by the degree of agreement among different administrators of the same test. These characteristics of measurement are so important that Chapter 7 is devoted to their calculation and use.

LEVELS OF MEASUREMENT

Measurements may be classified on the basis of the type of information they yield. For example, it would be possible to rank a group of students in height by inspection, or it would be possible to assess the height of each student using a measuring tape and recording the height in inches or centimeters. The type of information resulting from the two procedures is different. In the ranking procedure the results only permit statements such as "Sally is shorter than Betty," but use of the second procedure makes it possible to determine how much shorter Sally is than Betty. Measurements can be placed into four categories (nominal, ordinal, interval, and ratio) based on the information they provide.

Nominal measurement conveys a minimal amount of information. It permits only the assessment of equality or difference. Nominal measurement often uses word descriptors to classify people or objects into categories. For example, a person may be classified as a letter winner, a girl, having brown hair, and so on. Occasionally numerals are used in a nominal way. Baseball players, for example, are identified by numerals on their uniforms, but statements about the ordering or the number of times one baseball player is greater than another based on their identification numbers are not possible.

Ordinal measurement permits the ranking of the people or objects measured. Information regarding greater than or less than become relevant with ordinal measurement. Students' ability in handball may be ranked at the completion of a round robin tournament, for example.

Interval measurement permits the making of statements of equality of intervals. Temperature is an example of interval measurement. The same distance exists on the Fahrenheit scale between 20° and 40° as exists between 40° and 80°. However, it is not appropriate to say that 80° is twice as hot as 40° because the zero point on the Fahrenheit scale is an arbitrary point and does not really indicate no temperature. Likewise a fifth-grade boy who can do four chins is not twice as strong as another fifth-grade boy who can do only two chins because doing zero chins does not indicate the absolute lack of any upper arm strength.

Ratio measurement permits statements of comparison such as twice as much or one third as much. To achieve this level of measurement an absolute zero point is necessary. It is possible to say, for example, that a high jump of six feet is twice as high as a high jump of three feet.

Precision of measurement

Measurements are made in almost every phase of life. Some everyday measurements and the instruments used to make them are relatively simple. Examples include using a clock to measure the time required to complete a task, using a cloth tape to measure the circumference of the neck when buying a shirt, and using a scale to select three pounds of apples. Other measurements are rather complex and require sophisticated equipment. For example, using a laser beam to measure the distance between the earth and the moon, using an electron microscope to count the number of cells in a piece of tissue, and using chemical means to determine the amount of various pollutants in a river.

The examples above represent situations in which fairly precise measurements can be made. In other situations, however, measurements are not very exact—for a number of reasons, but due mainly to a lack of availability of precise instruments. Examples in this category include the measurement of personality characteristics, social qualities, and motivation. Thus measurements can be simple or complex and exact or inexact.

In physical education classes, which center around the body and its movement, measurements are often required. As in life, some of these measurements are simple, some complex, some exact, some inexact. The distance the shot is put can be determined with reasonable accuracy, whereas a measure of gymnastics potential is difficult to obtain. The time taken to run the 50-yard dash can be simply determined, whereas the stroke volume of the heart must be measured indirectly.

USES OF MEASUREMENT IN PHYSICAL EDUCATION

Whether done directly or indirectly, simply or with difficulty, exactly or vaguely, the physical educator has many reasons for making measurements. These reasons and a brief description of situations where they might apply are presented below.

1. *Classification of students into homogeneous groups.* Classification of students may be done at several times and in various ways. For example,

Classification methods facilitate placing students in similar ability groups and thus foster efficient instruction

it may be desirable before a particular unit to classify the students in a physical education class according to physical characteristics such as height and weight. Using classification methods students can be placed in similar ability groups and thus instruction can become more efficient. With the advent of modular and computer scheduling it is possible to change the student makeup of classes and thus eliminate the difficulties of trying to teach a swimming class in which students range from beginners to competitive swimmers.

2. *Motivation.* Comparison of achievements to local or national norms can provide interest and may foster the setting of goals. Although some controversy exists as to the pedagogical soundness of using tests as extrinsic motivators to encourage learning, there is little doubt that most students will try a little harder if they are aware that progress toward certain goals will be measured periodically.

3. *Measurement of improvement.* Measurements made before and after a particular unit can aid a teacher in evaluating the amount of improvement made by the students. This use of measurement is particularly valuable in an adaptive or remedial physical education situation.

4. *Measurement of achievement.* The most important function of measurement is the assessment of student achievement. It is on the basis of the results of these measurements that the most important evaluations and decisions, both by the teacher and the student, are made.

5. *Evaluation of progress.* To evaluate how a student is progressing toward

specified objectives implies periodic measurement. If progress is not evident perhaps teaching methods need to be altered or goals modified.

6. *Determination of potential.* For the most part, tests and measurements devised for the purpose of determining potential in physical activities have met with only partial success. With the current lack of adequate facilities and funds in many parts of the country, however, this type of test may become increasingly important.

7. *Diagnosis.* Various tests and measurements can be of use to a physical educator for investigating the reasons a student's physical achievements are less than adequate. For example, if a student is having difficulty in learning a particular gymnastic movement, it would be important for the instructor to know if a lack of strength, a lack of coordination, or some other problem was the cause of the failure. The results of such tests may indicate that a remedial program should be developed and undertaken before the student could be expected to accomplish certain goals.

8. *Public relations.* If the objectives of physical education are truly important for existing in our society, the public should be made aware of this fact. To "educate" the public requires public relations work, which in turn requires facts about physical education. These facts are obtained through careful measurement programs. Occasionally, too, physical educators are called upon to defend the retention of physical education classes in the schools, and having information concerning the effects of physical activity upon the body can be a valuable aid in this cause.

9. *Grading.* In most situations a physical educator is responsible for determining grades for the students in his or her classes. No matter what system of marking is used, proper test and measurement techniques can and should be a valuable part of the process of grading.

10. *Evaluation of instructional methods.* Descriptions of new methods, ideas, and instructional techniques for teaching physical skills and abilities are continually published in physical education literature. Because not all methods work equally well for all instructors, each instructor should be capable of evaluating the success or failure of one instructional method when compared to others.

11. *Establishment of norms.* Few physical education tests are available with accompanying national norms. This is in part due to great differences in interests and facilities through the United States. The resulting fact is that if norms are to be used they must be constructed locally. The development of norms requires that measurements be made, recorded, and treated mathematically in one of several ways.

12. *Research and research evaluation.* Obviously a knowledge of proper measurement techniques is a requirement for anyone seeking to do research in the area of physical education. However, teachers of physical education should be equipped with the same knowledge in order to intelligently read, evaluate, and make use of this research.

REFERENCES CITED

[1] Robert L. Ebel, *Measuring Educational Achievement* (Englewood Cliffs, N. J.: Prentice-Hall Inc.,) p. 415.

SECTION 2

BASIC STATISTICAL TECHNIQUES NECESSARY TO IMPLEMENT A MEASUREMENT PROGRAM

INTRODUCTION TO SECTION 2

A physical education teacher administers the standing long jump test to a class and later posts a sheet on the bulletin board on which is recorded each student's score. How much information has the physical educator passed on to the students in regard to their ability and level of performance on this particular test? Very little. From the posted results a student can learn what his or her own score is and, after studying the other scores, arrive at some notion of achievement compared to others in the class. If students' names are used for identification purposes, the typical student will often compare his or her performance with those of friends and perhaps the class "champ" and the class "chump." Wouldn't it be better if the teacher posted more information than just the raw scores so the students would be able to obtain additional information about their performances?

As an example, to tell Bill that his best effort for the standing long jump is 7'6" does not give him a great deal of information. What other information would be of value to Bill (and incidentally, to his parents, future teachers, and other interested persons)? Obviously, this depends on the activity and level of the students, but the questions below indicate some of the types of information that could be of value.

What were the highest and lowest scores in class? What was the class average? What score was most typical for this class? How far above or below the class average was Bill's score? How does a 7'6" long jump compare with other students who are Bill's age or have a similar physical stature? How can the teacher transform the raw score distribution to help answer some of these questions? How can Bill's performance on this test, which is measured in inches, be compared to his performance in the 100-yard dash, which is measured in seconds? What is the most efficient way for the teacher to handle all the scores obtained for several classes? How will these scores be used in the determination of grades? Is there some correlation between these scores and the scores on some other test? Is the average score in Bill's class significantly different from the average score in other similar classes?

The answers to these and many other questions can be determined by the physical educator knowledgeable in descriptive statistics. A knowledge of descriptive statistics enables one to organize, describe, and interpret a score within a group of scores or compare groups of scores. Inferential statistics, another portion of this branch of mathematics, can be used by the teacher in gathering evidence to support or reject various hypotheses.

The physical educator has many opportunities to increase students' awareness of their abilities and achievements. The major purpose of this section is to provide prospective physical educators with an opportunity to learn fundamental statistical techniques that can help to accomplish this increase in self-awareness.

Chapter 3 details the procedures involved in organizing a set of scores to determine trends and make calculations of various statistics efficient. The handling of data in both an ungrouped and a grouped manner is illustrated.

Chapter 4 is presented to acquaint the prospective physical educator with the definitions, methods of calculation, characteristics, and uses of various statistics in describing a score or a set of scores. Measures of central tendency and variability are the main concerns of this chapter.

Once the student is familiar with techniques of handling data and calculating various statistics, the interpretation of data is possible. In chapter 5 the usefulness of knowledge of the normal curve, standard scores, percentiles and percentile ranks, and norms for making a raw score or group of raw scores meaningful is explained.

Statistical techniques of some value to the physical educator are those of determining correlations and testing for significant differences between means. The results of these procedures are useful in evaluating parts of the physical educator's program as well as for evaluating performance and written tests devised by others. The procedures for calculating and the methods of interpreting correlation coefficients and differences between means are presented in Chapter 6.

Finally, the usefulness of measurements is directly related to their accuracy, which is primarily assessed by examining reliability, validity, and objectivity. These characteristics of measurement are examined in Chapter 7.

Chapter 3
Organizing the Data

Data are generally organized in some manner in order to make trends become apparent or to facilitate the calculation of various statistics used in describing characteristics of the data. To accomplish either of these goals the data may be handled in an ungrouped or grouped manner. The decision as to which organization of the data to use will depend on many factors, such as the degree of accuracy desired, the amount of data to be handled, the availability of a calculator, the eventual use of the data, and the personal preference of the person working with the data.

Before the appearance of the inexpensive hand calculator it was generally most efficient to handle large amounts of data in a grouped manner by placing scores similar in value together. Statistics are not now often calculated from grouped data because some degree of accuracy is lost, and the availability of the hand calculator has made this sacrifice unnecessary. But grouping data is still of value as a first step in preparing graphical representations of data, so both methods of organizing data will be presented.

The data in Table 3.1, representing sit-up scores achieved by sixty-five nine-year-old boys, will be used for illustrative purposes throughout this and subsequent chapters in this section.

ARRANGING DATA

Ungrouped

If the data are to be handled in an ungrouped manner, the only arranging necessary is to place the scores in chronological order. The data may be arranged in either ascending or descending order although it is common to put

Table 3.1   Sit-up scores for sixty-five nine-year-old boys

62	67	81	65	47	85	75
38	73	93	63	61	52	63
54	68	78	64	88	40	78
74	51	60	37	36	44	55
76	69	50	63	26	79	71
56	66	47	61	65	63	
83	56	65	70	81	55	
98	46	77	86	57	57	
64	53	59	67	71	72	
41	48	62	45	91	73	

the best score first. The sit-up scores listed in Table 3.1 are in random order as might result from the administration of the sit-up test in class. The scores are arranged in chronological order in Table 3.2.

Table 3.2   Chronological listing of the sit-up scores of Table 3.1

98	78	71	64	60	52	40
93	78	70	64	59	51	38
91	77	69	63	57	50	37
88	76	68	63	57	48	36
86	75	67	63	56	47	26
85	74	67	63	56	47	
83	73	66	62	55	46	
81	73	65	62	55	45	
81	72	65	61	54	44	
79	71	65	61	53	41	

Grouped

To handle the data in a grouped manner requires the use of a frequency distribution. A frequency distribution is, in fact, a display of the frequency with which score values fall into each of several groups. Certain procedures are commonly adopted in the construction of frequency distributions. Some of these procedures are mathematically sound, some are for convenience, and some are merely conventions. A frequency distribution of the sit-up scores appears in Table 3.3.

It is important to realize that for any given set of data it is possible to construct several different frequency distributions. For one particular set of data, however, some of the frequency distributions that could be structured are more acceptable than others due to mathematical considerations and mat-

Table 3.3   Frequency distribution of the sit-up scores of Table 3.1

Intervals	Tally	Frequency
95–99	I	1
90–94	II	2
85–89	III	3
80–84	III	3
75–79	ʬ I	6
70–74	ʬ II	7
65–69	ʬ III	8
60–64	ʬ ʬ I	11
55–59	ʬ II	7
50–54	ʬ	5
45–49	ʬ	5
40–44	III	3
35–39	III	3
30–34		0
25–29	I	1
		65

ters of convenience. Thus, although the frequency distribution presented in Table 3.3 is only one of many that could have been chosen to display the sit-up data, the decision as to which frequency distribution should be used is based on two major considerations. The frequency distribution should be convenient to work with, yet the loss of accuracy due to the grouping of scores should be minimal. To accomplish these two objectives, the construction of a frequency distribution should follow certain steps. These steps and the rationale for each are discussed below.

FREQUENCY DISTRIBUTION CONSTRUCTION

Step 1. Determine the range of the scores. The initial step in construction of a frequency distribution is to determine the *range* of the score values. The range is a numerical value indicating the number of different score values that exist between the extreme scores of a set of data. The range is determined by subtracting the lowest score value from the highest score value and adding one to the difference. Thus the formula is: Range = $(H - L) + 1$

Example: Determine the range for a set of data containing the following scores: 10,9,6,4,3

Range = $(H - L) + 1$
Range = $(10 - 3) + 1$
Range = $7 + 1$
Range = 8

Thus for this set of data there are eight different score values that could occur, namely 10,9,8,7,6,5,4 and 3.

The highest score value for the sit-up data of Table 3.1 is 98, and the lowest score value is 26. Therefore the range is $(98 - 26) + 1$, or 73.

Step 2. Determine the interval size. The size of each interval in a frequency distribution (that is, how many score values each interval contains) is represented by the symbol i. The value of i is determined by the range of the distribution and the number of intervals decided on. Generally the number of intervals in any frequency distribution should be somewhere between 12 and 18. As the number of intervals increases, the frequency distribution becomes unwieldy and the original purpose for grouping the data is defeated. As the number of intervals decreases, the degree of accuracy also decreases due to a loss of information about each particular score in the distribution.

The validity of these two statements can be examined by noting two extreme examples of frequency distributions that could be constructed for the sit-up data. If an interval size of one were chosen, the resulting frequency distribution would contain 73 intervals ranging from 98 to 26. This would not be an improvement over working with the 65 ungrouped scores. At the other extreme, if an interval size of 40 were chosen, the resulting frequency distribution would contain only two intervals. If these two intervals were, for example, 65–104 and 25–64, the first would contain the highest 30 sit-up scores and the second would contain the lowest 35 sit-up scores. Once arranged in this frequency distribution, however, the actual identity of each score would be lost. The resulting loss of information would reduce the degree of accuracy of computations made from this frequency distribution, and its descriptive properties would be minimal. Thus, the "12 to 18 interval" rule has evolved as a compromise.

To obtain an estimate of the largest interval size to be used for any distribution of scores, the range of the distribution (as obtained in step 1) is divided by 12.

> Example: Determine the largest interval size (i_L) that should be used in constructing a frequency distribution for the sit-up data (range = 73).
>
> $i_L = 73 \div 12$
>
> $i_L = 6.1$

To obtain an estimate of the smallest interval size to be used for a particular distribution, the range of the distribution is divided by 18.

> Example: Determine the smallest interval size (i_S) that should be used in constructing a frequency distribution for the sit-up data.
>
> $i_S = 73 \div 18$
>
> $i_S = 4.1$

From the two estimates of the possible extremes of interval size for the sit-up data it becomes apparent that an interval size of 4, 5, or 6 will result in a frequency distribution containing between 12 and 18 intervals. Although the quotients obtained in the two divisions above are decimal numbers, interval sizes are almost always whole numbers for ease in subsequent computations. For reasons that will be explained later it is also convenient to select, if possible, an uneven interval size. With these considerations in mind an interval size of 5 was chosen for the sit-up data (see Table 3.3).

Step 3. Determine the limits of the top interval. Two considerations are involved in determining the limits of the top interval of a frequency distribution. The interval must be of the size previously determined and it must contain the highest score in the distribution. These two restrictions can be met by more than one possible interval. For example, any of the following intervals could be selected for the top interval for the sit-up data and meet the requirements mentioned: 98–102, 97–101, 96–100, 95–99, or 94–98. Each of these intervals contains the highest sit-up score (98) and five score values (the interval size determined in step 2). However, a convention of using the interval for which the lower limit is a multiple of the interval size is often adopted. The only interval of those presented above to meet this criterion is the interval 95–99. The lower limit of this interval (95) is a multiple of the interval size (5).

Step 4. Complete the interval column. Once the interval size and the limits of the top interval are determined, the remainder of the interval column may be completed. The lower limit of each interval is determined by subtracting the interval size (i) from the lower limit of the interval above. The upper limit of each interval is determined by subtracting the value of i from the upper limit of the interval above. For example, the lower limit of the interval directly under the top interval in Table 3.3 is 90, obtained by subtracting 5, the interval size, from 95, the lower limit of the top interval. The upper limit of this interval, 94, is obtained in a similar manner.

The procedure for determining the interval limits is continued until finally the interval containing the lowest score in the distribution is reached. The lowest sit-up score of 26 is contained in the bottom interval having the limits of 25–29.

Step 5. Tally the score values in the appropriate intervals. The next step in constructing a frequency distribution is the clerical task of recording a tally mark in the proper interval for each score in the distribution. For example, a tally mark was made opposite the 60–64 interval to represent the sit-up score of 62, which is the initial value presented in Table 3.1. A tally mark was made opposite the 35–39 interval for the next score of 38 and so on until the final tally mark was made opposite the 70–74 interval for the last sit-up score of 71. The results of this step for the sit-up data are displayed in column two of Table 3.3.

Step 6. Construct the frequency column. The final step in the construction of the frequency distribution is to construct the frequency column. This step consists merely of counting and recording the number of tally marks for each interval. In the frequency column of Table 3.3 are displayed the results of this step for the sit-up data. It is wise to sum the frequency column as a check to determine whether or not any scores have been omitted from the frequency distribution.

FREQUENCY DISTRIBUTION CONSIDERATIONS

Although seldom done now that hand calculators are available, it is possible to calculate various statistics from a set of scores arranged in a frequency distribution. When this is done and when frequency distributions are used for graphing purposes, it is necessary to make an important assumption. Because the identity of each individual score is lost in a frequency distribution, it is necessary to assume that the scores in an interval are evenly distributed within that interval. From this assumption it follows that the mean of the scores within an interval is equal to the midpoint of the interval.

As an illustration, consider the frequency distribution of the sit-up scores displayed in Table 3.3. The interval 45– 49 contains five scores. The above assumption implies that these five scores are evenly distributed within the interval and that the mean of the five scores is 47. In reality the five tally marks made in this interval represent the scores 45, 46, 47, 47, and 48. The mean of these five scores is actually 46.6. The discrepancy between the assumption and reality is known as *grouping error*. Generally grouping error is so slight that it is seldom considered important in the computations made from a frequency distribution. In fact, the grouping error located in the upper intervals often tend to cancel out the grouping error located in the lower intervals due to the typical pattern in which score frequencies are commonly distributed in physical education (and other types of) data.

Further, it should be noticed that, in general, increasing the number of intervals in a frequency distribution decreases the range of each interval and thus reduces the amount of information about the individual scores that is lost resulting in less grouping error. Carried to the extreme, the number of intervals could be increased until the size of each interval became unity, at which point no loss of information and thus no grouping error would occur. Of course, the net result of such a procedure is to return to an ungrouped data situation.

The advantage in selecting an uneven interval size, as suggested in step 2, should now become apparent. The midpoint of an interval is often utilized in making various calculations from a frequency distribution and in graphing procedures. With an uneven interval size the midpoint of the interval is a whole number (integer).

Another consideration involves the nature of the interval limits and whether the data are discrete or continuous. *Discrete* data are expressed in whole numbers and usually represent counts of indivisible entities. In the sit-up data, for example, the scores represent the total number of complete sit-ups performed by each student. A score of 35½ (or any other fraction) was recorded as 35 because the student did not complete the thirty-sixth sit-up. Thus, in the sense that only whole number counts were recorded as scores, the data are considered to be discrete.

Data are classified as being *continuous* if it is possible for the score to correspond to any possible value of an unbroken scale. In other words, the trait being measured is, theoretically at least, capable of any subdivision. If the sit-up scores were obtained by recording the number of complete sit-ups plus any fractional part performed, the data would be considered continuous. As another example, an individual's weight can be obtained to the nearest pound, one-half pound, one-fourth pound, and so on. The eventual limiting factor is the accuracy of the measuring device, not the fact that smaller units do not exist.

The interval limits, as expressed in the frequency distribution in Table 3.3, appear to be relevant only for discrete data as the limits are expressed as integers. However, the interval identified by the interval limits of 95–99, for example, must be considered as actually extending from 94.5 to 99.4. This is because 95 represents any value from 94.5 to 95.4, and 99 represents any value from 98.5 to 99.4. Thus the *real limits* of an interval in a frequency distribution should be considered as extending one-half of a unit on either side of the integral units.

Chapter 4
Describing the Data

Originally it was stated that the purposes for organizing data are to identify trends and to facilitate the calculation of various statistics. One method of describing trends in data is through graphs. By following a few simple rules, data in a frequency distribution can be displayed in a histogram or a frequency polygon, making the data more interpretable.

HISTOGRAM (bar graph)

The histogram in Figure 4.1 represents the sit-up data from Chapter 3. To construct a histogram from a frequency distribution proceed as follows:

1. Obtain a piece of graph paper.
2. Draw a horizontal line (abscissa) for plotting score values.
3. Draw a vertical line (ordinate) for plotting frequencies.
4. Select a scale for score values and frequencies. A common rule of thumb is a 3:5 ratio for the length of the ordinate to the abcissa.
5. Locate the midpoints of the intervals from the frequency distribution on the horizontal line.
6. Record the frequency above each midpoint and construct the bar as shown.
7. Label both axes and the histogram.

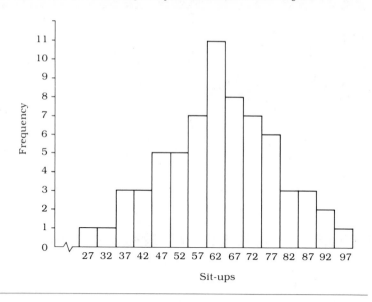

Figure 4.1   Histogram of sit-up data from sixty-five seventh-grade boys

FREQUENCY POLYGON

In the construction of a histogram, the assumption that the scores in an interval are evenly distributed over the interval is shown by the width of the bar. If the assumption is made that all the scores in an interval are concentrated at the midpoint of the interval, the resulting graph is labeled a frequency polygon. The procedures for constructing a frequency polygon are the same as those for a histogram; however, instead of constructing a bar to represent the interval, the points representing the frequency at each midpoint are connected. Figure 4.2 is a frequency polygon for the data shown in the histogram in Figure 4.1.

Construction of either a histogram or a frequency polygon permits a quick visual inspection of the data. The sit-up data displayed in Figures 4.1 and 4.2 appears fairly typical for many tests given in physical education—that is, the score frequencies are relatively low at the extremes and higher near the center of the distribution. It is even possible to make some preliminary comparisons between two or more sets of data using graphing techniques. For example, if the graphs of two different classes taking the same test resulted as in Figure 4.3, it might be concluded that for some reason the test was too difficult for the afternoon class.

The data for the afternoon class is described as being positively skewed (the direction of the tail is in a positive direction), which indicates that a large number of the scores were relatively low. A negatively skewed distribution is one having a relatively large number of high scores.

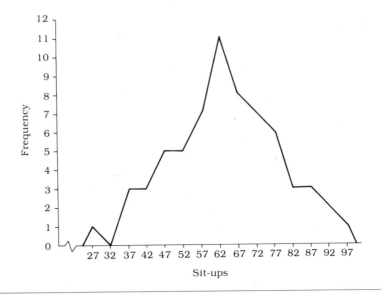

Figure 4.2   Frequency polygon of sit-up data from sixty-five seventh-grade boys

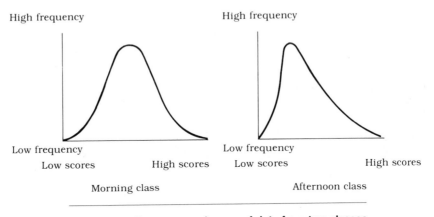

Figure 4.3   Frequency polygons of data from two classes

In addition to being useful in the construction of graphs, organizing data facilitates the calculation of various statistics that can then be used to describe the distribution. This is valuable for two reasons. First, these characteristics can be used in describing the similarities and differences among two or more sets of data. Second, the relationships that exist among the scores occurring within a set of data may be expressed in terms of these statistics.

MEASURES OF CENTRAL TENDENCY

One of the most important and useful characteristics of a set of scores is the location of its center point. Because the definition of the center point varies, several measures of central tendency exist. The computational procedures for obtaining three of them—the median, the mean, and the mode—and the advantages and disadvantages of each are presented below.

The median
Definition

The median of a distribution is the point on the score scale such that 50 percent of the scores fall above it and 50 percent of the scores fall below it. The median, usually represented by the symbol Mdn, is the 50th percentile of a distribution.

Calculation

The median is determined by locating the middle point of a distribution. With ungrouped data arranged in chronological order, this is merely a counting procedure. The formula, $\dfrac{N + 1}{2}$, where N is the total number of scores, can be used to determine the middle point of a distribution. Notice that when the number of scores (N) in a distribution is odd, the middle point, as determined by this formula, will be a whole number. For example, if a distribution contains fifteen scores, the middle point is the eighth score [(15 + 1) ÷ 2 = 8]. Thus, if

the fifteen scores are arranged in chronological order, the eighth score from the bottom (or from the top) is the median. However, when the number of scores in a distribution is even, the middle point is not a whole number. If, for example, a distribution contains sixteen scores, the middle point is the 8.5th score $[(16 + 1) \div 2 = 8.5]$. Since, in reality, there is no 8.5th score, the median is taken to be midway between the eighth and ninth scores. The following examples illustrate how the median of a distribution is obtained from ungrouped data.

1. What is the median of a distribution containing the scores 1, 7, 9, 15, 20?

   The middle score of the distribution is located by $\dfrac{N + 1}{2} = \dfrac{5 + 1}{2} = 3.$

   Thus the third score from the bottom (or top) of the chronologically arranged data is the median. Mdn = 9.

2. What is the median of a distribution containing the scores 1, 7, 9, 15, 20, 23?

   The middle point of the distribution is located by $\dfrac{N + 1}{2} = \dfrac{6 + 1}{2} = 3.5.$

   Since no 3.5th score exists, the median is assumed to be midway between the third and the fourth scores from the bottom (or top). Mdn = $(9 + 15) \div 2 = 12$.

Verify that the median for the sit-up data in Table 3.2 is the score point 63.

Characteristics

The median, by its definition, is related to the ranks of the scores rather than the actual values of the scores. This fact is illustrated by noticing that the median for each of the two following distributions is the same:

   Distribution A   1, 2, 6, 12, 14   Mdn = 6
   Distribution B   1, 2, 6, 12, 114   Mdn = 6.

From this example it can also be seen that the value of an extreme score (114 in distribution B) does not alter the value of the median. Because the median is not affected by extreme score values, it is often referred to as the most "typical" score in a distribution.

The mean
Definition

The mean of a set of scores is simply the arithmetic average of the scores or, in other words, the point on the score scale that corresponds to the sum of the set of scores divided by the number of scores in the set.

Calculation

Unlike the median, it is not necessary that the scores be listed in chronological order to facilitate the computation of the mean from ungrouped data. It is only necessary to determine the algebraic sum of all the scores in the distribution and the number of scores contributing to that sum. The symbolic representation of the definition of the mean is

$$\overline{X} = \frac{\Sigma X}{N},$$

where $\overline{X}$ (read, X bar) = symbol for the mean
Σ = the sum of
X = each individual score in the distribution
N = the number of scores in the distribution.

The following examples illustrate how the mean of a distribution is determined from ungrouped data:

1. What is the mean of a distribution containing the scores 9, 20, 1, 7, 15?

    The sum of the five scores is 52.

    $$\overline{X} = \frac{\Sigma X}{N}$$

    $$\overline{X} = \frac{52}{5}$$

    $$\overline{X} = 10.4.$$

2. What is the mean of a distribution containing the scores 15, −7, 13, 8, −3, −2, 11, 3?

    The sum of the eight scores is 38.

    $$\overline{X} = \frac{\Sigma X}{N}$$

    $$\overline{X} = \frac{38}{8}$$

    $$\overline{X} = 4.75.$$

    Verify that the mean for the sit-up data in Table 3.1 is the score point 63.40.

Characteristics

The most important characteristic of the mean is the fact that every score in the distribution affects the value of the mean. A change in any score will change the value of the mean. Previously two distributions were presented to show that the value of an extreme score had no effect on the value of the median. Notice, however, the effect of this same extreme score on the mean:

		Mdn	$\overline{X}$
Distribution A	1, 2, 6, 12, 14	6	7.0
Distribution B	1, 2, 6, 12, 114	6	27.0

Of course, if the score that changes is not an extreme score but rather one close to the mean, the value of the mean will not change as drastically, but it will nevertheless change. Consider the following two distributions and means:

		$\overline{X}$
Distribution A	1, 2, 6, 12, 14	7.0
Distribution C	1, 2, 8, 12, 14	7.4

The property of being affected by every score in a distribution results in the mean being the most sensitive of the three measures of central tendency. It is this characteristic that makes it the most valuable in a mathematical sense.

The mode
Definition
The mode of a set of scores is simply the value of the most frequently occurring score.

Calculation
An inspection of the data (more easily accomplished if the data are arranged in chronological order) is all that is needed to determine the mode. For example, examination of Table 3.2 reveals that 63 occurs with more frequency than any other score and is thus the mode of the sit-up data.

Characteristics
In a distribution where each score only occurs once (as in 1, 2, 6, 12, 14) or every score occurs more than once but with the same frequency (as in 1, 1, 2, 2, 6, 6, 12, 12, 14, 14), a mode cannot be determined. In a situation where two adjacent or nearly adjacent scores occur with equal frequency higher than the frequency of other scores, the mode is usually considered to be the mean of the two equally occurring scores. (The mode for a set of scores containing the values 1, 1, 2, 2, 6, 6, 6, 7, 7, 7, 12, 12, 14, 14 would be considered to be 6.5.) However, when two scores that are not close together both occur with the same frequency higher than for other scores, the distribution is described as being bimodal. In other words, both scores would be considered modes.
In a practical sense, the mode is of limited value because it is subject to judgment and does not lend itself to algebraic manipulation. Because the mode is a relatively crude measure of central tendency, it has little meaning unless the number of scores in the distribution is quite large.

Comparison of the median, mean, and mode
General considerations
The word *average* is a common term used to indicate a measure of central tendency. Although to most the word *average* is synonymous with the mean, the median and mode are also classified as averages. When reporting data it is important to specify which average has been computed. It is equally im-

portant to determine which average is being referred to by others reporting data. The example below demonstrates this importance.

A realtor was interested in influencing potential customers into buying a particular house. Attempting to indicate desirable features of the area in which the house was located, the realtor informed potential customers that the average yearly income of the seven families on the block where the house was located was over $25,000. In fact, the yearly incomes of the seven families were $9,000, $10,000, $12,000, $13,000, $14,000, $15,000, and $100,000. It is true that the mean yearly income of the seven families was over $25,000, but is is also true that only one of the seven families had an income of more than $25,000. In this case the median income ($13,000) represents a less misleading average. The point of this illustration is that the selection of the proper average depends on the situation for which it is to be used and the nature of the data from which it is derived.

Selection of an average

In almost all cases the mean is preferred. It is easily calculated, exactly defined, and amenable to algebraic manipulation. As indicated earlier a graph of data commonly obtained from physical education measurements, constructed by putting the score values on the abscissa and the frequency of occurrence of each score value on the ordinate, results in a bell-shaped curve. With this type of distribution the mean is the proper average to use in reporting central tendency.

When extreme scores, such as the $100,000 yearly income in the example above, are present in a set of data, the median becomes the proper average. The mean is pulled away from the center by the extreme score or scores, but the median is the most "typical" score in a distribution.

The mode, the least useful average, is seldom used to report central tendency, but it does have uses. For example, it would be very important for an equipment manager to know what size football jersey is most frequently required in order to keep a sufficient supply on hand. However, where a mean or median can be usefully calculated, the mode is seldom used.

In summary, the value of the median is not influenced by the particular values of the data but by their order and frequency. The value of the mean is not affected by the order of the data but by their value and frequency. Finally, the value of the mode is not influenced by the particular value or order of the data but only by their frequency.

MEASURES OF VARIABILITY

Thus far the characteristics of central tendency have been examined. Knowledge of this measure of the average performance is of some value in comparing this set of scores to other like sets of scores. For example, information of interest could be secured by comparing the mean of 63 sit-ups in Table 3.1 to the mean number of sit-ups done by a different sample of boys or by the same boys at a later date. It can also be used to compare performances within the group of 65 boys. At a minimum each boy can determine whether his performance was above or below the average performance.

Thus central tendency yields some valuable information but is not sufficient in itself to completely describe a set of scores. Consider the following two sets of scores:

Distribution D   2, 28, 50, 50, 72, 98
Distribution E   41, 47, 50, 50, 50, 53, 59.

The median, mean, and mode for both distributions are all equal to 50, but the two sets of scores have obvious differences. It becomes apparent that other characteristics must be examined to describe a set of scores adequately.

The most evident difference between distribution D and distribution E is the disparity in the distance between the extreme scores. This characteristic is referred to variously as dispersion, deviation, spread, scatter, and variability. As with central tendency, there are several statistics used to describe this characteristic.

The range
Definition and calculation
The definition and the procedures for calculating the range have been discussed in step 1 of constructing a frequency distribution. Since only the small-

est and largest scores are involved, it is not necessary that the data be organized in any particular fashion prior to determination of the range.

Characteristics

Although the range is the simplest measure of variability to obtain, it is also the least adequate. Its weakness lies in the fact that it does not account for the variability among any scores in a distribution except the two extreme scores. Because of this, two sets of data could vary greatly in respect to the compactness of their scores and yet have the same range. Further, the range is a misleading indicator of variability when an unusually low or high score occurs in a distribution.

The semi-interquartile range

To overcome some of the weaknesses of the range as a measure of variability, the distance between two specified points within a distribution, rather than the distance between the lowest and highest scores, is sometimes used to describe the characteristic of dispersion of the scores. The most common measure of this type is known as the semi-interquartile range.

Definition and calculation

The semi-interquartile range is half the distance between the 75th and 25th percentile scores. The initial step in calculating its value is to determine what score points in the distribution correspond to the 75th and 25th percentiles. Calculation is similar to that for the median, except that the points we are determining are such that 25 percent and 75 percent of the scores fall below them. The following example illustrates how a value of 10 was obtained for the semi-interquartile range for the ungrouped (but ordered) sit-up data displayed in Table 3.2.

The 25th percentile for the sit-up data occurs at the 16.25th score because there are sixty-five scores in the distribution ($65 \times .25 = 16.25$). Since the semi-interquartile range is a relatively crude measure of variability, the 16th score may be considered to represent the 25th percentile. By counting up sixteen scores from the lowest score the value of the 25th percentile is found to be 53. Following the same procedures the 75th percentile for these data is found to be the 49th score ($65 \times .75 = 48.75$), which has the value 73. Finally, from the definition:

$$\text{Semi-interquartile range} = \frac{\text{75th percentile} - \text{25th percentile}}{2}$$

$$= \frac{73 - 53}{2}$$

$$= \frac{20}{2}$$

$$= 10$$

Characteristics

The semi-interquartile range functions more adequately than the range as a measure of variability because it is more stable; that is, it it less likely to be influenced by extreme scores. However, the semi-interquartile range has two serious shortcomings that limit its usefulness as a statistic to describe variability. It does not take into consideration the value of each individual score within a distribution, and it would be possible for two distributions to have very similar semi-interquartile range values and yet end scores that vary widely. Thus, except when a crude but fairly stable measure of variability is all that is required, it is seldom worth the extra effort to calculate the semi-interquartile range even though it is in some ways an improvement over the range.

The mean deviation
Definition and calculation

Ideally a measure of variability should reflect the distance between each score in the distribution and the center of the distribution. One possible way to obtain such a value would be to determine the amount by which each score deviates from the mean. These deviation values could then be summed to obtain an indication of the variability of the distribution since, if the scores were widely scattered, the resulting sum would be greater than if the scores were all fairly close to the center of the distribution. However, if this procedure is followed in a strict algebraic sense, the resulting sum will always be zero. For example, consider the two following distributions:

Distribution A				Distribution D		
Scores	Mean	Deviation		Scores	Mean	Deviation
14	7	7		14	8	6
12	7	5		13	8	5
6	7	−1		12	8	4
2	7	−5		8	8	0
1	7	−6		6	8	−2
		$\Sigma = 0$		2	8	−6
				1	8	−7
						$\Sigma = 0$

To remove the problem, the absolute values of the deviations could be used (in other words, assume all deviation values to be positive). This results in the sum of the deviations for distribution A becoming 24 and that for distribution D becoming 30. It should be recognized that one reason the sum of distribution D is larger is that it contains more scores. If no further steps were taken to refine this measure of variability, it would be of no value because it would not be a function of the variability of the distribution. This problem is eliminated simply by dividing the sum of the absolute deviation values by the number of scores in the distribution. The resulting value is named the average deviation or, more precisely, the mean deviation. Symbolically the mean deviation is defined as follows:

$$MD = \frac{|\Sigma x|}{N} \qquad x = (x - \overline{X})$$

where MD = mean deviation
  Σ = the sum of
  x = deviation from the mean
  N = number of scores in the distribution
  $\overline{X}$ = the mean
  $|\ |$ = "absolute value."

Characteristics

The mean deviation reflects the information on variability contained in the data better than either the range or the semi-interquartile range because every score in the distribution affects the value of the mean deviation. It can very adequately be used to describe the extent to which the scores of a distribution are scattered along the score scale. Although this is true, the mean deviation is seldom used. The infrequent use is due to the involvement of absolute values and consequent unsuitability for algebraic values and more sophisticated statistical procedures. Elimination of this problem leads to the most commonly used measure of variability.

The standard deviation
Definition

An alternative to using absolute values is to square each deviation value before summing. The squares are summed and then divided by the number of scores in the distribution. To return to the units of the original scores, the square root of the resulting quotient must be found. The measure thus obtained is named the standard deviation and is symbolically defined as follows:

$$SD = \sqrt{\frac{\Sigma x^2}{N}} \qquad (x = x - \overline{X}),$$

where SD = standard deviation
  Σ = the sum of
  x^2 = each deviation value squared
  N = the number of scores in the distribution
  $\overline{X}$ = the mean.

The following example, using distribution A, is provided to clarify the computational procedures involved in determining the standard deviation from the definitional formula:

Score	Mean	Deviation	Deviation squared
14	7	7	49
12	7	5	25
6	7	-1	1
2	7	-5	25
1	7	-6	36
$\Sigma = 35$			$\Sigma = 136$

$$SD = \sqrt{\frac{\Sigma x^2}{N}}$$
$$= \sqrt{\frac{136}{5}}$$
$$= \sqrt{27.2}$$
$$= 5.21$$

Calculation

Direct calculation of the standard deviation using the definitional formula presented above can become a very tedious task. Fortunately, through algebraic manipulation of part of the definitional formula it is possible to arrive at a new formula that yields the sum of the squares of the deviations without actually determining each individual deviation value. When this new formula is substituted back into the definitional formula, the net result is a formula that can be used to determine the value of the standard deviation without having to use deviations.

It can be shown that the definitional formula for determining the value of the standard deviation is algebraically equivalent to the following formula:

$$SD = \sqrt{\frac{\Sigma X^2}{N} - \overline{X}^2} ,$$

where SD = standard deviation

Σ = the sum of

X^2 = each score, squared

N = the number of scores in the distribution

$\overline{X}^2$ = the mean of the distribution, squared.

Notice that the formula does not require any deviation values. To verify that this formula is indeed equivalent to the definitional formula and to clarify the computational procedures involved, the above formula is used in the following example to determine the value of the standard deviation for distribution A ($SD = 5.21$ from definitional formula):

Score (X)	(X)²
14	196
12	144
6	36
2	4
1	1
$\Sigma = 35$	$\Sigma = 381$

$\overline{X} = \dfrac{\Sigma X}{N}$

$\overline{X} = \dfrac{35}{5}$

$\overline{X} = 7$

$SD = \sqrt{\dfrac{\Sigma X^2}{N} - \overline{X}^2}$

$SD = \sqrt{\dfrac{381}{5} - (7)^2}$

$SD = \sqrt{76.2 - 49}$

$SD = \sqrt{27.2}$

$SD = 5.21$

As a practice exercise verify that the standard deviation of the sit-up data presented in Table 3.1 is 14.97.

The definitional and computational formulas presented here are used to describe the variability of scores from an entire population. Another branch of statistics, called inferential statistics, is concerned with estimating population values based on values obtained from samples of the population. For example, the director of physical education in a large school district may desire to know the average physical fitness level of children in the district. It may be impossible to measure every student, so a sample of students could be obtained (specific procedures need to be followed for identifying the students who would make up the sample) and estimates about the population made from the sample data.

In inferential statistics a slightly different formula is used for the standard deviation for reasons that are beyond the scope of this book. The formula is $SD = \sqrt{\dfrac{\Sigma x^2}{N-1}}$, where N = the number of students in the sample. Notice the only difference is $N-1$ rather than N in the denominator. As N becomes larger, this difference in the formulas becomes less significant.

This difference is pointed out because most hand calculators are programmed with the N-1 formula since they are used frequently for inferential statistics. Thus, if the standard deviation is calculated using the population formula and then checked using a hand calculator programmed to obtain the standard deviation, the values may differ slightly. It would not be proper to use the population formula for inferential statistical purposes, but either formula is adequate for most descriptive situations.

Characteristics

The standard deviation, with all its mathematical niceties, is far more easily defined in terms of symbols than in terms of words. The standard deviation is a unit of measurement to express the amount of variability present in a set of scores. It has several unique features and values, some of which are mentioned in later chapters of this book.

Considerations of measures of variability

Interpretation of measures of variability is more difficult than that of measures of central tendency. The information presented below may serve to elucidate the meaning and function of variability measures.

Measures of variability reflect the average amount of *deviation* from a center point among the scores in a distribution, whereas measures of central tendency reflect an average *position* in the distribution. Put another way, a measure of central tendency represents a particular point on a score scale; a measure of variability represents a particular distance on a score scale.

The absolute values expressing this distance are not in themselves very meaningful. For example, it is not reasonable to assume that, because the standard deviation for a set of standing long jump scores is 16 and for a set of 100-yard dash scores is 8, the standing long jump scores are twice as variable as the dash scores. The units in which these scores are expressed (inches and seconds) are not comparable, and thus standard deviations of the two distributions are not comparable. Calculation of the value of a measure of variability does reveal some information about the variability among the scores of the particular distribution in question, but it does not allow comparison to another distribution unless the scores for both are expressed in terms of the same unit. Methods of comparing distributions of scores involving different units of measure are presented in Chapter 5.

Chapter 5
Interpreting the Data

With information presented thus far, the reader should be able to calculate and express central tendency and variability in a variety of ways. The reader also should be able to express in a limited manner some information about a particular score in a distribution. For example, given that the mean and the standard deviation of a set of scores are 63 and 15, respectively, and that Bill's score is 83, one can determine that Bill's score is not only above average but more than one standard deviation above the mean.

But what does being one standard deviation above the mean indicate? How does Bill's score rank in class? How does Bill's score on this test compare with his score on some other test? To intelligently assess the nature of a particular score within a set of scores and to compare it to a score from another distribution requires some knowledge about the normal curve, standard scores, percentiles, and norms.

THE NORMAL CURVE

The normal curve is a mathematical phenomenon of great importance in statistical theory. Although a complete treatment of the significance of the normal curve is beyond the scope of this book, a knowledge of certain elementary considerations and applications of various properties of the normal curve is required in interpreting data.

It happens that the normal curve (based on certain unique relationships between the height of the curve at the mean and the height of the curve at various distances from the mean) accurately describes the form of the distribution of many types of actual data. The properties of the normal curve are especially useful to the physical educator because it has been demonstrated that measures of many physical traits approximate the normal curve if the measures are obtained from a group of subjects who are relatively homogeneous in regard to factors that affect the trait being measured. For example, a distribution of height measures will closely approximate the normal curve if a large number of subjects who are the same age, race, and sex are involved in the sample. Care must be taken not to make too many assumptions of normality, but knowledge of some of the characteristics of the normal curve is useful in interpreting a set of scores.

Characteristics of the normal curve

Some of the important characteristics of the normal curve are illustrated in Figure 5.1. The three measures of central tendency described earlier—the mean, median, and mode—are all located at the same point. If a line is drawn from this point on the baseline to the curve, the line bisects the curve into two symmetrical halves. In theory, the normal curve extends continuously on either side of the mean, continually approaching the baseline but never touching it. Distances from the mean are marked off in terms of standard deviation units.

The height of the normal curve above any point on the baseline is a function of the distance that point is from the mean. From this it follows that the area under the curve between the same two random points on the baselines of different normal curves, will always be the same proportion of the total area

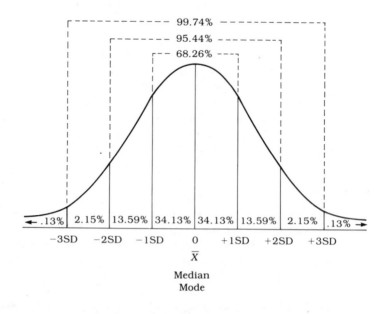

Figure 5.1   The normal curve

under the curve. This is true for any normal curve, regardless of the units in which it is plotted. The fact that the location and the distance between two points on the baseline are related to the area under the curve between the two points is the single most important characteristic of the normal curve.

The values in the body of Table 5.1 are the decimal fractions of the total area under the curve between the mean and the standard deviation units listed on the perimeter of the table. For example, .1517 (or 15.17 percent) of the area lies between the mean and 0.39 standard deviation units. Several interesting

Table 5.1   Areas of the normal curve

	.00	.01	.02	.03	.04	.05	.06	.07	.08	.09
.00	.0000	.0040	.0080	.0120	.0159	.0199	.0239	.0279	.0319	.0359
.10	.0398	.0438	.0478	.0517	.0557	.0596	.0636	.0675	.0714	.0753
.20	.0793	.0832	.0871	.0971	.0948	.0987	.1026	.1064	.1103	.1141
.30	.1179	.1217	.1255	.1293	.1331	.1368	.1406	.1443	.1480	.1517
.40	.1554	.1591	.1628	.1664	.1700	.1736	.1772	.1808	.1844	.1879
.50	.1915	.1950	.1985	.2019	.2054	.2088	.2123	.2157	.2190	.2224
.60	.2257	.2291	.2324	.2357	.2387	.2422	.2454	.2486	.2517	.2549
.70	.2580	.2611	.2642	.2673	.2703	.2734	.2764	.2794	.2823	.2852
.80	.2881	.2910	.2939	.2967	.2995	.3023	.3051	.3078	.3106	.3133
.90	.3159	.3186	.3212	.3238	.3264	.3289	.3315	.3340	.3365	.3389
1.00	.3413	.3438	.3461	.3485	.3508	.3581	.3554	.3577	.3599	.3621
1.10	.3643	.3665	.3686	.3707	.3729	.3749	.3770	.3790	.3810	.3830
1.20	.3849	.3869	.3885	.3907	.3925	.3944	.3962	.3980	.3997	.4015
1.30	.4032	.4049	.4066	.4082	.4099	.4115	.4131	.4147	.4162	.4177
1.40	.4192	.4207	.4222	.4236	.4251	.4265	.4279	.4292	.4306	.4319
1.50	.4332	.4345	.4357	.4370	.4382	.4394	.4406	.4418	.4429	.4441
1.60	.4452	.4463	.4474	.4484	.4495	.4505	.4515	.4525	.4535	.4545
1.70	.4554	.4564	.4573	.4582	.4591	.4599	.4608	.4616	.4625	.4633
1.80	.4641	.4649	.4656	.4664	.4671	.4678	.4686	.4693	.4699	.4706
1.90	.4713	.4719	.4726	.4732	.4738	.4744	.4750	.4756	.4761	.4767
2.00	.4772	.4778	.4783	.4788	.4793	.4798	.4803	.4808	.4812	.4813
2.10	.4821	.4826	.4830	.4834	.4838	.4842	.4846	.4850	.4854	.4857
2.20	.4861	.4864	.4868	.4871	.4875	.4878	.4881	.4884	.4887	.4890
2.30	.4893	.4896	.4898	.4901	.4904	.4906	.4909	.4911	.4913	.4916
2.40	.4918	.4920	.4922	.4925	.4927	.4929	.4931	.4932	.4934	.4936
2.50	.4938	.4940	.4941	.4943	.4945	.4946	.4948	.4949	.4951	.4952
2.60	.4953	.4955	.4956	.4957	.4959	.4960	.4961	.4962	.4963	.4964
2.70	.4965	.4966	.4967	.4968	.4969	.4970	.4971	.4972	.4973	.4974
2.80	.4974	.4975	.4976	.4977	.3977	.4978	.4979	.4979	.4980	.4981
2.90	.4981	.4982	.4982	.4983	.4984	.4984	.4985	.4985	.4986	.4986
3.00	.4987									

facts can be obtained from this table. As an illustration, if a set of scores is assumed to be normally distributed, approximately two thirds of the scores should fall within the distance one standard deviation above and below the mean. This information is obtained by noticing that the area between the mean and +1.00 standard deviation unit is 34.13 percent of the total area under the curve. Since the normal curve is symmetrical, the same percentage of the curve must lie between the mean and −1.00 standard deviation unit for a total of 68.26 percent (approximately two-thirds) of the total area under the curve.

Table 5.1 can be used to determine the area under the curve between almost any two points on the baseline of a normal curve. For example, the area between +1.5 and +2.5 standard deviation units can be determined to be 6.06 percent of the total area by subtracting .4332 (area between mean and 1.5) from .4938 (area between mean and 2.5). Verify that 84.84 percent of the total area under the normal curve lies between −1.32 and +1.57 standard deviation units. The relevancy of this information concerning the normal curve will become increasingly apparent in the remainder of this chapter.

STANDARD SCORES

Measures sometimes cannot be directly compared because they are expressed in different units. One solution to this problem is to convert each distribution of scores into a standard form.

z-scores

An example of such a standard measure is the z-score. The formula to determine the z-score value corresponding to any raw score is as follows:

$$z = \frac{X - \overline{X}}{SD},$$

where z = the standard score
X = the particular raw score being converted to standard form
$\overline{X}$ = the mean of the raw score distribution
SD = the standard deviation of the raw score distribution.

The resulting z-score actually designates how many standard deviation units the particular score deviates from the mean of the distribution. For example, Bill's score of 83 in the distribution having a mean of 63 and a standard deviation of 15 corresponds to a z-score of 1.33.

$$z = \frac{83 - 63}{15} = \frac{20}{15} = 1.33$$

This z-score indicates that Bill's score is 1.33 standard deviation units above the mean. A score of 50 from this same distribution corresponds to a z-score of −0.86.

$$z = \frac{50-63}{15} = \frac{-13}{15} = -0.86$$

Thus, a raw score of 50 is 0.86 standard deviation units *below* the mean. From the z-score formula it should be evident that positive z-scores are obtained when the raw score lies above the mean, and negative z-scores are obtained when the raw score lies below the mean.

It is not necessary to assume that a distribution is normal or approximately normal before converting it to a standard form. The conversion does nothing to alter the form of the original raw score distribution. However, if the raw score distribution is normally distributed or approximately so, the z-score conversion becomes especially meaningful. For example, if the sit-up scores are assumed to be normally distributed, Bill's score of 83 surpasses approximately 91 percent of the distribution. This value (actually 90.82) is obtained by adding 40.82, which is the percentage of the area under the curve between the mean and 1.33 standard deviations above the mean (Table 5.1) and 50.00, which is the percentage of the area under the curve occurring below the mean. As a further illustration, consider the raw score of 50 corresponding to a z-score of −0.86. Since the percentage of the area under the curve between the mean and 0.86 standard deviation units is 30.51 and because the negative sign indicates this score is below the mean, the raw score of 50 exceeds approximately 19.5 percent of the scores (50 − 30.51 = 19.49) if the sit-up data are in fact normally distributed.

Besides providing information about an individual score in a distribution, z-scores can be used to compare a score from one distribution to a score from another. The example below illustrates how this is done.

Bill learned that his standing long jump score was 97 inches and that his softball throw for distance score was 225 feet. Comparison between the two raw scores reveals very little because of the differing units and the dissimilarity of the tasks. When informed that the class mean on the standing long jump test was 85 inches and on the softball throw, 180 feet, Bill can determine that his performance on both tests was above average but is still unable to ascertain which of the two was the better performance. However, knowledge of the z-score corresponding to Bill's two scores can be used to compare the two performances. Notice that to obtain the z-score values it is necessary to determine the mean and standard deviation for each raw score distribution. The necessary statistics and calculations are shown below.

Standing long jump test	*Softball throw for distance test*
$\overline{X}$ = 85 inches	$\overline{X}$ = 180 feet
SD = 9 inches	SD = 30 feet
Bill's score = 97 inches	Bill's score = 225 feet
z-score $= \dfrac{97-85}{9}$	z-score $= \dfrac{225-180}{30}$
$= \dfrac{12}{9}$	$= \dfrac{45}{30}$
$= 1.33$	$= 1.5$

Assuming that the two tests were administered to the same group of students, it is now possible to conclude that Bill's performance in the softball throw was superior to that for the standing long jump test.

Another popular standard score scale is the T-scale, which has a mean of 50 and a standard deviation of 10. The formula for converting a raw score into a T-score is as follows:

$$\text{T-score} = 50 + \frac{10(X - \overline{X})}{SD},$$

where   T-score = the standard score

X = the particular raw score being converted into a T-score
$\overline{X}$ = the mean of the raw score distribution
SD = the standard deviation of the raw score distribution.

Bill's sit-up score of 83, which corresponded to a z-score of 1.33, is equivalent to a T-score of 63.

$$\text{T-score} = 50 + \frac{10(83 - 63)}{15}$$
$$= 50 + 13 = 63$$

Considerations of standard scores

Although the T-score scale eliminates the inconvenience of working with signs and decimals, it introduces a new problem — interpretation. Virtually all (99.73 percent) of the scores in a normal distribution are located between points three standard deviations below and three standard deviations above the mean. For this reason, and because the T-scale has a mean of 50 and a standard deviation of 10, the T-score values obtained by conversion of a raw score distribution that approximates the normal curve will seldom have a value less than 20 or greater than 80. An unknowing student may interpret a T-score of 80, extremely high, as mediocre unless educated as to the interpretations and uses that can be made of standard scores.

One further use of standard scores is in deriving composite scores. This is an extremely valuable procedure for the physical educator. Frequently it is necessary to combine scores from several different tests to arrive at a single score for each student. Because in physical education the scores on various tests are often expressed in different units, the raw scores cannot be added together to arrive at a meaningful composite score. In a track unit, for example, it would not be reasonable to add together the time in seconds for a student to run a 100-yard dash and the distance in feet that the shotput was thrown. Even if scores from various tests are expressed in the same units, unless certain conditions are met it is not valid to simply add them together to obtain a composite score. Because this use of standard scores has its greatest implications in the area of grading, a discussion of how and why standard scores are used to obtain composite scores will be deferred until Chapter 21.

Finally, depending on the size of the distribution of scores, it may be more efficient to construct a conversion table than to determine the standard score corresponding to each raw score. Such a conversion table for T-scores can be constructed in the following manner:

Step 1. Write the numbers from 20 to 80 in a vertical column. These numbers represént T-score values.

Step 2. Place the mean of the raw score distribution opposite the T-score of 50.

Step 3. Multiply the standard deviation of the raw score distribution by 0.1. (This value is derived from the fact that for the T-score scale 5 standard deviation units are divided into 50 T-score values.)

Step 4. Add the product obtained in step 3 to the mean and place this sum opposite the T-score 51.

Step 5. Add the product obtained in step 3 to the value placed opposite the T-score 51 and place this sum opposite the T-score 52.

Step 6. Continue in this fashion until the T-score of 80 is reached.

Step 7. Subtract the product obtained in step 3 from the mean and place the difference opposite the T-score 49.

Step 8. Subtract the product obtained in step 3 from the value placed opposite the T-score 49 and place this difference opposite the T-score 48.

Step 9. Continue in this fashion until the T-score of 20 is reached.

Step 10. Round off the scores opposite the T-score values.

The results of this procedure for the sit-up data are displayed in Table 5.2.

Table 5.2   Conversion of raw scores to T-scores

T-scores		Raw scores	T-scores	Raw scores	T-scores		Raw scores
73	97.9	98	57	73.9	74	41	49.9	50
72	96.4	96	56	72.4	72	40	48.4	48
71	94.9	95	55	70.9	71	39	46.9	47
70	93.4	93	54	69.4	69	38	45.4	45
69	91.9	92	53	67.9	68	37	43.9	44
68	90.4	90	52	66.4	66	36	42.4	42
67	88.9	89	51	64.9	65	35	40.9	41
66	87.4	87	50	63.4	63	34	39.4	39
65	85.9	86	49	61.9	62	33	37.9	38
64	84.4	84	48	60.4	60	32	32.4	36
63	82.9	83	47	58.9	59	31	34.9	35
62	81.4	81	46	57.4	57	30	33.4	33
61	79.9	80	45	55.9	56	29	31.9	32
60	78.4	78	44	54.4	54	28	30.4	30
59	76.9	77	43	52.9	53	27	28.9	29
58	75.4	75	42	51.4	51	26	27.4	27
						25	25.9	26

Because the highest number of sit-ups performed was 98 it was necessary to continue step 6 only to the T-score value of 73. Likewise because the lowest number of sit-ups done was 26, step 9 was continued only to the T-score value of 25.

$\overline{X}$ = 63.40
SD = 14.97
Step 3 14.97 × 0.1 = 1.497 = 1.5 rounded off.

In the listing of the data in Table 3.1 there appears a score of 76 sit-ups. However, in Table 5.2 there is no value of 76 in the raw score column. What T-score should be assigned to this score? Actually it makes little difference if a T-score of 58 or 59 is chosen as long as whatever procedure is adopted is used consistently. In this particular case, a T-score of 58 is probably more correct than 59 because 76 is slightly closer to 75.4 than to 76.9.

PERCENTILES AND PERCENTILE RANKS

Another method is sometimes employed to indicate the relative standing of a particular score in a distribution. This method, less precise than standard scores because it is limited to the determination of the rank of a score within a set of scores, involves rank-order scales.

One obvious procedure would be to simply arrange a set of scores in chronological order and determine the rank of each score in the set by counting. This technique, though somewhat meaningful when only one set of scores is being examined, does not allow comparison among sets of scores unless the sets all contain an equal number of scores. Merely ranking scores gives little more information than the raw scores unless the size of the distribution is also known, and even then comparison to other rankings is difficult if different size distributions are involved.

This problem is solved by expressing the rank of a score in terms of the total number of scores in the distribution. This generally is accomplished by stating the percentage of the scores in the distribution that fall below the particular score in question. Ranks reported in this manner are called percentile ranks.

A *percentile rank* of a point on a score scale is defined as the percentage of scores in the set of scores that are below this point. The *percentile* is the score point below which a given percentage of the scores lie. For example, in the sit-up data, 13 of the 65 scores occur below the score point of 51. Thus the *percentile rank* of the score point 51 is 20 ($13 \div 65 = .20$). Conversely, the 20th *percentile* has the value 51 in this distribution.

Calculation of percentiles and percentile ranks

The method for determining one particular percentile—the median, defined as the point on the score scale below which 50 percent of the scores fall—has already been presented. Also, in determining the semi-interquartile range it was necessary to calculate the score points corresponding to the 25th and the 75th percentiles. The basic procedure is the same for determining any percentile of interest. As an example, assume it is necessary to determine the 60th percentile for the sit-up data. Since there are 65 scores in this distribution the value of the 60th percentile must lie just above the 39th score ($65 \times .60 = 39.0$). By referring to Table 3.2 it can be determined that the 39th score from the bottom of the distribution has the value of 66. Thus, 39 scores fall below the score of 67 which is then the value of the 60th percentile.

Although this procedure could be repeated to find any or all percentiles desired, it is usually of more value to be able to calculate the percentile ranks of each score in the distribution. As with standard scores, if the distribution is relatively large, construction of a table to convert each score is more efficient than converting each score individually. To construct a conversion table, such as Table 5.3, the following steps must be taken:

> *Step 1.* Set up a frequency distribution having an interval size of 1. The top interval is the highest score and the bottom interval is the lowest score in the distribution. Record the frequency of occurrence of each score in the frequency (f) column.

Table 5.3   Conversion of raw scores to percentile ranks: Sit-up data

Interval	Frequency (f)	Cumulative frequency (cf)	Cumulative frequency of midpoint (cfm)	Percentile rank (pr)	Interval	Frequenc (f)
98	1	65	64.5	99	74	1
97		64	64	98	73	2
96		64	64	98	72	1
95		64	64	98	71	2
94		64	64	98	70	1
93	1	64	63.5	98	69	1
92		63	63	97	68	1
91	1	63	62.5	96	67	2
90		62	62	95	66	1
89		62	62	95	65	3
88	1	62	61.5	95	64	2
87		61	61	94	63	4
86	1	61	60.5	93	62	2
85	1	60	59.5	92	61	2
84		59	59	91	60	1
83	1	59	58.5	90	59	1
82		58	58	89	58	
81	2	58	57	88	57	2
80		56	56	86	56	2
79	1	56	55.5	85	55	2
78	2	55	54	83	54	1
77	1	53	52.5	81	53	1
76	1	52	51.5	80	52	1
75	1	51	50.5	78	51	1
					50	1

Step 2. Construct the cumulative frequency (cf) column. The cumulative frequency for any interval is the sum of the frequency for the interval plus the total of every interval below it.

Step 3. Construct the cumulative frequency of the midpoint (cfm) column. The cfm value for any interval is determined by adding one-half the f value for the interval to the cf value of the next lower interval. For example, the score 65 occurs three times in this distribution and 35 scores occur that are lower than 65. Thus the cfm value for this interval is 36.5 obtained by adding 1.5 (3÷2) to 35. The value of the cfm is based on the assumption that scores in an interval are evenly distributed within that

Cumulative frequency (f)	Cumulative frequency of midpoint (cfm)	Percentile rank (pr)	Interval	Frequency (f)	Cumulative frequency (cf)	Cumulative frequency of midpoint (cfm)	Percentile rank (pr)
50	49.5	76	49		12	12	18
49	48	74	48	1	12	11.5	18
47	46.5	72	47	2	11	10	15
46	45	70	46	1	9	8.5	13
44	43.5	67	45	1	8	7.5	12
43	42.5	65	44	1	7	6.5	10
42	41.5	64	43		6	6	9
41	40	62	42		6	6	9
39	38.5	60	41	1	6	5.5	8
38	36.5	56	40	1	5	4.5	7
35	34	52	39		4	4	6
33	31	48	38	1	4	3.5	5
29	28	43	37	1	3	2.5	4
27	26	40	36	1	2	1.5	2
25	24.5	38	35		1	1	2
24	23.5	36	34		1	1	2
23	23	35	33		1	1	2
23	22	34	32		1	1	2
21	20	31	31		1	1	2
19	18	28	30		1	1	2
17	16.5	25	29		1	1	2
16	15.5	24	28		1	1	2
15	14.5	22	27		1	1	2
14	13.5	21	26	1	1	0.5	1
13	12.5	19					

interval. Thus 1.5 of the three scores occurring in the interval 65 are assumed to be below and 1.5 of the three scores are assumed to be above the midpoint of this interval.

Step 4. Divide the number of scores in the distribution into 100 to obtain the constant necessary to convert the cfm values into percentages. For the example given, the value of this constant is 1.54 ($100 \div 65 = 1.54$).

Step 5. For each interval multiply the cfm value by the constant obtained in step 4. Since each interval encompasses only one raw score value, the resulting product for each interval is the percentile rank (pr) associated with a different score in the distribution.

Considerations of percentile scores

No score in a distribution can be higher (or lower) than 100 percent of the scores in that distribution. For this reason it is not possible to obtain a percentile rank of 100 or 0 (although these values may be approached with very large sets of data). In these cases percentile ranks such as 0.4 and 99.7 may result. Occasionally, though incorrectly, these values are rounded off to 0 and 100.

Notice in Table 5.3 that in a few instances more than one raw score value corresponds to the same percentile rank and yet in other areas of the table some percentile ranks are missing. This is a result of the sample size and the range of the raw score values. Although it is true that for very large and widely variable distributions this does not happen as often as with small and narrow distributions, the value and usefulness of percentile ranks is not lessened by this occurrence.

The greatest advantage in using percentiles lies in their relatively simple interpretation. Generally, most students are aware that 84 percent of the scores in a distribution fall below the score given a percentile rank of 84. Although helpful in making raw scores meaningful to students by indicating relative position in a distribution, percentiles are not as useful as standard scores for obtaining composite scores. In fact, percentiles should not be used for combining or averaging scores.

NORMS

A raw score is not high or low in any absolute sense. It is, however, higher or lower than other scores. To determine whether a particular raw score is high or low implies comparison to some standard. This standard often takes the form of a set of norms. Norms, then, are generally constructed for the purpose of interpreting data. There are several different types of norms.

Types of norms

A raw score can be related to a general frame of reference in two ways. One is to compare the score to a sequential series of groups to see where it fits best. The other is to determine where, in a particular group, a score falls. With sequential groups, each may represent a particular chronological age (age norms) or a grade in school (grade norms). With a particular group, the location of the score may be given in terms of the percentage of the group the score surpasses, (percentile norms) or in terms of the mean and standard deviation of the distribution from which it came (standard score norm). Each of these methods of interpreting physical education data has some advantages and disadvantages.

Age norms

Many physical characteristics change with age, and it is for these traits that age norms should be used. Age norms are constructed by determining the average value of the trait in question for any particular age. For example, if a representative sample of ten-year-old boys is given a sit-up test and the average number of sit-ups performed is determined, the result is the norm for sit-ups for ten-year-old boys. This procedure could be repeated for 11-year-old boys, 12-year-old boys, and so forth.

A frequency polygon (see Figure 5.2) could be constructed and the line connecting the determined values assumed to be continuous so estimates could be made for ages between those for which data are available. For example, the norm value for the average 11½-year-old could be estimated from Figure 5.2 to be 48.

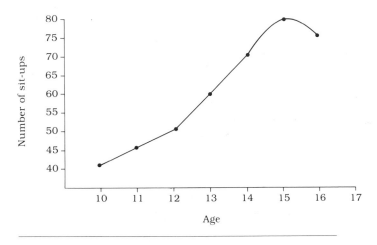

Figure 5.2   Frequency polygon for number of sit-ups and age

It is also possible to read this graph from the other direction. A boy capable of doing 50 sit-ups can be described as being able to perform sit-ups as well as the average 12-year-old boy. If the boy's actual age is known, it is then possible to interpret his performance as being superior, average, or poor for his age. The major advantage of age norms lies in their convenience and familiarity. It is simple and meaningful to report that "He is as strong as a 14-year-old!"

Age norms do have some disadvantages that should be recognized. Comparisons of various traits are very tenuous when done on the basis of age norms because rates of change and the ages when maximums are reached differ greatly. For example, average scores on the standing long jump test continue to improve through age seventeen, whereas average sit-up scores peak at age fifteen. Thus for a 14-year-old to have reached the 16-year-old level represents entirely different degrees of superiority for these two measures. Also, because of the changing improvement rate, a two-year acceleration may have substantially different meaning depending on when it happens. In performing sit-ups, for example, an 11-year-old scoring at the 13-year-old level represents a greater accomplishment than a 14-year-old scoring at the 16-year-old level.

Another problem arises in trying to classify a performance that results in a score not located on the graph. For example, the performance of a boy who does 90 sit-ups cannot be classified as average for any age.

Grade norms

Grade norms are very similar to age norms, differing only in the fact that the reference groups are grade groups instead of age groups. Consequently, the advantages and disadvantages of grade norms are virtually the same as those mentioned for age norms.

The major limitation of grade norms is the lack of assurance that growth of one grade is the same amount of growth at all grades. The use of grade norms is only reasonable for those subjects in which instruction is continuous through all or a major portion of the school program. Grade norms are thus more useful in elementary school than in high school.

Grade norms must be interpreted with care. If, for example, on a standardized physical education test given at the end of the year a fourth-grade student obtains a score for which the grade equivalent is 7.0, this should not be interpreted as indicating that the student has a mastery of all or even a large part of the physical education concepts taught in the fifth and sixth grades. The score this student achieved is as high as the average beginning seventh-grade student, but the high score is very probably the result of a high degree of mastery of fourth-grade work. This high score should not be interpreted as indicating that the student is ready to enter seventh-grade physical education.

Percentile norms

Age norms and grade norms aid in interpreting a score by determining the age or grade in which the score would be average. Percentile norms aid in interpretation of a score by comparing it to scores obtained by similar students. In fact, the process of converting the sit-up scores to percentile scores described earlier in this chapter is in actuality the construction of a set of norms.

Although percentile norms are widely used and are applicable to almost any situation, they have two major shortcomings. The first problem involves the norming group. If a set of raw scores for a single class of students is converted to percentile ranks for interpretative purposes, no problem exists. However, if it is desirable to compare the performance of a group or an individual with that of another class, school, city, state, or other population group, the comparability of the group or individual to the other population must first be established. For example, it is not reasonable to obtain a score for a sixth-grade girl on the standing long jump test and then determine the percentile rank of this score from a set of norms established on ninth-grade boys.

To use percentile norms, then, it is necessary to have a set constructed on the basis of scores achieved by students and under conditions very similar to those for whom the norms are to be used. This is one of the major reasons so few physical education tests are accompanied by percentile norms. This also underscores the importance of each physical educator being capable of constructing norms. Even for tests such as the American Alliance for Health, Physical Education, Recreation, and Dance (AAHPERD) Youth Fitness Test, for which national norms are available, the local conditions, facilities, and type of students may dictate that local norms be developed. Often local norms can provide more significant interpretations of scores than national norms.

Unfortunately the second shortcoming of percentile norms is more serious than that involved with the norming group. Percentiles assume equal distances between scores. In other words, percentiles are the points on the score scale that divide the distribution into 100 equal-sized groups. However, as previously pointed out, scores on most physical education measures tend to approximate the normal distribution by piling up in the center and becoming less frequent as the extremes are approached. Thus, the range of percentile ranks needed to encompass some percentage of the scores at one of the extremes is much greater than the range of percentile ranks needed to encompass the same percentage of the scores in the center of the distribution. For example, to encompass approximately 12 percent (eight scores) of the sit-up scores (see Table 5.3) at the lower extreme it is necessary to go from a percentile rank of 26 to 45 while in the center of the distribution the same percentage of scores is encompassed by the percentile ranks 62 to 64.

This problem usually manifests itself when looked at from the other direction. The student performing 62 sit-ups (percentile rank of 43) notices that if he would have done but one more sit-up his percentile rank would have increased to 48. On the other hand, the student doing 88 sit-ups would have to do 3 more to increase his percentile rank from 95 to 96. This result is due simply to the fact that transformation of scores into percentile ranks alters the form of the distribution. For this reason it is necessary to use some form of standard scores to obtain composite scores.

Standard score norms

The conversion of a set of raw scores into z-scores, T-scores, or any other of several standard forms is, in effect, the construction of a set of standard score norms.

The major advantage of standard score norms over percentile norms is the equality of the unit throughout the entire range of values. Recall that converting a raw score to a z-score results in an expression of the raw score in terms of its number of standard deviation units above or below the mean of the raw score distribution. This standard unit of measure has substantially the same meaning from test to test. Other standard score scales have been devised with various means and standard deviations due to varying philosophies. However, for whatever scale is selected, as long as the same score scale and comparable norming groups are used for all tests given, the results from different tests are directly comparable.

In summary, for standard scores as for percentiles the interpretation of a score is based on its relationship to a particular reference group. However, unlike percentiles, standard scores are expressed in supposedly equal units which are based on the standard deviation of the reference group. Several different standard score scales have been devised, but all are modifications of the basic z-score scale.

Quotients

Although helpful for interpreting the score of one individual, it is difficult to compare the performance of two or more students using age norms. For example, which performance is superior—a nine-year-old obtaining an age equivalent of 11.5 years or a fifteen-year-old obtaining an age equivalent of seventeen years? In an effort to answer this type of question and thus develop an index that would include an indication of rate of progress, the quotient was devised. Generally, a quotient is simply an obtained score divided by an appropriate norm value. (The result of the division, a quotient, is commonly multiplied by 100 to avoid decimal numbers.)

Probably the most well-known quotient is the intelligence quotient, or IQ. The formula for IQ is as follows:

$$IQ = \frac{MA}{CA} \times 100,$$

where   IQ = intelligence quotient
   MA = mental age (score on an intelligence test)
   CA = chronological age.

Assuming the question in the previous paragraph involved intelligence test data, the IQ's of the two students would be as follows:

$$IQ = \frac{11.5}{9} \times 100 = 128 \qquad IQ = \frac{17}{15} \times 100 = 113$$

Notice that the two performances can be compared in this way and the performance of the younger student is revealed as being superior.

Quotients have not been used extensively in physical education. Rogers[1] in 1926 and McCloy[2] in 1939 published what amount to strength quotients. In each case the obtained score is secured through a battery of strength tests and the norm value is based on the factors of sex, age, and body weight. The awesome task of accumulating the appropriate normative data is undoubtedly one of the major reasons why the quotient is seldom used in physical education and other disciplines.

Profiles

The raw scores on two or more different tests are not meaningful if compared directly. However, through the use of norms the scores can be expressed in common units and thus compared. When this procedure is followed involving a series of scores for one individual the result is called a profile. Profiles are commonly used to interpret the results of diagnostic and other test batteries.

A great variety of types of profile charts are possible because the type of norms, methods of graphing, and formats for presenting the information vary considerably.

In physical education measurement probably the most frequent use of profiles is made in conjunction with physical fitness test batteries. Figure 5.3 is a profile chart that can be used with the AAHPERD Youth Fitness Test. The student records, in the appropriate column, the percentile norm corresponding to the obtained raw score for each of the six items in the test battery. Frequently a line joining the percentile ranks for each test is constructed to increase the visual impact of the profile. The results of several administrations of the entire test battery can be plotted on the same profile chart by using different colors each time.

The greatest advantage of using profiles lies in the pictorial summary obtained for interpreting the test scores. At a glance the student can see how he or she stands in relation to any standard included in the profile. In Figure 5.3, for example, a line corresponding to the 50th percentile has been made darker than the others to serve as a reference point. It would be possible to include on the profile chart the average score for the group tested, for each test in the battery. This information would reveal the strengths and weaknesses of the individual in relation to the other students in the group. Further, if the same profile chart is used for consecutive administrations of the test battery, improvement, or lack of it, is easily and quickly noticeable.

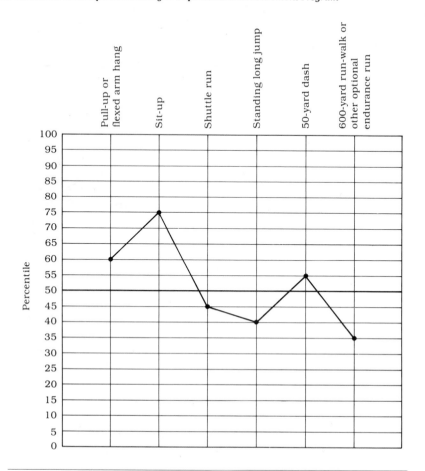

Figure 5.3   Sample profile record for American Alliance for Health, Physical Education and Recreation, and Dance (AAHPERD) Youth Fitness Test

Two important considerations must be recognized when using profile charts to interpret scores. First, the normative data for each test represented on the profile chart must be based on comparable populations and appropriate for the student's scores being plotted on the profile. The development of local norms based on a common group is the best way to satisfy this requirement. If separately developed tests are plotted together, unless the populations on which the norms are based are comparable, the resulting profile chart would be very misleading.

The second consideration involves the reliability of testing procedures. For a great variety of reasons test scores cannot be assumed to be perfectly accurate. Thus, some portion of the fluctuation of the line on a profile chart is due to chance and some part due to actual differences in ability on the tests involved. Unfortunately it is not possible to separate the portions of the fluctuation due to each of these factors. However, it is known that, as the reliability of the measurements decreases, the amount of fluctuation due to chance increases. For this reason, small differences among scores on a profile chart should not be regarded as important but should be attributed to chance. Also, as the reliability of the measurements decreases, larger differences among scores are probably due to chance and must be interpreted with this in mind. The interpretation must be based on common sense and take into account the unreliability of some testing procedures.

REFERENCES CITED

[1]Frederick R. Rogers, *Physical Capacity Tests in the Administration of Physical Education* (New York: Bureau of Publication, Teachers College, Columbia University, 1926).

[2]C. H. McCloy and Norma D. Young, *Tests and Measurements in Health and Physical Education* (New York: Appelton-Century-Crofts, Inc., 1954).

Chapter 6

Correlation and Group Comparisons

The techniques previously explained for arranging, describing, and interpreting data primarily involve one set of scores. At times the physical educator may be interested in comparing two sets of scores. For example, it may be of interest to determine whether scores from a measure of strength are in any way associated with scores from a gymnastics performance test. Correlational techniques could be employed in this case. As another possibility, a physical educator might be interested in comparing the average strength score obtained by one class to that obtained by another class. A statistical procedure called a t-test might be used to make this comparison.

CORRELATION TECHNIQUES

When measures of two traits are obtained for a class of students it may be noticed that the two scores for each student tend to be related in some way. They may have approximately the same relative position in each distribution, or the first score may be above average while the second is below average. The correlation coefficient can be used as a method of quantifying these relationships.

Not a correlation coefficient, but somewhat descriptive, a scatter diagram may be constructed to examine visually the nature of the relationship between two sets of scores. This is done by plotting both scores for each student on one graph. The following example involving the heights and weights of twenty-five seventh-grade students listed in Table 6.1 illustrates the procedures for constructing a scatter diagram.

Table 6.1   Heights and weights of twenty-five students

Student	Height (inches)	Weight (pounds)	Student	Height (inches)	Weight (pounds)
1	50	49	14	58	110
2	52	62	15	59	69
3	55	69	16	59	100
4	56	65	17	60	63
5	56	72	18	60	91
6	56	78	19	61	100
7	57	70	20	61	105
8	57	73	21	61	120
9	57	75	22	62	124
10	57	83	23	62	126
11	57	94	23	63	110
12	58	74	25	65	131
13	58	84			

Examination of Table 6.1 and Figure 6.1 reveals that heights and weights of these particular students are related to some degree because there is a tendency for taller students to be heavier and shorter students to be lighter. This type of situation (high scores on one trait associated with high scores on the other trait) is called a positive relationship. A negative relationship occurs when high scores on one trait are associated with low scores on a second trait. The relationship between the average velocity and the time required to run a mile is an example of a negative relationship (the higher the average velocity, the less time required). Notice that the general pattern of the plotted points of a scatter diagram of a negative relationship would run from the lower right corner to the upper left corner of the graph. This is the opposite of the pattern displayed in Figure 6.1, in which a positive relationship is plotted. Thus the words positive and negative refer to the direction of the relationship.

Another consideration is the degree of the relationship between two sets of scores. Are the two traits closely related or is the relationship tenuous at best? Two traits are related to some degree if all students in the class who have the same score on the first trait exhibit less variability on the second trait than the variability of all the students in the class. For example, height and weight for most populations chosen are related to some degree because the variability of the weights for a group of students all of the same height is less than the variability of the weights of all the students in a class. The amount of the reduction of the variability is what determines the degree of the relationship.

If the variability is reduced so far that none remains, the relationship is considered to be perfect. If there is no reduction in the variability (that is, the variability of the scores on the second trait is the same for a group of students having identical scores on the first trait as it is for all the students in the class), no relationship exists between the two sets of scores. For example, given the

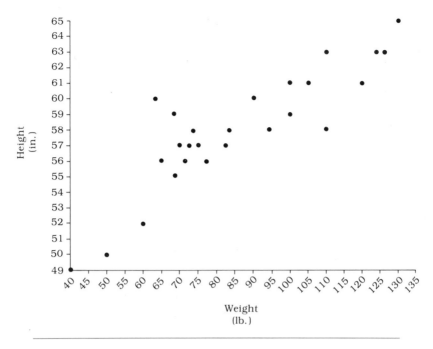

Figure 6.1   Scatter diagram of twenty-five pairs of heights and weights

length of the side of a square, the area can only be one value. Thus the relationship between a set of scores representing the length of the side of a square and a second set of scores representing the area of the corresponding square is perfect because no variation exists among the area values for all squares having a given side length. On the other hand it is generally accepted that no relationship exists between height and intelligence. Thus the variability of the IQ scores for a group of students, say 56 inches tall, is not significantly different from that of the variability of the IQ scores for a group of students of differing heights.

The degree as well as the direction of the relationship existing between two traits is reflected by the general pattern of the points plotted in a scatter diagram. If a perfect relationship is plotted, the result is a line since no variation exists among the scores. As the degree of the relationship becomes increasingly less than perfect and approaches the situation where no relationship exists, the pattern of the plotted points changes from a line to an ever-widening oval and finally into a random pattern of dots.

Although the scatter diagram can be used to obtain a general notion of the relationship existing between two sets of scores, it is difficult to interpret and compare with other scatter diagrams. For these reasons, a single index reflecting the degree and direction of the relationship is desirable. Such an index, the correlation coefficient, has been devised.

The correlation coefficient includes all the values from $+1.00$ to -1.00. The symbol r is generally used to represent a correlation coefficient and the sign indicates the direction of the relationship, positive or negative. As the degree of the relationship between two variables increases, the absolute value of r increases until a perfect correlation is indicated by 1.00 (either positive or negative). An r of 0.00 indicates that no correlation exists.

USES OF CORRELATION COEFFICIENTS

Definitions of reliability, validity, and objectivity were presented in Chapter 2. Quantifying these concepts is one of the primary uses of the correlation coefficient because they all involve determining the degree of relationship that exists between two or more sets of scores. The specific procedures involved are explained in Chapter 7. Correlational techniques can also be used in predictive and inferential statistical situations but these procedures are not often required of the physical educator and thus are not presented.

CALCULATION OF CORRELATION COEFFICIENTS

Pearson product-moment correlation coefficient

Karl Pearson, an English statistician, introduced a measure of relationship, called the Pearson product-moment correlation coefficient, based on the conversion of the raw scores into z-scores. The definitional formula derived by Pearson is:

$$r_{XY} = \frac{Z_X Z_Y}{N} \, ,$$

where

$$r_{XY} = \text{the correlation between the } X \text{ scores and the } Y \text{ scores}$$
$$Z_X Z_Y = \text{the sum of the cross products obtained by multiplying,}$$
for each student, the z-score corresponding to the
X-score by the z-score corresponding to the Y-score
$$N = \text{the number of pairs of scores.}$$

From this definitional formula many computational formulas have been devised. Although the formula below looks much more complicated than the definitional formula, it has the advantage of involving raw scores rather than z-scores. In other words, the steps involved in converting each set of scores into z-scores are incorporated into this formula so that by substituting the appropriate raw score values the correlation coefficient is obtained directly:

$$r_{XY} = \frac{N(\Sigma XY) - (\Sigma X)(\Sigma Y)}{\sqrt{[\, N(\Sigma X^2) - (\Sigma X)^2 \,]\, [\, N(\Sigma Y^2) - (\Sigma Y)^2 \,]}}$$

where

$$r_{XY} = \text{the correlation between the } X\text{-scores and the}$$
Y-scores
$$N = \text{the number of pairs of scores}$$
$$\Sigma XY = \text{the sum of the cross products obtained by}$$
multiplying, for each student, the X-score by the
Y-score
$$\Sigma X = \text{the sum of the } X\text{-scores}$$
$$\Sigma Y = \text{the sum of the } Y\text{-scores}$$
$$\Sigma X^2 = \text{the sum of the squared } X\text{-scores}$$
$$(\Sigma X)^2 = \text{the square of the sum of the } X\text{-scores}$$
$$\Sigma Y^2 = \text{the sum of the squared } Y\text{-scores}$$
$$(\Sigma Y)^2 = \text{the square of the sum of the } Y\text{-scores.}$$

Table 6.2 illustrates the data arrangement and the calculation of the various values necessary to compute the Pearson product-moment correlation coefficient with ungrouped data. The data used in the illustration are the 25 heights and weights listed in Table 6.1.

The values (which may be relatively simply obtained using a calculator with the capacity to accumulate squares or products) necessary to determine the Pearson product-moment correlation coefficient for the 25 pairs of heights and weights are as follows:

$$N = 25$$
$$\Sigma XY = 129{,}549$$
$$\Sigma X = 1{,}457$$
$$\Sigma Y = 2{,}197$$
$$\Sigma X^2 = 85{,}181$$
$$\Sigma Y^2 = 205{,}659$$
$$(\Sigma X)^2 = 2{,}122{,}849$$
$$(\Sigma Y)^2 = 4{,}826{,}809$$

$$r = \frac{25(129{,}549) - (1457)(2197)}{\sqrt{[25(85{,}181) - (1457)^2]\,[25(205{,}659) - (2197)^2]}}$$

$$r = \frac{3{,}238{,}725 - 3{,}201{,}029}{\sqrt{[(2{,}129{,}525) - (2{,}122{,}849)]\,[5{,}141{,}475 - 4{,}826{,}809]}}$$

$$r = \frac{37{,}696}{\sqrt{(6{,}676)(314{,}666)}}$$

$$r = \frac{37{,}696}{\sqrt{2{,}100{,}710{,}216}}$$

$$r = \frac{37{,}696}{45{,}834}$$

$$r = .82$$

The resulting correlation between height and weight for the 25 students in the example is +.82. The fact that the sign of the correlation is positive is not surprising if an examination is made of the data in Table 6.1 and of the scatter diagram in Figure 6.1. The degree of the relationship between the two traits is given by the absolute value of the correlation coefficient, namely .82. Methods of interpreting the meaning of the value of the correlation coefficient are presented later in this chapter.

Rank difference correlation coefficient

Calculation of the rank difference correlation coefficient is a simple method for obtaining a relatively quick estimate of the relationship between two sets of scores. This method requires the conversion of the two sets of scores into ranks. Some information about the absolute value of the scores is lost while ranking, so the rank difference correlation coefficient is an estimate of the Pearson product-moment correlation coefficient. Generally, the accuracy of the estimate increases as the number of pairs of scores increases and as the number of tied ranks decreases. The Greek rho (ρ) is used to identify the rank difference correlation coefficient. The formula for this correlation is:

$$\rho = 1 - \frac{6\Sigma D^2}{N(N^2-1)},$$

where ρ = the rank difference correlation coefficient

ΣD^2 = the sum of the squared differences between each pair of ranks

N = the number of pairs of ranks

**Table 6.2   Calculation of Pearson product-moment correlation coefficient:
Ungrouped data**

Student	Height (X) (inches)	Weight (Y) (pounds)	X²	Y²	XY
1	50	49	2,500	2,401	2,450
2	52	62	2,704	3,844	3,224
3	55	69	3,025	4,761	3,795
4	56	65	3,136	4,225	3,640
5	56	72	3,136	5,184	4,032
6	56	78	3,136	6,084	4,368
7	57	70	3,249	4,900	3,990
8	57	73	3,249	5,329	4,161
9	57	75	3,249	5,625	4,275
10	57	83	3,249	6,889	4,731
11	57	94	3,249	8,836	5,358
12	58	74	3,364	5,476	4,292
13	58	84	3,364	7,056	4,872
14	58	110	3,364	12,100	6,380
15	59	69	3,481	4,761	4,071
16	59	100	3,481	10,000	5,900
17	60	63	3,600	3,969	3,780
18	60	91	3,600	8,281	5,460
19	61	100	3,721	10,000	6,100
20	61	105	3,721	11,025	6,405
21	61	120	3,721	14,400	7,320
22	62	124	3,844	15,376	7,688
23	62	126	3,844	15,876	7,812
24	63	110	3,969	12,100	6,930
25	65	131	4,225	17,161	8,515
	1,457	2,197	85,181	205,659	129,549

Table 6.3 illustrates the data arrangement and the methods for obtaining
the values for substitution into the rank difference correlation coefficient
formula.

The values necessary to determine the rank difference correlation coefficient for the 25 pairs of heights and weights are as follows:

$$\Sigma D^2 = 551$$
$$N = 25$$
$$\rho = 1 - \frac{6\Sigma D^2}{N(N^2-1)}$$
$$\rho = 1 - \frac{6(551)}{25(625-1)}$$
$$\rho = 1 - \frac{3306}{15600}$$
$$\rho = 1 - .21$$
$$\rho = .79.$$

Table 6.3   **Rank difference method of obtaining a correlation coefficient between twenty-five heights and weights**

Student	Height (inches)	Weight (pounds)	Height (rank)	Weight (rank)	D	D^2
1	50	49	25	25	0	0
2	52	62	24	24	0	0
3	55	69	23	20.5	2.5	6.25
4	56	65	21	22	1	1.0
5	56	72	21	18	3	9.0
6	56	78	21	14	7	49.0
7	57	70	17	19	2	4.0
8	57	73	17	17	0	0
9	57	75	17	15	2	4.0
10	57	83	17	13	4	16.0
11	57	94	17	10	7	49.0
12	58	74	13	16	3	9.0
13	58	84	13	12	1	1.0
14	58	110	13	5.5	7.5	56.25
15	59	69	10.5	20.5	10	100.0
16	59	100	10.5	8.5	2	4.0
17	60	63	8.5	23	14.5	210.25
18	60	91	8.5	11	2.5	6.25
19	61	100	6	8.5	2.5	6.25
20	61	105	6	7	1	1.0
21	61	120	6	4	2	4.0
22	62	124	3.5	3	.5	0.25
23	62	126	3.5	2	1.5	2.25
24	63	110	2	5.5	3.5	12.25
25	65	131	1	1	0	0
						551.00

Notice that the two values obtained through the Pearson product-moment correlation method and the rank difference correlation method compare quite favorably.

Multiple correlation coefficient

Multiple correlation is a technique for quantifying the relationship between a criterion score and a combination of two or more other sets of scores. The following situation illustrates a possible incidence where practical application of the multiple correlation technique might be made.

A teacher has devised four different tests of handball playing ability, all of which show reasonable validity. The validity of each test was checked by correlating the test scores with a criterion measure of handball playing ability, in this case the results of a round-robin tournament. By comparing the four correlation coefficients the teacher determined which one of the four sets of

test scores correlated highest with the criterion measure. However, by calculating a multiple correlation the teacher can determine the correlation coefficient between the criterion and a combination of all four tests (or between the criterion and any combination of two or three of the tests). The combined use of all four tests will result in a higher correlation with the criterion than the use of only the best single test, although the improvement may be slight. Possibly a combination of two of the tests might result in an acceptable correlation, thus allowing less time spent administering tests and more time spent in instruction. Determining the best combination can result in a more efficient use of teaching time than might otherwise be the case.

The symbol, $R_{0.12 \ldots n}$, is used to designate a multiple correlation coefficient. The R represents the multiple correlation. The multiple correlation coefficient reflects the correlation between the criterion, symbolized by 0, and the combination of from two to n tests (n is the general symbol to represent any number).

In general, most of the variety of equivalent procedures described for the calculation of a multiple correlation coefficient require a knowledge of matrix algebra. Unless the prospective physical educator possesses this knowledge or has access to a computer center in which computer programs for calculating the multiple correlation coefficient are available, the computation of $R_{0.12 \ldots n}$ is tedious and time consuming. It will not be presented here.

INTERPRETATION OF CORRELATION COEFFICIENTS

Two parts, the sign and the actual value, of the correlation coefficient require interpretation. As mentioned previously the sign of a correlation coefficient indicates the direction of the relationship, and the value of a correlation coefficient denotes the degree to which the sets of scores are related.

Sign

A positive sign preceding a correlation coefficient signifies a relationship in which the high scores in one distribution are associated with the high scores of the second distribution. (If no sign preceeds the correlation coefficient it is assumed to be positive.) A negative sign in front of a correlation coefficient signifies that the high scores in one distribution are associated with the low scores in another. The sign of a correlation coefficient indicates nothing about the degree of relationship that exists between the sets of scores.

A negative correlation can have a positive meaning if a low score indicates a good performance in one of the sets of scores. Timed events and golf are examples of instances in which such measures are used. For example, if one set of scores representing the time required to run the initial 50 feet of the pole vault approach and another set of scores representing the height cleared in the pole vault correlate negatively, the interpretation would be in a positive direction. That is, the faster the initial 50 feet of the approach is run the higher the vault. The negative sign would result from the fact that the best performance in running the initial 50 feet of the approach is assigned the lowest score in terms of time.

Value

The value of the correlation coefficient denotes the degree of relationship that exists between sets of scores. Yet once a single value is obtained to indicate the relationship, it is necessary to interpret that value.

If only general descriptions of the degree of relationship are required, visual inspections of scatter diagrams will probably be sufficient. But being more precise, even with the correlation coefficient, is difficult. With the exception of $r = .00$ and $r = \pm 1.00$, various authorities would undoubtedly differ as to the word description assigned to the various values of the correlation coefficient. Several factors affect the interpretation of a correlation coefficient of a particular value. Four of these factors and how they influence interpretation are explained below.

Purpose of obtaining correlation coefficients

If two separate correlation coefficients are calculated and identical values of, say .80 result, the same degree of relationship is, of course, present between each of the two sets of scores. However, depending on the purpose for which the two correlation coefficients are calculated, one might be considered high while the other, even though equal in value, might be regarded as only fair. For example, when correlation coefficients are used to report reliability, objectivity, or validity, higher values are usually expected for reliability and objectivity than for validity. This is because reliability coefficients result mainly from correlations of a test with itself whereas validity coefficients usually result from correlations between a test and another measure of the same characteristic.

In this text the use of the correlation coefficient is limited mostly to the function of determining and reporting reliability, objectivity, and validity. When correlational techniques are used for other purposes the degree of relationship expressed by a particular value of the correlation coefficient may have still other interpretations.

Method of obtaining correlation coefficients

Whether the value of the correlation coefficient is calculated through the use of the Person product-moment or the rank difference formula, the differences in the actual value obtained generally will be only slight. However, both formulas require two sets of scores from which the correlation coefficient is calculated. The procedures for obtaining the two sets of scores can vary and the interpretation of the meaning of a particular value of the correlation coefficient is influenced by the method used.

Some procedures for determining the two sets of scores contain more factors that affect the value of the correlation coefficient. For this reason the degree of relationship reflected by two correlation coefficients equal in value but calculated from sets of scores acquired in two different ways might be interpreted differently. The following example illustrates how two different methods of obtaining two sets of scores affect the interpretation of the correlation coefficient.

Teacher A administers a 100-item multiple-choice examination and, in an effort to secure information regarding the reliability of the examination, records two scores for each student, one indicating how many even-numbered items, and the other, how many odd-numbered items were answered correctly. Teacher A reasons that if the examination measures consistently a student should correctly answer approximately the same number of even-numbered items as odd-numbered items. That is, a student who does well on the examination should have a high proportion of both the even-numbered and odd-numbered items correct, while a student who does poorly on the examination should have a low proportion of both even-numbered and odd-numbered items correct. Thus a correlation coefficient calculated for the two sets of scores reflects the reliability of the examination.

Teacher B constructed two different 50-item multiple-choice examinations and administered them on two consecutive Fridays. The examinations contained different items but were equivalent in that each covered the same material. Teacher B secured reliability information by calculating a correlation coefficient between the scores on the first examination and the scores on the second examination.

In each case two sets of scores were obtained and each set of scores was in effect a measure of the same thing. However, notice the differences that exist. Since the two sets of scores obtained by Teacher A were both achieved during a single testing period and those secured by Teacher B were achieved at two testing periods separated by one week's time, differences in the students and the environmental conditions under which the examinations were administered would probably have a greater effect on the scores obtained by

Teacher B than those obtained by Teacher A. For example, if a student in Teacher A's class did poorly on the examination for some reason (illness, anxiety, noisy class in adjacent room), it would likely affect both scores (even-numbered and odd-numbered items) to a similar degree. Thus the student's two scores would probably rank in nearly the same place in both sets of scores. However, if a student for some reason did poorly on Teacher B's first examination and if the removal of this reason resulted in an improved performance on the second examination, this student's two scores would not occupy similar locations in the two distributions, and the net result would be a lowering of the correlation coefficient.

The method used by Teacher B to obtain two sets of scores contains more factors that could reduce the value of the correlation coefficient than the method used by Teacher A. Thus, even if both teachers calculated identical correlation coefficient values and even though the purpose (examining reliability) was the same in both cases, the interpretation of the values would differ.

Variability of scores

Another factor influencing the interpretation of a correlation coefficient is the variability of the scores involved. Generally, if the variability of the scores is small the correlation coefficient will be less than if the variability of the scores is large. Consequently higher correlation coefficients can be expected to occur when measures are obtained from classes with a wide range of talent than when measures are from classes of students nearly equal in ability. For example, consider two golf classes, one advanced and one intermediate, both containing ten students. Assume that the advanced class contains students who shoot close to par golf and the intermediate class contains students who vary from poor to excellent in their golf ability. In Table 6.4 are displayed the results of fictional tournaments held in each class.

Table 6.4   Golf tournament results from an advanced and an intermediate golf class

Student	Advanced class		Intermediate class	
	First day	Second day	First day	Second day
1	69	73	75	79
2	70	72	80	76
3	70	70	84	85
4	71	73	88	84
5	71	75	91	93
6	71	69	95	92
7	72	70	101	103
8	72	72	106	102
9	73	74	110	114
10	74	73	121	125

The value of the Pearson product-moment correlation coefficient between the two days' results in the advanced class is .18, which is considerably less than the value of .98 obtained for the similar situation in the intermediate class. Therefore, to interpret the meaning of a correlation coefficient it is important to be aware of some characteristics of the group from which the measurements or scores were obtained. Of particular interest is the variability of the group on the trait or traits measured.

Exactness of scores

Some measurements in physical education can be made very accurately but others cannot. This factor too must be considered when interpreting correlation coefficients. For example, after proper instruction and warm up, performances on the standing long jump test will be fairly consistent (until fatigue becomes a factor). Further, these performances can be measured relatively accurately, usually to the nearest inch at least. Because of their nature, however, some traits (such as creativity, social adjustment, rhythm, and others) cannot be assessed with great accuracy. Due to its lack of precision, a test to measure creativity may classify a student high one time and average another, whereas a student who performs well on the initial standing long jump trial will likely do well on the second trial. It is thus more difficult to achieve high values of the correlation coefficient when inexact measures are used than when relatively precise scores can be obtained. This is another factor to be aware of when interpreting correlation coefficients.

CONSIDERATIONS OF CORRELATION COEFFICIENTS

Two important considerations about correlation coefficients should be understood. First, a correlation coefficient is specific to the group from, the time at, and the conditions under which it is obtained. A correlation coefficient calculated on sets of scores obtained from a different group of students, or from the same students but at a different time or under different conditions will in all probability differ somewhat from the original correlation coefficient. A consequence of this fact is that a test does not have a single reliability or a single validity. A test given to fourth-, fifth-, and sixth-grade students may exhibit a reliability of .90, but when the same test is administered only to fifth-grade students the reduction in the range of talent may reduce the reliability to .50. Therefore, when pondering the information conveyed by a correlation coefficient, the specific situation from which it was derived must also be considered.

A second important consideration regarding correlation coefficients is that, although indicating the existence of a relationship between two sets of scores, the correlation coefficient does not necessarily imply that a cause-and-effect relationship is present. For example, a high correlation exists between the height of elementary school children and grade status. Logically, however, a particular child's height is not "caused" by grade status, nor is grade status "caused" by height.

A high correlation coefficient suggesting a cause-and-effect relationship may be due to the fact that both traits involved in the correlation are related to another trait (or to several other traits). For example, if a correlation coefficient between a measure of softball throwing ability and a measure of reading ability of elementary school children was calculated, the value obtained would likely be fairly high. Obviously, the ability to throw a softball well does not cause a student to read well nor does the ability to read well cause the student to be able to throw a softball well. Instead, both of these abilities increase with age, reading due to training in school, and softball due to growth and maturation.

Another example serves to illustrate how the result of two traits being related to a third can give rise to misinterpretation if a cause-and-effect relationship is assumed. A correlation coefficient calculated between the order in which test papers are turned in and the order of the test papers arranged from the best performance to the poorest performance is almost always positive (unless an extremely difficult test is involved). It would not be wise, however, to conclude on the basis of the correlation coefficient that turning in a test paper as quickly as possible would cause a student to perform well on the test. The positive correlation is due to the fact that the more intelligent student is generally able to finish a test sooner than the less intelligent student and that intelligence is, generally, positively related to the performance on a test.

Interpretations involving cause-and-effect relationships should be based on logical evidence, not correlational evidence. The correlation coefficient may suggest that a cause-and-effect relationship exists but cannot be used to prove such a condition.

GROUP COMPARISON TECHNIQUES

A portion of the branch of statistics called inferential statistics is concerned with the comparison of the average performances from various groups and involves concepts useful to the physical educator. No attempt will be made here to explain the derivation of the various formulas and facts involved or the assumptions underlying the procedures described. An abundance of elementary statistics textbooks are available to the interested reader.

Perhaps the best way to present inferential statistics is through illustration and explanation. Imagine that a physical educator is interested in determining whether girls or boys are more coordinated. Assume for the purposes of this illustration that the physical educator has a valid and reliable method for assessing coordination and that the results of the administration of this test to a sample of girls and boys in the schools are those shown in Table 6.5.

Notice that there is a difference in the mean score for girls (20) and for boys (18). Assuming that high scores indicate better coordination, are the girls more coordinated than the boys? Is it possible that the difference between the means (2) is due to the fact that, even though girls and boys are really equal on this test, the means obtained reflect sampling error? (That is, it would be reasonable to assume that the means calculated for several samples taken from the same population would vary somewhat). The t-test for independent sam-

Table 6.5 Coordination scores for fourteen girls and boys

	Girls (x_1 scores)	*Boys* (x_2 scores)
	20	16
	18	20
	25	15
	29	11
	15	19
	13	25
		10
		28
N =	6	8
ΣX =	120	144
$\overline{X}$ =	20	18
ΣX^2 =	2584	2872

ples described below allows a choice to be made between these two questions.

First an estimate of the population variance, s^2, is obtained using the following equation:

$$s^2 = \frac{[\Sigma X_1^2 - (\Sigma X_1)^2/N_1][\Sigma X_2^2 - (\Sigma X_2)^2/N_2]}{N_1 + N_2 - 2},$$

where

s^2 = estimate of population variance
ΣX_1^2 = sum of the girls scores after they are squared
$(\Sigma X_1)^2$ = square of the sum of the girls scores
N_1 = number of girls
ΣX_2^2 = sum of the boys scores after they are squared
$(\Sigma X_2)^2$ = square of the sum of the boys scores
N_2 = number of boys

$$s^2 = \frac{[2584 - (120)^2 / 6] + [2872 - (144)^2 / 8]}{6 + 8 - 2}.$$

$$s^2 = \frac{184 + 280}{12}$$

$$s^2 = \frac{464}{12}$$

The estimate of the population variance is then used to obtain a statistic called the standard error of the difference between the means:

$$s_{\bar{X}_1 - \bar{X}_2} = \sqrt{\frac{s^2}{N_1} + \frac{s^2}{N_2}},$$

where

$s_{\bar{X}_1 - \bar{X}_2}$ = standard error of the difference between two means
s^2 = estimate of population variance
N_1 = number of girls
N_2 = number of boys

$$s_{\bar{X}_1 - \bar{X}_2} = \sqrt{\frac{38.67}{6} + \frac{38.67}{8}}$$

$$s_{\bar{X}_1 - \bar{X}_2} = \sqrt{6.45 + 4.83} = 3.36.$$

Finally a t-ratio is formed by dividing the difference between the means by the standard error of the difference between the means:

$$t = \frac{\bar{X}_1 - \bar{X}_2}{s_{\bar{X}_1 - \bar{X}_2}}$$

t = t-ratio
$\bar{X}_1$ = girl's mean
$\bar{X}_2$ = boy's mean
$s_{\bar{X}_1 - \bar{X}_2}$ = standard error of the difference between two means

$$t = \frac{20.0 - 18.0}{3.36} = \frac{2.0}{3.36} = 0.595.$$

The value thus obtained is compared to the values in a table called critical values of t. An abbreviated version of such a table is presented in Table 6.6. If the obtained value is greater than the table value, it is concluded that the

Table 6.6   Critical value of *t*

Degrees of freedom	Level of significance (two-tailed)	
	.05	.01
1	12.71	63.66
2	4.30	9.93
3	3.18	5.84
4	2.78	4.60
5	2.57	4.03
6	2.45	3.71
7	2.37	3.50
8	2.31	3.36
9	2.26	3.25
10	2.23	3.17
11	2.20	3.11
12	2.18	3.06
13	2.16	3.01
14	2.15	2.98
15	2.13	2.95
16	2.12	2.92
17	2.11	2.90
18	2.10	2.89
19	2.09	2.86
20	2.08	2.85
25	2.06	2.79
30	2.04	2.75
40	2.02	2.70
60	2.00	2.66
120	1.98	2.62

means are significantly different from one another. That is, the chances of the differences between two sample means drawn from the same population being so large as to result in a t-ratio larger than the table value are so slight that it is concluded the means must be coming from different populations.

To enter the table of critical values of *t* (Table 6.6) to make the comparison, two pieces of information are required. One is a concept called degrees of freedom. In an independent t-test this value is given by the equation $N_1 + N_2 - 2$. For the example being used the degrees of freedom are 12 (6 + 8 − 2).

In addition, a level of significance must be selected. In table 6.6 only two choices (.05 or .01) are listed. The level of significance has to do with the probability of deciding that two means are significantly different when in reality no such difference exists. If the .05 level of significance is used, the chance of making this error is 1 out of 20. The chance of making this error is 1 out of

100 if the .01 level of significance is selected. Several factors beyond the scope of this book enter into this choice of a significance level.

With the data given in the example the physical educator would conclude that there is no significant difference in coordination between boys and girls. This results from the fact that the obtained t-ratio (0.595) is not larger than the table value of 2.18, given 12 degrees of freedom and a .05 level of significance.

In the previous illustration the t-test for independent samples was described because the students in each sample were independent of one another. In some cases the samples may be correlated as in the case where the same students are tested under two different conditions. The following contrived situation illustrates a t-test for correlated samples.

Assume a physical educator wanted to determine if exposure to a particular curriculum increased students' coordination and that the physical educator administered a valid and reliable instrument to measure coordination before and after the students participated in the curriculum. The resulting scores are given in Table 6.7.

Table 6.7   Before and after coordination scores

Student	Before	After	D	D^2
1	9	15	−6	36
2	21	20	1	1
3	15	17	−2	4
4	28	32	−4	16
5	17	24	−7	49
6	11	12	−1	1
7	12	16	−4	16
8	18	15	3	9
9	24	24	0	0
10	16	25	−9	81
11	16	20	−4	16
12	23	25	−2	4
13	29	27	2	4
14	10	19	−9	81
15	12	15	−3	9
ΣX	261	306	−45	327
$\overline{X}$	17.4	20.4	−3.0	

The mean coordination score after exposure to the curriculum (20.4) is higher than the before mean coordination score (17.4). But, as in the previous example, is the difference (3.0) large enough to be significant or could it be reasonably explained by chance due to sampling error? The approach taken is to examine for each student the difference between the two coordination scores. If the exposure to the particular curriculum involved had little effect, the differences between the scores should be small and the sum of the D column should be close to zero. Thus the t-test for correlated samples described below is actually a test to determine whether the mean of the D scores is significantly different from zero.

A convenient computational formula for this t-test is:

$$t = \frac{\Sigma D}{\sqrt{[N\Sigma D^2 - (\Sigma D)^2] \ / \ (N-1)}}$$

where　　t = t-ratio
　　　　Σ = the sum of
　　　　D = difference between before and after score
　　　　N = number of pairs of scores
　　　　D^2 = square of each D score.

For the illustration, the t-ratio is found as follows:

$$t = \frac{-45}{\sqrt{[15(327) - (-45)^2] \ / \ 15 - 1}}$$

$$t = \frac{-45}{\sqrt{(4905 - 2025) \ / \ 14}}$$

$$t = \frac{-45}{\sqrt{205.71}} = \frac{-45}{14.34} = -3.14.$$

This value (-3.14) is compared to the appropriate value in Table 6.6 to determine whether the mean D value (-3.0) is significantly different from zero. The negative sign may be ignored for purposes of comparison to the table value. (It merely indicates the direction of the difference.) In the illustration, since the after scores were subtracted from the before scores, the negative sign indicates the change was in the direction desired by the physical educator.

To enter the table of critical values of t it is again necessary to determine the degrees of freedom and select a significance level. For a correlated t-test the number of degrees of freedom is N-1, or 14 in the example. The obtained value of 3.14 is found to exceed the table values of 2.13 (.05) and 2.95 (.01). The physical educator can conclude that the coordination scores after exposure to the particular curriculum are significantly better than the coordination scores before. Whether the physical educator can claim that exposure to the curriculum was the factor that caused these scores to improve is dependent on the design of the experiment and the control of other conditions (which were not a part of this discussion).

The inclusion of these two examples is provided merely to introduce a very large and interesting area of statistics. The introduction is very basic and incomplete. It is intended only to point out possibilities, not to provide the reader with all skills and knowledges necessary to be a competent statistician. The t-tests presented only scratch the surface of inferential statistics, the study of which would benefit any teacher.

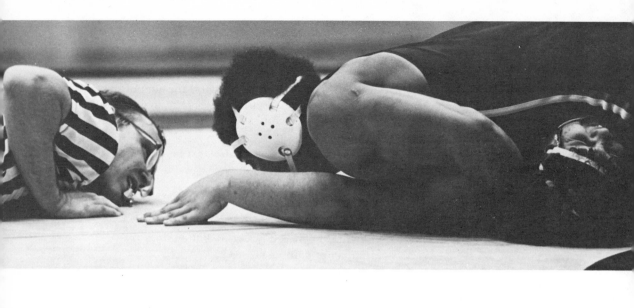

Chapter 7

Validity, Reliability, and Objectivity

The usual outcome of the application of a measuring instrument is a set of symbols, most often numerical values, supposedly quantifying the characteristic being measured. For example, if a pull-up test is administered to a group of students, the number of correctly performed executions of the exercise is generally understood to indicate a particular student's upper arm muscular endurance. The numerical values obtained for a class of students can then be handled and interpreted in many ways, depending on the interests of the physical educator. Each student's score can be compared to the group average, norms can be developed, correlations between upper arm muscular endurance and other parameters can be calculated, and so on.

The usefulness and worth of a set of scores depends, however, on three characteristics of measurement: validity, reliability, and objectivity. A test can be said to have validity if it actually measures the parameter of interest. For example, does the number of pull-ups completed reflect only upper arm muscular endurance, or might other factors, such as grip strength or differences in motivation, be affecting the results? A test can be said to be reliable if its repeated application results in consistent values. For example, if enough rest was permitted to eliminate the effects of muscle fatigue and the pull-up test was administered a second time, would the students' scores match those obtained on the first administration? A particular type of reliability is called objectivity. Do the scoring procedures followed by a particular test administrator affect the resulting scores? For example, if all other conditions were to remain constant and one person administered the pull-up test very strictly (that is, allowed no kipping action or resting and made certain the arms were completely extended) and another person did not enforce these constraints, the resulting two sets of scores might differ considerably. The lack of consistency (an issue of reliability) in this case would be due to the different approaches of the test administrators (an issue of objectivity). A set of scores is virtually worthless, regardless of the amount of effort expended in obtaining the scores, if it represents the results of tests that lack validity, reliability, and objectivity.

VALIDITY

The most common definition of validity is the degree to which a test measures what it is intended to measure. Upon close examination, however, this seemingly simple concept becomes somewhat complex, and complete development of the concept is beyond the scope of this book. Nevertheless, it is important for physical educators to be aware of the need to examine whether or not scores from any measurement procedure actually assess the traits or abilities of interest.

Various types of validity have been defined and methods for their calculation or examination devised. In general, two approaches can be used to examine validity. The qualitative approach involves logic and subjective judgment, although numerical evidence also may be used. The quantitative approach involves the correlation coefficient (in this case renamed the validity coefficient). Four types of validity and the approaches used to examine each type are discussed below.

Content validity

Content validity is assessed by determining the degree to which a measuring instrument contains tasks that provide evidence about the traits or capabilities to be measured. The content validity of a measuring instrument is usually examined qualitatively. For example, the content validity of written achievement tests is generally subjectively determined by the extent to which the individual test items represent a sufficient sample of the educational objectives included in the course of instruction. In other words, by examining a copy of a test being considered for use, a teacher can decide the degree of content validity the test has for a particular situation. It is important to follow the proper procedures for constructing a written test, especially the formulation and use of a table of specifications (see Chapter 8) to ensure that a test possess content validity.

Content validity also can be determined by logically examining the actions required to complete a physical performance measurement device. The content of a 50-yard-dash test is a valid indicator of how fast a student can run, but the content validity of tests purporting to measure volleyball playing ability, for example, may be more difficult to assess. Often for these tests experts in the ability to be measured are called upon to determine content validity.

Concurrent validity

The concurrent validity of a measuring instrument is determined quantitatively. To determine how valid a test is it is necessary to compare how well a test measures whatever it actually measures with whatever it is supposed to measure. To make such a comparison requires a method of obtaining criterion scores that accurately measure whatever the original test is designed to assess. If this requirement can be met, a correlation coefficient (called a validity coefficient) between the two resulting sets of scores provides evidence for a type of validity known as concurrent validity.

Methods for obtaining criterion scores include administering a previously constructed test having previously established validity (but too costly, time consuming, or difficult for any other reason to use all the time); securing ratings of experts about each student's abilities in the activity being measured; and obtaining a ranking of a student's abilities through the use of some type of a tournament, such as a round robin.

Once the criterion scores are obtained they are correlated with the scores from the test being examined for concurrent validity. If the validity coefficient is high, the new test must be measuring approximately the same traits as the criterion measure. The selection of the criterion measure is critical; unless the criterion scores are accurate measures of the traits desired, the evidence for concurrent validity is not worthwhile.

Predictive validity

Another type of validity that is examined through correlational techniques is predictive validity. If a measuring instrument, test, or test battery has high predictive validity, its scores will have a high correlation with some future measure. For example, a manufacturer has devised a new type of running shoe and is interested in hiring sales personnel who will successfully sell the product. A test battery is devised that purportedly measures selling ability, and the test is administered to all sales personnel hired. Six months later success in selling is assessed for each sales person by determining the number of pairs of shoes sold. The number of pairs of shoes is the criterion score. The predictive validity of the test designed to measure selling ability is examined by correlating the criterion scores with the test scores. If the correlation coefficient is high, the test can be said to possess predictive validity.

Construct validity

Such attributes as athletic ability, anxiety, and intelligence are examples of constructs. Although these attributes are intangible, they are believed to exist because they explain observable behavior. For example, some people appear to be very ceative; others do not. Thus it seems logical to assume that a construct of creativity exists.

The usual approach to demonstrating the degree of construct validity of a test is to conduct several experiments in which specific outcomes are hypothesized. For example, Mood[1] devised a test to measure the construct of physical fitness knowledge and then hypothesized that students enrolled in a large number of classes where they are exposed to information on physical fitness (such as conditioning, exercise physiology, and the like) will score higher on the test than students not enrolled in such classes. Confirmation of this hypothesis can be used as one piece of evidence that the test actually measures the construct of physical fitness knowledge but it is certainly far from conclusive proof. The construct validity of a test is generally examined over repeated uses and examination of the results obtained. Construct validation is not only an assessment of the test itself but also an appraisal of the existence of the construct.

Considerations of validity

Validity is a matter of degree; tests are neither completely valid nor completely invalid. A measure or assessment of the degree to which a test measures what it is intended to measure is a function of many factors. The environmental conditions under which validity is assessed, the attributes (e.g., age, sex, and ability level) of the particular group of students involved, and the criterion measure selected must be considered when a validity coefficient is presented. It does not seem logical, for example, that a test shown to be valid for measuring the basketball playing ability of high school boys would be valid for measuring this ability in elementary school girls.

The validity of a test is also related to its reliability. A test that does not result in consistent scores cannot be a valid measure of a specific trait.

RELIABILITY

Reliability concerns the consistency or dependability of measurement. If the same score is obtained when a measurement is repeated, the measurement is said to possess high reliability.

Reliability is related to precision and the reduction of error. Some traits can be measured more precisely and thus more reliably than others. For example, a student's weight can be measured very exactly but the measurement of a student's volleyball playing ability involves less precise methods. Anytime a measurement is made some error is introduced. Using a steel tape to measure the distance a discus was thrown is undoubtedly more accurate than using a yardstick. However, error is still possible with the steel tape, which is likely to expand or contract with fluctuations in temperature.

Various methods have been devised for obtaining reliability estimates to accommodate the fact that various sources of errors in measurement are possible. A student may perform a task differently for any of several possible reasons. For example, the two distances recorded for a student on two trials of the standing long jump may differ because of differences within the individual or differences in measurement techniques.

The complexities of most physical movements do not allow them to be performed in the same way physiologically and anatomically every time. In addition, individual motivational states and interest levels may cause different performances. The inconsistencies in repeated measurements caused by these differences are not due to measurement error but nevertheless must be noted when determining the appropriate reliability coefficient.

Inconsistent application of test directions and scoring procedures, differences in environmental conditions, and changes in equipment used between test administrations are examples of measurement errors that can reduce reliability. The degree to which any of these occur and thus alter scores from one administration to the next will affect the reliability of a test.

Calculating reliability coefficients

To examine the consistency of a measuring procedure it is necessary to obtain at least two sets of scores. The conditions under which the scores are obtained and the time between their collection introduce differing error components and thus necessitate various methods of estimating reliability.

Test-retest method

If a test is administered twice to the same group of students, a correlation coefficient computed for the resulting two sets of scores will serve as an indicator of the test's reliability. A high correlation would be possible only if the students' scores remained consistent from one administration to the next. If, for any reason (fatigue, stopwatch differences, variations in scoring procedures), the students score differently on the second administration of the test, the resulting scores will change and the correlation coefficient will be lowered.

In evaluating a reliability coefficient obtained by the test-retest method, it is important to know the time interval between testings. If the test is read-ministered immediately, it would be logical to assume that such factors as environmental conditions and test administration procedures would not affect the reliability coefficient although such factors as fatigue or motivation would. If a substantial amount of time occurs between testings, however the fatigue factor might be eliminated but other factors, such as increases in skill because of practice, changes in strength, or differences in the environmental conditions, might affect the value of the reliability coefficient.

If the time between testings does not exceed three days, the test-retest method is one of the best ways to assess the reliability of a performance test. If the time between testings exceeds three days, changes in students' abilities might begin to affect the reliability coefficient, and these changes should not be considered as measurement error. The test-retest method is somewhat time consuming because the entire test must be readministered to obtain scores to use in calculating the reliability coefficient. This method is not recommended for determining the reliability of a written test.

Split-halves method

To estimate the reliability of a measuring instrument by the split-halves method, the test is split into two parts, each part is scored and the resulting two sets of scores are correlated. For performance tests, an even number of trials are given. Usually the scores for the odd-numbered trials and the scores for the even-numbered trials are used as the two sets of scores. The odd-even split is generally adopted so that the effects of learning and fatigue are equally represented in both sets of scores. When the split-halves method is used to measure the reliability of written tests, it is common to use an odd-even split. However, any split might be considered; if a teacher desires, an attempt could be made to divide the written test so that comparable items appear on each half.

The reliability of a test is related to its length. Since the reliability coefficient obtained using the split-halves method is based on one half the length of the test, the coefficient should be "stepped up" to reflect the actual length of the test. To accomplish this it is necessary to apply a special form of the Spearman-Brown Prophecy formula. The split-halves method and application of the Spearman-Brown Prophecy formula are best explained through an example.

Suppose a throwing for accuracy test consists of twelve throws at a particular target and each throw is scored according to its closeness to the center of the target. To determine the reliability of this test the sum of each student's scores on the odd-numbered trials (1, 3, 5, 7, 9, 11) can be correlated with the sum of the scores on the even-numbered trials (2, 4, 6, 8, 10, 12). Assume for illustrative purposes that the correlation coefficient obtained is .74. Each of the two scores for each student consists of the sum of six trials; however, since the test actually consists of twelve trials, the value of .74 is substituted into the special form of the Spearman-Brown Prophecy formula to obtain an estimate of what the reliability coefficient would be if the twelve-trial test were administered twice and the test-retest method used. The formula is:

$$r_{(est)} = \frac{2 \times r_{(obt)}}{1 + r_{(obt)}},$$

where $r_{(est)}$ =   estimated reliability of the full-length test

          $r_{(obt)}$ =   correlation obtained using the split-halves procedure.

For the example we obtain:

$$r_{(est)} = \frac{2 \times .74}{1 + .74}$$

$$r_{(est)} = \frac{1.48}{1.74}$$

$$r_{(est)} = .85.$$

The advantage of the split-halves method is that it eliminates retesting simply for the purposes of obtaining a reliability coefficient. However, the split-halves method does not allow for day-to-day changes since all the scores are obtained on the same day. Thus it tends to overestimate the reliability obtained using the test-retest method.

Other Methods

A method that examines more accurately than the correlation coefficient the amount of variance in a set of scores that is attributable to various sources uses the relatively advanced statistical technique of analysis of variance. Although this method is beyond the scope of this book, the reader should be aware that through analysis of variance it is possible to examine the various sources of measurement error in a set of scores and thereby obtain accurate reliability coefficients.

Other methods of calculating reliability coefficients are available. Some of these are specifically used with written test scores and are considered on p. 105.

Interpreting Reliability Coefficients

Because the various methods of calculating the reliability coefficient reflect different sources of error, an interpretation of the coefficient must consider the method by which it is derived. In general, however, the higher the reliability coefficient, the more consistently does a test measure whatever it does measure. It is sometimes helpful to think of a measurement, or an observed score, as being made up of two parts: a true score and an error score. It can be shown that the variance of the observed scores (σ_o^2) is equal to the variance of the true scores (σ_t^2) plus the variance of the error scores (σ_e^2). Within this theoretical model reliability is defined as the ratio of the variance of the true score to the variance of the observed score, or reliability $= \dfrac{\sigma_t^2}{\sigma_o^2}$. Only when no error is present in the observed scores could the value of the reliability coefficient be 1.0. As the amount of error increases, the value of σ_o^2 increases, and thus reliability decreases.

Another method that is useful in interpreting the meaning of a reliability coefficient is to use the reliability coefficient in calculating a statistic called the standard error of measurement. This statistic can be used to determine the amount of confidence that can be placed in a student's observed score. It is calculated from the following formula:

$$SE_{meas} = SD_O \sqrt{1 - r} \, ,$$

where

SE_{meas} = standard error of measurement

SD_O = standard deviation of the observed scores

r = reliability coefficient.

Using this formula, verify that the SE_{meas} for a test having a standard deviation of 10 and a reliability coefficient of .64 is 6.

Since the SE_{meas} is actually the standard deviation of the error scores for the group tested, and because error scores are considered to be normally distributed with a mean of zero, the SE_{meas} can be used to determine limits within which the true scores lie. For example, on a test having a reliability coefficient of .81 and a standard deviation of 9.17, Jeff received a score of 54. By calculating the Se_{meas} to be 4 and knowing that in a normal curve approximately 68 percent of the scores are located between one standard deviation above and below the mean, the teacher could assume (with a 32 percent risk of being wrong) that Jeff's true score lies between 50 and 58 (54 ± 4). To reduce the risk of being wrong to slightly less than 5 percent, the values of 2× SE_{meas} could be added to and subtracted from Jeff's score to find limits containing his true score 95% of the time ($2 \times 4 = 8$; $54 \pm 8 = 46 - 62$). Finally, to reduce the risk of being wrong to less than 1%, 2.6 × SE_{meas} could be added to and subtracted from Jeff's score to find limits containing his true score slightly more than 99 percent of the time ($2.6 \times 4 = 10.4$; $54 \pm 10.4 = 43.6 - 64.4$).

To be reasonably certain that a student's true score is "captured," the range of scores becomes increasingly wider. Also, by examining the formula to obtain the SE_{meas}, notice that the less reliable the test, the greater the value of the SE_{meas} and thus the greater the range of the limits necessary to be certain the true score is contained within them. With knowledge of the standard error one can reduce the temptation to misuse test results by placing undue emphasis on rather small differences between students' scores.

Factors affecting reliability

It has already been indicated that the reliability coefficient is related to the length of the test and that its value is a function of the method used in its calculation. In general, increases in test length increase its reliability. It is logical that the more times a student is measured the more likely the resulting score will reflect this student's ability because the effects of chance are re-

duced. If a throwing for accuracy test, for example, consisted of one trial and the student hit the center of the target, the hit could be due to accurate throwing ability or luck. However, if the student hit the center of the target 8 out of 10 times, the hits are likely to be due to accurate throwing ability, not luck. A special case of the Spearman-Brown Prophecy formula was presented above to show the effect on estimated reliability of doubling the length of a test. The general form of the Spearman-Brown Prophecy formula can be used to estimate the reliability of a test increased by any proportion. The general form of the formula is:

$$r_{(est)} = \frac{N \times r_{(obt)}}{1 + (N - 1)\, r_{(obt)}},$$

where $r_{(est)}$ = estimated reliability coefficient of the lengthened test

$r_{(obt)}$ = reliability coefficient of the test before lengthening

N = proportion of increase in length.

Suppose a throwing for accuracy test with a reliability coefficient of .70 when six trials are used is increased to eighteen trials. The length of the original test is increased three times, thus $N = 3$. Substituting into the formula, we get:

$$r_{(est)} = \frac{3\,(.70)}{1 + (3-1)\,(.70)}$$

$$r_{(est)} = \frac{2.1}{1 + 1.40}$$

$$r_{(est)} = \frac{2.1}{2.4}$$

$$r_{(est)} = .875.$$

Thus, if a test constructor wants to use a throwing for accuracy test but feels a reliability coefficient of approximately .90 is necessary for the purposes the test is to be used, he or she would have to decide between inclusion of this test with the inconvenience of tripling the test length and finding some other method of measuring this trait. Notice how increasing the number of trials affects the estimated reliability.

Trials	Reliability
6	.70
12	.82
18	.88

The general form of the Spearman-Brown Prophecy formula can be rearranged to solve for N and thus be used to estimate the number of trials necessary to achieve a desired reliability. The rearrangement of the formula is:

$$N = \frac{r_{(est)}\,(1 - r_{(obt)})}{r_{(obt)}\,(1 - r_{(est)})},$$

where

N = proportion of increase in test length

$r_{(obt)}$ = reliability coefficient obtained before lengthening

$r_{(est)}$ = reliability coefficient desired.

Suppose that the administration of a test involving six trials results in a reliability coefficient of .60, but a reliability coefficient of at least .80 is desired. Substitution into the above formula reveals that the test would have to be increased approximately 2⅔ times, or from six to sixteen trials ($6 \times 2.67 = 16$) to achieve the desired reliability:

$$N = \frac{.80\,(1 - .60)}{.60\,(1 - .80)}$$

$$N = \frac{.80\,(.40)}{.60\,(.20)}$$

$$N = \frac{.32}{.12}$$

$$N = 2.67.$$

Another factor that must be considered when examining the reliability coefficient is the range of talent of the group for which the reliability coefficient was calculated. For example, a test designed for third-grade students will demonstrate a larger reliability coefficient if it is administered to students in grades K through 6 than if administered only to third-grade students. The sixth-grade students would be expected to perform consistently well on the test, and the kindergarten students would be expected to perform consistently poorly on the test. Thus, the reliability coefficient, being a measure of consistency, will be higher when a wide range of talent is measured and lower when a narrow range of talent is measured.

In other words, the reliability coefficient is much like the validity coefficient in that it is specific to the situation in which it is obtained. A test is neither reliable nor unreliable, but it is reliable to some degree. The method of calculation, the condititions under which the measurements were taken, and the characteristics of the students on whom the scores were collected must be considered when interpreting the reliability coefficient.

Written test reliability

The test-retest method of obtaining a reliability coefficient is not suitable for written test data. The split-halves method can be used for this purpose, but other techniques are available.

Equivalent forms method

One way to include the sampling of items error in expression of reliability of a written test is to construct and administer two tests of equal length built around the same table of specifications. The equivalent forms method results in a reliability coefficient reflecting most of the possible sources of error and is considered an accurate means of expressing the reliability of a written test. However, the additional time consumed in constructing, administering, and scoring an entirely new test solely for the purpose of determining reliability makes this method impractical for the teacher. It is used primarily by professional test construction agencies.

Kuder-Richardson method

The split-halves method of determining test reliability is considered a measure of internal consistency because other sources of error (e.g., day-to-day variations in students, changes in test administration conditions) are not reflected in the resulting reliability coefficient. The procedure for halving a test, considering the large number of possibilities, is somewhat arbitrary, however. Several authorities, Kuder and Richardson among them, have devised various methods of utilizing all the information concerning consistency of performance from item to item within a test. Two of the more useful formulas for estimating reliability thus derived are known as the K-R_{20} and K-R_{21}

To calculate the reliability coefficient resulting from K-R_{20}, let

$$r_{K\text{-}R_{20}} = \frac{k}{k\text{-}1} \times \left(1 - \frac{\Sigma pq}{\sigma^2}\right),$$

where
$r_{K\text{-}R_{20}}$ = Kuder-Richardson 20 reliability coefficient
k = number of items on the test
p = proportion of correct responses
q = proportion of incorrect responses
σ^2 = variance of the test scores (standard deviation squared).

This formula is applicable only when items on a test are scored one point if answered correctly and zero points if answered incorrectly or omitted.

To calculate $r_{K\text{-}R_{20}}$ it is necessary, for each item on the test, to multiply the proportion of students answering the item correctly (p) by the proportion of students answering the item incorrectly (q) and to sum over all items the resulting products. Notice that $q = 1 - p$.

Using the formula presented above, confirm that the $r_{K-R_{20}}$ for a forty-item test having a variance of 34 and a Σpq of 8.86 is .76.

The reliability coefficient resulting from the K-R$_{21}$ is less time consuming to calculate but is an underestimate of reliability if the level of difficulty of test items varies widely. If a test includes many items that nearly all students answer correctly or incorrectly (or both) the underestimate can be quite large. In any other case, however, the ease of computation makes the K-R$_{21}$ a valuable formula to know.

To calculate the reliability coefficient resulting from K-R$_{21}$, let

$$r_{K-R_{21}} = \frac{k}{k-1} \times \left(1 - \frac{\overline{X}\left(1 - \frac{\overline{X}}{k}\right)}{\sigma^2}\right),$$

where

$r_{K-R_{21}}$ = Kuder-Richardson 21 reliability coefficient

k = number of items on the test

$\overline{X}$ = mean score on the test

σ^2 = variance of the test scores (standard deviation squared).

Using the formula above, verify that the $r_{K-R_{21}}$ for a sixty-item test having a mean score of 40 and a variance of 50 is .75.

OBJECTIVITY

Objectivity is actually a form of reliability in which one source of error — that of differences in test administrators — is examined. Possibly the best way to explain the meaning of the term objectivity is by illustration. Assume that two different testers each administer separately an abdominal muscular endurance test to the same group of students. Further assume that all factors that could cause a difference to exist between the two sets of measures are carefully controlled. If these assumptions are correct, the only reason for differences to exist between the measures obtained by the two testers is the fact that two different people administered the test. Thus a measure of the objectivity of this test would be made by comparing the two sets of measures obtained by the two testers.

Tests such as measuring height, taking pulse rates, and determining standing long jump distances are reasonably high in objectivity because the procedures for obtaining these measures are fairly standard and the possibilities of measurement error are not as great as when administering some other tests. Measures of rhythm and dance skills, sports potential, and motor educability are examples of tests that typically are low in objectivity because they involve a high degree of subjective judgment on the part of the tester.

Objectivity of tests can be increased by carefully planning and adhering to test administration and scoring procedures. Test scores that are "contaminated" by the test administrator are of little value in evaluating the abilities of students.

RELATIONSHIP AMONG VALIDITY, RELIABILITY, AND OBJECTIVITY

The three characteristics of measurement under discussion are related in some ways. A test cannot be valid without being reliable. In other words, if it is possible to demonstrate that a test actually does measure cardiovascular fitness, then that test must necessarily measure cardiovascular fitness consistently or else the demonstration would not be possible. However, a test can be reliable without being valid. For example, the cardiovascular fitness test might give very consistent results but upon further investigation the test might be found to be measuring the muscular endurance of the legs. This test could thus be considered reliable but not valid for measuring cardiovascular fitness.

A test may be reliable but not objective. An example of this situation involves skinfold measurements. One person, with some practice, may become adept at taking these measurements and arriving at consistent results. However, if this person's measurements are compared to those obtained on the same subjects by someone else, equally adept, the results might differ considerably. Thus, even though both testers are able to take reliable measures, the objectivity of the measurements is low.

From this introductory material it is important to realize that for a measurement to be of any value, it must 1) actually measure the trait it purports to measure; 2) measure the trait consistently; and 3) result in the same measurement no matter who administers it.

REFERENCES CITED

[1]Dale Mood, "Test of Physical Fitness Knowledge: Construction, Administration and Norms," *Research Quarterly* (December 1971), 423–29.

SECTION 3

MEASURING MENTAL OBJECTIVES

INTRODUCTION TO SECTION 3

Since most physical education programs include objectives in the cognitive or mental domain, it is logical to assume student achievement of these objectives should be measured. Unfortunately, in the past these objectives generally have been poorly measured if considered at all.

The most efficient method of measuring achievement of mental objectives, if well done, is the written test. Many disciplines have long had nationally standardized tests available. Only recently, however, have the publishers of such tests begun to explore the area of physical education. In 1970 a series of tests was published, developed cooperatively by the Educational Testing Service, an advisory committee from AAHPERD, and a group of specialists chosen to represent various geographical areas, school levels, and areas of specialization.

Textbook publishers occasionally include written tests constructed especially for use with their books. Again, however, the availability of textbooks for elementary and secondary school physical education has been limited. Using written tests provided by textbook publishers involves some problems when a particular instructor's objectives differ somewhat from those of the author of the text or the test constructor. Further, these tests are sometimes more of a promotional item for the textbook than excellently constructed measuring devices.

Some state departments of education provide written tests for use in statewide testing programs but the major intent of such programs usually involves comparisons of schools, districts, or geographical areas rather than the measurement of achievement of each individual student. For this reason the objectives of a particular teacher may differ considerably from those measured by these tests.

For a combination of reasons, written testing in physical education generally has been of poor quality or ignored completely. Some of these reasons include omission of mental achievements as a legitimate objective of physical education, a lack of professionally prepared written tests available to physical educators, a lack of written tests that measure the precise objectives desired, and a general lack of knowledge on the part of physical educators in respect to the proper procedures for constructing adequate written tests.

The purpose of this section is to remedy the final reason mentioned above by presenting information regarding the planning, administration, scoring, and evaluation of written tests. The classroom teacher knows exactly what the objectives of his or her course are and thus should be capable of constructing a more valid written test than anyone else. With a knowledge of proper techniques for constructing written tests, the teacher can also assure that the tests are reliable and efficient.

In addition to learning how to plan, construct, administer, score, and evaluate written tests, a teacher must meet four other general requirements. The first is the rather obvious qualification of having a thorough knowledge of the subject area. Without this it is very difficult to construct meaningful questions for inclusion on a test. Second, a test constructor must be fairly skilled in written expression. Questions devised by a teacher lacking in this skill are often characterized by ambiguity. This reduces the validity and reliability of a written test because there is no way of distinguishing whether an incorrect answer is due to a lack of knowledge or to an error in interpreting the question. Third, the teacher must have an awareness of the level and range of understanding in the group to be tested. This is necessary so that questions of appropriate difficulty can be constructed (as will be explained later, this affects the efficiency of the test). Finally, the prospective test constructor must be willing to spend a considerable amount of time on the task. Effective written tests are not constructed overnight.

Before discussing the tests themselves, we must consider the differences between mastery, or criterion-referenced, tests and achievement, or norm-referenced, tests. A mastery test is used to determine whether or not a student has achieved enough to meet some minimum requirement set by the tester. It is not used to determine the relative ranking of students, only to determine each student's compliance, or lack of, with some previously set standard or criterion. A familiar example of the mastery type test is the spelling test in which all students are expected to have perfect or nearly perfect scores.

The purpose of achievement tests, on the other hand, is to discriminate among different levels of achievement. It is not reasonable to expect every student to achieve 100 percent of every objective put forth in any particular course, so the identification of each student's progress toward meeting the objectives is of great interest. For this reason, the majority of written tests administered in the classroom are of the achievement type.

In physical education both types of tests have important uses. For example, in a potentially dangerous activity such as gymnastics or swimming, the use of a mastery test of the safety rules might be prudent. For the most part, however, this section deals with the various phases of constructing and using achievement tests. The discussion is divided into four parts: planning, constructing and scoring, administering and analyzing, and locating sources of previously constructed tests.

Chapter 8

Planning the Written Test

There are two important decisions to make when planning a written test. The first and most important of these involves determining *what* is to be measured. The objectives of (and what to measure in) a course depend on several variable factors such as size of the class, ability level of the students; time, space, and equipment available; and so on. The decision must be made for each instance. A technique for ensuring that a written test measures the desired objectives and that the correct emphasis is given to each objective is the development and use of a table of specifications. The procedures involved in this technique are explained later.

The second fundamental decision in planning a written test involves the answering of several relatively mechanical questions, basically concerned with *how* to measure. Such issues as the frequency and timing of testing, the number and type of questions to be used, and the format and scoring procedures to be employed need to be settled.

WHAT TO MEASURE

If teaching is done properly this question should, for the most part, be answered before the class convenes for the first time. The objectives of the course, the experiences to be used to meet these objectives, and the implementation and sequence of these experiences must all be thought out and planned ahead of time if teaching is to be efficient. These elements may be altered and modified as the course progresses, but radical changes should seldom be necessary. Measurement is used to determine the degree to which objectives are being accomplished and to aid in the evaluation of where any problems may be. When the objectives are cognitive, the initial step in designing the test is the development of a table of specifications.

Table of specifications

The table of specifications is to a test as a blueprint is to a building. The table denotes the relative importance of each item on the test by giving it a percentage value. It is a two-way table with course content objectives along one axis and educational objectives (example lists of these are given later) along the other.

The example below demonstrates the process of formulating a table of specifications for a 60-item multiple-choice written test to be used in a coeducational high school class in badminton. The course content objectives and the approximate amount of time spent on each are:

History	5%
Values	5%
Equipment	10%
Etiquette	10%
Safety	10%
Rules	20%
Strategy	15%
Techniques of play	25%

The educational objectives and the weighting for each as determined by the teacher are:

Knowledge	30%
Comprehension	10%
Application	30%
Analysis	20%
Synthesis	0%
Evaluation	10%

Once the relative percentages are decided upon, the table of specifications can be constructed. The result of the preceding example is shown in Table 8.1. The course content objectives and their weighting factors are located on the vertical axis, and the educational objectives and their weighting factors are on the horizontal axis. The weight associated with any single cell of the table is found by determining the product for the intersection of the appropriate column and row. The resulting product for any cell is an expression of the approximate percentage of the test that should be made up of items combining the two types of objectives intersecting at that cell. The actual number of questions of each type is found by multiplying the percentage by the proposed length of the test. In Table 8.1 each cell is divided into two halves; the upper number represents the percentage of the test to be made up of items combining the appropriate course content and educational objectives, and the bottom number represents the number of questions of this type based on a total test length of 60 items.

Table 8.1   Table of specifications for a sixty-item multiple-choice written test

Educational objectives

Course content Objectives	Weight	Knowledge 30%	Comprehension 10%	Application 30%	Analysis 20%	Synthesis 0%	Evaluation 10%	100%	Total number items for each course objective
History	5%	.15% / .9	.05% / .3	.15% / .9	.10% / .6	0 / 0	.05% / .3		3
Values	5%	.15% / .9	.05% / .3	.15% / .9	.10% / .6	0 / 0	.05% / .3		3
Equipment	10%	.30% / 1.8	.10% / .6	.30% / 1.8	.20% / 1.2	0 / 0	.10% / .6		6
Etiquette	10%	.30% / 1.8	.10% / .6	.30% / 1.8	.20% / 1.2	0 / 0	.10% / .6		6
Safety	10%	.30% / 1.8	.10% / .6	.30% / 1.8	.20% / 1.2	0 / 0	.10% / .6		6
Rules	20%	.60% / 3.6	.20% / 1.2	.60% / 3.6	.40% / 2.4	0 / 0	.20% / 1.2		12
Strategy	15%	.45% / 2.7	.15% / .9	.45% / 2.7	.30% / 1.8	0 / 0	.15% / .9		9
Techniques of play	25%	.75% / 4.5	.25% / 1.5	.75% / 4.5	.50% / 3.0	0 / 0	.25% / 1.5		15
	100%								
Total number of items for each educational objective		18	6	18	12	0	6		60

Obviously it is not possible to include .9 of a question (as indicated by the upper left cell of the table) on the test but the numbers in the table of specifications are to be taken only as guides; usually some rounding and adjusting is necessary. If followed fairly closely, the use of a table of specifications should result in a test containing questions in proportion to the percentages of weighting desired for each category.

Some resource material is available for helping the teacher determine educational objectives. Various authors have listed and defined objectives. The list used in the table of specifications in Table 8.1 is published in the *Taxonomy of Educational Objectives*.[1] In the book each educational objective is defined and divided into several categories, and many examples of test items are given illustrating the type of cognitive behavior associated with each type of objective. Briefly, knowledge is defined as remembering and being able to recall specifics; comprehension, as the lowest level of understanding; application, as the use of abstractions in concrete situations; analysis, as a division of a communication into its parts in such a way as to make clear the relationship between the expressed ideas; synthesis, as the putting together of elements and parts so as to form a whole; and evaluation, as judgments about the extent to which methods and materials satisfy criteria.

Another list of educational objectives that includes terminology, factual information, generalization, explanation, calculation, prediction, and recommended action has been proposed by Ebel.[2] These two examples are presented to indicate some of the possibilities that can be used in constructing the table of specifications. It is entirely conceivable and probable that the teacher of a particular unit might devise his or her own list.

Although the example deals with a multiple-choice test, the formulation of a table of specifications should be the first step in the construction of *any* type of achievement test. It is an objective statement of what is to be tested and the proportion of the test that is to deal with each area of concern, and as such is a most useful blueprint.

HOW TO MEASURE

As mentioned, determining how to measure usually involves the answering of several relatively mechanical questions. These answers are often partially resolved by school or departmental policies or practical considerations, but frequently the answers require a knowledge of the outcomes of using various testing procedures.

When to test

Certain institutional policies partially dictate the times testing is done. The type and frequency of grade reporting, the school policy on setting aside certain class periods for testing, and various class scheduling practices have a bearing on the decision of when to test. Most frequently, tests are administered during a regularly scheduled class period at or near the end of a particular unit. Often the lengths of these units are designed to coincide with the school grading periods. These practices are justifiable for the type of test (achievement) discussed in this chapter. There may be, however, valid reasons for administering tests at other times during a unit of instruction. A mastery test to ensure a knowledge of safety rules near the beginning of a unit or a test near the middle of a unit to help evaluate progress toward certain objectives are possibilities.

Testing should be frequent enough to assure that reliable results are obtained and yet not so frequent that instructional time is needlessly reduced. For obvious reasons, there is no set percentage of time that should be reserved for measurement purposes. However, it is probably safe to surmise that in general too little rather than too much time has been spent measuring achievement in physical education.

How many questions?

Generally the reliability of an achievement test increases as its length increases. This is because the more often an assessment of a student's achievement is made the less opportunity there is for chance occurences to affect the results. Flipping a coin twice and obtaining two "heads" is rather meager evidence to support the contention that the coin has two "head" sides. However, if the coin is "tested" fifty times and fifty heads occur, the contention becomes quite tenable because the chance occurence of such an event with a normal coin is extremely remote.

The length of a test is a function of factors other than the desire for reliable results. The three most important factors determining the number of questions on a test are 1) the time available for testing, 2) the type of questions used, and 3) the attention span of the students being tested.

In most situations the length of the class period is the limiting factor on achievement test length. Only the typical 45–60 minutes of class are available. The number of questions that can be answered in this time will depend largely on the type of questions used (e.g., essay, true-false, multiple-choice). The student response required may vary considerably not only among the different types of questions but also within one type. For example, very few essay questions requiring extensive answers can be completed within one class period, but many more essay questions requiring a one- or two-sentence answer could be included. A test comprised mainly of factual multiple-choice items usually contains more questions than one made up of items requiring application of knowledge to novel situations because the fact items involve mostly recall, whereas the application items require additional thinking. Finally, differences in the length of attention spans of students at different levels influence the decision regarding the number of questions included on a test. This factor is often accounted for, however, by the difference in the length of class periods at the various levels.

Another aspect to consider when determining the number of questions to include on a test is the fact that not all students work at the same rate. What percentage of students should be able to complete the test? In most physical education situations, all or nearly all of the students should be able to finish the test. With a few possible exceptions, such as a sports officiating unit in which one objective might be teaching the ability to make rapid and correct rule interpretations, it is generally true that in physical education a measurement of the ability to answer questions correctly is of more value than a measurement of the speed with which answers can be produced. Further, to construct a test of more questions than can be completed by most or all of the students is an inefficient use of the test constructor's time, since the final test questions are seldom used.

The innumerable combinations of the factors of available time, question type, attention span, and work rates described above make a certain amount of trial and error experimentation regarding the number of questions on a test inevitable. However, some general guidelines can be mentioned. Per minute of testing time, most high school students should be able to complete three true-false questions, three matching items, one to two completion questions, two recognition-type multiple-choice items, or one application-type multiple-choice item. Few guidelines can be given regarding the number of essay questions. However, the time necessary to organize an answer should be allowed for, and generally many short essay questions measure more effectively than a few lengthy ones. Again, these are very general guidelines and should be adjusted to meet particular situations.

What format should be used?

Achievement tests are most commonly presented in an oral fashion, by projection, or in some form of printed material. Expense, convenience, and minimization of the opportunities for cheating all affect the decision as to what format should be used. Most importantly, the format used should maximize the opportunity for every student to understand and complete the required task or tasks.

Oral presentation of test questions is, in general, an unsatisfactory procedure for most types of items, with the possible exception of true-false questions. Although the expense is minimal and the preparation of this format for the test constructor is simple, all the students are forced to work at the set pace and there is no opportunity for the students to check over answers. Projection of the test by means of slides, filmstrips, or overhead projector has basically the same disadvantages as oral presentation. In addition, there is the expense and time-consuming preparation. Probably the most common and efficient method of presenting achievement tests is in some written form with each student receiving a copy of the test questions. Although this method like projection, requires advance preparation (in this case, typing, proofreading, duplicating, and possibly compiling), the convenience to the students is maximized. Each student may work at his or her own rate, the answers may be checked if time permits, and the questions may be answered in any order. The test administrator is free to monitor the test and answer questions.

Attention to various layout practices can help to cut the cost and time of preparation of the test booklet, as well as enhance the accuracy of the student responses. For example, when a student actually knows the correct answer to a question but because of an illegible test copy makes an incorrect response, the reliability and validity of the test are reduced. Also, careful proofreading can avoid the use of time allotted for testing to correct typing and other errors in the test booklet.

If various types of questions are used in one test it is common practice to group questions of the same type together. This reduces the number of fluctuations in the types of mental processes required of the students. Following this same reasoning, it is usually considered best to group questions of similar content on achievement tests. Although the practice of ordering the test question from easiest to hardest is not generally recommended, the practice of including a relatively simple question or two at the beginning of a test may serve to reduce students' anxiety about the test.

For multiple-choice tests presented in printed form the students' task is made easier if the responses are listed with each response starting on a new line rather than immediately following one after another. Also, unless each response for the majority of the multiple-choice items on the test is quite long (an unlikely event), it is more efficient in terms of the amount of paper necessary to print the items in double columns instead of across the page. Using letters instead of numbers to identify the responses avoids confusion between the number of the item and the possible answers. Questions are more easily comprehended if completed in the column or on the page where begun, and groups of related questions should be separated by a space or dotted line from other groups. Several of these practices are illustrated in Figure 8.1.

Tests involving essay questions are most conveniently presented to each student in printed form also. (If few questions are involved they may be written on the chalk board with equal effectiveness.) The procedure of spacing essay questions so that sufficient room is left to answer each (as decided on by the test constructor) helps the student perceive the value of each question but may penalize those students with large handwriting. Listing the questions and indicating the point value of each in the margin is a convenient and helpful format.

Two interesting variations of the typical classroom test are the open-book test and the take-home test. Each has advantages and disadvantages and under certain conditions can be used effectively in physical education. The greatest benefit of both types is the reduction of anxiety on the part of the student taking the test. In addition, use of the open-book test usually results in fewer trivial questions and more application questions. The test constructor is forced to invent novel situations rather than present questions based entirely on circumstances presented in the textbook or lectures. Also the possibilities for cheating are reduced somewhat with open-book tests.

One of the problems encountered when open-book tests are used is a reduction in the incentive to overlearn and a possible general reduction in the time spent by the students in studying. Evidently students tend to rely on being able to obtain answers from their notes and books during the test and thus spend less time learning. Due to the practice of "looking up" answers it is necessary to set time limits on open-book tests or some students (usually unprepared and in effect studying while taking the test) will take an inordinate amount of time to finish. If an open-book test is well constructed, most students will find that the textbook and notes are of little value except for looking up formulas and tables.

Take-home tests can be used in situations where more time is required to complete a test than the teacher has available in a classroom period. The major problem with them lies in the inability to be certain that each student does his or her own work. Thus take-home tests should not be used to measure

Don't print questions across the page:

1. What type of keel is suitable for use in both open and white water?
   *A. Shoe keel
   B. Standard
   C. Bilge
   D. Ridge

Do use double columns:

2. When tandem paddling, bowman on the port and sternman on the starboard, what stroke combination will result in the canoe moving sideward to port?
   A. Bowman-pushover; Sternman-draw
   *B. Bowman-draw; Sternman-pushover
   C. Bowman-sculling; Sternman-sculling
   D. Bowman-reverse sculling; Sternman-reverse sculling

Do list responses:

3. Which badminton shot requires the greatest expenditure of energy?
   A. Underhand backhand clear
   B. Overhead backhand clear
   C. Deep singles serve
   *D. Smash

Don't put responses in following order:

4. How does a doubles badminton court differ from the singles court for the serve?
   *A. It is shorter and wider. B. It is wider and deeper. C. There is no difference on the serve. D. The outside lines are used in doubles.

Don't break an item from one column or page to another:

5. Which has the greatest degree of difficulty: a dive performed on the one-meter board or the same dive performed on the three-meter board?
   A. The dive performed on the one-meter board
   B. The dive performed on the three-meter board
   *C. This varies from dive to dive
   D. Most dives have the same degree of difficulty at both heights.

Do use letters to identify the responses:

6. How many strikes constitute a "turkey" in bowling?
   A. 1
   B. 2
   *C. 3
   D. 4

Don't use numerals to identify responses:

7. How many more fouls are allowed per player in professional basketball than in collegiate basketball?
   1. 0
   *2. 1
   3. 2
   4. 3

Do complete each item in the column or on the page it starts:

8. What canoeing term does NOT refer to a part of a paddle?
   A. Tip
   B. Loom
   C. Grip
   *D. Stem

Figure 8.1   Some dos and don'ts for layout of multiple-choice tests

student achievement but might be used for illustrating what the students should study and as homework assignments.

What questions should be used?

The various types of questions that exist may be classified into the three general categories of objective, semiobjective, and essay. Characteristically, the task of the student in responding to an objective question is to select the correct answer from a list of two or more possibilities provided by the test constructor. This type of question is considered objective because scoring consists of matching the student's response to a previously determined correct answer; checking whether or not the student circled the proper letter, marked the correct space, or some similar procedure. Scoring is free of any subjective or judgmental decision. Types of questions classified as objective include true-false, matching, multiple-choice, and classification items.

When responding to an essay question the task of the student is to compose the correct answer. Usually the question provides some direction by including such terms as "compare," "describe," or "explain." Other constraints are often imposed on the answer by inclusion of such phrases as "limit your discussion to" or "restrict your answer to the year . . . " in the question. The essay question is considered to be subjective because the scoring usually involves judgmental decisions.

Questions in the semiobjective category have characteristics of both of the other categories. There are three types of questions in this category: short-answer, completion, and mathematical problem. For these questions, the task of the student involves composition of the correct answer, but one so short that little or no organization is necessary. While some subjectiveness may be used in scoring (for example, awarding partial credit for the correct procedures but wrong answer for a mathematical problem), procedures are generally very similar to those used for objective questions; the student's response is checked to see whether or not it matches the previously determined correct answer.

The type of response required of the student (selection or composition) and the type of decisions necessary when correcting that response (objective or subjective) determine the category of each question. But there are several other related differences, of particular consequence to either the student or the test constructor.

Much of the time available for testing is consumed in writing (essay questions), reading (objective or semiobjective questions), or determining the answer (mathematical problems). Hence, because reading is less time-consuming than writing or figuring, more objective questions can generally be included on a test than can questions from the other categories. Also, students with a weakness in one of these areas may be at a disadvantage in taking tests comprised mainly of questions requiring the skill in which they are weak. A poor reader, for example, may do worse on an objective test than on an essay test of the same material.

Differences especially significant to the test constructor are the laboriousness of item construction and scoring. Essay and semiobjective questions are simpler to prepare than objective questions. The situation is reversed, however, for scoring the various types of questions. In addition, the quality of an objective test is dependent almost entirely on the ability of the test constructor rather than the scorer, whereas the situation is reversed for an essay or semiobjective test. Thus the decision regarding the type of test to be constructed might be influenced, in part, by the time available for construction and scoring, or whether the abilities of the teacher lie in constructing or scoring tests.

One other possible difference among the categories, although evidence is very inconclusive, is that students study differently for different types of tests. It is plausible to suspect that objective tests promote the study of factual information and details, whereas essay tests focus on the recognition of broad and general concepts. The validity of this assumption rests mainly on the mistaken belief that objective questions cannot measure the depth of a student's achievement. Although it is often more difficult to construct, a test composed of objective questions can measure the achievement of almost any objective as well as a test made up of essay questions. The type of studying promoted by a test is more a function of the quality of the question than the type of questions.

Thus, almost any educational objective can be measured with any type of question, although one type of question is often much more efficient than another in particular situations. It would be difficult, for example, to conceive how the quality of a student's handwriting might be measured efficiently with an objective test or how the ability to solve mathematical problems might be measured any more validly by a test composed of other than mathematical problem questions. The fact that it may be more efficient to use objective questions to measure factual knowledge and essay questions to measure the organization and integration of knowledge has stereotyped the way certain questions are used. Also, conditions may preclude the use of the seemingly most efficient type of question. For example, it is usually impractical to correct an essay test given to a great number of students. Thus, an objective test may be used even though the measurement involves more than just factual information. The use of objective questions on nationally standardized tests is an example of this situation.

Despite the names of the three categories of questions, subjectiveness is a part of every test constructed. Subjective decisions are required in the scoring of essay questions and, to a lesser degree, semiobjective questions. Subjectiveness is present in the construction of all types of questions. The decisions involved in both determining what questions to ask and how they are to be phrased are subjective in nature. To increase the reliability of classroom tests, the amount of subjectiveness involved in their construction and scoring should be reduced as much as possible. Practices such as formulating a table of specifications and consulting with colleagues are ways in which this may be accomplished.

Regardless of the type or types of questions that are used on a test, the usefulness of the resulting scores is dependent on their stability. A test is designed and constructed to measure the achievement of certain objectives, and the scores resulting from the administration and correction of the test are supposed to express the degree of achievement that has occurred. If a different construction, administration, or correction of the test by the same or a different teacher resulted in a different set of scores and a corresponding different ordering of the students in regard to their achievements, the stability and thus the value of the scores would be reduced. The type of questions included on a test affect the stability of the scores in various ways. For example, if two teachers were instructed to construct a test over the same unit of instruction, it is more likely that the two tests would contain similar questions if an essay test rather than an objective or semiobjective test was constructed. On the other hand, if two teachers each corrected an objective test, a semiobjective test, and an essay test, concurrence is much more probable for the objective test than for the semiobjective or essay test.

Knowledge of the similarities and differences among the types of questions, along with an awareness of the advantages and disadvantages of each type of question (see the following chapter), is useful in selecting the most efficient type or types of questions for each particular situation. This knowledge, plus proficiency in the general requirements for test construction, can lead to the development of valid and reliable written achievement tests.

REFERENCES CITED

[1]Benjamin S. Bloom, ed., *Taxonomy of Educational Objectives* (New York: David McKay Company, Inc., 1956), 207 pp.

[2]Robert L. Ebel, *Measuring Educational Achievement* (Englewood Cliffs, N.J.: Prentice Hall Inc., 1965), 481 pp.

Chapter 9

Constructing and Scoring Written Tests

ESSAY QUESTIONS

When to use

Although almost any type of question can effectively measure the extent to which a student can organize, analyze, synthesize, and evaluate information, essay questions are easier to construct for this purpose than any other type. The contention that the use of essay questions promotes the study of generalizations rather than facts is reasonable but has not been and probably never will be conclusively substantiated. However, the essay question is undoubtedly the most effective measurement of opinions and attitudes.

In some situations, the use of essay questions is more efficient or convenient, regardless of the mental processes or subject matter involved. For example, the time required for the construction and correction of an essay test is often less than the time for other types of questions. If a test is to be used only once, an essay test may prove to be most economical in terms of time. When a test is used on several occasions, the time spent in question construction is lessened considerably after the initial administration. Only the revision of some items may be necessary for subsequent administrations.

Two other conditions possibly motivating the use of essay questions involve the preferences and time schedule of the teacher. A teacher having confidence in his or her ability to construct and score essay questions but lacking that confidence for other types of questions should probably use essay tests. However, the teacher should be aware of the weaknesses of essay questions and how they can be minimized or eliminated. Finally, when scheduling circumstances dictate little time for test construction but ample time for test correction, the essay test should be used.

Weaknesses

Even with careful preparation and scoring methods, some problems arise when essay questions are used to measure achievement. These problems involve 1) the inability to obtain a wide sample of student achievement, 2) inconsistencies inherent in the scoring procedures, and 3) difficulties in analyzing the effectiveness of the test.

Essay tests have fewer questions than objective tests due to the time required to organize and write down the essay answer. It is not always possible to include enough essay questions on a test to measure the achievement of each content and educational objective desired. Since the test does not measure all it is assumed to be measuring there is some lack of content validity. This problem can be alleviated by construction of a table of specifications, use of numerous essay questions requiring relatively short answers rather than a few questions requiring extended answers, and use of frequent tests to reduce the amount of material measured by each.

The most serious problem of the essay question is the unreliability of the scoring procedures. Not only does it take a substantial amount of time to correct an essay question properly, but several factors cause inconsistencies in the scores obtained. Because of the freedom given to the student in constructing the essay answer, it is often necessary for the teacher correcting the test to decide, sometimes subjectively, whether or not a student has achieved an objective. The subjectivity can be reduced if the teacher is very knowledgeable in the subject matter tested and if the task required of the student for each question is made very specific. But it is probably never completely eliminated.

Another problem is the "halo effect" or "generalization," the reflection of a teacher's overall opinion of a student on the score the student receives on an essay question or test. Giving the benefit of the doubt on one question to a student who has done well on most of the other questions on a test or to a student who has impressed the teacher favorably in the past is an example of this phenomenon. By divising some coding system so that students' names need not appear on the answer sheets and by correcting the test questions by question rather than paper by paper, the consequences of this problem may be diminished.

Several irrelevant elements can also affect the scoring of essay answers. Handwriting, spelling, and grammar, for example, can positively or negatively affect the teacher correcting an essay answer. Unless these are specific objectives of the test, the scores should not reflect these elements but should only be influenced by the achievement in the area being measured.

After a test has been constructed, administered, and corrected, analysis of how well the test measured what it was intended to measure is of value, especially if the test is to be used again. Analyzing the test generally includes obtaining indications of the overall reliability, validity, and objectivity of the test, and the strengths and weaknesses of the test's individual items. Although some of these characteristics can and should be investigated for essay tests, essay questions do not lend themselves to scrutiny as conveniently as do objective questions.

Recommendations for construction

Attention to the following six suggestions concerning the construction of essay questions will help overcome some of the weaknesses and problems associated with their scoring.

1. Phrase the question in such a manner that the mental processes required of the student are clearly evident. The objective of a question might be to determine whether or not a student has a mastery of factual material, to ascertain the degree to which learned material can be applied to novel situations, or to evaluate a student's ability to organize an answer in a logical manner. The student should be able to recognize the type of answer required by the manner in which a question is stated.

2. Use several essay questions requiring relatively short answers as opposed to few questions requiring extended answers. This practice usually leads to two positive results: a wider sampling of the students' knowledge is obtained and the teacher is forced to ask relatively specific questions, the answers to which can normally be scored more reliably.

3. Phrase the question in such a manner that the task of the student is specifically identified. Avoid asking for opinions when measuring educational achievement. Begin essay questions with such words or phrases as, "Explain how . . . ," "Compare . . . ," "Contrast . . . ," and "Present arguments for and against . . . ." Do not start essay questions with words or phrases such as, "Discuss . . . ," "What do you think about . . . ," or "Write all you know about . . . ." Also, unless the purpose of a question is to measure the mastery of relatively factual material, do not begin an essay question with words such as "List . . . ," "Who . . . ," "Where . . . ," or "When . . . ."

4. Set guidelines to indicate to the student the scope of the answer required. This can be done in several ways. Limiting factors may be built into the question as in the following examples, "Explain how, during the years 1970– 72 . . . ," or "Limiting your answer to team games only, compare . . . ." Other methods of indicating how involved the answer should be are to specify the amount of time to be spent on the answer, the number of points the answer is worth, or the amount of space in which the answer is to be completed.

5. Prepare an ideal answer to the question. Because this requires that the teacher identify exactly what the question is intended to measure, ambiguities often become apparent. This practice also aids in increasing the reliability of the scoring process.

6. Avoid giving a choice of essay questions to be answered. If an essay test is designed to measure achievement of the objectives of a group of students all exposed to the same instruction, each student should be required to answer the same questions. The common base of measurement is lost if a choice of questions is given. The use of optional questions adds another variable and increases the possibility of inaccurate scoring.

Recommendations for scoring

Certain practices, if followed, reduce some of the unreliability inherent in the process of scoring an essay answer. Several of these procedures are related to or follow from the previous suggestions for construction.

1. Decide in advance what the essay question is intended to measure. If an essay question is designed to measure application of facts, the answer to the question should be evaluated on that basis and not on the basis of organization, spelling, grammar, neatness, or some other standard. An attempt should be made to ignore elements not dealing with the question's objective.

2. Use the ideal answer previously prepared as a frame of reference for scoring each answer. This is especially important if an independent rating of the answers is secured as is suggested and explained later.

3. Determine the method of scoring to be used. One of three systems — analytic, global, or relative — may be employed. The analytic method involves identifying specific facts, points, or ideas in the answer and awarding credit for each one located. An answer receiving a perfect score would necessarily include all the specific items occurring in the ideal answer. This type of scoring is especially effective when the objective of the question involved is to measure the acquisition of relatively factual material.

    Global scoring consists of reading the answer and converting the general impression obtained into a score. In theory, the general impression is a function of the completeness of the answer in comparison to the ideal answer. Of the three grading methods, global is the most subjective and the one most likely to be affected by extraneous factors.

    The relative method of scoring the answers to an essay question consists of reading all the answers to one question and arranging the papers in order according to their adequacy. This may be accomplished by setting up a number of categories (such as Good, Fair, Poor, or Excellent; Above Average, Average, Below Average) and assigning each answer to one of the categories. Second, third, and possibly more readings may be necessary to arrange the papers within each category and occasionally to shift one paper to another category. The end result will be an ordering of all the papers in respect to the correctness of the answers.

After the sorting is completed scores may be assigned to each answer. There is no reason the top paper must be assigned an "A" or the bottom paper an "F." The teacher's evaluation should also be influenced by the comparison of each answer to the ideal answer. This ordering of the papers helps assure consistency in the scoring procedure and is especially effective when the object of a question is to measure relatively complex mental processes.

4. Develop a system so that the scorer does not know whose paper is being scored. Students could sign their names on a piece of paper next to a number corresponding to the number on their test booklet or mark their test copy with a unique design or pattern that only they will recognize. Having each answer recorded on a separate sheet of paper also helps to eliminate the bias caused by noticing the scores given to a student's other answers. If several answers do occur on one answer sheet (as would be the case if short answers are required), scores can be recorded on a separate sheet of paper, thus eliminating the halo effect. This procedure is also very useful if tests are rescored to check reliability. The second reader, who may or may not be the same as the first scorer, will not be influenced by the score previously awarded.

5. Score all the students' answers to one question rather than each student's answers to all the questions. This process is a requisite if the global or relative systems of scoring are used and, although not required for the analytic method, usually leads to more consistent scoring because it is easier to compare all the answers to one question if answers to other questions do not intervene.

6. Arrange for a second scoring of the question. Examination of the reliability and objectivity of the scoring procedure used to mark an essay test requires that each answer be scored twice and the two resulting scores compared. These two scores should be awarded by two different scorers to ensure that they are independently obtained. If it is possible to arrange for another teacher knowledgeable in the area covered by the test to score the papers, it is important to supply that teacher with the ideal answers to the questions so that the two scores thus obtained have a common basis. However, if it is not feasible to obtain an independent scoring of the papers, the same teacher might score the answers on two different occasions, perhaps separated by a week, in an effort to secure some evidence about the consistency of the scoring procedures used.

As should be obvious by this point, the process of constructing and scoring a reliable essay test can be very tedious and time consuming. However, to be fair to the students the procedures explained above should be followed if an essay test is employed to measure educational objectives.

SEMIOBJECTIVE QUESTIONS

The three types of questions in this category are short answers, completion, and mathematical problem. The short-answer question and the completion question differ only in format. The completion item is presented as an incomplete statement, whereas the short answer item is presented as a question. The task required to answer a mathematical problem is specified either by various symbols or by words as in a "story problem." The uses, advantages, disadvantages, construction, and scoring suggestions for all three types of questions are described simultaneously due to their similarities.

When to use

The semiobjective question is especially useful for measuring relatively factual material such as vocabulary words, dates, names, identification of concepts, and mathematical principles. It is also particularly suitable for assessing recall rather than recognition since the student supplies the answer. The advantages of the semiobjective question include relatively simple construction, almost total reduction of the possibility of guessing on the part of the students, and simple and rapid scoring.

Weaknesses

Due to the limited amount of information that can be given in one question or incomplete statement, it is often necessary to include additional material to prevent semiobjective questions from being ambiguous. Even when a situation is explained in fair detail, the danger of ambiguity is not completely removed, especially for completion items. Occasionally, a blank left in a sentence can be filled by a word or phrase that can be defended as being correct although it is not precisely what the teacher desired. For example, consider the following completion item: Basketball was invented by _____ .
The name "James Naismith" or the phrase "an American" are two possibilities that correctly complete the sentence. When this situation occurs, a decision involving whether or not to award credit is necessary. This introduces some subjectivity and thus the possibility of inconsistency in the scoring procedure. Use of certain construction techniques can help alleviate but seldom eliminate this problem.

Recommendations for construction

Of the three types of semiobjective questions, ambiguity is most likely to occur with the completion item. Rephrasing the incomplete sentence into a question and, thus, a short answer item, often resolves several problems. However, if the completion item is used, following the suggestions listed below may reduce some ambiguities.

  1. Avoid indefinite statements for which several answers may be correct and sensible. This can be done, in part, by specifying in the incomplete state-

ment what type of answer is required. For example, the item "Basketball was invented by ＿＿＿＿＿＿＿＿." could be reworded to read, "The name of the person who invented basketball is ＿＿＿＿＿＿＿＿." Another similar method for eliminating ambiguity is to present the item as: "Basketball was invented by ＿＿＿＿＿＿＿＿."
(person's name)

2. Construct the incomplete sentences, when possible, in such a way that the blank occurs near the end of the statement. When this is done the specific type of answer required is generally better identified than when the blank space occurs early in the statement. For example, "The ＿＿＿＿＿＿＿ system of team play in doubles badminton is recommended for beginners." The desired correct answer is "side by side" but the blank could logically be filled in with the phrase "least complex" because it is not clear that it is the name of the system that is desired. Rewording the statement so that the blank occurs near the end helps solve this problem. "The type of team play recommended for beginners in doubles badminton is called the ＿＿＿＿＿＿＿ system."

3. Do not leave so many blanks in one statement that the item becomes indefinite. "The name of the ＿＿＿＿＿＿＿ who invented ＿＿＿＿＿＿＿ is ＿＿＿＿＿＿＿." As shown by this example, the more blanks in the statement the less information given to the student, and answering the question becomes a guessing game. Additional information should be given by either explaining what is required or making several items from the one.

4. Do not give inadvertent clues. Occasionally the phrasing of the statement or the use of a particular article or verb reduces the number of possible words or phrases that might complete a statement. For example, "Basketball was invented by an ＿＿＿＿＿＿＿." The article "an" suggests
(nationality)
that the answer begins with a vowel and thus eliminates several possible responses. This may be corrected by including both the articles "a" and "an" thusly: "Basketball was invented by a(n)＿＿＿＿＿＿＿." If more
(nationality)
than one blank occurs in a statement, each blank should be the same length to avoid giving the student information about the length of the correct response.

5. If a numerical answer is required, indicate the units and degree of accuracy desired. Specifying this information simplifies the scorer's task and eliminates one source of confusion for the student.

6. Use short answer questions where possible to reduce ambiguity. Scoring consistency is enhanced because the student's task is typically more clearly identified than with completion items. It is important that the short-answer item be phrased in such a way that the limits on the length of the response are obvious.

Recommendations for scoring

If semiobjective questions are well constructed and no problems are encountered (as when two or more answers are plausible for one item), the scoring process is simple, objective, and reliable. The answers can be scored easily by persons other than the teacher.

If the test consists of completion items, a keyed answer sheet can be prepared by cutting out a rectangular area where each blank occurs on a test copy. Immediately below or adjacent to the rectangular area the correct answer is written. When this answer sheet is superimposed on a completed test copy, each student response can be quickly matched with the keyed answer.

The use of separate answer sheets for short-answer items speeds the scoring process. Since only one-word or short-phrase answers are expected, an answer sheet, previously prepared to accommodate the correct number of responses, may be distributed with each test copy. The answer sheet should provide a numbered blank space corresponding to each test item. Usually, two columns of answers can be placed on one side of a standard-sized piece of paper. Efficient scoring can be accomplished by placing a keyed answer sheet, constructed by recording the correct responses on a copy of the answer sheet, alongside each student's answer sheet. This procedure eliminates searching through the pages of all the test booklets to locate the answers.

OBJECTIVE QUESTIONS

Questions requiring the student to select one of two or more given responses can be scored with minimal subjective judgment. Thus, they are categorized as objective questions. There are many similarities among the various types of objective questions but separate consideration is given to true-false, matching, classification, and multiple-choice items because there are also many differences.

True-false questions

Perhaps unfortunately, true-false questions have been very popular and widely used by teachers, probably because their construction and scoring is relatively simple and quickly accomplished. Although there are advantages unique to true-false questions and situations where their use is justifiable, several weaknesses cause this type of item to be among the least adequate of the objective questions.

When to use

Like the various semiobjective questions, true-false items are particularly suited for measuring relatively factual material such as names, dates, and vocabulary words. The advantages of using true-false items in this situation include the ease with which they can be constructed, administered, and scored and the fact that per unit of testing time more true-false items can be answered than any other type of question. The minimal amount of time spent reading and the simple procedure for answering result in a maximum number of samples of a student's knowledge in a given time period.

Weaknesses

Many of the major weaknesses of true-false questions stem from the fact that a totally unprepared student, by chance alone, might answer one-half of the items correctly. This makes it difficult to assess the level of achievement attained by a student or a class of students. A correct answer could be an indication of complete understanding of the concept, a correct blind guess, or any shade of understanding between these two extremes. In addition, the inordinately excessive influence of chance lowers the amount of differentiation among good and poor students and consequently the reliability of the test.

To be fair and avoid ambiguity, a true-false item should be absolutely true or absolutely false. This requirement is difficult to meet except when factual knowledge is involved. True-false questions are not well suited for measuring complex mental processes. Because of this, ill-composed true-false tests can include many trivial questions and reward sheer memory rather than understanding.

Recommendations for construction

Generally, the writing of good true-false questions involves the ability to avoid ambiguity. Suggestions for accomplishing this and several practical considerations are presented below.

1. Avoid using an item whose truth or falsity hinges on one insignificant word or phrase. To do so results in measuring alertness rather than knowledge.

2. Beware of using indefinite words or phrases. A question whose response depends on a student's interpretation of such words or phrases as "frequently," "many," or "in most cases" is usually a poor item.

3. Include only one main idea in each true-false question. Combining two or more ideas in one statement often leads to ambiguity. If the combination introduces the slightest amount of falsity in an otherwise true statement, the student is forced to decide whether to mark true or false on the basis of the amount of truth rather than on the basis of absolute truth.

4. Avoid taking statements directly out of textbooks or lecture notes. Out of context, the meaning of the resulting item is often confusing. Very few statements made in a text or lecture can stand alone meaningfully. In addition, the practice of using textbook sentences as true-false items results in the rewarding of memorization.

5. Use negative statements sparingly and avoid the use of double negatives completely. The insertion of the word "not" to make a true statement false borders on trickery and may result in a measurement of vigilance

rather than knowledge. Statements containing double negatives, especially if false, are often needlessly confusing and complex.

6. Beware of giving clues to the correct choice through the use of specific determiners or statement length. Specific determiners are words or phrases that inadvertently provide an indication of the truth or falsity of a statement. For example, true-false items containing words such as "absolutely," "all," "always," "entirely," "every," "impossible," "inevitable," "never," or "none" are more likely to be false than true because exceptions can usually be found to any such sweeping generalizations. On the other hand, qualifying words such as "generally," "often," "sometimes," or "usually" are more common in true statements than in false statements. Because it often takes several qualifications to make a statement absolutely true, care must be taken to avoid a pattern of long statements being true and false statements being short.

7. Write separate true-false items in pencil on separate cards to facilitate revision and item selection and placement on the test.

8. Include approximately the same number of true and false statements on a test. There is some evidence that false statements are slightly more discriminating, perhaps because an unprepared student is more inclined to mark true. For this reason it may be advantageous to include a slightly higher percentage of false statements.

9. Do not arrange a particular pattern of correct responses. The placement of true and false statements should be regulated by chance to avoid the possibility of students detecting a pattern of responses.

10. If possible, arrange for a colleague to review the true-false questions before administering them to the students. Occasionally some ambiguity can be removed by following this procedure.

Modifications

Attempts have been made to modify the true-false question with the intent of reducing excessive blind guessing. One method is to require the student to identify the portion of a false statement that makes it false. A further modification requires the student to correct the inaccurate portion. Although these two modifications partially eliminate the effect of chance on the final score, unfortunately they simultaneously introduce other problems. Ambiguity may result, as in the following: "James Naismith invented the game of volleyball." The statement is false but may be corrected by replacing the name James Naismith with the name William Morgan or by replacing the word "volleyball" with the word "basketball." Some subjectivity is conceivably introduced into the scoring of these kinds of true-false questions. Further, the advantage of quick scoring is lost.

Another area of modification for true-false questions involves changing the answering and scoring procedures to reflect the degree of confidence students have in their responses. The intent of this variation is to discriminate between those students who get an answer wrong because they do not know the correct response and those who know something but not enough to prevent a "bad luck" choice. Several scoring systems have been devised to accomplish a confidence weighting of the response to a true-false item. One of these systems is presented in Table 9.1

Table 9.1   System for confidence weighting answers to true-false questions

Response	Mark	Scoring procedure	
		Correct	Incorrect
Definitely true	A	2	−2
Likely true	B	1	0
Omit or don't know	C	.5	.5
Likely false	D	1	0
Definitely false	E	2	−2

This modification, while increasing the discriminatory power of a true-false test, possibly introduces some undesirable variables. For example, differences in personality traits among students (some more willing to gamble than others) and the importance not only of knowledge in the subject being tested but also an awareness about the nature of one's knowledge become factors influencing the final test results. Thus these modifications may well increase the reliability and discriminatory power but simultaneously reduce the validity of a true-false test.

Recommendations for scoring

As is true of most semiobjective and objective questions, the use of a separate answer sheet facilitates the scoring procedure. Because of the similarity between the letters T and F, it is not a good idea to have students write these responses on a sheet of paper when completing a true-false test. A previously prepared answer sheet on which students block out, circle, or underline the correct response helps eliminate scoring problems. Special answer sheets that can be scored by machine are available for most objective questions including true-false questions. Scoring by hand can be efficiently accomplished by matching each response on a student's answer sheet with a previously prepared correct answer sheet. Further, this task can be performed by someone not familiar with the subject matter being tested.

Matching questions

Matching questions generally involve lists of related questions and possible answers. The task of the student is to match the correct answer to the proper question. At times, instead of a question-answer format, this type of question involves matching an item in one list with the item most closely associated with it in the second list.

When to use

As with true-false questions, matching questions are most efficient for measuring relatively superficial types of knowledge. Measurements of vocabulary, dates, events, and simple relationships such as authors to books can be effectively obtained with matching questions. Basically they are used to make measurements of who, what, where, and when rather than how or why. Among the advantages of matching questions are the relative ease of construction and the rapidity, accuracy, and objectivity with which they can be scored. One requirement for using this type of objective item is the necessity of developing a cluster of similar questions and similar answers. Usually the most discriminating matching questions are those used in conjunction with a graph, chart, map, diagram, or similar device in which labels on the pictorial presentation are matched with functions, names, or similar categories of answers.

Weaknesses

It is difficult, although not impossible, to construct matching questions requiring the use of high-order mental processes. However, the most limiting aspect of matching questions is the requirement for similarity among each of the two lists comprising the item. As compliance to this requirement lessens, the discriminating power of the matching item also usually diminishes.

Recommendations for construction

Because it is easier to write questions that measure relatively superficial knowledge than it is to write questions that measure cognitive processes such as application, analysis, and evaluation, it is necessary when constructing matching questions to refer often to the table of specifications drawn up for a test to ensure that the desired balance among the areas measured is achieved. Unless caution is exercised, a test composed mainly of matching items may concentrate more heavily on factual material than warranted by the table of specifications. Suggestions for constructing matching questions are presented below.

1. Present clear and complete directions. In general, the directions to a matching question should include three details: 1) the basis for matching the items in the two lists, 2) the method by which the student is to record the answers, and 3) whether or not a response in the second column may be used more than once. A sentence such as "Match the statements in column I with those in column II" does not include any of the three points. An example of a complete set of directions is as follows: "For each type of physical activity listed in column I select the physical benefit from column II that is most likely to be derived from it. Record your choice on the line preceding the question number. An item in the physical benefit column may be used more than once."

2. Use complete sentence questions rather than a fill-in-the-blank format. This procedure usually reduces ambiguity for the student.

3. Avoid clues. Every word or phrase in the second column must be an acceptable answer to every question in the first list in both a logical and grammatical sense. Verb tenses, the use of singular and plural words, and articles are the most common areas of grammatical clues.

4. Avoid including too many questions in one matching item. To be effective, the list of questions and the list of answers in a matching item must be homogeneous. As the length of the list increases, the ability to meet this requirement becomes increasingly difficult. In most cases five or six questions is the practical limit for each matching item.

5. Do not start a matching item on a page if it cannot be completed on that page.

6. Include a greater number of answers than questions or allow the repeated use of some answers. This removes the possibility of using the process of elimination to obtain the answer to one part of a matching item.

7. Keep the parts of the matching questions as short as possible without sacrificing clarity. The list of possible answers must be completely reread for each question and thus valuable testing time is consumed with needlessly lengthy answers.

8. Arrange the two lists of questions and answers in a random fashion. There should not be any particular pattern to the sequence of correct responses for a "test-wise" student to perceive.

9. Place the answers in a logical order if one exists. This allows the student who knows the answer to locate it quickly.

Recommendations for scoring

Since matching questions are generally answered on the test booklet rather than on a separate answer sheet, the items should be arranged on the test booklet so that a key can be placed next to the margin for quick scoring. Scoring a matching item is quite objective and can be done by someone not familiar with the subject matter tested.

Multiple-choice questions

The multiple-choice question is made up of two parts: the stem, which may be in the form of a question or an incomplete statement, and at least two responses, one of which either best answers the question or best completes the statement. The task of the student is to select the correct or best response to the question presented in the stem.

For several reasons, some of which are obvious, multiple-choice questions are used on almost all nationally standardized tests. These items can be scored efficiently, quickly, and reliably. Analysis of how each item and the entire test functioned can be conveniently accomplished. Ambiguity, although never completely eliminated, is probably less of a problem with multiple-choice questions than with other types of questions. Although they share many of the advantages of true-false questions, multiple-choice questions having more than two responses are not as susceptible to chance errors caused by blind guessing. Finally, it is easier to construct questions that measure the high-order cognitive processes such as application and analysis using multiple-choice questions. In fact, almost any educational objective can be measured using multiple-choice questions.

When to use

Since multiple-choice questions are capable of measuring all levels of cognitive behavior, are applicable for nearly any subject or grade level, and can be used to measure virtually any educational objective, they can be used in almost any situation. If a large group of students is to be tested or if a test or parts of it are to be reused, a multiple-choice test is indicated because when the total time for test constructing, administering, scoring, and analyzing is considered, the multiple-choice test is most efficient.

In the event that fairly rapid feedback is important, the multiple-choice item, because of its quick and accurate scoring characteristics, should be used. Generally a fairly large number of multiple-choice questions can be included on a test because the time required to answer each item is short. This, coupled with the fact that multiple-choice questions can be constructed to measure most educational objectives, results in it being less difficult to construct a test fitting the table of specifications by using multiple-choice questions than any other type of test item. Finally, as with all of the objective and most of the semiobjective test items, the scoring procedures are quick and can be done by someone not familiar with the subject area.

Weaknesses

The multiple-choice question, because of its versatility, does not have many intrinsic weaknesses. The required investment of time makes multiple-choice inefficient for small groups or one-time use. A few objectives are not as efficiently measured by multiple-choice questions as by other types of questions. Although multiple-choice questions could probably be devised to measure organization, grammatical construction of sentences, and other writing characteristics, if these are objectives to be measured by a test, essay questions would seem the logical choice.

Recommendations for construction
General considerations

1. Realize that each multiple-choice question will probably require future revision and write the initial draft accordingly.

Use pencil and double space so that erasure and revision requiring the addition of information are possible. Write each item on a separate sheet of paper or index card to allow for ease in assembling the items into a test. Record with each question the course objectives and educational objectives it measures so its place in the table of specifications may be determined quickly. Also record with each question the location of the source for the idea around which the question is built, as this information is often lost with the passage of time.

2. Base each multiple-choice question on an important, significant, and useful concept.

Usually the most successful multiple-choice questions are those based on generalizations and principles rather than on facts and details. For example, a question requiring the student to know the general organization of Bloom's *Taxonomy of Educational Objectives* is more valuable than a question requiring the student to know that the third category of the taxonomy is that of Application.

3. Use novel situations when possible.

Generally, effective questions result when the specific illustrative materials used in the textbook or lectures are avoided as the basis for questions and novel situations requiring the application of knowledge are used.

4. Phrase each multiple-choice question in such a manner that one response can be defended as being the best alternative.

It is not always necessary that the response keyed as being correct be the best of all possible answers to the question, but it must be the best of the choices listed. Also in this regard it is unwise to ask a question that requests an opinion of the student because this results in a "no best answer" situation. For example, consider the following stem: "What do you consider to be the best defense against the fast break in basketball?" Since this asks for the student's opinion, any choice marked must be regarded as correct, whether or not it agrees with the opinions of basketball authorities.

5. Phrase each multiple-choice question in as clear and concise a manner as possible.

Ideally the stem should contain enough information so that every student understands what is being asked and yet be brief enough that no testing time is wasted reading unnecessary material. Occasionally it is necessary to include a sentence or two to clarify a situation and avoid ambiguity. However, the practice of teaching on the test or including unnecessary information (called "window dressing" by some test construction experts) should be avoided.

The tendency to use flowery and imaginative language should also be avoided as this practice can lead to ambiguity due to the increase in possible interpretations. The use of negatively stated questions should be kept to a minimum; when they are used the negative word(s) should be capitalized, underlined, or both. The purpose of asking a question is to determine whether or not the student knows the answer, not to see if the student reads carelessly or can work through the confusion that sometimes arises with negatively stated questions.

6. Do not include a multiple-choice question that all or nearly all students will answer correctly or incorrectly unless it is determined that the question must be included to increase the validity of the test.

A question that is answered correctly (or incorrectly) by every student is of little value on an achievement test because no discrimination among the students results. In fact, it has been shown mathematically that maximum discrimination can occur only when a question is of middle difficulty; that is, when approximately half the students answer the question correctly and half incorrectly. Although it is quite difficult to estimate the proportion of students who will answer a question correctly the first time the question is used, the test constructor should attempt to structure multiple-choice questions so that they will be of middle difficulty. Recall that one of the requirements for writing good test questions is to have an awareness of the level and range of understanding of the group being tested.

The difficulty of a multiple-choice question is most effectively altered by changing the homogeneity of the responses. The more homogeneous the responses, the more difficult the question. A method for obtaining an index describing the difficulty of a multiple-choice question is presented later.

7. Arrange to have the multiple-choice questions reviewed, if possible, by someone teaching in the same subject area.

Often ambiguities, grammatical mistakes, idiosyncracies and clues, all of which can affect a test negatively, can be located by an independent review. If it is not possible to arrange for another teacher to review the questions, the test constructor should reread them a few days after they have been written. Notice that the implication of this suggestion is that the questions are not written the night before the test is to be administered. One of the requirements for writing good test questions is the willingness to spend a considerable amount of time on the project.

Writing the stem

If a multiple-choice question is to be meaningful and important, the teacher should have in mind a definite concept around which the question is constructed. The most important part of the multiple-choice question in regard to the expression of this concept is the stem, and it is the first part constructed.

The stem can take two forms, a direct question or an incomplete sentence. It is usually wise (especially for novice question writers) to use the question rather than the incomplete stem so that the students' task is clearly defined. No matter which form is used it is important that when the student finishes reading the stem a definite problem has been identified so that the search for the correct response can begin. A stem such as "Badminton experts agree that . . . " does not provide a specific question or task because badminton experts agree on many things. The student is forced to read through all the responses to determine what is actually being asked. This stem would not be improved greatly by changing it to the question, "On what do badminton experts agree?" The problem with this stem is still the lack of direction regarding what the student is to do. If revised to "On what do badminton experts agree regarding the learning of the rotation strategy by beginning badminton players?" the student can begin reading the responses to locate the correct one rather than to determine what is being asked. The use of incomplete sentence stems is generally more likely to result in no question or task being specified than the use of direct questions.

Other suggestions, such as using negatives sparingly, avoiding teaching and window dressing, using qualifying information to reduce ambiguity, and using vocabulary and writing techniques familiar to all students, have been presented under the heading of general considerations but are especially germain to the stem of a multiple-choice question.

Writing the response

Following the stem of a multiple-choice question are usually four or five words, phrases, or sentences known as the responses. One of the responses is predetermined by the teacher as the correct response (usually called the keyed response). The remaining responses are labeled foils or distractors.

When constructing a multiple-choice question, the keyed response should be written immediately after the writing of the stem. Following this procedure helps ensure that the teacher is basing the question on an important concept. The question is formulated and then answered. On the test, of course, the position among the responses of the keyed response should be determined by some random procedure.

Care must be taken not to word the keyed response more precisely than the distractors in an effort to assure that it is absolutely correct. Recall that the keyed response needs only to be the best of the listed choices, not unequivocally correct under any circumstances. The length of the keyed response should seldom differ significantly from the length of the distractors. In fact, all responses should be as similar as possible in respect to appearance and grammatical structure to avoid the selection of any response for reasons other than thinking it is correct.

As with the stem, simple, clear, and concise expression of the responses is desirable to avoid ambiguity and to keep reading time to a minimum. If a natural order exists among the responses (such as dates) they should be listed in that order to remove one possible source of confusion.

The distractors, the last part of the multiple-choice question to be developed, should not be constructed for the purpose of tricking the student into selecting one of them. The distractors, however, should be attractive to the unprepared student. All the responses should be plausible answers to the question. Often the use of true statements (but not answering the question) or stereotyped words or phrases as distractors is an effective method for making them attractive to unprepared students.

The use of a ridiculous distractor unlikely to be chosen by any student is a waste of testing time. There is no reason a multiple-choice question must contain any set number of responses nor do all the multiple-choice questions on a test have to have the same number of responses. Four or five responses are commonly used because this represents a compromise between the problem of finding several adequate, plausible possibilities and including enough responses that chance does not become an important factor as with true-false questions.

Often when no other plausible distractors can be invented, it is tempting to use "None of these" as the final response. To avoid confusion, however, this should not be done unless the keyed response is absolutely correct (as in a mathematical problem) and not merely the best response. When several responses are partially correct (even if one of them is more correct than the others according to the "experts") the response "None of these" might be defended as being correct because none of the partially correct answers is absolutely correct. A similar problem exists with the response, "All of these." If these types of responses are to be used they should be the keyed response occasionally (especially early on the test) so the students realize they are to be considered seriously as possible correct answers.

Clues

Ideally a student should answer a multiple-choice question correctly only if he or she knows the answer and incorrectly if the answer is unknown. Two factors can negatively affect this situation. A student could blindly guess the correct answer to a question, and there is no way for the teacher to determine whether a correct response indicates knowledge or luck. However, in the long run, every student has an equal chance to be lucky, and the effects of chance can be mathematically accounted for. The second and more serious factor is that of clues included within multiple-choice questions or tests. Because all students are not equally adept at spotting clues, the effects are not as predictable as those for chance. The only way to eliminate the problem is to eliminate the clues.

Some clues are rather obvious; others are quite subtle. For example, it is usually fairly easy to spot the use of a key word in both the stem and the correct response, or a keyed response that is the only one that grammatically agrees with the stem. Clang associations (words that sound as if they belong together, such as shoes and socks) are often relatively difficult to spot.

Using stereotyped words or phrases was suggested as a method of securing attractive distractors. However, these should not be used in the correct response because an unprepared student may select the keyed response because it "sounds good" rather than because he or she knows it to be the correct answer.

Items that interlock also provide clues for the test-wise student. In the process of asking one question, information can be given that answers another item on the test. This is especially likely to happen if a test is constructed by selecting several questions from a file of possible questions or if new questions are added or old questions are revised on a subsequent administration of a test. To prevent interlocking items the test must be read in its entirety once assembled.

Variations

Several variations of the multiple-choice question have been devised to meet the needs of various situations. For example, the classification question, an example of which is presented below, is an efficient form of the multiple-choice format if the same set of responses is applicable to many questions.

> For questions 89 through 98 you are to determine the type of test *best* described by each statement or phrase. For each item blacken answer space
>
> > A. if an essay test is described
> > B. if a true-false test is described
> > C. if a matching test is described
> > D. if a classification test is described
> > E. if a multiple-choice test is described
>
> 89. Test limited by difficulty in securing sufficiently similar stimulus words or phrases
> 90. Responses generally cover all possible categories
> 91. Quality determined by skill of reader of answers
> 92. Simplest to prepare
> 93. Etc.

Another example of a variation of the multiple-choice involves the use of pictures or diagrams. This is illustrated below.

> If the shaded circle represents a top view of a tennis player making a crosscourt forehand stroke, in what location should the ball be when contracted by the racket, A, B, C, or D?

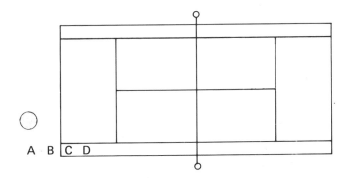

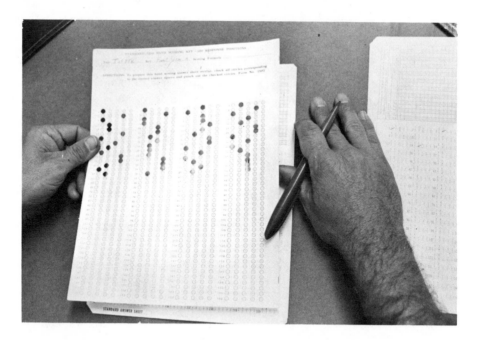

Many other variations can be created to serve particular functions as needed so long as the students are able to understand their task in answering. Most of the suggestions presented above will apply to these diverse variations.

Recommendations for scoring

Typically the answers to multiple-choice questions are recorded on the test booklet or on a separate answer sheet. A slight reduction in the chances of a student mismarking an answer and the convenience when discussing a test with the students after it has been administered are two advantages of having students mark the answers on the test booklet. If this procedure is used, the scoring process can be facilitated by arranging the questions in such a manner that the answers are recorded along the margins of the test booklet. An answer key overlay spaced to match each page can then be used effectively.

Although not as convenient to the student, the procedure of recording answers on a separate answer sheet has many advantages to the scorer. The answer sheets may be scored quickly and accurately by constructing a key from one of the answer sheets. Holes, corresponding to the positions of the keyed responses, are punched in the answer sheet. When superimposed on a student's answer sheet, the number of correct responses can be counted.

Separate answer sheets, when used with special pencils, have the further advantage of being machine scorable. Some of the machines available for this task also have the capacity to punch a computer card corresponding to each answer sheet. These cards can be used for analyzing the test and its items by means of a computer program.

Chapter 10

Administering and Analyzing Written Tests

ADMINISTERING THE WRITTEN TEST

As we have been noting, there are problems involved in testing. For example, prior to and during a testing session the anxiety level of some students can increase beyond desirable levels, during a testing session cheating can occur, and afterward, when the scores are posted, students may experience feelings of humiliation or haughtiness. Notice that these undesirable circumstances can occur but that they do not have to occur. Although the written test itself and the scoring procedures used have some influence on these circumstances, the administration of the test itself probably has the greatest impact on whether or not problems will arise before, during, and after the test. The suggestions presented below, if followed, should serve to eliminate or at least reduce many of the objectionable events that are often associated with testing.

Before the test

1. Prepare the students for the test

   Generally less anxiety is associated with a test that is announced well in advance than with surprise or "pop" tests. This is also true if the content of the test comes as no surprise to the students. It is not logical to include on an achievement test questions on topics not covered or assigned in class. In fact, a discussion about an upcoming test can help reduce student apprehension. Items such as the general areas to be measured, the approximate amount of testing time devoted to each area, the type(s) of questions that will be asked (essay, multiple-choice, etc.), the length of the test, and similar information represent legitimate concerns of the students. In the final analysis the written test, if properly constructed, should be a rather precise expression of the teacher's course objectives. It is difficult to imagine a situation in which knowledge of these objectives should be withheld from the students.

2. Eliminate, as much as possible, the test-wise advantage possessed by some students.

Most of this is accomplished through the use of proper test construction techniques (by avoiding grammatical clues, specific determiners, interlocking items, and the like). In addition, however, several suggestions on how to take a written test might equalize this skill to some degree. For example, the following recommendations might be made to the class:

> Realize that all the material measured by a good test cannot be learned the night before the test. This time should be spent reviewing but not learning.

> Read the directions to the test before beginning to answer the questions.

> Know how the test will be scored. Are all questions worth the same value? Will neatness, grammar, and organization be accounted for in the score? Will a correction for guessing formula be applied?

> Pace yourself.

> Plan an essay answer before starting to write it down.

> Check often to see that answers are located in the correct place if a separate answer sheet is used.

> Check over your answers if time permits.

3. Give any unusual or lengthy instructions the period prior to the one during which the test is to be administered.

This will save time on the day the test is to be given but more importantly, will enable the students to begin the test as near the beginning of the period as possible. This reduces the time available for anxiety to build, especially for those students who feel pressured by time.

4. Proofread the test before it is reproduced.

The effort required to proofread the master copy of a test carefully is time well spent. Proofreading helps ensure that each student will receive a legible copy free of typographical, spelling, and other errors. It also eliminates or at least reduces the time spent during the test clearing up these errors.

During the test

1. Organize an efficient method for distributing and collecting the tests.

With a small class, efficient distribution and collection of test booklets is seldom a concern. However, with sixty students spread out around a gymnasium floor, some problems can occur. If a great deal of time has been spent constructing a test and it (or part of it) is to be used in the future, an efficient collection procedure is vital to keep the test secure.

2. Help the students pace themselves.

   This can be accomplished by quietly marking the time remaining on the blackboard. A rough estimate of the portion of the test the students should be on might also be given.

3. Answer individual questions carefully and privately.

   To avoid disturbing others, an individual question should be answered privately at the student's desk or at the teacher's desk. However, care should be taken not to give any student an advantage over the others by the answer that is given. Careful proofreading should eliminate most of the problems caused by individual questions.

4. Control cheating.

   Obviously, cheating negates the validity of a set of test scores. Even a more serious problem than this, though, is the negative attitude generated toward the students who cheat, the teacher who does not control cheating, and testing in general.

5. Control the environment.

   In the final analysis any factor that prevents a student from doing his or her best on a written test lowers the reliability, validity, and useability of the resulting set of scores. Some of these factors — for example, student desire, reading habits — are not under the direct control of the teacher, although they can be influenced. However, other factors can be controlled by the teacher. Some simple yet important considerations deal with the regulation of the environment: providing adequate lighting, eliminating noise distractions, maintaining a comfortable temperature, and providing adequate space in which to work.

After the test

1. Correct the tests and report the scores to the students as quickly as possible.

   The rapidity of this operation of course depends on the type and length of the test administered. However, students generally appreciate prompt knowledge of results.

2. Report test scores anonymously.

   The decision as to whether or not a student desires to make his or her score known to others should rest with each student. Using some type of identification number system when posting scores allows this condition to exist.

3. Avoid misusing and misinterpreting test scores.

By following the suggestions in this section, physical educators will be able to improve the reliability and validity of their written tests. However, it is important to remember that no test is without some error; that is, no test is perfectly reliable and valid. Because of this, crucial decisions should not be based on the results of one written test. A one-point variation between the test scores of two students on a written test should not be interpreted as showing a significant difference between those students. These are examples of misuses of test scores. Along with other forms of measurement, written test results should be considered when evaluating students but they should be only as influential in these decisions as their accuracy permits.

ANALYZING THE WRITTEN TEST

To determine the amount of confidence that can be placed in the set of scores resulting from a test administration, the reliability and the validity of the test should be examined. This is based on how closely (validity) and how consistently (reliability) the test actually measures what is intended.

Reliability

If a test were perfectly reliable each student's observed score would be an exact representation of his or her level of achievement of whatever the test measures. Each observed score would be a true score uncontaminated by error. In actuality, of course, a student's observed score consists of two parts—the true score and the error score. The error score may be positive or negative, increasing or decreasing the observed score. As the error portion of the observed score increases, reliability decreases. Unfortunately there are several sources of error for written tests.

Sources of error

The actual questions that appear on a test represent only a sample of the infinite population of possible questions that could be selected. Error is introduced if, for any of several possible reasons, the sample selected does not adequately represent the desired population of possible questions. The failure of a student to be credited with understanding or penalized for not comprehending a particular notion because no question was included on the test to measure that comprehension is a practical example of how sampling error might reduce test reliability.

A student's mental and physical condition can affect the reliability of a test. Such possibilities as illness, severe anxiety, overconfidence, or fatigue can alter a student's score and thus lower the reliability of a test.

Conditions under which the test is administered can also be important. Poor lighting, poor temperature control, excessive noise, or any other similar variable that negatively affects concentration can cause observed scores to misrepresent true scores.

Because each student has, in theory at least, the same chance for good luck (and bad luck) when blindly guessing at an objective test, it would seem that in the long run the total effect would balance out and there would be no error introduced. However, one administration of a test does not represent "the long run" and test reliability might be reduced because some students could on one administration of a test be luckier guessers than their peers.

Sometimes error is introduced not by the measuring instrument, but by the fact that the variable being measured is changeable. Lack of a consistent definition (for example, authorities do not agree as to the definition of physical fitness) and fluctuations in the amount of the attribute being measured (for example, attitude toward physical education can change from time to time) make construction of a reliable test difficult in some areas.

Thus many factors, some of which are under at least partial control of the teacher, can introduce error and consequently reduce the reliability of a written test. As indicated in chapter 7 there are several methods of calculating a coefficient to express the reliability of a test and each of these methods reflects one or more of the sources of error.

Validity

If a written test does not measure what it is designed to measure, though it may measure something consistently, the resulting test scores are of little value. As pointed out in Chapter 7, there are various types of validity and several methods of assessing validity.

For a written test one of the most important types of validity is content validity. This is generally subjectively determined by the extent to which the individual test items represent a sufficient sample of the educational objectives a course of instruction has included. In other words, by examining a copy of a test being considered for use the teacher decides the degree of content validity the test has for the particular situation. Following the proper procedures for constructing a written test, especially the formulation and use of a table of specifications, helps assure that a teacher-made test will possess content validity.

Item analysis

Student response to the test items should be analyzed for several reasons, the most important of which is eventual improvement of the items and consequently the test. The difficulty level and the discriminating power of each item are the keys to item improvement.

Item analysis can also lead to improved teaching through identification of weakness in the students as a group, in teaching methods, or in the curriculum. It can also contribute to an improvement in the skill of written test construction. Most of the illustrations and examples presented involve multiple-choice questions because there are efficient methods available for analyzing them. However, most of the techniques of item analysis described can be modified for other types of objective items and in general the principles involved may be applied to any type of question.

Procedures

Step 1. Score the tests.

Step 2. Arrange the answer sheets in order according to score.

Step 3. Separate the answer sheets into three subgroups.

    A. The upper group consists of the upper 27 percent (approximately) of the answer sheets.

    B. The middle group consists of the middle (approximately) 46 percent of the answer sheets.

    C. The lower group consists of the same number of answer sheets as placed in the upper group.

Only the answer sheets of the two extreme groups—the upper and the lower—are used in the item analysis. As a compromise between having as many responses as possible and maximizing the differences between the types of responses, test authorities suggest the two groups be composed of the 27 percent of the answer sheets located at the two extremes of the score scale. Generally, as long as an equal number occur in each of the two groups, the use of the most convenient number of answer sheets between 25 and 33 percent for each group is satisfactory. For example, if 60 answer sheets were available for analysis, the highest and lowest 15–20 could be used.

Step 4. Count and record for each item the frequency of selection of each possible response by the upper group.

Step 5. Count and record for each item the frequency of selection of each possible response by the lower group.

Steps four and five require the most time consuming portion of the item analysis. Several procedures can help reduce the tedium of this task. Possibilities include using previously prepared "score cards" for each item, using a typewriter to speed the process of recording responses (five adjacent keys are used to represent each of five possible responses, for example, so that responses can be tabulated without lifting the eyes from the answer sheet), cooperating with another teacher (or a student) with one person reading and the other recording, or if possible, key punching computer cards by hand or using an optical scanner in order to have a computer accomplish these steps.

At the completion of step five the necessary data are available to calculate indexes of difficulty and discrimination for each item. An example of a possible organization of these data is shown in Figure 10.1. The data shown are used in the following paragraphs to illustrate the calculation of the difficulty and discrimination indexes and to illustrate how change suggested by the response pattern can improve an item. These data were obtained from a question included on a nationally standardized test of physical fitness knowledge administered to senior physical education majors.

Source: *Handbook of Physical Fitness*									Topic: *Physical Fitness*									

First Draft: In the opinion of most authorities, three of the following factors have contributed to a lowering of the national level of physical fitness. Which has NOT had this effect?

  A. An increase in life-span.

  B. A decrease in the physical effort required for daily living.

  C. An increase in the number of occupations involving sedentary activity.

*D. An increase in school consolidation.

Revision: In the opinion of most authorities, three of the following have contributed to a lowering of the national level of physical fitness. Which has NOT had this effect?

  A. An increase in the number of senior citizens.

  B. A decrease in the physical effort required for daily living.

  C. An increase in the number of occupations involving sedentary activity.

*D. An increase in school consolidation.

Item: 5	Test: Form D Trial		Date: 6/68		*N*: 185			Item: 25	Test: Final Form A		Date 9/70		*N*: 1,112		
Responses	A	B	C	*D	E	omit	Diff.	Disc.	Responses	A	B	C	*D	E	omit	Diff.	Disc.
Upper 27% = 50	28	2	1	19		0	36%	.04	Upper 27% = 300	69	10	5	216		0	53%	.37
Lower 27% = 50	24	8	1	17		0			Lower 27% = 300	89	52	54	104		1		

Figure 10.1   Data organization for item analysis

Step 6. Calculate and record the index of difficulty for each item. Substitution into the following formula results in this index.

$$\text{Diff} = \frac{U_c + L_c}{U_n + L_n} \times 100 \text{ (expressed as a percentage)}$$

where

Diff = index of difficulty
U_c = number of students in the upper group answering the question correctly
L_c = number of students in the lower group answering the question correctly
U_n = number of students in the upper group
L_n = number of students in the lower group
(Recall that $U_n = L_n$)

Inspection of this formula reveals that the index of difficulty is actually the percentage of students answering the question correctly, thus the higher the difficulty index the easier the question. The following examples using the data displayed in Figure 10.1 illustrate the use of the index of difficulty formula.

First draft results: $N = 185$, therefore 50 students are represented in each extreme group ($185 \times 27\% = 50$)

$$\text{Diff} = \frac{19 + 17}{50 + 50} \times 100$$

$$= \frac{36}{100} \times 100 = 36\%$$

Revision results: $N = 1{,}112$, therefore 300 students are represented in each extreme group ($1{,}112 \times 27\% = 300$)

$$\text{Diff} = \frac{216 + 104}{300 + 300} \times 100$$

$$= \frac{320}{600} \times 100 = 53\%$$

As previously mentioned, the maximum amount of discrimination can only occur when an item has an index of difficulty of 50%. If this criterion could be met by every question on a test the mean score of such a test would necessarily be equal to one-half the number of items on the test. For example, the mean score of such a test containing eighty items would be forty. However, this is not quite true because the element of chance must be considered. On an 80 item multiple-choice test on which each item had four possible responses, random marking of the answer sheet should produce approximately twenty correct responses. Thus, considering chance, the mean score of the test described here should be fifty.

In summary, the mean score ideally should be approximately halfway between the chance score and the highest possible score. If the difficulty index of each of the eighty items was 62.5% the mean score for the test would be fifty (80 × 62.5% = 50).

Obviously it is not possible, especially on the first draft, to produce an item having exactly some predetermined difficulty index. The point is, that in an attempt to maximize an item's discrimination power it should be written in such a manner that half or slightly more than half of the students will answer it correctly. One further point should be noted. Maximum discrimination *can* only occur for a middle difficult item but meeting this condition does not necessarily guarantee that it will occur.

Step 7. Calculate and record the index of discrimination for each item. Substitution into the following formula results in this index.

$$\text{Disc} = \frac{U_c - L_c}{U_n \text{ or } L_n} \quad \text{(expressed as a decimal)}$$

where

Disc = index of discrimination

U_c = number of students in the upper group answering the item correctly

L_c = number of students in the lower group answering the item correctly

U_n = number of students in the upper group

L_n = number of students in the lower group ($U_n = L_n$)

Notice that the denominator for this formula is not the sum of the number of students in both groups but is the number in one group (either, since $U_n = L_n$). The following examples, again using the data presented in Figure 10-1, illustrate the use of the index of discrimination formula.

First draft results: $N = 185$, therefore each extreme group $N = 50$

$$\text{Disc} = \frac{19 - 17}{50} = \frac{2}{50} = .04$$

Revision results: $N = 1112$, therefore each extreme group $N = 300$

$$\text{Disc} = \frac{216 - 104}{300} = \frac{112}{300} = .37$$

The criterion used to examine the discriminating power of an item is usually the test on which the item appears. In general, if the students who did well on the entire test did well on the item and the students who did poorly on the entire test did poorly on the item, the item is considered to be a good discriminator. If approximately the same numbers of "good" and "poor" students answer an item correctly it is considered to possess little or no discriminatory power. Finally, if the item is answered correctly by more of the "poor" students than by the "good" students it is considered to be a negative discriminator.

The index of discrimination presented here is known as the Net D and is only one of several discrimination indexes that have been devised. The Net D is presented here because it is relatively simple to calculate, uses the same data as required to determine the difficulty index, and is fairly simple to interpret.

Notice that the higher the value of the decimal the higher the discriminating power of the item, and that the Net D formula could produce a negative decimal indicating an item that discriminates negatively. In fact, the value obtained is actually the net percentage of "good" or positive discrimination achieved by an item. The following example illustrates this concept.

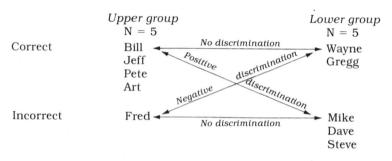

No discriminations occurred between Bill, Jeff, Pete, Art, Wayne, and Gregg because all these students answered the item correctly. Similarly, no discriminations occurred between Fred, Mike, Dave, and Steve because all these students answered the item incorrectly. The discrimination that occurred between Bill (or Jeff, Pete or Art) and Mike (or Dave or Steve) is considered a "good" or positive discrimination because of the groups in which these students have been placed based on their total test scores. Altogether a total of twelve positive discriminations occurred. Conversely the discrimination that occurred between Fred and Wayne (or Gregg) is considered a "bad" or negative discrimination because Fred is in the upper group and Wayne and Gregg are in the lower group. A total of two negative discriminations occurred. The total number of discriminations that could occur with five students in each group is twenty-five (5×5). Of these twenty-five, twelve were positive, two were negative, and thirteen did not occur. Subtracting the two negative discriminations from the twelve positive discriminations results in a net of ten positive discriminations. The ratio of net positive discriminations to the total possible (10/25) is .40. Using the Net D formula presented above results in this same value.

$$\text{Disc} \ = \ \frac{4-2}{5} \ = \ \frac{2}{5} \ = \ .40$$

Although the teacher should attempt to keep the index of difficulty of an item slightly above 50% for an achievement test, the index of discrimination should be as high as possible. Generally, most test construction authorities agree that an item having a discrimination index of .40 or higher is a very good item. Items having an index of discrimination below .20, and especially those with negative discrimination indexes, are poor and should probably be discarded. Discrimination indexes between .20 and .40 are considered acceptable but generally indicate possible revision especially as the value approaches .20.

Step 8. Examine the pattern of responses to determine how an item might be improved.

Although it is often difficult to understand why certain responses are selected or ignored and even more difficult to determine possible alterations of the responses or stem that will improve an item, examination of the response patterns often suggests possibilities. For example, the first response for the initial draft of the item displayed in Figure 10.1 was chosen by over 50% of the students even though it is incorrect. Rewording this distractor in the revision resulted in the keyed response becoming more attractive than the first response and especially so to the students in the upper group. The changes in the difficulty and discrimination indexes indicate that the alteration of this one response improved the item considerably.

Chapter 11

Sources of Physical Education Written Tests

When a written test is given in a physical education class the chances are great that the examination was constructed by the teacher. This is true for a variety of reasons, the major one being that the number of sources for written tests in physical education is relatively limited. With the exceptions of the AAHPERD Cooperative Physical Education Tests and a handful of projects, theses, and dissertations, no nationally standardized physical education written tests are available.

In the process of constructing a written test it is often helpful to examine other similar tests to obtain ideas for questions. The possible sources for similar tests include 1) professionally constructed tests; 2) text books; and 3) periodicals, theses, and dissertations. Examples under each of these categories are given here.

PROFESSIONALLY CONSTRUCTED TESTS

AAHPERD cooperative physical education tests[1]

Currently these are the only physical education written tests available from a professional test construction organization. Two alternative and comparable test forms contain 60 multiple-choice questions each for three levels. The levels are grades 4–6, grades 7–9, and grades 10–12. The tests center on three major content areas: performance of activity, the effects of activity, and factors that modify performance. National norms for each grade, four through twelve, are available.

TEXTBOOKS

Physical education textbooks often contain written tests or include suggestions for possible questions. An example is a thirty-item true-false test on basketball in a book by J.C. Bliss[2] published in 1929. This test is often cited as the first published written test in physical education. A similar example is provided by Thompson[3] in *Fundamentals of Rhythm and Dance.* Matching, short-answer, and essay questions for tests covering rhythms, and creative, tap, and folk dance are given at the end of the book's chapters.

Many textbooks describing the history, rules, equipment, and techniques for learning physical activities have been published over the years. In many cases, either at the end of each chapter or in a separate manual to accompany the book, written tests are provided for each activity in the book. Some examples include:

Fait, Shaw, Fox and Hollingsworth.[4] True-false, short-answer, matching, and multiple-choice questions are given for thirty-six activities described in the book.

Kireilis, Cobb, and Segrest.[5] A ten-item true-false test and five discussion questions for each of twenty activities are given.

Evans.[6] Chapters dealing with nineteen different activities are followed by several question formats including matching, essay, short answer, and multiple-choice.

Dintman and Barrow.[7] Using matching and short-answer questions the authors present written tests for twenty-four activities.

Armbruster, Musker and Mood.[8] In a manual to accompany their book describing thirty-two activities, the authors present written tests made up of true-false, multiple-choice, short-answer, and essay questions.

Brown Activity Series. Another approach to the publication of information about physical activities is demonstrated by the W.C. Brown activity series. Thirty-four separate booklets, each dealing with a separate activity, are available, and written tests are included in them. For example, Allsen and Witbeck[9] present sixty-three true-false, forty-four multiple-choice, and six short answer questions at the end of the booklet dealing with racquetball and paddleball. Umbach and Johnson[10] similarly present twenty matching, thirty short-answer, and forty-seven true-false questions in the *Wrestling* booklet.

Ideas for questions can also be found in the sports guides published by the National Association for Girl's and Women's Sports (formerly the Division for Girl's and Women's Sports). These guides, covering a wide variety of sports, often contain specific articles including objective written tests. In addition, many of the guides contain a section titled "Study Questions," which usually includes multiple-choice and true-false items on rules and officiating.

PERIODICALS, THESES, AND DISSERTATIONS

Periodical articles, theses, and dissertations provide the largest source for physical education written tests. Most often these journal articles or the research efforts of graduate students involve the development of a written test for a single aspect of physical education, although in a few cases several areas are covered either in a single test or through a battery of tests.

In the annotated list presented here only sources containing 1) the tests, 2) sample items from the tests, or 3) a footnote explaining where a copy of the test may be secured are included. The purpose of the list is to identify sources of tests from which possible ideas for questions can be obtained. The sources are numbered and listed alphabetically by author. Table 11.1 has been constructed to aid the reader in finding materials for a specific sport or area.

Table 11.1   Sources of physical education tests by topic

Topic	Identification number*
Archery	6,24,39
Badminton	6,7,9,14,17,24,30,37
Baseball	2,13,32,39,40
Basketball	13,14,24,33,34,39
Bowling	6,11,14,24
Field hockey	5,14,20,39
Football	13
Golf	6,24,28,39,42
Gymnastics	8
Handball	13
Horseback riding	39
Lacrosse	16,46
Physical education knowledge and principles	4,10,18,19,38,39,45
Physical fitness	27,41
Recreational sports	13
Self defense	13
Soccer	12,13,21,24,39,47
Softball	14,17,24,43
Speed-a-way	29
Statistics	3
Swimming	9,25,35
Tennis	1,6,13,14,15,17,26,36,39,44
Vocabulary	31
Volleyball	13,14,17,23,24,39
Wrestling	22

*Numbers refer to the annotated list of tests in the text.

1. Bogisich Tennis Test[11]

   The thesis contains a forty-item multiple-choice test; several of the items are pictorial.

2. Bradley Baseball Test[12]

   Designed for testing baseball knowledge of male physical education majors, the test contains eighty four-option multiple-choice questions. T-score norms are provided.

3. Burkhardt Statistical Test[13]

   Two parallel forms consisting of fifty multiple-choice questions each were devised to measure the understanding of physical education graduate students of the statistical techniques and methods frequently appearing in the *Research Quarterly.* National norms are included.

4. Cowell Physical Education Principles Test[14]

   Eight sample multiple-choice items are given in the article describing the construction of the test.

5. Deitz and Freck Field Hockey Test[15]

   The test, designed for girls in grades 9 through 12, contains a total of seventy-seven items. Some items are short answer, some are true-false, and some are multiple-choice.

6. Farrow Sports Tests[16]

   Five multiple-choice tests for the sports of archery, badminton, bowling, golf, and tennis are presented.

7. Fox Badminton Test[17]

   Designed for college women, the test contains 106 items of the following types: twenty-three multiple-choice; thirty-seven short answer; thirty-eight multiple true-false; and eight identification.

8. Gershon Gymnastics Apparatus Test[18]

   One hundred items (forty-five true-false, fifty-five multiple-choice) comprise the test to measure knowledge of male college physical education students about gymnastics apparatus. Norms are available.

9. Goll Badminton and Swimming Tests[19]

   A forty-seven-item multiple-choice test for swimming and a forty-three-item multiple-choice test for badminton are presented in the thesis.

10. Hambright Fifth-Grade Jumping and Ball Handling Test[20]

    The author constructed a written test for fifth-grade students to measure their knowledge of principles associated with jumping and ball handling skills.

11. Hardin Bowling Test[21]

    A 120-objective-item test for measuring bowling knowledge of college students.

12. Heath and Rodgers Soccer Test[22]

Designed for boys in grades 5 and 6, this test is made up of 100 true-false items.

13. Hempbill Physical Education Tests[23]

Hempbill constructed a variety of written tests for high school boys. Tests for baseball, basketball, football, self-defense (boxing and wrestling), health, minor sports (soccer, handball, tennis, volleyball), and recreational activities (hiking, golf, fishing and hunting, swimming, riding and horsemanship, camping and picnicking, and horseshoes) were constructed.

14. Hennis Sports Tests[24]

Written tests for seven activities for use by college women were constructed by Hennis. All the tests consist of four-option multiple-choice questions. The activities involved and the number of questions are: badminton–37, basketball–35, bowling–35, field hockey–32, softball–33, tennis–35, and volleyball–35.

15. Hewitt Tennis Tests[25]

Two forms of a tennis knowledge test consisting of a variety of question formats were devised by Hewitt for college men and women in 1937. The two forms were revised in 1964.

16. Hodges Lacrosse Test[26]

A forty-item multiple-choice test for college women was constructed by Hodges to measure knowledge about lacrosse.

17. Hooks Sports Tests[27]

Badminton, softball, tennis, and volleyball written tests, each composed of fifty multiple-choice items, were constructed by the author. National norms for college men are provided.

18. Karst Potential Achievement Tests[28]

Physical Education Knowledge Concepts Tests were developed by the author for boys and girls in grades 3, 6, and 9 through 12.

19. Kelley and Lindsay Physical Education Knowledge Test[29]

A test called "Inventory of Recent Knowledge in Physical Education" was constructed by the authors. The inventory consists of fifty-two multiple-choice items in each of the areas of adaptive physical education, athletic training and conditioning, curriculum, exercise physiology, and methodology.

20. Kelly and Brown Field Hockey Test[30]

A test to measure field hockey knowledge of female physical education majors was devised using eighty-eight five-option multiple-choice questions.

21. Knighton Soccer Test[31]

    Twenty-five true-false, five multiple-choice, and five short answer questions make up this soccer test.

22. Kraft Wrestling Test[32]

    Kraft constructed a fifty-item short-answer and multiple-choice test of wrestling for use by non-physical-education majors. Norms are provided.

23. Langston Volleyball Test[33]

    National norms are provided for this 100-item (70 true-false, 30 multiple-choice) volleyball knowledge test designed for male physical education majors.

24. Ley Sports Tests[34]

    Four-option multiple-choice tests in eight sports activities were constructed by Ley. The activities and number of questions are: archery— 36, badminton– 40, bowling– 55, golf– 40, basketball– 47, soccer– 45, softball– 40, and volleyball– 50.

25. Manuel Water Safety Instructor Test[35]

    Designed for college students, this test covering knowledge from a water safety instructor's course is made up of eighty-three multiple-choice questions.

26. Miller Tennis Test[36]

    A 100-item (30 true-false and 70 multiple-choice) test to measure tennis knowledge of female physical education majors is presented with national norms.

27. Mood Physical Fitness Knowledge Test[37]

    Two parallel forms consisting of sixty multiple-choice questions each and national norms for the assessment of knowledge of physical fitness concepts were constructed by the author.

28. Murphy Golf Test[38]

    Ninety-three items of various types make up this test that measures golf knowledge of college women.

29. Palmer Speed-a-Way Test[39]

    This test was designed for use by college women.

30. Phillips Badminton Test[40]

    National norms for scores on a test made up of forty-five multiple-choice and fifty-five true-false items for college women are presented by the author.

31. Rhoda Technical Vocabulary Test[41]

    Ninety multiple-choice items, thirty each from the areas of physiology, measurement, and evaluation, and restricted and correctives make up this test of technical vocabulary for senior and graduate-level physical education majors. The item stems consist of a definition, and the responses are vocabulary terms relevant to physical education.

32. Rodgers and Heath Playground Baseball Test[42]

This is a 100-item true-false test designed for fifth- and sixth-grade boys.

33. Schwartz Basketball Test[43]

A knowledge test for senior high school girls concerning girls' basketball was constructed by Schwartz. The test contains 100 items of various formats.

34. Scott Basketball Officials' Test[44]

Sample items are given for a basketball officials' test. Check marks are made in appropriate boxes on a chart in response to various situations that are presented.

35. Scott Swimming Tests[45]

An elementary swimming test consisting of thirty multiple-choice and twenty-six true-false items, and an intermediate swimming test made up of twenty-two multiple-choice and thirty-six true-false questions were devised by Scott for college students.

36. Scott Tennis Tests[46]

Multiple-choice and true-false questions were used to construct an elementary and an intermediate tennis knowledge test for college students.

37. Scott Badminton Test[47]

An eighty-item test for assessing badminton knowledge of college students is presented by Scott.

38. Sefton Source Material Test[48]

A 160-item test using a yes-no format was devised to measure knowledge of source material in physical education. Fifteen different areas, such as periodicals, indexes, and government agencies, are covered in the test.

39. Snell Physical Education Knowledge Tests[49]

Several multiple-choice tests for college women were constructed and published by Snell. The activities included are 1) fundamentals, 2) archery, 3) field hockey, 4) hygiene, 5) volleyball, 6) soccer, 7) basketball, 8) golf, 9) horseback riding, 10) tennis, and 11) baseball.

40. Steitz Baseball Test[50]

Steitz devised a written test to compare baseball knowledge between male and female fans.

41. Stradtman and Cureton Physical Fitness Test[51]

The authors constructed a 100-item multiple-choice test to measure physical fitness knowledge of junior and senior high school boys and girls. Norms are provided.

42. Waglow and Rehling Golf Test[52]

    A 100-item true-false golf knowledge test was constructed by the authors for college students.

43. Waglow and Stephens Softball Test[53]

    College students' softball knowledge is measured by this 100-question test. The question format is varied.

44. Wagner Tennis Test[54]

    Wagner presents some sample questions from her multiple-choice test designed to measure tennis knowledge of beginners.

45. Walker Physical Education Foundations Test[55]

    Two forms, each having ninety four-option multiple-choice questions, were constructed by Walker as a general knowledge inventory for a physical education foundations course for college freshmen.

46. Warren Lacrosse Test[56]

    A thirty-two item examination and percentile norms for high school girls are presented by Warren.

47. Winn Soccer Test[57]

    A 100-item test for college men and T-score norms were constructed by Winn. Two sixty-five-item short forms of the test are also presented.

REFERENCES CITED

[1] *AAHPER Cooperative Physical Education Tests* (Princeton, N.J.: Educational Testing Service, 1970).

[2] J.C. Bliss, *Basketball* (Philadelphia: Lea and Febiger, 1929), 202 pp.

[3] Betty Lynd Thompson, *Fundamentals of Rhythm and Dance* (New York: A.S. Barnes, 1933), 230 pp.

[4] Hollis F. Fait, John H. Shaw, Grace I. Fox, and Cecil B. Hollingsworth, *A Manual of Physical Education Activities, 2nd ed.* (Philadelphia: Saunders Publishing Company, 1961), 327 pp.

[5] Ramon W. Kireilis, John W. Cobb, and Herman W. Segrest, *Handbook of Physical Activities for Men* (Philadelphia: F.A. Davis Company, 1969), 272 pp.

[6] Virden Evans, *Physical Education Activities* (Berkeley, Ca.: McCutchan Publishing Corp., 1969), 219 pp.

[7] George B. Dintman, and Loyd M. Barrow, *A Comprehensive Manual of Physical Education Activities for Men* (New York: Appleton-Century-Crofts, 1970), 487 pp.

[8] David Armbruster, Frank Musker and Dale Mood, *Sports and Recreational Activities for Men and Women, 7th ed.* (St. Louis: The C.V. Mosby Company, 1979), 390 pp.

[9] Philip E. Allsen, and Alan R. Witbeck, *Racquetball/Paddleball, 2nd ed.* (Dubuque, Iowa: W.C. Brown Company Publishers, 1977), 74 pp.

[10] Arnold Umbach, and Warren Johnson, *Wrestling, 2nd ed.* (Dubuque, Iowa: W.C. Brown Company Publishers, 1977), 82 pp.

[11] Randall K. Bogisich, "The Relationship of a Preinstruction Written Test of Physical Ability to Final Class Ranking in Tennis," Thesis, University of Colorado, 1973, 61 pp.

[12]William B. Bradley, "Standardization of a Baseball Knowledge Test for College Men Majoring in Physical Education," Dissertation, Indiana University, 1959, 164 pp.

[13]Edward Burkhardt, Donald Casady, and Robert Forsyth, "Statistical Comprehension for Graduate Students in Physical Education: Test and Norms," *Research Quarterly* (Oct. 1971), 235–43.

[14]Charles C. Cowell, "Test of Ability to Recognize the Operation of Certain Principles Important to Physical Education," *Research Quarterly* (Oct. 1962), 376–80.

[15]Dorothea Deityz and Beryl Freck, "Hockey Knowledge Test for Girls," *Journal of Health and Physical Education* (June 1940), 366, 387.

[16]Andrea C. Farrow, "Skill and Knowledge Proficiencies for Selected Activities in the Required Program at Memphis State University," Dissertation, University of North Carolina-Greensboro, 1970, 370 pp.

[17]Katherine Fox, "Beginning Badminton Written Examination," *Research Quarterly* (May 1953), 135–46.

[18]Ernest Gershon, "Apparatus Gymnastics Knowledge Test for College Men in Professional Physical Education," *Research Quarterly* (December 1957), 332–41.

[19]Lillian M. Goll, "Construction of Badminton and Swimming Knowledge Tests for High School Girls," Thesis, Illinois State University, 1956, 112 pp.

[20]Joanne Hambright, "A Written Knowledge Test for the Fifth Grade Students at Archer Elementary School," Thesis, University of North Carolina, 1965, 76 pp.

[21]Ruby Low Hardin, "The Construction of an Information Examination for College Students Enrolled in Bowling Classes," Thesis, Texas Women's University, 1961, 78 pp.

[22]Marjorie L. Heath, and Elizabeth G. Rodgers, "A Study in the Use of Knowledge and Skills Tests in Soccer," *Research Quarterly* (Dec. 1932), 33–53.

[23]Fay Hemphill, "Information Tests in Health and Physical Education for High School Boys," *Research Quarterly* (Dec. 1932), 82–96.

[24]Gail Hennis, "Construction of Knowledge Tests in Selected Physical Education Activities for College Women," *Research Quarterly* (Oct. 1956), 301–09.

[25]Jack E. Hewitt, "Comprehensive Tennis Knowledge Test," *Research Quarterly* (Oct. 1937), 74–84; and Jack E. Hewitt, "Hewitt's Comprehensive Tennis Knowledge Test-Form A and Form B Revised," *Research Quarterly* (May 1964), 147–55.

[26]Carolyn V. Hodges, "Construction of an Objective Knowledge Test and Skill Tests in LaCrosse for College Women" Thesis, University of North Carolina-Greensboro, 1967, 123 pp.

[27]Edgar W. Hooks, "Hook's Comprehensive Knowledge Test in Selected Physical Education Activities for College Men," *Research Quarterly* (Dec. 1966), 506–14.

[28]Ralph Karst, "The Development of Standards for Potential Achievement in Physical Education," Dissertation, University of Wisconsin, 1967, 416 pp.

[29]E.J. Kelley, and Carl A. Lindsay, "Knowledge Obsoloscence in Physical Educators," *Research Quarterly* (May 1977), 463–74.

[30]Ellen D. Kelly, and Jane E. Brown, "The Construction of a Field Hockey Test for Women Physical Education Majors," *Research Quarterly* (Oct. 1952), 322–29.

[31]Marian Knighton, "Soccer Questions," *Journal of Health and Physical Education* (Oct. 1930), 29, 60.

[32]George C. Kraft, "The Construction and Standardization of a Wrestling Knowledge Test for College Men Majoring in Physical Education," Dissertation, Indiana University, 1971, 174 pp.

[33]Dewey F. Langston, "Standardization of a Volleyball Knowledge Test for College Men Physical Education Majors," *Research Quarterly* (March 1955), 60–68.

[34]Katherine L. Ley, "Constructing Objective Test Items to Measure High Levels of Achievement in Selected Physical Education Activities," Dissertation, State University of Iowa, 1960, 188 pp.

[35]Kathryn A. Manuel, "A Standardized Knowledge Test for a Water Safety Instructor Course," Dissertation, Indiana University, 1975, 423 pp.

[36]Wilma K. Miller, "Achievement Levels in Tennis Knowledge and Skill for Women Physical Education Major Students," *Research Quarterly* (March 1953), 81–90.

[37]Dale P. Mood, "Test of Physical Fitness Knowledge: Construction, Administration and Norms," *Research Quarterly* (Dec. 1971), 423–30.

[38]Mary A. Murphy, "Criteria for Judging a Golf Knowledge Test," *Research Quarterly* (Dec. 1933), 81–88.

[39]Wendall L. Palmer, "An Evaluation of a Speed-a-way Knowledge Test," Thesis, Ft. Hays State College, 1961, 101 pp.

[40]Marjorie Phillips, "Standardization of a Badminton Knowledge Test for College Women," *Research Quarterly* (March 1946), 48–63.

[41]William P. Rhoda, "The Construction and Standardization of a Test of Technical Vocabulary in Selected Areas of Physical Education for Senior and Graduate Levels," Dissertation, University of Oregon, 1951, 52 pp.

[42]Eliz. G. Rodgers, "The Standardization and Use of Objectives Type Information Tests in Team Game Activities," *Research Quarterly* (March 1939), 102–12; and Eliz. G. Rodgers, and Marjorie L. Heath, "An Experiment in the Use of Knowledge and Skill Tests in Playground Baseball" *Research Quarterly* (Dec. 1931), 113–31.

[43]Helen Schartz, "Knowledge and Achievement Tests in Girls' Basketball on the Senior High School Level," *Research Quarterly* (March 1937), 143–56.

[44]M. Gladys Scott, "Written Test for Basketball Officials," *Journal of Health and Physical Education* (Jan. 1937), 41, 60.

[45]M. Gladys Scott, "Achievement Examinations for Elementary and Intermediate Swimming Classes," *Research Quarterly* (May 1940), 100–111.

[46]M. Gladys Scott, "Achievement Examinations for Elementary and Intermediate Swimming Classes," *Research Quarterly* (March 1941), 40–49.

[47]M. Gladys Scott, "Achievement Examinations in Badminton," *Research Quarterly* (May 1941), 242–53.

[48]Alice A. Sefton, "Knowledge Test on Source Material in Physical Education Including Aspects of Health Education and Recreation," *Research Quarterly* (May 1936), 124–36.

[49]Catherine Snell "Physical Education Knowledge Tests," *Research Quarterly* (Oct. 1935), 78–94; Catherine Snell, "Physical Education Knowledge Tests," *Research Quarterly* (March 1936), 73–82; and Catherine Snell, "Physical Education Knowledge Tests," *Research Quarterly* (May 1936), 77–91.

[50]Stephan E. Steitz, "A Comparison of Basketball Knowledge Between Male and Female Fans," Thesis, Springfield College, 1974, 39 pp.

[51]Alan D. Stradtman, and T.K. Cureton. "A Physical Fitness Knowledge Test for Secondary School Boys and Girls," *Research Quarterly* (March 1950), 53–57.

[52]I.F. Waglow, and C.H. Rehling, "A Golf Knowledge Test," *Research Quarterly* (Dec. 1953), 463–70.

[53]I.F. Waglow, and F. Stephens, "A Softball Knowledge Test," *Research Quarterly* (May 1955), 234–43.

[54]Miriam M. Wagner, "An Objective Method of Grading Beginners in Tennis," *Journal of Health and Physical Education* (March 1935), 24–25, 79.

[55]William P. Walker, "The Development of a General Knowledge Inventory Test and a Resource Syllabus for a Foundations Course in Physical Education for College Freshmen," Dissertation. Florida State University, 1965, 155 pp.

[56]Margaret S. Warren, "Construction of a Knowledge Test in Lacrosse," Thesis, University of Iowa, 1971, 54 pp.

[57]Jerome E. Winn, "Soccer Knowledge Test for College Men," Dissertation, Indiana University, 1957, 106 pp.

SECTION 4

MEASURING
SOCIAL
OBJECTIVES

173

INTRODUCTION TO SECTION 4

In addition to physical, motor, and mental objectives, physical educators often claim to modify students' behavior in another area by listing goals under a general heading of social objectives. A great number of vaguely defined terms can be found in the literature that might be placed in this category. Sportsmanship, leadership, values, adjustment, attitudes, personality, self-concept, and acceptance are a few of the characteristics sometimes listed under the social heading. As in the cognitive and motor domains, attempts have been made to classify and organize some of the social characteristics. The most notable is by Krathwohl, Bloom and Masin.[1] These authors have devised a taxonomy of educational objectives for the affective domain. In general, the affective domain is defined by those human traits concerned with feelings or emotions.

As with written tests, the availability of nationally used tests in the social domain is relatively limited. In fact, with the possible exception of measurement of attitudes toward physical education and physical activity, the amount of physical education literature in this area is not great although it is increasing at an accelerated rate. It is interesting that social objectives have been claimed by physical educators throughout history and yet the measurement of these objectives is seldom done in any objective manner. Whenever assessments in this area are made they are generally used for counseling purposes rather than for grading.

The purpose of this section is to present 1) methods that are commonly employed in the measurement of social characteristics and 2) sources for tests that have been devised for possible use or for ideas that might be helpful in constructing a test for local use.

---

[1] D. R. Krathwohl, B. S. Bloom, and B. B. Masin, *Taxonomy of Educational Objectives: The Classification of Educational Goals, Handbook II: Affective Domain* (New York: David McKay Company Inc., 1964).

Chapter 12

Methods of Measuring Social Characteristics

Even with the various attempts to structure social traits, the approach to their measurement remains varied. Four different (although somewhat overlapping) methods of assessment are used to quantify social characteristics:

1. Self-report: Through a variety of techniques, such as interviews, questionnaires, and inventories, information can be obtained directly from the individuals being assessed.

2. Impressions made on others: The measurement devices most commonly used with this approach are letters of recommendation, rating scales, and sociograms.

3. Observable actions: Situational tests, systematic observation, and anecdotal records are among the assessment tools used to quantify observable actions.

4. Imagination and make-believe: Through the use of expressive and projective techniques, such as analyzing the comments made when shown a series of inkblots or relatively vague pictures, insights can be gained about some emotional traits. Johnson[1] suggests more use of these techniques should be made in the study of attitude toward health and physical education.

Many of the measuring instruments and techniques listed above are impractical for the physical educator. For example, situational tests that require placing an individual or a group of individuals into a controlled problem-solving or role-playing situation are generally inefficient in terms of time. They also often require several administrators to provide the situations. The projective techniques require extensive training on the part of the administrator and are generally impractical. A relatively brief description of only the more practical assessment devices and their construction is presented here. Considered are 1) anecdotal records, 2) interviews, 3) sociometric devices, 4) rating scales, and 5) questionnaires and inventories.

ANECDOTAL RECORDS

The anecdotal record is a method of systematically cataloging individual behavior. The value of such a procedure is not in the independent observations but in trends that become apparent over time. The purpose of actually writing down such observations is to overcome the fallability of human memory and to avoid having one or a few striking occurrences overly influence perceptions of an individual. The most severe restriction is the time required to record specific events and accurately summarize the observations. A less obvious difficulty is the care and consistency that must be exercised in the recording procedure. The following guidelines are suggested if this technique is adopted.

1. Record the anecdote as soon as possible after the occurrence of the incident. Delay usually results in forgetting important information.
2. Provide an accurate description of the specific incident.
3. Provide enough background information to give the incident meaning.
4. Include an evaluative statement but be certain that it is clearly identified as such.
5. Indicate whether the incident is either representative of the individual or is important because it is very much different from usual behavior.
6. Record anecdotes frequently in order to establish accurate trends.
7. Record anedcotes in such a fashion (index cards, for example) that filing and sorting is facilitated.
8. Summarize findings from time to time to determine behavior trends.

Examples of the use of anecdotal records in the physical education setting (as well as several of the other techniques presented here) are provided by Cassidy.[2]

INTERVIEWS

Common sense dictates that the best way to find out about a person is to ask the individual questions and evaluate the answers. If done orally in a face-to-face situation, the technique is called an interview. The greatest advantage of this procedure is its flexibility. The interviewer can structure the interview in the most suitable way based on the responses to previous questions. Unfortunately, this same element is also one of the interview's greatest weaknesses, creating difficulty in trying to compare results of several interviews. Another

disadvantage of the interview technique is the time required to sample a relatively small number of people.

To reduce the subjectivity associated with the interview while still maintaining most of its advantages, it is possible to develop a structured interview. A set of questions for the interview are prepared ahead of time and then adhered to rather strictly. Obviously the interviewer still must use judgment and develop additional questions as the need arises (otherwise this becomes a questionnaire read to the respondent), but this technique assures adequate coverage of all areas for which the interview was originally designed.

An example of the structured interview technique is provided by Moore[3] in her study to examine the attitudes of college women toward physical activity as a means of recreation.

SOCIOMETRIC INSTRUMENTS

Sociograms and social distance scales are the two instruments described here. Both are examples of assessments of social characteristics based on data secured from others. The procedures for obtaining these data are relatively simple, but the process of interpretation is more complex. The pioneer work done in this area was by Moreno.[4]

A typical procedure is to ask each member of a group to write down the names of others in the group he or she would most like to be with. Sometimes a restriction is placed on the number of names that can be listed. More specific situations might also be used, such as "who would you like most to have on your team" or "who would you like to have in your squad?" Additional information is sometimes obtained by requesting not only the names of those desired but also the names of those definitely not wanted in the group.

The following data were contrived for illustrative purposes. Each member of a group of ten boys was asked to list at least three names of those boys in the group they would most like for friends. Their choices were:

Child		Choices
Art	:	Chuck, Dave, John
Bob	:	Ian
Chuck	:	Art, Ed, John
Dave	:	Art, John, Hank
Ed	:	Chuck, Hank, John
Fred	:	
George	:	Art, Dave, Hank
Hank	:	Dave, Ed, John
Ian	:	Bob
John	:	Art, Ed, Hank

The resulting sociogram is shown in Figure 12.1. The most immediately revealing observations are that 1) Fred was chosen by no one nor did he choose anyone (isolate); 2) Bob and Ian chose only each other (an isolate group); 3) George chose three friends but was not chosen himself (fringer); and 4) the rest of the group is fairly cohesive with John, Art, and Hank being chosen most often (stars).

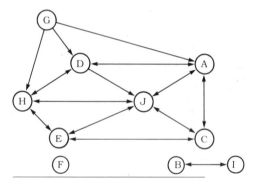

Figure 12.1 Example of a sociogram

Although observant teachers are usually aware of most of the information obtained from sociograms before collecting the data, occasional surprises occur. This is usually because a teacher may judge a student by adult criteria whereas the sociogram reveals the student's standing as measured by peer standards. It should be remembered that 1) group structures are not permanent, 2) the limitations (choose only three friends) used can affect results, and 3) the situation described (asking students who they would like on their basketball team may put a premium on height instead of friendship, for example) all can influence the outcome. These factors suggest care is needed in evaluating sociograms.

Another method of using data from others to examine social characteristics is the social distance scale first proposed by Bogardus.[5] Defining social distance as "the degree of sympathetic understanding that exists between two persons or between a person and a group,"[6] Bogardus obtained the reactions of 100 judges regarding the social distance inherent in sixty statements by having them place the statements into one of seven catagories. The resulting instrument contained the following statements used to judge the individuals in a group.

1. Would marry
2. Would have as a regular friend
3. Would work beside in an office
4. Would have as one of several families in my neighborhood
5. Would have merely as a speaking acquaintance
6. Would have live outside my neighborhood
7. Would have live outside my country

Although administrative and scoring procedures are given in the source, no evidence regarding the reliability or validity of the instrument is provided.

RATING SCALES

Examining social characteristics through the use of sociograms and social distance ballots makes use of data obtained from others, usually peers of the individuals of interest. Letters of recommendation and rating scales also make use of data from others, but usually not peers. The rating scale was probably developed because of the very subjective nature of the letter of recommendation. Rating scales usually list several personality traits, such as honesty, ability to get along with others, and creativity, and provide a scale on which each of these traits is to be assessed by the rater. The scale may vary from "does not possess this trait" and "does possess this trait" to a line representing from 0 percent to 100 percent on which the rater is to mark an estimate of the amount of the trait possessed by the individual being rated.

The two greatest problems with rating scales center on the willingness and ability of raters. If a rater does not care to take the time or for some reason is unwilling to make a rating that may "hurt" the individual being rated, the validity of the instrument suffers. In addition, insufficient opportunity to observe the individual, or differing interpretations of the names of the traits to be rated or the descriptors used will lessen the usefulness of the data from the instrument. The terms *self-esteem* or *feelings of insecurity* and descriptors such as *outstanding* or *satisfactory* have different meanings to different people.

Some techniques to improve rating scales are:

1. Define the traits to be rated with a short sentence by providing brief examples or requiring evaluations of several aspects of a single trait.

2. Define the rating scale. For example, "Superior" might be qualified by "among top 5 percent."

3. Use a graduated scale for the rating such as

Superior   Poor

4. Choose only raters who are capable of and interested in completing the ratings.

5. Give complete directions to be sure the raters understand the task.

6. Where possible, obtain several ratings and pool the information. This can only be done when several qualified raters are available. The various ratings should be made independently.

INVENTORIES

Far and away the most common type of instrument used in the assessment of social characteristics is the questionnaire or inventory. The information comes from the individuals being measured and is usually obtained by having the respondents indicate choices of, or degree of agreement with, various statements. Several similar yet variable methods for constructing these instruments have been devised. Five of these approaches are identified here.

The adjective check list.

A large number of adjectives that relate to a particular situation are collected. By various means the list is narrowed to those appearing on the final instrument. For example, Davidson and Lang,[7] in a study of children's perceptions of their teachers' feelings toward them, started with 200 adjectives and considered 1) how commonly each adjective was used to describe how people feel and think of others; 2) the appropriate level of vocabulary (ten to sixteen years of age); and 3) an end result of an approximately equal number of positive and negative adjectives. The remaining adjectives were then judged by thirty-five

teachers and fifty students as favorable, unfavorable, or neutral. After eliminating those words not put into one of these three categories at least 80 percent of the time and screening out the remaining adjectives having duplicate meanings, the initial 200 adjectives were reduced to thirty-five. Examples of the remaining adjectives are: a nuisance, neat, loving, clever, and shy. Each adjective was assigned a favorable or unfavorable rating. The individuals under study were asked to indicate for each adjective if the teacher felt this way toward them most of the time, half of the time, seldom, or never. The checklist, scoring procedures, and reliability and validity data are given in the source.

Another adjective checklist, constructed by Gough and Heilbrun[8] contains 300 adjectives commonly used to describe attributes of a person (such as absent minded, determined, honest, reckless, and trusting). The list can be self-administered or used by raters. According to the authors, twenty-four scales, or indicies, such as defensiveness, self-confidence, and aggression, can be identified with the list. Norms, definitions, the 300-word list, and several reliability and validity studies are presented in the reference. These adjective checklists have been applied to physical education settings. Reynolds[9] used the Davidson Adjective Check List to compare personality to maturity and physical and mental characteristics of thirteen-year-old boys. Brunner[10] found a significant difference on eight of the scales of the Gough and Heilbrun Adjective Check List between adults who do or do not participate in vigorous physical activity.

Q-sort technique

Most often used to assess various personality characteristics, this technique requires the respondent to place a relatively large number of words or statements into a prescribed number of categories. The number of statements that can be placed into each category is set in such a way as to force the responses into an approximately normal distribution. For example, the directions might specify the placing of seventy-five statements thus:

Most like me								Least like me
1	2	3	4	5	6	7	8	9
Two state-ments	Five state-ments	Nine state-ments	Fourteen state-ments	Eighteen state-ments	Fourteen state-ments	Nine state-ments	Five state-ments	Two state-ments

Generally the respondent is asked to complete the Q-sort twice—once as the individual sees himself or herself and again as the individual views the ideal or perfect self. The correlation between the two sets of scores thus obtained is interpreted as the degree of agreement between "myself" and "my ideal."

Thurstone-Chave questionnaire[11]

The measurement of attitudes is most commonly accomplished through the use of a questionnaire. One of the earliest suggested methods for the construction of such a questionnaire was presented by Thurstone and Chave. Over the years the technique has been modified somewhat, and a brief description of the main procedures is presented here.

A large number of statements, each of which reflects a positive or negative feeling, are constructed. Edward[12] lists fourteen criteria for editing such statements. These criteria were collected from several sources and contain such advice as avoid statements that may be interpreted in more than one way and avoid statements containing universals such as "all," "always," "none," and "never" as these often introduce ambiguity. After editing, the statements are submitted to a panel of judges. These judges are asked to place the statements into a set number of categories (Thurstone suggested eleven, but seven or five are now more commonly used) based on their degree of favorableness or unfavorableness. The median of these ratings is used to give each statement a scale value reflecting the degree of favorableness of the statement. Items placed in a wide range of the possible categories by the judges are discarded or modified to eliminate ambiguity. Once the final list of statements is composed, it is administered with the directions to check only those items with which one agrees. The instrument is scored by determining the mean scale value for the items chosen by the respondent.

Likert questionnaire[13]

As with the Thurstone-Chave method, the initial procedure involves the collection of a number of clearly written positive and negative statements relative to some object or situation about which an attitude measure is desired. Judges are used to determine whether the statements are positive or negative, but not to assess their degree of favorableness. The statements selected for the final instrument are then presented to the respondents with the directions to indicate their degree of agreement with each statement. The scale for indicating agreement might range from a simple "agree," "disagree" to a ten-point scale with "totally agree" on one end and "totally disagree" on the other. Seven-, five-, or three-point scales are often used; the five-point scale of "strongly agree," "agree," "undecided," "disagree," and "strongly disagree" probably is the most common. Even-numbered choice scales are sometimes used to eliminate the "undecided" or "I don't know" response. Scoring the Likert-type questionnaire requires the assigning of points (5 for strongly agree, 4 for agree, and so forth) to positively worded statements, reversing the weighting for negatively worded statements, and obtaining a total score for each individual by summing the choices selected.

A great number of surveys dealing with attitudes toward physical education, athletic competition, and similar concepts have been conducted.

Semantic differential[14]

Instead of positive or negative statements the semantic differential is constructed of sets of bipolar adjectives. Examples might be good-bad, full-empty, fast-slow, and the like. Between the two adjectives are usually seven spaces, one of which is to be checked as a reflection of the respondent's attitude toward the object of the measurement. For example, the individual may be asked to give his or her feeling toward athletic competition by marking spaces between adjectives such as

Feminine   _ _ _ _ _ _   Masculine

Important   _ _ _ _ _ _   Unimportant

Worthwhile   _ _ _ _ _ _   Valueless

etc.

Osgood, Suci, and Tannenbaum[15] have determined that three basic factors (evaluation, potency, and activity) are revealed through this semantic differential procedure. The evaluation factor seems to be most reflective of the attitude of the respondents toward the concept or object measured. Thus adjective pairs such as good-bad, positive-negative, and wise-foolish are commonly used to assess this factor. The potency factor is measured by adjectives generally suggestive of strength, size, and depth. Weak-strong, hard-soft, and shallow-deep are examples of such pairs. Finally, adjectives describing motion, such as quick-slow, passive-active, and tense-relaxed, measure the activity factor. Usually semantic differential instruments contain twenty to twenty-five pairs of adjectives. Scoring is done in much the same manner as for the Likert-type questionnaire where three scores, one for each factor, are obtained.

REFERENCES CITED

[1]Warren Johnson, "An Approach to Attitude Studies in Health and Physical Education," *The Physical Educator* (March 1961), 20– 22.

[2]Rosalind Cassidy, *Counseling in the Physical Education Program* (New York: Appleton-Century-Crofts, 1959), 156 pp.

[3]Beverly Y. Moore, "The Attitude of College Women toward Physical Activity as a Means of Recreation," *Research Quarterly* (Dec. 1941), 720– 25.

[4]Jacob L. Moreno, *Who Shall Survive?* (Washington, D.C.: Nervous and Mental Disease Publishing Co., 1934).

[5]Emory S. Bogardus, "A Social Distance Scale," *Sociology and Social Research,* 17 (1932– 33), 265– 71.

[6]Ibid., p. 268.

[7]Helen Davidson and Gerhard Lang, "Children's Perceptions of Their Teachers' Feelings toward Them Related to Self-Perception, School Achievement, and Behavior," *Journal of Experimental Education* (Dec. 1960), 107– 18.

[8]Harrison Gough and Alfred Heilbrun, *The Adjective Check List Manual* (Palo Alto, Ca.: Consulting Psychologists Press, Inc., 1965), 33 pp.

[9]Robert M. Reynolds, "Responses on the Davidson Adjective Check List as Related to Maturity, Physical and Mental Characteristics of Thirteen Year Old Boys," Ed. D. Dissertation, University of Oregon, 1965, 205 pp.

[10]Burton C. Brunner, "Personality and Motivating Factors Influencing Adult Participation in Vigorous Physical Activity," *Research Quarterly* (Oct. 1969), 464 – 69.

[11]L. L. Thurstone and E. J. Chave, *The Measurement of Attitude* (Chicago: Chicago University Press, 1929), 96 pp.

[12]Allen L. Edwards, *Techniques of Attitude Scale Construction* (New York: Appleton-Century-Crofts, 1957), 256 pp.

[13]Rensis A. Likert, "Technique for the Measurement of Attitudes," *Arch. Psychology No. 140* (1932), 5 – 55.

[14]Charles E. Osgood, George Suci, and Percy Tannenbaum, *The Measurement of Meaning* (Urbana, Ill.: University of Illinois Press, 1957), 364 pp.

[15]Ibid.

Chapter 13

Sources of Measuring Devices for Physical Education Social Characteristics

One of the best methods for examining the variety of instruments available for assessing social characteristics is to locate studies in which the tests are employed. The examples presented in this chapter were selected to illustrate the many approaches described in the previous chapter.

ANECDOTAL RECORDS

An example of the use of anecdotal records is provided in a study by Dawley, Troyer, and Shaw.[1] These investigators compiled anecdotal records on 179 elementary school children. They found little relationship between actual behavior as reflected by the anecdotal records and scores from a written test designed to determine how well each child knew proper behavior.

SOCIOMETRIC SCALES AND STUDIES

Sociograms and social distance scales

Skubic[2] was one of the earliest investigators to report the use of sociometric measurement in a physical education setting. The subjects were 326 freshmen and sophomore college women enrolled in swimming, dance, and volleyball classes. Skubic obtained from them an acquaintance score (a list of names of persons in class with whom each girl was familiar) and, from each girl, the five most and least desired classmates as teammates on the basis of skill and the five most and least desired as friends. She found very little relationship between choices as teammates and acquaintances and only a slight positive relationship between choices as friends and acquaintances. The acquaintance measure doubled over six weeks.

Breck,[3] using the same questions as Skubic, examined the applicability and stability of the sociometric technique in the physical education setting. She examined various scoring methods and selected choices minus rejections as the most adequate, including use for physical education.

Using sociometric devices similar to those described previously, investigators have examined 1) the relationship between teammate status and measures of skill in volleyball,[4] (2) sociometric status and athletic ability of junior high school boys,[5] 3) the relationship of physical fitness to selected measures of popularity,[6] and 4) the effect of various class organization procedures on sociometric status.[7]

A social distance ballot somewhat similar to the one constructed by Bogardus was reported by Cowell[8] and has been used in physical education and athletic settings. With Cowell's Personal Distance Ballot each member of a class is asked to indicate the degree of willingness to accept each of the other students by placing a check in one of the following columns: 1) into my family as a brother, 2) as a very close pal or chum, 3) as a member of my gang or club, 4) on my street as a neighbor, 5) into my class at school, 6) into my school, 7) into my city. The scores given to each student are summed and the total divided by the number of respondents to obtain a final score. The higher the score, the less the degree of acceptance. The ballot has been used in such diverse ways as to investigate the sociometric differences between motivated and nonmotivated bowling classes[9] and to assess the relationships among social integration, athletic ability, and football playing ability.[10] Percentile norms, some discussion of validation techniques, and several other sociometric devices are described in the source.

RATING SCALES

McCloy,[11] Blanchard,[12] and O'Neil,[13] in the 1930s, developed rating scales for the purpose of measuring elements of character. Blanchard's final instrument requires the rater to mark "never," "seldom," "fairly often," "frequently," or "extremely often" for twenty-four statements such as "is popular with classmates," "grumbles over decisions of classmates," and "is liked by others." The twenty-four statements are divided and classified under the nine categories of 1) leadership, 2) positive active qualities, 3) positive mental qualities, 4) self-control, 5) cooperation, 6) social action standards, 7) ethical social qualities, 8) qualities of efficiency, and 9) sociability.

Cowell[14] developed a rating scale to measure social adjustment of students. The instrument contains two forms, one for rating ten positive behavior trends and the other for rating ten negative behavior trends.

ATTITUDES—INVENTORY CONSTRUCTION

A great number of instruments have been developed to assess the attitudes of various subgroups of the population toward physical education in general, athletic competition, and related areas. An annotated listing of many of these is presented here in chronological order.

Bullock and Alden[15]—A three-part questionnaire (home life and play experiences, high school experiences, and university physical education situation) was developed and used to examine the differences in attitudes of college freshmen women who liked physical education and those who disliked it.

Carr[16]—Using the Thurstone-Chave method, Carr devised an attitude questionnaire and administered it to 355 freshmen high school girls to compare their attitudes to success in physical education as measured by grades and performance on a battery of athletic events.

Nemson[17]—Also using the Thurstone-Chave technique, Nemson constructed a 121-item questionnaire to measure what aspects of physical education classes were most annoying to junior and senior high school boys. These scores were compared to an instructor's rating of attitude. Only sample questions are provided in the reference.

Wear[18]—Beginning with 289 statements, Wear, through editing, pilot studies, try out tests, and reliability and validity considerations, constructed a forty-item attitude inventory for college male freshmen. The inventory, administrative and scoring procedures, and T-score norms are given in the first source. Four years later, Wear reported a refinement of the instrument by introducing two thirty-item equivalent forms with the items classified into the four categories of physiological-physical, mental-emotional, social, and general. The two forms and data regarding their reliability, validity, and parallelness are given in the second source. The Wear Attitudes Inventory has served as the basis for several instruments and has been used in a great number of studies involving the measurement of attitude toward physical education.

McCue[19]—A seventy-seven-item questionnaire to assess attitudes toward intensive competition in team games was reported by McCue in 1953. The instrument is of the Likert-type, with a five-point scale, and is intended for college students and teachers.

Scott[20]—Parents, teachers, and school administrators were assessed with a revised form of McCue's instrument to determine their attitudes toward athletic competition in elementary schools. The seventy-nine-item Likert-type inventory is presented in the article but no evidence of reliability or validity is given.

Kappes[21]—This twenty-item Likert-type attitude inventory was included in a study to determine the attitudes of college women toward physical education and student services of the physical education department. Reliability and validity data are given with the inventory in the source.

Leyhe[22]—A checklist containing eighty-one statements about competition, fifteen statements about the National Section for Girl's and Women's Sports, and a four-item general attitude scale was used to measure the attitudes of women members of AAHPERD toward competition for females.

McGee[23]—A seventy-item attitude scale for determining the attitudes of parents and teachers toward competition for high school girls is presented. Statistical analysis of the data obtained from over 1,300 subjects is also given.

Sheehan[24]—A six-page questionnaire requesting demographic data and containing forty-six questions designed to gain an overview of attitudes toward athletes, coaches, and the administration of sports was devised by Sheehan. Although no reliability or validity data are presented, the questionnaire is given in the appendix of the thesis.

Kneer[25]—After determining that high school girls did not understand some words and concepts contained in Wear's Attitude Inventory, Kneer modified the instrument based on suggestions from 490 high school girls and their teachers. The reliability and validity of the new instrument were examined and the report of these investigations appears with the modified inventory in the thesis.

Hunter[26]—On the basis of information obtained from 687 college females enrolled in required physical education classes, Hunter developed an instrument to measure women students' attitudes toward physical education.

Bowman[27]—A twenty-item questionnaire for parents and a twenty-six-item questionnaire for fifth-grade children were constructed to measure attitudes toward physical education as part of a study to compare these attitudes to the children's skill levels. The instruments, directions for administration, and considerations for reliability, validity, and scoring are all contained in the thesis.

Cutler[28] — The details for the construction of a thirty-eight-item Likert-type attitude survey to assess the attitudes of male junior college students toward physical education are presented in the thesis.

Galloway[29] — As part of a study to determine the effectiveness of physical education experiences in the development of attitudes of college women toward certain values, Galloway devised a sixty-eight-item attitude inventory. In addition to the survey and directions for its administration, Galloway presents T-score norms. The attitude inventory was later revised by Mercer[30] for use with high school girls.

Drinkwater[31] — Drinkwater constructed parallel forms containing thirty-six items each to assess high school girls' attitudes toward physical education as a career for women. The Likert-type five-point scale is used, and the statistical data relevant to the instrument's construction, along with the forms, are given in the source.

Richardson[32] — Two nineteen-item tests, scoring directions, and comments about reliability and validity are given in this article by Richardson. The tests are designed to measure the attitudes of college students toward physical fitness and exercise.

Adams[33] — Using the Thurstone-Chave method and 245 teacher college students as subjects, Adams constructed two twenty-item scales for measuring attitude toward physical education. The scales can be scored either by the Thurstone-Chave or the Likert procedure.

Sheehan[34] — The semantic differential technique was used to measure attitudes toward thirty-two concepts before and after exposure to a physical education teaching model designed to affect attitude formation. Examples of the concepts measured are working alone, too many cooks spoil the broth, and encouraging others in the group. Each of the thirty-two concepts was tested with a ten-item semantic differential list containing the following bipolar adjectives: good-bad, wise-foolish, successful-unsuccessful, and true-false (evaluation); strong-weak, tough-fragile, and brave-cowardly (potency); and motivated-aimless, active-passive, and interesting-boring (activity).

Moyer, Mitchem, and Bell[35] — These investigators modified Wear's original forty-item attitude inventory, added ten questions specific to the program at Northern Illinois University, and measured the attitudes toward physical education of freshmen and junior college women.

Penman[36] — Through pilot study and suggestions from English teachers, Penman modified the Wear forty-item inventory for use by inner-city junior high school girls. As an example of the changes made, Wear's item "Associations in physical education activities give people a better understanding of each other" was changed to "Playing together in gym helps us understand one another better." The revised thirty-item form and reports of reliability and validity checks are given in the thesis.

Campbell[37] — Campbell concludes that Form A of Wear's Physical Education Attitude Inventory is applicable to junior high school boys.

Kenyon[38] — Believing that attitude toward physical activity consisted of more than one dimension, Kenyon devised two six-factor attitude scales, one for males and one for females. The six factors measured are physical activity 1) as a social experience, 2) for health and fitness, 3) as the pursuit of vertigo, 4) as an aesthetic experience, 5) as catharsis, and 6) as an ascetic experience. The scale for men contains fifty-nine items and the scale for women fifty-four, all scored on a seven-point Likert scale ranging from very strongly agree to very strongly disagree. Factor analysis techniques confirmed the viability of the six factors. Since their appearance, Kenyon's attitude scales have been used in several studies.

Edgington[39] — A final scale consisting of sixty-six items and scored on a six-point Likert scale was devised by Edgington to assess the attitude of high school freshmen boys toward physical education.

McPherson and Yuhasz[40] — These two investigators constructed an attitude scale to measure the attitude of adult males toward physical activity and exercise. It is a fifty-item five-point Likert scale, but only sample items are given in the article.

O'Bryan and O'Bryan[41] — Using the semantic differential technique and sampling a wide variety of males (eleventh-grade students, first year physical education majors, third year physical education majors, and non-physical-education graduate students, academic staff, and junior and senior high school teachers), O'Bryan and O'Bryan constructed an instrument to determine attitudes of males toward selected aspects of physical education.

Seaman[42] — To investigate the attitude of a population that differed slightly from those reported so far, Seaman devised a forty-item Likert-type questionnaire to measure the attitudes of physically handicapped children toward physical education. Neither evidence regarding the reliability and validity nor the instrument are presented in the source.

Simon and Smoll[43] — Using a semantic differential approach based on Kenyon's conceptual model, Simon and Smoll constructed an instrument to assess children's attitudes toward physical activity. Reliability and interrelationships of the subdomains are discussed in the article. Although the instrument is not given, a footnote explains how a copy may be obtained.

Selby and Lewko[44] — A twenty-item Likert-type questionnaire called CATFIS

(Children's Attitudes Toward Females in Sports) was constructed for use in a study by Selby and Lewko. The instrument is not given in the article.

ATTITUDES—STUDIES IN PHYSICAL EDUCATION AND ATHLETICS

Each entry in the annotated bibliography just presented represents a study either specifically to develop an attitude measuring instrument or necessitating such development as a side effect. Thus, in all the studies mentioned, a different instrument was constructed (although some were modifications of others). A great number of studies have been reported in which one of these "ready-made" attitude surveys has been adopted for use. The Wear Physical Education Attitude Inventory, for example, was used by Bell,[45] Broer,[46] Keogh[47] Brumbach,[48] and Campbell[49] to determine the attitudes of college students toward physical education. The Wear Inventory has also been used to examine the relationship between attitudes toward physical education and various other attitudes such as strength,[50] success in physical education,[51] and fitness and social adjustment.[52]

Recently the Kenyon attitude scales have become increasingly popular for use in studies involving the measurement of attitudes. For example, O'Brian[53] used it in determining the relationship between personality and attitude toward physical activity, Alderman[54] used it with champion athletes, and Straub and Felock[55] used it to compare attitudes of delinquent and nondelinquent junior high school girls.

PERSONALITY ASSESSMENT

Using some of the methods previously described, several instruments have been constructed to measure personality characteristics. Most of these report scores on several aspects of personality (such as sociability, thoughtfulness, and masculinity). The most common of these tests used in physical education settings is the Cattell 16 Personality Factor Questionnaire.[56] Others sometimes used included the California Psychological Inventory,[57] the Minnesota Multiphasic Personality Inventory,[58] the Gordon Personal Profile,[59] and the Edwards Personal Preference Schedule.[60] Some investigators[61] have devised their own instruments for measuring personality, usually by combining portions of tests constructed by others.

The notion of determining relationships between personality measures and concerns of physical education and athletics is a relatively recent phenomenon. In reviewing the literature dealing with athletics, activity, and personality, Cooper,[62] in 1969, reported on only twenty-five studies—fourteen of which were done in 1955 or after. These studies might be classified into four categories.

Effects of various experiences on personality —Examples include studies to

determine the effects of judo,[63] cycling and jogging,[64] and a physical fitness program[65] on personality.

Comparison of personality traits of various groups — Examples of groups compared are athletes and nonathletes,[66] women in team sports and women in individual sports,[67] baseball players and tennis players,[68] superior and average college basketball officials,[69] female teacher education and physical education students,[70] and regular and nonregular adult male exercisers.[71]

Relationship between personality and other characteristics — For example, the relationships between personality traits and athletic achievement,[72] recreational preferences,[73] motor achievement,[74] somatotype,[75] and football injuries[76] have been studied.

Personality traits of various types of people — Studies have been designed to determine personality traits of athletes,[77] successful swimming coaches,[78] champion level female fencers,[79] weightlifters,[80] and women educators.[81]

Measures of single personality traits

In addition to the recent trend of investigating how overall personality relates to concerns of physical educators and coaches, another relatively recent development is the study of single aspects of personality such as self-concept, body image, and sportsmanship in similar settings. For example, descriptions of the self-concepts of athletes,[82] and the relationship between self-concept and sports interest,[83] motor ability[84] and body image[85] are studies involving the measurement of self-concept. Other individual personality traits assessed and related to physical education or sport situations include self-image,[86] self-determination,[87] self-esteem,[88] and masculinity-femininity.[89]

Two personality traits of special interest to physical educators are body image and sportsmanship. The body image of women athletes,[90] the relationships among body image, physiological measures,[91] and motor skills,[92] comparisons of body image among various sport groups,[93] and the effect of physical activity on body image[94] are representative of the studies involving this trait. Tests designed to assess sportsmanship have been devised by several investigators[95] and used to measure this trait among elementary school children[96] and various groups of athletes.[97]

REFERENCES CITED

[1]Dorothy Dawley, Maurice E. Troyer, and John H. Shaw, "Relationship between Observed Behavior in Elementary School Physical Education and Test Responses," *Research Quarterly* (March 1951), 71–76.

[2]Elvera Skubic, "A Study in Acquaintanceship and Social Status in Physical Education Classes," *Research Quarterly* (March 1949), 80–87.

[3]Sabrina J. Breck, "A Sociometric Measurement of Status in Physical Education Classes," *Research Quarterly* (May 1950), 75–82.

[4]Ruth E. Fultan, "Relationship between Teammate Status and Measures of Skill in Volleyball," *Research Quarterly* (Oct. 1950), 274–76.

[5]L.W. McCraw and J. W. Tolbert, "Sociometric Status and Athletic Ability of Junior High School Boys," *Research Quarterly* (March 1953), 72–80.

[6]C.D. Yarnall, "Relationship of Physical Fitness to Selected Measures of Popularity," *Research Quarterly* (May 1966), 286–88.

[7]Jack K. Nelson and Barry L. Johnson, "Effects of Varied Techniques in Organizing Class Competition upon Changes in Sociometric Status," *Research Quarterly* (Oct 1968), 634–39.

[8]Charles C. Cowell, "Validating an Index of Social Adjustment for High School Use," *Research Quarterly* (March 1958), 7–18.

[9]E.C. Walters, "A Sociometric Study of Motivated and Non-Motivated Bowling Groups," *Research Quarterly* (March 1955), 107–12.

[10]Charles C. Cowell and A.H. Ismail. "Validity of a Football Rating Scale and Its Relationship to Social Integration and Athletic Ability," *Research Quarterly* (Dec. 1961), 461–67.

[11]C.H. McCloy, "Character Building through Physical Education," *Research Quarterly* (Oct. 1930), 41–61.

[12]B.E. Blanchard, "A Behavior Frequency Rating Scale for the Measurement of Character and Personality in Physical Education Classroom Situations," *Research Quarterly* (May 1936), 56–66.

[13]F.W. O'Neal, "A Behavior Frequency Rating Scale for the Measurement of Character and Personality in High School Physical Education Classes for Boys," *Research Quarterly* (May 1936), 67–76.

[14]Cowell, "Validating an Index of Social Adjustment."

[15]Marguerite Bullock and Florence Alden, "Some of the Factors Determining the Attitudes of Freshmen Women at the University of Oregon toward Required Physical Education," *Research Quarterly* (Dec. 1933), 60–70.

[16]Martha G. Carr, "The Relationship between Success in Physical Education and Selected Attitudes Experienced by High School Freshmen Girls," *Research Quarterly* (Oct. 1945), 176–91.

[17]Edward Nemson, "Specific Annoyances in Relation to Student Attitude in Physical Education Classes," *Research Quarterly* (Oct. 1949), 336–47.

[18]Carlos L. Wear, "The Evaluation of Attitudes toward Physical Education as an Activity Course," *Research Quarterly* (March 1951), 114–26; and Carlos L. Wear, "Construction of Equivalent Forms of an Attitude Scale," *Research Quarterly* (March 1955), 113–19.

[19]Betty F. McCue, "Constructing An Instrument for Evaluating Attitudes toward Intensive Competition in Team Games," *Research Quarterly* (May 1953), 205–09.

[20]Phebe M. Scott, "Attitudes toward Athletic Competition in Elementary Schools," *Research Quarterly* (Oct. 1953), 353–61.

[21]Eveline E. Kappes, "Inventory to Determine Attitudes of College Women toward Physical Education and Student Services of the Physical Education Department," *Research Quarterly* (Dec. 1954), 429–38.

[22]Naomi L. Leyhe, "Attitudes of the Women Members of the American Association for Health, Physical Education, and Recreation toward Competition in Sports for Girls and Women," Doctoral Dissertation, University of Indiana, 1955, 270 pp.

[23]Rosemary McGee, "Comparison of Attitudes toward Intensive Competition for High School Girls," *Research Quarterly* (March 1956), 60–73.

[24]Thomas J. Sheehan, "Attitudes of Senior Male Students at the Ohio State University Concerning the Athlete and Intercollegiate Competition," M.A. Thesis, Ohio State University, 1956, 85 pp.

[25]Marian E. Kneer, "The Adaptation of Wear's Physical Education Attitude Inventory for Use With High School Girls," M.S. Thesis, Illinois State Normal University, 1956, 131 pp.

[26]Sammie R. Hunter, "Attitudes of Women Students toward College Physical Education," Doctoral Dissertation, University of Florida, 1956, 147 pp.

[27]Mary O. Bowman, "The Relationship between Students and Parent Attitudes and Skills of Fifth Grade Children," Doctoral Dissertation, University of Iowa, 1958, 166 pp.

[28]Russel K. Cutler, "Attitudes of Male Students toward Physical Education in Selected Junior Colleges of California," Doctoral Dissertation, Stanford University, 1958, 265 pp.

[29]June P. Galloway, "An Exploration of the Effectiveness of Physical Education Experiences in the Development of Attitudes of College Woman toward Sociological, Psychological, and Spiritual Values as Related to These Experiences," M.Ed. Thesis, University of North Carolina at Greensboro, 1959, 74 pp.

[30]Emily L. Mercer, "An Adaptation and Revision of the Galloway Attitude Inventory for Evaluating the Attitudes of High School Girls toward Psychological, Moral-spiritual, and Sociological Values in Physical Education Experiences," M.Ed. Thesis, University of North Carolina at Greensboro, 1961, 57 pp.

[31]Barbara L. Drinkwater, "Development of an Attitude Inventory to Measure the Attitude of High School Girls toward Physical Education as a Career for Women," *Research Quarterly* (Dec. 1960), 575–80.

[32]Charles E. Richardson, "Thurstone Scale for Measuring Attitudes of College Students toward Physical Fitness and Exercise," *Research Quarterly* (Dec. 1960), 638–43.

[33]R.S. Adams, "Two Scales for Measuring Attitude toward Physical Education," *Research Quarterly* (March 1963), 91–94.

[34]Thomas J. Sheehan, "The Construction and Testing of a Teaching Model for Attitude Formation and Changes through Physical Education," Doctoral Dissertation, Ohio State University, 1965, 154 pp.

[35]Lou J. Moyer, John Mitchem, and Mary Bell, "Women's Attitudes toward Physical Education in The General Education Program at Northern Illinois University," *Research Quarterly* (Dec. 1966), 515–19.

[36]Mary M. Penman, "An Adaptation of Wear's Physical Education Attitude Inventory for Inner-city Junior High School Girls," M.Ed. Thesis, Wayne State University, 1967, 92 pp.

[37]Donald E. Campbell, "Wear Attitude Inventory Applied to Junior High School Boys," *Research Quarterly* (Dec. 1968), 888–93.

[38]Gerald Kenyon, "Six Scales for Assessing Attitude toward Physical Activity," *Research Quarterly* (Oct. 1968), 566–74.

[39]Charles W. Edgington, "Development of an Attitude Scale to Measure Attitudes of High School Freshman Boys toward Physical Education," *Research Quarterly* (Oct. 1968), 505–12.

[40]B.D. McPherson and M.S. Yuhasz, "An Inventory for Assessing Men's Attitudes toward Exercise and Physical Activity," *Research Quarterly* (March 1968), 218–20.

[41]Maureen H. O'Bryan and K.G. O'Bryan, "Attitudes of Males toward Selected Aspects of Physical Education," *Research Quarterly* (May 1969), 343–52.

[42]Janet A. Seaman, "Attitudes of Physically Handicapped Children toward Physical Education," *Research Quarterly* (Oct. 1970), 439–45.

[43]Julie Simon and Frank L. Smoll, "An Instrument for Assessing Children's Attitudes toward Physical Activity," *Research Quarterly* (Dec. 1974), 407–15.

[44]Rosemary Selby and John H. Lewko, "Children's Attitudes toward Females in Sports: Their Relationship with Sex, Grade, and Sports Participation," *Research Quarterly* (Oct. 1976), 453–63.

[45]Margaret Bell and C.E. Walters, "Attitudes of Women at the University of Michigan toward Physical Education," *Research Quarterly* (Dec. 1953), 379–91.

[46]Marion Broer, K.S. Fox and E. Way, "Attitude of University of Washington Women Students toward Physical Education Activity," *Research Quarterly* (Dec. 1955), 379–84.

[47]Jack Keogh, "Analysis of General Attitudes toward Physical Education," *Research Quarterly* (May 1962), 239–44; and Jack Keogh, "Extreme Attitudes toward Physical Education," *Research Quarterly* (March 1963), 27–33.

[48]Wayne B. Brumbach and John Cross, "Attitudes toward Physical Education of Male Students Entering the University of Oregon," *Research Quarterly* (March 1965), 10.

[49]Donald E. Campbell, "Student Attitudes toward Physical Education," *Research Quarterly* (Oct. 1968), 456–62.

[50]Janet A. Wessel and Richard Nelson. "Relationship between Strength and Attitudes toward Physical Education Activity Among College Women," *Research Quarterly* (Dec. 1964), 562–69.

[51]Marilyn F. Vincent, "Attitudes of College Women toward Physical Education and Their Relationship to Success in Physical Education," *Research Quarterly* (March 1967), 126–31.

[52]Mary L. Young, "Personal-social Adjustment, Physical Fitness, Attitude toward Physical Education of High School Girls by Socioeconomic Level," *Research Quarterly* (Dec. 1970), 593–99.

[53]Carol K. O'Brian, "The Relationship between Personality and Attitude toward Physical Activity," M.S. Thesis, University of Wisconsin, 1966, 125 pp.

[54]Richard B. Alderman, "A Sociopsychological Assessment of Attitude toward Physical Activity in Champion Athletes," *Research Quarterly* (March 1970), 1–9.

[55]William F. Straub and Thomas Felock, "Attitudes toward Physical Activity of Delinquent and Non-delinquent Junior High School Age Girls," *Research Quarterly* (March 1974), 21–27.

[56]Raymond B. Cattell, Herbert W. Eber, and Maurice M. Tatsuoka, *Handbook for the Sixteen Personality Factor Questionnaire* (Champaign, Ill.: The Institute for Personality and Ability Testing, 1970).

[57]Harrison C. Gough, *California Psychological Inventory, rev. ed.* (Palo Alto, Ca.: Consulting Psychologist Press, 1964).

[58]S.R. Hathaway and J.G. McKinley, *The Minnesota Multiphasic Personality Inventory Manual* (New York: Psychological Corporation, 1951).

[59]Leonard V. Gordon, *Gordon Personal Profile Manual* (New York: Harcourt, Brace and World, 1963).

[60]Allen L. Edwards, *Edwards Personal Preference Schedule Manual* (New York: Psychological Corporation, 1959).

[61]Lance Flanagan, "A Study of Some Personality Traits of Different Physical Activity Groups," *Research Quarterly* (Oct. 1951), 312–23; Franklin M. Henry, "Personality Differences in Athletes and Physical Education and Aviation Students," *Psychological Bulletin* (1941), 745; A.P. Sperling, "The Relationship between Personality Adjustment and Achievement in Physical Education Activities," *Research Quarterly* (Oct. 1942), 351–63; and John B. Thune, "Personality of Weightlifters," *Research Quarterly* (Oct. 1949), 296–306.

[62]Lowell Cooper, "Athletics, Activity and Personality," *Research Quarterly* (March 1969), 17–22.

[63]John Pyecha, "Comparative Effects of Judo and Selected Physical Education Activities on Male University Freshman Personality Traits," *Research Quarterly* (Oct. 1970), 425–31.

[64]Victor A. Buccola and William J. Stone, "Effects of Jogging and Cycling Programs on Physiological and Personality Variables in Aged Men," *Research Quarterly* (May 1975), 134–39.

[65]R.J. Young and A.H. Ismail, "Personality Differences of Adult Men before and after a Physical Fitness Program," *Research Quarterly* (Oct. 1976), 513–19.

[66]Richard A. Berger and Donald H. Littlefield, "Comparison between Football Athletes and Nonathletes on Personality," *Research Quarterly* (Dec. 1969), 663–69; Donald H. Hunt, "A Cross Racial Comparison of Personality Traits between Athletes and Nonathletes," *Research Quarterly* (Dec. 1969), 704–11; and Kathleen A. O'Connor and James L. Webb, "Investigations of Personality Traits of College Female Athletes and Nonathletes," *Research Quarterly* (May 1976), 203–10.

[67]Sheri L. Peterson, Jerome C. Weber, and William W. Trousdale, "Personality Traits of Women in Team Sports vs. Women in Individual Sports," *Research Quarterly* (Dec. 1967), 686–90.

[68]Robert N. Singer, "Personality Differences between and within Baseball and Tennis Players," *Research Quarterly* (Oct. 1969), 582–88.

[69]Mel R. Fratzke, "Personality and Biographical Traits of Superior and Average College Basketball Officials," *Research Quarterly* (Dec. 1975), 484–88.

[70]James H. Widdop and Valerie A. Widdop, "Comparison of the Personality Traits of Female Teacher Education and Physical Education Students," *Research Quarterly* (Oct. 1975), 274–81.

[71]R.J. Young and A.H. Ismail, "Comparison of Selected Physiological and Personality Variables in Regular and Nonregular Adult Male Exercisers," *Research Quarterly* (Oct. 1977), 617–22.

[72]Lowell G. Biddulph, "Athletic Achievement and the Personal and Social Adjustment of High School Boys," *Research Quarterly* (March 1954), 1–7.

[73]Hilmi Ibrahim, "Recreational Preference and Personality," *Research Quarterly* (March 1969), 76–82.

[74]Philip K. Wilson, "Relationship between Motor Achievement and Selected Personality Factors of Junior and Senior High School Boys," *Research Quarterly* (Dec. 1969), 841–44.

[75]Mary Slaughter, "An Analysis of the Relationship between Somatotype and Personality Traits of College Women," *Research Quarterly* (Dec. 1970), 569–75.

[76]Rex B. Brown, "Personality Characteristics Related to Injuries in Football," *Research Quarterly* (May 1971), 133–38.

[77]E.G. Booth, "Personality Traits of Athletes as Measured by the MMPI," *Research Quarterly* (May 1958), 127–38; William L. Lakie, "Personality Characteristics of Certain Groups of Intercollegiate Athletes," *Research Quarterly* (Dec. 1962), 566–

73; and Theresa M. Malumphy, "The Personality and General Characteristics of Women Athletes in Intercollegiate Competition," Doctoral Dissertation, Ohio State, 1966, 223 pp.

[78] L.B. Hendry, "A Personality Study of Highly Successful and 'Ideal' Swimming Coaches," *Research Quarterly* (May 1969), 299–304.

[79] Jean M. Williams, Barbara J. Hoepner, Dorothy L. Moody, and Bruce C. Ogilvie, "Personality Traits of Champion Level Female Fencers," *Research Quarterly* (Oct. 1970), 446–53.

[80] John B. Thune, "Personality of Weightlifters," *Research Quarterly* (Oct. 1949), 296–306.

[81] Sheila Brown, "Personality Characteristics of Selected Groups of Women Educators," *Research Quarterly* (May 1975), 127–33.

[82] Marguerite A. Clifton and H.M. Smith, "Comparison of Expressed Self-Concepts of Highly Skilled Males and Females Concerning Motor Performance," *Perceptual and Motor Skills* (Feb. 1963), 199–201; and Hilmi Ibrahim and Nettie Morrison, "Self-Actualization and Self-Concept among Athletes," *Research Quarterly* (March 1976), 68–79.

[83] Donald W. Felker, "Relationship between Self-Concept, Body Build and Perceptions of Father's Interest in Sports in Boys," *Research Quarterly* (Oct. 1968), 513–17.

[84] Anna May Doudlah, "The Relationship Between Self-Concept, the Body Image and the Movement-Concept of College Freshman Women with Low and Average Motor Ability," M.S. Thesis, University of North Carolina at Greensboro, 1962, 62 pp.

[85] Sara M. Nelson, "An Investigation of the Relationship between the Real Self-Concept, Ideal Self-Concept and Motor Ability of Eighth Grade Girls in Physical Education," M.Ed. University of North Carolina at Greensboro, 1965, 77 pp.

[86] Pearline P. Yeatts and Ira J. Gordon, "Effects of Physical Education Taught by a Specialist on Physical Fitness and Self-Image," *Research Quarterly* (Oct. 1968), 766–70.

[87] Barbara L. Callahan, "Self Determination Measurement in Physical Education," M.S. Thesis, University of California at Los Angeles, 1962, 91 pp.

[88] Daniel C. Neale, Robert J. Sonstroem, and Ken F. Metz, "Physical Fitness, Self-esteem, and Attitudes toward Physical Activity," *Research Quarterly* (Dec. 1969), 743–49.

[89] Elizabeth Y. Brown and Carl N. Shaw, "Effects of a Stressor on a Specific Motor Task on Individuals Displaying Selected Personality Factors," *Research Quarterly* (March 1975), 71–77; and Daniel M. Landers, "Psychological Femininity and the Prospective Female Physical Educator," *Research Quarterly* (May 1970), 164–70.

[90] Eldon E. Snyder and Joseph E. Kivlin, "Women Athletes and Aspects of Psychological Well-Being and Body Image," *Research Quarterly* (May 1975), 191–99.

[91] William J. Vincent and Don S. Dorsey, "Body Image Phenomena and Measures of Physiological Performance," *Research Quarterly* (Dec. 1968), 1101–06.

[92] Marcella D. Woods, "An Exploration of Developmental Relationships between Children's Body Image Boundries, Estimates of Dimensions of Body Space, and Performance of Selected Gross Motor Skills," Doctoral Dissertation, Ohio State, 1966, 192 pp.

[93] Ellington Darden, "A Comparison of Body Image and Self-Concept Variables among Various Sport Groups," *Research Quarterly* (March 1972), 7–15.

[94] Edwin G. Belzer, "Effect of Physical Activity upon Body Image as Measured by an Aniseikonic Technique," M.A. Thesis, University of Maryland, 1962, 41 pp.

[95] George Bovyer, "Children's Concepts of Sportsmanship in the Fourth, Fifth, and Sixth Grades," *Research Quarterly* (Oct. 1963), 282–87; Mary Jane Haskins, "Problem Solving Test of Sportsmanship," *Research Quarterly* (Dec. 1960), 601–06; Marion L. Johnson, "Construction of Sportsmanship Attitude Scale," *Research Quarterly* (May 1969), 312–16; William L. Lakie, "Expressed Attitudes of Various

Groups of Athletes toward Athletic Competition," *Research Quarterly* (Dec. 1964), 497–503; and Robert A. McAffee, "Sportsmanship Attitudes of Sixth, Seventh, and Eighth Grade Boys," *Research Quarterly* (March 1955), 120.

[96]Bovyer, "Children's Concepts of Sportsmanship in the Fourth, Fifth, and Sixth Grades"; and McAffee, "Sportsmanship Attitudes of Sixth, Seventh, and Eighth Grade Boys."

[97]William L. Lakie, "Expressed Attitudes of Various Groups of Athletes toward Athletic Competition," *Research Quarterly* (Dec. 1964), 497–503.

SECTION 5

MEASURING PHYSICAL PERFORMANCE OBJECTIVES

INTRODUCTION TO SECTION 5

The most unique objective of physical education in comparison with other school subjects is the teaching of physical skills. Consequently it is this area that has received the most attention and for which measurement tools are most abundant.

There are probably as many ways to categorize these tests as there are people who would care to attempt it. The following chapters are presented to aid the prospective physical educator in selecting and scoring a previously constructed test, as well as providing ideas for "home-made" tests. Following Chapter 14, which presents the procedures for constructing a performance test, are chapters giving examples and sources of tests for classification, physical stature, physical condition, sports skills, and dance and rhythm.

Chapter 14

Performance Test Construction

The construction of a valid and reliable test to measure physical performance is a difficult and time-consuming task. It is not something that can be accomplished in one day, nor can a beginning physical education teacher expect to construct a performance test for each activity taught during the school year. However, there is no reason that a performance test devised by someone else cannot be used if the test is appropriate for the situation. Knowledge of the proper procedures for constructing performance tests can be of value in determining whether or not the test is appropriate. Further, over a period of years it is possible to establish a collection of performance tests, self-made and selected from the literature, so that an efficient measurement program is developed. A blend of objective and subjective evidence and practical considerations affect the final makeup of a performance test. This blend is illustrated in the following fourteen-step procedural outline for constructing a performance test and the ensuing hypothetical example.

PROCEDURES FOR CONSTRUCTING A PERFORMANCE TEST

Step 1—Examine the pertinent literature

As will become apparent in the remainder of the chapter, a great deal of time can be saved if a suitable performance test can be found in the literature. For this reason the physical educator is encouraged to become aware of sources of published tests. Articles in the various physical education journals and textbooks, primarily those in the measurement area, are two major sources. Perusal of education and psychology journals and discussions with other physical educators may also prove fruitful in locating possible tests.

If a test is located, determination of its suitability is generally based on the answers to the following five questions: 1) What does the test measure? 2) How was the test constructed? 3) What are the characteristics of and how many subjects were used in establishing the test? 4) What criterion measure was used? 5) How reliable and valid is the test and how were these statistics determined? The answers to these questions will become increasingly clear throughout the remainder of this chapter.

Practical matters such as necessary equipment, space, or time must also be considered. If an appropriate test cannot be found, the physical educator should construct one to obtain the desired measurements.

Step 2—Select specific characteristics to be measured

When the failure to locate an appropriate test calls for the construction of a performance test, the initial procedure is to select the specific characteristics to be measured for the given situation. For example, if softball playing ability is the general concern, a possible list of important characteristics might include throwing, hitting, fielding skills, and speed. The particular characteristics to be measured will differ from one class to another depending on the type, age, and ability level of the students and the objectives of the instructor. In an advanced softball class, for example, the general skill of hitting may be broken down into specific skills such as bunting, hitting to certain fields, and hitting for power. Similarly the general skill of throwing might be divided into pitching, throwing from third to first, and throwing from the outfield to home plate. In general, as the level of achievement to be measured increases, the characteristics to be measured become increasingly specific.

A list of the important characteristics required by an activity can be compiled in many ways. Certainly personal knowledge and familiarity with the activity will greatly benefit the physical educator. Observation can be helpful and attention to the frequency with which the various skills are used should provide evidence as to the importance of each skill. If available, experts in the activity might be polled and their opinions used as the basis for a list of the important characteristics to be measured. Finally, if step one was followed, the physical educator should obtain several suggestions from the literature as to what characteristics other test constructors have concluded are important to the activity.

Step 3—Formulate tenative tests

Once the list of important characteristics required by the activity is compiled it is necessary to locate or devise tests to measure these characteristics. The perusal of the literature in step one should provide several suggestions of possible tests that might be used or modified. Knowing exactly what is to be measured and what facilities and equipment are available, the physical educator can often invent tests to fit the specific situation. In selecting, modifying, or originating tentative tests, several factors should be considered. Although it is highly unlikely that every test finally used will conform to each of the following standards, it is desirable to come as close as possible:

1. Each test item must be valid — that is, each test item must actually measure the characteristic it is intended to measure. If this is not the case, the time spent in compiling the list of important characteristics is wasted. In this same regard, each test item should require correct techniques and proper form. A test item should not be used if it is possible to score well by using improper skill execution, poor form, or violation of the rules of the activity being measured. If high scores can be achieved through any of these methods, the test item is not measuring the actual characteristic required by the activity, and thus the validity is reduced.

2. Each test item must be reliable. If a test item is incapable of measuring each student consistently, it is of little value and should be discarded or modified in such a way that the reliability increases.

3. Each test item must discriminate among the students in class. This means that students who possess a great deal of the characteristic being measured should score high on the test item and students who possess little of the characteristic should score low. Further, almost all students should achieve some score in order for the test item to discriminate. As an example, a pull-up test administered to a class of fourth-grade students does not discriminate well because a great number of the students will score zero. Thus no differentiation occurs among the students scoring zero, although differences probably exist in the arm strength and endurance of these children.

4. Each test item should be as objective as possible. Although complete objectivity is difficult to achieve, clearly written test directions, development of easy and accurate scoring procedures, and, where necessary, development of ranking scales and check lists, can help meet this standard.

5. Each test item should be practical in terms of time, expense, and personnel required for administration.

6. The score resulting from the administration of each test item should reflect only the amount of the characteristic possessed by the student being measured and not be influenced by another student or the test administrator. Measuring how well a student hits a softball that is pitched by another student is an example of a violation of this standard.

7. To help assure that students are motivated to put forth thier best efforts, the test items should be as interesting and as much like the activity in question as possible.

Again, it is seldom possible to select or devise all tentative test items that conform to each of these standards. Usually, a great deal of experimentation and modification of the original idea for each test item must occur. This often includes trying out a test item on a small number of students to check its conformance to these standards.

The number of tentative test items selected depends on the number of important characteristics identified and on the degree of specificity of each of these characteristics. For practical reasons it is seldom necessary to identify more than six characteristics and probably three tentative test items for each characteristic is the maximum necessary. If a characteristic is relatively general, such as throwing, probably two or three tentative test items—perhaps distance, speed, and accuracy—might be selected. Conversely, if the characteristics are quite specifically identified, such as speed in base running, a single tentative test item may be sufficient. Generally the higher the number of tentative test items included, the greater are the chances that the final test battery will be an accurate measuring device. However, practical considerations usually limit the list of tenatative test items to a workable number.

Step 4—Select a procedure to obtain a criterion score

At this point a procedure must be devised for securing an accurate assessment of each student's achievement in the activity for which the performance test is being constructed. This assessment is known as the criterion score. Obviously, determining an accurate assessment of achievement in the activity is precisely the reason for constructing the performance test in the first place. However, the method used to determine the criterion score is usually one that is impractical for use (due to cost, time, space, equipment, or personnel limitations) every time such a measurement is desired. It should also be noticed that the determination of the criterion score is a procedure used only during the construction of a performance test and is not part of the performance test once it is completed.

There are several methods of obtaining a criterion score. A previously constructed performance test that would be suitable for use except for some practical problems can be used if the problems can be overcome for the one administration necessary to establish the criterion score. For example, a performance test may be located that except for the requirement of too much time and too many administrators might otherwise be suitable. If these two inconveniences can be surmounted for one administration, the resulting score could be used as the criterion score.

If the activity for which the performance test is being constructed is of an individual nature, such as handball, tennis, or badminton, a round-robin tournament in which each student competes with every other student can be used to obtain the criterion score. At the completion of a round-robin tournament it is possible to rank the participants fairly accurately. If a continuous, interval score is desirable (recall that rankings represent discrete, ordinal data), the average number of points scored by each student throughout the tournament may be determined.

When a performance test is constructed to measure ability in a team activity, such as softball, volleyball, or basketball, the round-robin method for establishing a criterion score cannot be used efficiently. If qualified judges are available their ratings can be used to establish a criterion score for each student. In general, this method consists of obtaining a rating from each of a number of "experts" of the ability of each student in the activity for which the performance test is being constructed. The success of this method depends on many factors.

Obviously, the accuracy of the judges in determining each student's level of competence is crucial. The use of a well-constructed and unambiguous rating sheet is very important for securing valid ratings. Allowing the judges to discuss and practice with the rating sheet before the actual ratings are obtained will usually result in an increase in the consistency among the judges. Discrmination between students will generally increase with an increase in the number of judges doing the rating. It is important that the judges have sufficient time to observe each student and that during the observation periods each student performs the various aspects of the activity that are to be rated. To be fair to each student the physical set-up and the level of competition should be as similar as possible during all observation periods. Spreading the judges around the room helps to ensure that student performances are seen from more than one angle and that the ratings are made independently. In the likely event that the judges do not know the names of the students, some means of identification, such as numbered pinnies, should be provided.

The fact that one judge's ratings seem to be lower (or higher) than the other judges' is not necessarily a problem as long as that judge is fairly consistent in scoring each student low (or high). An investigation of the consistency of the judges can and probably should be made by correlating the ratings of each judge with the ratings of the other judges. A low correlation between the ratings of two judges indicates that the two judges did not rate the students similarly. In the event that one judge's ratings do not correlate well with most or all of the other judges' ratings, it may be necessary to eliminate that judge's ratings. Although the degree of correlation is affected by the complexity of the activity and the amount of subjectivity required to obtain the rankings, if the conditions described in the previous paragraph are generally present correlation coefficients below .80 signify inconsistency.

For example, assume five judges were used in obtaining ratings and that the ten correlation coefficients necessary to make all possible comparisons were as follows:

Judge	2	3	4	5
1	.90	.85	.75	.92
2		.81	.62	.91
3			.81	.87
4				.59

Elimination of the ratings of Judge 4 is warranted since this judge's ratings are evidently not in general agreement with the other judges. The ratings of the other judges are fairly consistent, and each student's criterion score should be considered the sum (or mean) of these judges.

A few other methods can be used for obtaining a criterion score, although they are generally less common and more complex than the methods described above. A technique resulting in what is called an internal criterion score involves summing for each student the T-score (or some other standard score) equivalents of the raw scores achieved on each of the tentative tests. The composite score thus obtained is used as the criterion score. This procedure assumes that each tentative test is at least somewhat valid so that the sum achieved over all the tentative tests ranks the students accurately in their ability in the activity. Any individual tentative test that does not rank the students in approximately the same order as the composite scores is considered to lack validity. This procedure is similar to that used in investigating the value of individual test items on a written test. Using a composite score as a criterion measure is becoming less common because evidence is mounting that physical skills are quite specific rather than general among individuals. This makes it very difficult to interpret or compare composite scores obtained by combining various individual measures.

Another method for examining validity is to administer each tentative test to two contrasting groups. If the tentative test is valid, the mean score achieved by one group, consisting of students who are known to be proficient in the activity, should be substantially better than the mean score achieved by the second group consisting of students known to be beginners in the activity. The contrasting group method presents many problems such as 1) locating two groups of students relatively equal in everything but the level of ability for the particular activity in question and 2) determining what degree of difference between the two groups' mean scores is required to label the tentative tests as valid.

In summary, some method must be determined for assessing each student's level of ability in the activity for which the performance test is being constructed. This criterion score is needed to evaluate the validity of each of the tentative tests and help in deciding which of the tentative tests should be excluded and which should be retained in the final test battery.

Step 5—Select the students

Consideration needs to be given to the procedures for selecting a group of students from which tentative test scores and criterion scores can be obtained. Attention to the characteristics and the number of students is especially critical.

The students selected should be as similar as possible in terms of sex, age, skill level, and physical characteristics to those students for whom the performance tests will eventually be used. It is illogical to gather evidence about the tentative tests by administering them to high school boys if the performance test is being constructed for use in classes of junior high school girls.

Within practical limits, the greater the number of students used for obtaining data on the tenative tests the better. Greater confidence can be placed on the results obtained from a large group than from a small group. Although no single number can be given as a minimum because of the great differences existing among situations in which performance tests are constructed, the use of at least 50 and preferably 100 students is recommended.

Step 6—Administer the tentative tests and obtain the criterion scores
At the completion of step six each student should have at least one score for each tentative test and a criterion score. Depending on the method selected for investigating the reliability of each tentative test (see step seven) it may be necessary to obtain two scores for each student on some tests.

Obviously the conditions under which each test is completed should be as similar as possible for each student. Each student should receive the same complete set of instructions, be allowed the same amount of time for completion of the test, and operate under the same environmental conditions (amount of light, noise level, etc.) as the other students. Time can be saved by previously instructing any testing assistants and using previously constructed score cards.

Step 7—Determine the reliability of the tentative tests
Steps seven, eight, and nine involve statistical computations executed to determine how each tentative test correlates with (1) itself (reliability); (2) the criterion measure (validity); and (3) the other tentative tests (intercorrelations). The several correlation coefficients obtained for each tentative test provide statistical data that are combined with the subjective and practical considerations to decide which tests should be retained in the final battery.

The various approaches for determining reliability of the tentative tests were outlined in Chapter 7.

If a tentative test is to be retained in the final battery it must measure consistently—that is, it must be reliable. Thus, once the reliability coefficient for each tentative test is determined, the selection of tests to be retained in the final battery can begin. Although it is difficult to set a minimum reliability coefficient because other evidence needs to be considered (e.g., validity coefficients and intercorrelation coefficients), in general, tests having reliability coefficients below .70 should be discarded or altered in such a way as to increase their reliability.

In the event that the reliability of a seemingly important tentative test is below the desired limit, some practices, if followed, may increase the reliability enough to make the test acceptable. One response involves changing the scoring procedures of the test. A second is to lengthen the test. Both of these techniques increase reliability through a reduction of chance occurences.

Unless the reliability coefficient is quite low, making the tentative test beyond saving, the decision as to whether or not the scoring procedures should be altered or the test lengthened in an effort to improve its reliability will be based, in part, on the other statistical data gathered. A test with questionable reliability may be worth the effort required to improve it, for instance, if it demonstrates fair validity and measures a unique aspect of the ability for which the performance test is being constructed.

Step 8—Determine the validity of the tentative tests

A validity coefficient, obtained for each test by correlating the scores on the test with the criterion scores (obtained in step four), is useful in determining which tests should be retained. Generally the validity coefficients obtained are not as high as the reliability coefficients. This is due to the fact that each tentative test is intended to measure a limited part of the activity while the criterion score represents an assessment of overall competence in the activity. As with the reliability coefficient, it is difficult to set a minimun validity coefficient to determine retention or rejection of each tentative test because the validity coefficient is not the only evidence that is involved in this decision. As a general rule, however, tentative tests having validity coefficients below .60 can be discarded unless retention is warranted for some other reason.

At this point it is important to notice that a change in any of several factors (e.g., a different group of students, a different floor surface, a change in student motivation) might cause the reliability and/or the validity coefficients of a test to change. In other words, a test does not have "a" reliability or "a" validity. When reporting a reliability coefficient for a test it is important to describe the conditions under which and the students from whom the scores were obtained. In addition to these, a description of the procedure for obtaining criterion scores should accompany the reporting of a validity coefficient.

Step 9—Determine the intercorrelation coefficients among the tentative tests

There is little sense in retaining in the final battery tests that measure the same or nearly the same aspect of the activity. To determine whether two of the tentative tests measure a common element, a correlation coefficient is calculated between the scores achieved by the students on the two tests. The resulting correlation coefficient is called an intercorrelation. At this point the intercorrelations among all remaining tentative tests are calculated. A high correlation between two tentative tests indicates both are measuring much the same thing; a low intercorrelation reveals that the two tests measure unique aspects of the activity. When a high intercorrelation between two tentative tests is encountered, the poorer test (in terms of reliability and validity) can be eliminated.

Step 10—Determine which tentative tests remain for the final battery

With the subjective and statistical data gathered to this point, it is usually possible to eliminate several of the tentative tests. The statistical information (reliability, validity, and intercorrelation coefficients), the subjective judgments (practical considerations of time, expense, space, equipment, and personnel), and knowledge gained concerning the success or failure of the scoring systems adopted and the reactions of the students to the various tentative tests are all combined in determining which of the tentative tests should be retained.

Step 11—Obtain the multiple correlation coefficient

The validity coefficient for any single one of the tentative tests will rarely be above .85. If the scores for one tentative test did correlate very highly with the criterion, this single test could be used as the final performance test. Since this almost never occurs, the final performance test is usually made up of a combination, or battery, of several fairly valid tests. One of the purposes of calculating the multiple correlation coefficient is to determine how well the test battery correlates with the criterion, or in other words to determine the validity of the test battery.

The procedures for calculating the multiple correlation coefficient are fairly complex and time consuming if done by hand. Computer assistance is generally advisable at this point. The validity coefficient for each test and the intercorrelations among the tests are used to calculate the value of $R_{0.12...n}$. The value of R cannot be less than the highest validity correlation of the retained tentative tests.

The list of tentative tests retained to this point can sometimes be further reduced by calculating the multiple correlation coefficient several times, each time omitting one of the tentative tests. Omitting the weakest tentative test may result in a very small decrease in the value of the multiple correlation coefficient. This is especially convenient if the omitted test is one that for any of several possible reasons is laborious to administer. Unfortunately, determining which of the tentative tests is the weakest is not necessarily an easy task since two factors (the value of the validity coefficient and the values of the intercorrelations) are involved. In general, the tests with the lowest validity coefficient and the highest intercorrelations are the ones that should be scrutinized for possible ommision. Since it is possible for a test to have a low validity coefficient but also low intercorrelations or to have a high validity coefficient and high intercorrelations, some trial and error experimentation may be necessary to determine the most efficient battery of tests possessing an acceptable validity with the criterion.

Step 12—Obtain the regression equation

Once it is decided which of the tentative tests are to be retained in the final battery, it is necessary to compute a regression equation to determine how the various tests should be weighted. The raw scores cannot merely be summed for each student because the various score units may differ, and the variability of each set of scores affects the amount of weight each score has on a composite score. The regression equation accounts for the differences in the variability of the test score distributions as well as in the variability and the intercorrelation coefficients. If the test battery is valid (as shown by the value of R) the list of activity proficiency scores should rank the students in the same or nearly the same order as the criterion scores.

The regression equation calculation, due to its complexity, should be handled by someone familiar with the statistical manipulations necessary. To reduce the number of cumbersome multiplications required by the regression equation it is possible to determine the ratios that exist between the weighting constants and use this information in obtaining the activity proficiency scores. The ratios can be determined by dividing all the constants by the value of the smallest constant.

Step 13—Establish norms

Through administration of the tests remaining after step eleven and substitution of the resulting test scores into the regression equation obtained in step twelve, a number indicating proficiency in the performance of the activity is determined for each student. Accordingly the students tested can be ranked in their ability to perform the activity. However, it may sometimes be desirable to use this information in other ways, some of which require norms rather than the raw scores resulting from the regression equation. For example, a student may wish to compare proficiency in one activity with that in another activity. A teacher may want to combine the proficiency scores from a performance test with the written test scores for each student. In both cases the raw scores must be converted to some type of norms to accomplish the desired results. Percentile norms or some form of standard score norms can be used, although standard score norms are preferred if the performance scores are to be combined with other scores.

The development of norms is somewhat difficult until a relatively large group of students has been tested. Norms may have to be recalculated fairly often until the data increase and stability is achieved.

Step 14—Publish the performance test

The initial step in the process of testing activity performance involves examining the pertinent literature to determine whether or not a suitable performance test is already available. Failure to locate such a test leads to the construction of a performance test as outlined above. To complete the circle, the final step is to publish a report of the final test battery and the procedures leading to its development. Thus other physical educators might be saved the time of constructing a performance test.

HYPOTHETICAL EXAMPLE—TEST OF SOFTBALL PLAYING ABILITY

Assume that a physical educator desires to measure the softball playing ability of junior high school boys through the use of a performance test. The following hypothetical example illustrates the procedures outlined above for constructing such a test.

Step 1—Examine the pertinent literature

In actuality, several softball tests have been devised and reported (see Chapter 17), one of which could probably be used. However, so that the hypothetical example may continue, it will be assumed that no test was located that fit the particular situation involved.

Step 2—Select specific characteristics to be measured

Through a discussion with colleagues, an examination of textbooks concerning the teaching of softball, and a scrutiny of the particular objectives of the softball unit, the physical educator compiled a list of the important characteristics to be measured. The list included the skills of batting, fielding, throwing, and running.

Step 3—Formulate tentative tests
Batting

Test 1: Fungo batting:

Standing in the batters' box the student throws a ball in the air and attempts to hit it into the outfield on the fly. The student attempts to hit the first ball into left field, the second into right field, the third into left field, and so on for twenty trials. Any time a ball is hit by the bat it counts as one trial. A complete miss is not counted as a trial. A ball must pass between first and second base or second and third base to be considered hit into right field or left field, respectively. Balls landing in the outfield on the fly count five points, balls hitting first in the infield but rolling into the proper field count three points, and foul balls in the proper direction count one point. Balls to the wrong field or not going past the infield count no points. The maximum score possible is 100 points.

Batting for distance

Test 2: Batting for distance

A batting tee is placed at the goal line of a football field. After several warm-up hits during which the batting tee may be adjusted for height, the student is given ten trials to hit the softball as far as possible. The score is the sum of the ten distances achieved (measured to the nearest foot). Each distance is measured from the batting tee to the spot where the ball first hits the ground. Any swing in which the softball and/or the batting tee is hit counts as one of the ten trials.

Fielding

Test 3: Fielding ground balls

A test included in the AAHPERD Softball Skills Test[1] battery was selected to measure the ability to field ground balls. A rectangular area 17' × 60' is marked off as shown in Figure 14.1. The total area is divided into three smaller rectangles two of which are 25' × 17' and the other 10' × 17'. To begin the test the student stands in the smaller rectangle and the tester stands behind the throwing line. The tester throws softballs overhand and with fair speed at the rate of one every five seconds in such a manner that each ball bounces at least once in the first rectangle. The student's task is to field the ground ball clearly, hold it momentarily, and discard it. After the test is begun the student may field the ground balls anywhere inside the center rectangle.

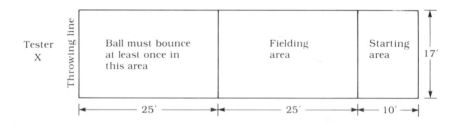

Figure 14.1   Markings for fielding ground balls test

The tester should not deliberately try to make the student miss the ball but should place approximately one-half of the throws to each side of the student. After a few practice trials, twenty test trials are given and scored on a pass-fail basis. Each throw results either in a score of one point or zero. The maximum score is twenty.

Test 4: Fielding fly balls

The student stands behind a restraining line drawn on the floor ten feet from a smooth wall surface on which a line twelve feet from the floor has been drawn. At the signal to start the student throws a softball against the wall above the line and catches it in the air. This process is continued until fifteen successful catches are made. The ball may be caught in front of the restraining line but must be thrown each time from behind this line. After a few practice catches, the test is begun; the score is the amount of time required to complete the test.

Test 5: Repeated throws fielding test

The test described below is included in a battery of tests devised by Jacqueline Shick to measure defensive softball skills of college women.[2] Its purpose is to measure a student's ability to field a ground ball and to throw the ball quickly after fielding it. The student stands behind a restraining line fifteen feet from a smooth wall surface. On the wall a line is drawn four feet above the floor. The task is to throw a ball, using any type of throw, hit the wall below the line, and field the ball as it returns. This is continued as many times as possible for a period of thirty seconds. Four thirty-second trials are given. (The second trial is administered after each student has completed the first trial.) The score for each trial is the number of acceptable hits (below the four-foot mark and thrown from behind the restraining line) made in the thirty seconds. The total score for the test is the sum of the four trial scores.

Test 6: Fielding footwork test

A softball fielding test devised by the Research Committee of the Central Association for Physical Education for College Women is reported by Scott and French.[3] The test measures a combination of fielding, throwing, and footwork skills. To administer the test two smooth wall surfaces at right angles to each other are required. On one wall a target is placed consisting of five concentric circles. The radii of the five circles are three inches, twelve inches, twenty-one inches, thirty inches, and thirty-nine inches, with the center of the target being located 48 inches from the floor. Located forty-five feet directly in front of the target is a one-foot square base. The base is located thirty feet from the non-target wall (See Figure 14.2).

At the command "Ready, Go!" the student, with one foot touching the base, throws the ball at the blank wall, fields the ball as quickly as possible, touches the base, and throws at the target. This task is repeated ten times after a few practice trials. A rest may be required between the first and last five trials.

Both the accuracy of the throws and the time required to complete the ten trials are involved in the scoring. The accuracy portion of the score is the sum of the points obtained by hitting the target; a hit in the center circle counts five points, and the point value decreases by one for each successive circle. The time portion of the score is computed by recording the time required to complete each trial (from the time the ball is released toward the blank wall until it hits the target) and summing over the ten trials. If the time is above a fixed maximum (which must be determined in an experimental run of the test, since it will vary for students of differing ages and for differing wall surfaces), one point is subtracted from the accuracy portion of the score for

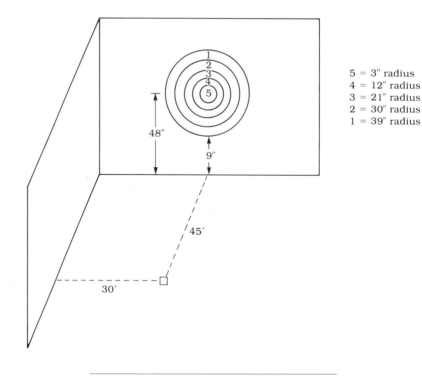

Figure 14.2   Markings for fielding footwork test

each excessive two seconds. If the total time is below the maximum, the final test score is simply the sum of the accuracy points.

Throwing
Test 7: Repeated throws test
This is a common test found in various forms in many softball performance tests. The student stands behind a restraining line which is ten feet from a smooth wall surface. On the signal to start, the ball is thrown by the student so that it hits above a line marked on the wall ten feet from the floor. The ball is caught on the rebound (in the air or on the bounce) and thrown again. This is repeated as many times as possible in thirty seconds. The student must recover any ball getting out of control with the loss of time being sufficient penalty. One point is awarded each time the ball hits above the line as long as the throw was made from behind the restraining line. The score for the test is the sum of the scores for four thirty-second trials.

Test 8: Throwing for accuracy and power
A smooth wall and a clear area at least forty-five feet in front of the wall are required for this test designed by Shick.[4] The dimensions and the necessary

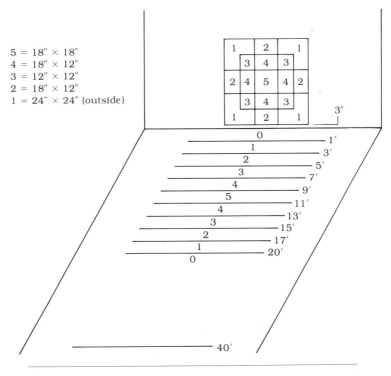

Figure 14.3   Markings for throwing for accuracy and power test

floor markings are shown in Figure 14.3. The target is sixty-six inches square with its center thirty-six inches from the floor. The test consists of two trials of ten throws each. All throws are made from behind the restraining line forty feet from the target. Two practice throws are allowed.

For each throw a score is recorded for accuracy (point value of where the ball hits the target) and for power (point value of where the ball first strikes the floor). The maximum score for one throw is ten (five for accuracy and five for power). Thus the maximum score for the entire test consisting of twenty throws is 200. (Note: As this test was constructed for use by college women it is probable that the floor markings would need to be altered if the test is used for measuring other types of students.)

Test 9: Throw for distance
The student, starting from within a six-foot restraining area, throws the softball as far as possible on a marked field such as a football field. After proper warm-up, three throws are allowed; the distance of the best throw, to the nearest foot, is recorded as the score for the test. The measurement is made at right angles to the restraining line, not from the point of release to the point of landing.

Running

Test 10: Running the bases

A batting tee and ball are set up on home plate and the student stands in the batters' box. When ready, the student hits the ball, drops the bat, and runs a complete circuit around the bases. (The batting tee should be removed before the student returns.) Each base must be contacted and in the proper order. A stop watch is started when the ball is contacted with the bat and stopped when the student touches home plate. After one practice trial, three trials are administered; the best time is recorded as the score for the test. The direction or the distance the ball is hit does not enter into the scoring.

Test 11: Running to first base

The student stands in the right-hand batters' box with the left side facing the pitcher's mound as if actually batting. At the command "Ready, Go!" the student runs to (and continues past) first base as quickly as possible. A stop watch is started on the command "Go!" and stopped when the student contacts first base. After a practice trial, four trials are administered; the sum of the four trial times is the score for the test.

Step 4—Select a procedure to obtain a criterion score

Five colleagues agree to serve as judges in ranking the softball playing ability of the students to be used as subjects in the softball test construction project. The colleagues are all physical education instructors and relatively knowledgeable in the area of teaching softball skills. Although it may be difficult to schedule times when all five of the judges can observe the students, once the softball playing ability test is constructed this procedure will not have to be repeated.

A rating sheet is constructed and given to each judge so that each judge will be rating the students on the same basis. For example, in assessing a student's batting ability, each judge rates the following characteristics from one to five: bat selection, grip, location in the batters' box, stance, readiness and concentration, swing mechanics, ability to determine a ball from a strike, power, placement, and reactions after hitting the ball. A similar list is prepared and used for the other skills rated.

The observation periods are set up in such a manner that all five judges are present each period and are scheduled frequently enough that each judge has adequate time to properly rate each student. By correlating each judge's ratings with the other judges' ratings it is determined that all five judges are consistent. Thus for each student the five rankings are combined and the resulting sum used as the criterion score.

Step 5—Select the students

The softball performance test was constructed for measuring the softball playing ability of junior high school boys. Therefore, only boys are selected as subjects and an attempt is made to include an approximately equal number of students from each grade in the school. Sixty students are selected as subjects in the construction of the softball performance test.

Step 6—Administer the tentative tests and obtain the criterion scores

With the help of several test administrators, the eleven tentative tests are administered to the sixty students. It is decided that due to the few trials involved in tests 4, 9, 10, and 11, evidence of the reliability of these tests will be determined through the test-retest method. Thus these tests are administered twice to each student. Tests 1–3 and 5–8 are administered once and the split-halves method and the Spearman Brown Prophecy formula used to estimate their reliability.

In addition, a criterion score is obtained for each student by summing the five judges' ratings. A score card (see Figure 14.4) is devised for recording the information for each student efficiently and in an accessible manner for determining reliability and validity coefficients.

Steps 7, 8, and 9—Determine the reliability, validity, and intercorrelations for the tentative tests

The computational procedures for determining correlation coefficients are explained in Chapter 6, and the techniques for applying these procedures in calculating reliability, validity, and intercorrelation coefficients are presented in Chapter 7. Although the computation of these coefficients will not be represented here, a listing of the fictitious coefficients is presented in order that the hypothetical performance test construction may continue (see Tables 14.1 and 14.2)

Step 10—Determine which tentative tests remain for the final battery

On the basis of the validity coefficients obtained, tests 1, 10, and 11 are eliminated from further consideration. The .52 validity coefficient of test 6 causes this test to be classified as questionable pending further evidence. Investigation of the reliability coefficients reveals that tests 5 and 6 did not measure consistently. Thus test 5 is eliminated on the basis of poor reliability, and the combination of poor reliability and questionable validity removes test 6 from further consideration.

An investigation of the intercorrelations among the remaining tentative tests reveals the following information:

Test 2 measures a relatively unique trait not measured to any great extent by the other remaining tests. Test 3 measures a relatively unique trait not measured to any great extent by the other remaining tests.

The intercorrelations between tests 4 and 7 and between tests 4 and 9 are relatively high. The intercorrelation between tests 7 and 8 is relatively high.

On the basis of these facts and further examination of the reliability and validity coefficients, tests 4 and 8 are eliminated. Since both tests 7 and 9

Name _____ Class _____ I.D. No. _____

	Judge					Total
	1	2	3	4	5	

Criterion score _____

Test												
1.	Trial	1	3	5	7	9	11	13	15	17	19	Total for odd trials	Total score
	Trial	2	4	6	8	10	12	14	16	18	20	Total for even trials	
2.	Trial	1	3	5	7	9						Total for odd trials	Total score
	Trial	2	4	6	8	10						Total for even trials	
3.	Trial	1	3	5	7	9	11	13	15	17	19	Total for odd trials	Total score
	Trial	2	4	6	8	10	12	14	16	18	20	Total for even trials	
4.												Score for trial 1	Best score
												Score for trial 2	
5.	Trial	1	3									Score for odd trials	Total score
	Trial	2	4									Score for even trials	
6.	Throw	1	3	5	7	9						Score for odd throws	Total score
	Throw	2	4	6	8	10						Score for even throws	
7.	Trial	1	3									Total for odd trials	Total score
	Trial	2	4									Total for even trials	

Figure 14.4   Score sheet used for softball performance test construction

Figure 14.4   continued

Test													
8.	Throw	1	3	5	7	9	11	13	15	17	19	Total for odd throws	Total score
	Throw	2	4	6	8	10	12	14	16	18	20	Total for even throws	
9.	Trial 1	1	2	3								Best throw for trial 1	Best throw
	Trial 2	1	2	3								Best throw for trial 2	
10.	Trial 1	1	2	3								Best time for trial 1	Best time
	Trial 2	1	2	3								Best time for trial 2	
11.	Trial 1	1	2	3	4							Total time for trial 1	Best total time
	Trial 2	1	2	3	4							Total time for trial 2	

Table 14.1   Reliability and validity coefficients of eleven tentative tests

Test	*Reliability coefficient*	*Validity coefficient*
1. Fungo batting	.72	.49
2. Batting for distance	.80	.65
3. Fielding ground balls	.71	.62
4. Fielding fly balls	.92	.63
5. Repeated throws fielding	.61	.60
6. Fielding footwork	.59	.52
7. Repeated throws	.94	.67
8. Throwing for accuracy and power	.85	.61
9. Throwing for distance	.95	.79
10. Running the bases	.78	.42
11. Running to first	.73	.33

Table 14.2   Intercorrelations among eleven tentative tests

Test	2	3	4	5	6	7	8	9	10	11
1	.62	.31	.25	.58	.24	.38	.37	.42	.21	.17
2		.25	.61	.52	.19	.40	.54	.48	.34	.29
3			.45	.70	.65	.48	.31	.33	.27	.37
4				.58	.56	.85	.63	.71	.26	.25
5					.81	.82	.24	.48	.31	.34
6						.50	.39	.35	.29	.38
7							.49	.52	.17	.24
8								.81	.10	.23
9									.24	.19
10										.90

possess reliability and validity coefficients superior to those obtained for test 4, this test is eliminated. Similarly, test 9 is retained and test 8 eliminated because they measure much the same aspect of softball playing ability and test 9 has higher reliability and validity than test 8.

Step 11—Obtain the multiple correlation coefficient

To determine the validity of the combination of the remaining four tests, a multiple correlation coefficient is calculated. The validity coefficients and the intercorrelation coefficients used to compute $R_{0.2379}$ are presented in Table 14.3.

Table 14.3   Validity and intercorrelation coefficients used in calculating the multiple correlation coefficient

Test	Validity coefficient	Test	Intercorrelation coefficients		
			3	7	9
2	.65	2	.25	.40	.48
3	.62	3		.48	.33
7	.67	7			.52
9	.79				

Combining the four tests with the characteristics shown in Table 14.3 results in an $R_{0.2379}$ of .93. To investigate the possibility of reducing the list of remaining tests even further without significantly affecting the validity of the test battery, a multiple correlation coefficient is calculated for each of the four possible combinations of three tests. The results are as follows:

$$R_{0.379} = .89 \quad \text{(omit test 2)}$$
$$R_{0.279} = .88 \quad \text{(omit test 3)}$$
$$R_{0.239} = .92 \quad \text{(omit test 7)}$$
$$R_{0.237} = .85 \quad \text{(omit test 9)}$$

Thus, a battery of tests composed of tests 2, 3, and 9 is nearly as valid as the battery containing all four tests. It is decided that the minimal loss of validity encountered when using the three-test battery is justified by the reduction of time and effort required to administer test 7.

Step 12—Obtain the regression equation
The three tests comprising the final battery, batting for distance (2), fielding ground balls (3), and throwing for distance (9) are renumbered as tests 1, 2, and 3, respectively. A regression equation is calculated to determine the proper weighting of the scores resulting from each test.
The resulting regression equation is as follows:

Softball Playing Ability = 1.05 test 1 + 3.86 test 2 + .54 test 3

For each student, an index of softball playing ability (SPA) could be found by multiplying the three test scores by the proper constant indicated by the regression equation and summing the resulting three products. However, some of the tedium of the computational procedure is eliminated by dividing the two larger constants (1.05 and 3.86) by the smallest constant (.54), resulting in the values of 1.94 and 7.14. Rounding these values to 2 and 7, respectively, results in the following regression equation:

SPA = 2 × test 1 + 7 × test 2 + test 3

This regression equation, with very minimal loss of accuracy in comparison to the regression equation involving decimal constants, is used to determine an index of softball playing ability for each student.

Step 13—Establish norms
Over a period of a few years, records are kept of the frequency with which various softball playing ability indexes are obtained. Eventually these data are converted to percentile and standard score norms. The percentile norms are valuable for informing students of their standing in relation to their peers in regard to softball playing ability. The standard score norms are particularly valuable for combining each student's performance with other measures, such as achievement on the softball written test.

Step 14—Publish the performance test
Since this example of the construction of a performance test is completely hypothetical, it is not published in any journal or book (save this one). However, if the amount of work and effort required to construct such a performance test

is put forth and if the results are favorable, the project should be written up and submitted for publication to benefit other physical educators.

REFERENCES CITED

[1]*AAHPER Skills Test Manual: Softball for Boys,* David K. Brace, Test Consultant (Washington, D.C.: American Association for Health, Physical Education and Recreation, 1966).

[2]Jacqueline Shick, "Battery of Defensive Softball Skills Tests for College Women," *R.Q.,* Vol. 41, No. 1 (March 1970). 82–87.

[3]M. Gladys Scott and Esther French, *Measurement and Evaluation in P.E.* (Dubuque, Iowa: Wm. C Brown, 1959), 204–06.

[4]Shick, "Battery of Defensive Softball Skills Tests for College Women."

Chapter 15
Classification Methods

Although the W. T. Harris plan put into effect in St. Louis in 1867 is often cited as one of the first organized attempts at what is now termed "homogeneous ability grouping," the regular practice of classifying students according to ability is a relatively recent innovation in education. The popularity, use, and variations of classification methods have fluctuated since the initial attempts, but, in general, ability grouping has been practiced earnestly for the past seventy to eighty years and its results studied for approximately forty years. Although summaries of the studies investigating whether or not ability grouping is advantageous are typically inconclusive, the general purpose of classifying students into homogeneous groups is to improve the efficiency of teaching.

Until fairly recently very little ability grouping has been done in physical education classes. A form of classification seen in the past was that of segregation of boys and girls, usually starting around the fifth or sixth grades. Also in some school systems (usually large ones), provision of special physical education classes for students handicapped in some way might be regarded as a form of ability grouping. Recent federal legislation has all but eliminated these practices of separating students. With the advent of computer and modular scheduling and the resulting increase in flexibility in assigning students to classes and teachers, the possibilities for ability grouping in physical education have expanded greatly. As with other subject areas, classification of physical education students can be accomplished in any of several ways.

TYPES OF CLASSIFICATION

Specific classification

It would be most desirable to reclassify students according to ability for each unit taught in the physical education curriculum. However, several factors, such as the time required to accomplish this amount of measurement, the lack of availability of good classification tests for all activities, and the improbability of having sufficient scheduling flexibility to shuffle students among classes during the school year, usually make classification for each unit impractical.

Some school systems classify students according to swimming ability and use this information to assign students to classes for the entire semester. This procedure results in having ability grouped classes during the portion of the semester in which swimming is taught, but, for other units during the semester, this grouping is of minimal value. This system has merit, however, because swimming is perhaps one of the most difficult subjects to teach with heterogeneous classes.

Classification by indexes combining age, height, and weight information

Instead of reclassifying physical education students on the basis of ability for each unit taught, a general grouping according to various physical characteristics may sometimes be employed. Commonly the physical characteristics of age, height, and weight are considered. Two similar methods of combining these factors into one classification index were developed by McCloy and by Neilson and Cozens. These methods are easily applied, require little equipment, and take little time.

McCloy classification index

The first to investigate the possibilities of combining age, height, and weight into a single index for classification purposes was C. H. McCloy.[1] The following three formulas resulted from his work:

Classification Index I (Junior + Senior High School) = 20 × age (yr) + 6 × height (in) + weight (lb)

Classification Index II (College) = 6 × height (in) + weight (lb)

Classification Index III (Elementary) = 10 × age (yr) + weight (lb)

As can be seen by the formulas, McCloy found at the college level (actually after seventeen years of age) that age was no longer important, and that at the elementary level height contributed little to the classification index. Table 15.1 shows the categories suggested by McCloy for classifying elementary school, junior high school, senior high school, and college students based on the value of the corresponding index.

The following example illustrates the use of the McCloy Classification Index: A senior high school boy is fifteen years old, weighs 125 pounds, and is 5 feet 6 inches tall. Substituting these values in Classification Index I

$$(20 \times 15) + (6 \times 66) + 125$$

yields an index of 821, which places this student in the D class if he is in a small group, or in the C class if he is in a large group.

Neilson-Cozens classification index

Shortly after McCloy's Classification Index was published, N. P. Neilson and Frederich Cozens[2] reported a similar technique for categorizing elementary and junior high school boys and girls. One of the advantages of the Neilson-Cozens Classification Index is the exponent system they devised for determining a student's classification. A chart (see Table 15.2) was constructed for converting height in inches, age in years, and weight in pounds to exponents. The three exponents are totaled and the sum compared to the bottom portion of the chart to determine a student's class.

Classification systems are sometimes used to report normative data. The most common method is to report norms by sex and/or age. Occasionally a classification index is used in this manner also. The following example illustrates the use of the Neilson-Cozens Classification Index: A ninth-grade girl is 14 years and 1 month of age, 58 inches tall, and weighs 75 pounds. From the chart the corresponding exponents of 9 for age, 8 for height, and 3 for weight are determined. The sum of the three exponents (20) places this girl in the D class.

Classification index considerations

The similarity of these two classification systems is demonstrated by the fact that a correlation coefficient of over .98 has been obtained between them and very similar correlation coefficients have been obtained between the McCloy

Table 15.1 Categories suggested by McCloy for classification indexes

Classification Index I

	Senior high school Range 685–955			Junior high school Range 540–900		
Class	*For a small group*	*Class*	*For a large group*	*Class*	*For all groups*	
A	890 and over	A	900 or over	A	875 and over	
B	860	B	845	B	845	
C	830	C	815	C	815	
D	800	D	785	D	785	
E	770	E	755	E	755	
F	740	F	725	F	725	
G	739 and under	G	695	G	695	
		H	665	H	665	
		I	664 or under	I	664 or under	

Classification Index II — College

Range 490–600

Class	*For a small group*	*Class*	*For a large group*
A	570 and over	A	580 and over
B	550	B	560
C	530	C	540
D	529 and under	D	520
		E	519 and under

Classification Index III — Elementary

Range 160–320

Class	*For a small group*	*Class*	*For a large group*
A	275 and over	A	275 and over
B	260	B	265
C	245	C	255
D	230	D	245
E	215	E	235
F	200	F	225
G	185	G	215
H	184 and under	H	205
		I	195
		J	185
		K	184 and under

Source: C. H. McCloy and N. D. Young, *Tests and Measurements in Health and Physical Education* (New York: Appleton-Century-Crofts, 1939), p. 47.

Table 15.2   Neilson-Cozens classification chart for elementary and junior high school boys and girls

Exponent	Height (inches)	Age (years)	Weight (pounds)
1	50 to 51	10 to 10-5	60 to 65
2	52 to 53	10-6 to 10-11	66 to 70
3		11 to 11-5	71 to 75
4	54 to 55	11-6 to 11-11	76 to 80
5		12 to 12-5	81 to 85
6	56 to 57	12-6 to 12-11	86 to 90
7		13 to 13-5	91 to 95
8	58 to 59	13-6 to 13-11	96 to 100
9		14 to 14-5	101 to 105
10	60 to 61	14-6 to 14-11	106 to 110
11		15 to 15-5	111 to 115
12	62 to 63	15-6 to 15-11	116 to 120
13		16 to 16-5	121 to 125
14	64 to 65	16-6 to 16-11	126 to 130
15	66 to 67	17 to 17-5	131 to 133
16	68	17-6 to 17-11	134 to 136
17	69 and over	18 and over	137 and over

Sum of exponents	Class	Sum of exponents	Class
9 and below	A	25 to 29	E
10 to 14	B	30 to 34	F
15 to 19	C	35 to 38	G
20 to 24	D	39 and above	H

Source: N. P. Neilson and F. W. Cozens, *Achievement Scales in Physical Education Activities for Boys and Girls in Elementary and Junior High School* (New Jersey: A. S. Barnes and Company, 1934).

Classification Index and a battery of track and field tests and between the Neilson-Cozens Classification Index and the track-and-field battery.[3] Consequently, use of either of these indexes will result in approximately the same categorization of students.

Some evidence[4] indicates that only moderate correlations exist between classification indexes and various sports and measures of overall motor ability. This indicates that classification indexes may serve to categorize students only into relatively broad classes, after which further specific classification may be necessary. Other evidence[5] indicates that the classification indexes do not classify senior high school and college females as successfully as they classify males.

Classification by motor ability tests

In the past some success has been achieved by equating groups of students on the basis of measures of motor abilities thought to be important to most physical activities. Both measures of one motor ability and batteries of tests involving measures of several motor abilities have been used. The latter are usually called tests of General Motor Ability.

The singular measures usually involve an assessment of strength or power. Various strength indexes (Rogers, McCloy) and some power tests (standing long jump, vertical jump) have been found to correlate moderately with ability in a variety of activities.[6] Like the classification indexes, these tests are relatively simple to administer and can be used to classify students into rather broad categories.

To increase the accuracy of classification (at the expense of administrative convenience, however), test batteries were designed on the premise that certain motor abilities, such as agility, balance, coordination, endurance, power, speed, and strength, are basic to physical performance. These General Motor Ability test batteries typically contain three to six test items, each of which measures one or a combination of these "basic elements." Much current research (starting in the latter 1950s[7]) indicates that motor abilities are specific rather than general. This conclusion, based on the findings of several investigators, stems from the fact that little relationship has been found among the abilities thought to be "basic to activity." However, to the degree that the individual test items on a General Motor Ability test battery represent a sampling of the many specific abilities underlying physical performance, these batteries can be used with fair success for classification purposes.

Over the years several General Motor Ability tests have been devised. For purpose of illustration, one of these — the Barrow Motor Ability Test — is described in detail below. Following this description is an annotated list of several other General Motor Ability test batteries.

General motor ability tests
Barrow motor ability test[8]

The Barrow Motor Ability Test was initially designed for college men and norms were developed later for junior and senior high school boys. Originally twenty-nine test items measuring eight basic factors (agility, arm-shoulder coordination, balance, flexibility, hand-eye coordination, power, speed, and strength) were selected on the basis of expert opinion and administered to over 200 college men. Two test batteries were then established. A mutiple correlation coefficient of .95 was obtained between the first battery (consisting of the standing long jump, the softball throw for distance, a zigzag run, a wall pass, a six-pound medicine ball put, and the sixty-yard dash) and the criterion measure (the score on all twenty-nine items). A multiple correlation of .92 was obtained between the criterion and the second battery (consisting of the standing long jump, the zigzag run, and the medicine ball put). Reliabilities (test-retest method) of the test items used in the batteries range from a low of .79 for the wall pass to a high of .89 for the standing long jump.

Test item directions (Second battery)

Standing long jump

The only equipment necessary for this test is an area (either floor space or a tumbling mat) marked with parallel lines indicating the distance from a take-off line. Chalk or, preferably, tape can be used to make the lines. The student starts from behind the take-off line and by bending the knees and swinging the arms jumps as far forward as possible. Three trials are permitted; the final score is the best of these measured to the nearest inch. The measurement is made from the take-off line to the body part landing closest to the take-off line. Students should have an opportunity to practice the required movement so that learning does not reduce the reliability and validity of the scores.

Zigzag run

A stop watch and five standards to indicate turns are required for this test item. The standards are arranged as shown in Figure 15.1. After demonstrating the path to be taken, allowing the students to jog through the course, and indicating that the test consists of three laps around the entire circuit, each student is given one trial. If a student follows an incorrect path or grasps a standard to aid in a turn, a retest should be given. Tennis shoes should be worn and the floor surface should be cleaned to avoid slipping. The final score is time (to the nearest tenth of a second) required to run the complete course three times.

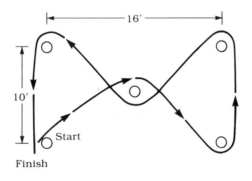

Figure 15.1   Barrow motor ability test: zigzag run

Source: H. M. Barrow and R. McGee, *A Practical Approach to Measurement in Physical Education* (Philadelphia: Lea & Febiger, 1971).

Six-pound medicine ball put

An area approximately 90 feet × 25 feet is recommended and a six-pound medicine ball is required for this test. The put is made from within an area bounded by two lines fifteen feet apart. Each student is allowed three trials to put (not throw) the medicine ball as far as possible. The final score for the event is the distance of the best put measured to the nearest foot. Measuring can be facilitated by marking regularly spaced arcs on the floor previous to the administration of the test. If a student fouls by stepping over the restraining line, it counts as a trial. However, if three fouls occur, the student is permitted to try until a legal put is made. As with any skill test the students should be permitted to practice the required movement so that learning does not interfere with the reliability and validity of the test.

Normative data

Although it is undoubtedly best for each physical educator to establish his or her own norms because of the variables that might affect them, the T-score norms presented in Tables 15.3 - 15.6 were established by Barrow for college men and for junior and senior high school boys.

Carpenter motor ability test[9]

The Carpenter Motor Ability Test was designed to measure the motor ability of boys and girls in the primary (one through three) grades. Multiple correlation coefficients of .84 for girls and .82 for boys were obtained between the test battery (consisting of the standing long jump, a four-pound shot put test, and body weight) and the criterion (total points score on a battery of eight physical performance items). Although no normative data are given, the two following multiple regression equations for obtaining a general motor ability score (GMAS) from which local norms could be constructed were computed:

Girls: GMAS = 1 long jump + 1.5 shot + 0.05 weight

Boys: GMAS = 2 long jump + 2.5 shot + 0.5 weight

Directions for administering the items are presented in reference 9.

Table 15.3   Barrow motor ability test: T-score for college men

T-score	Standing long jump (inches)	Zigzag run (seconds)	Medicine ball put (feet)
80	113 and over	20.8 and under	58 and over
75	109–112	21.6–20.9	55–57
70	105–108	22.4–21.7	52–54
65	101–104	23.2–22.5	48–51
60	97–100	23.9–23.3	45–47
55	93–96	24.7–24.0	42–44
50	89–92	25.5–24.8	39–41
45	85–88	26.3–25.6	35–38
40	81–84	27.1–26.4	32–34
35	77–80	27.8–27.2	29–31
30	73–76	28.6–27.9	26–28
25	69–72	29.4–28.7	23–25
20	68 and under	29.5 and over	22 and under

Source: H. M. Barrow and R. McGee, *A Practical Approach to Measurement in Physical Education* (Philadelphia: Lea & Febiger, 1971).

Table 15.4   Barrow motor ability test: Standing long jump (inches)
T-scores for junior and senior high school boys

			Grade		
T-score	7	8	9	10	11
80	90 and over	97 and over	103 + ↑	105 + ↑	112 + ↑
75	86–89	92–96	98–102	101–104	107–111
70	82–85	88–91	93–97	97–100	103–106
65	77–81	83–87	88–92	92–96	97–102
60	73–76	78–82	83–87	88–91	93–96
55	69–72	73–77	79–82	83–87	88–92
50	65–68	69–72	74–78	79–82	83–87
45	61–64	64–68	69–73	75–78	78–82
40	56–60	59–63	64–68	71–74	74–77
35	52–55	54–58	59–63	66–70	69–73
30	48–51	50–53	54–58	62–65	64–68
25	44–47	45–49	49–53	58–61	59–63
20	43 and under	44 and under	48 + ↓	57 + ↓	58 + ↓

Source: H. M. Barrow and R. McGee, A Practical Approach to Measurement in Physical Education (Philadelphia: Lea & Febiger, 1971).

Table 15.5   Barrow motor ability test: Zigzag run (seconds)
T-scores for junior and senior high school boys

			Grade		
T-score	7	8	9	10	11
80	20.1 and under	17.8 and under	20.2 + ↓	21.6 + ↓	21.5 + ↓
75	21.4–20.2	19.5–17.9	21.3–20.3	22.7–21.7	22.6–21.6
70	22.7–21.5	21.2–19.6	22.4–21.4	23.8–22.8	23.7–22.7
65	24.0–22.8	22.8–21.3	23.5–22.5	24.8–23.9	24.7–23.8
60	25.2–24.1	24.5–22.9	24.6–23.6	25.8–24.9	25.8–24.8
55	26.5–25.3	26.2–24.6	25.7–24.7	26.9–25.9	26.8–25.9
50	27.8–26.6	27.8–26.3	26.8–25.8	27.9–27.0	27.8–26.9
45	29.0–27.9	29.5–27.9	27.9–26.9	28.9–28.0	28.9–27.9
40	30.3–29.1	31.2–29.6	29.0–28.0	29.9–29.0	29.9–29.0
35	31.6–30.4	32.8–31.3	30.1–29.1	31.0–30.0	31.0–30.0
30	32.8–31.7	34.5–32.9	31.2–30.2	32.1–31.1	32.0–31.1
25	34.1–32.9	36.2–34.6	32.3–31.3	33.1–32.2	33.0–32.1
20	34.2 and over	36.3 and over	32.4 + ↑	33.2 + ↑	33.1 + ↑

Source: H. M. Barrow and R. McGee, A Practical Approach to Measurement in Physical Education (Philadelphia: Lea & Febiger, 1971).

Table 15.6   Barrow motor ability test: Medicine ball put (feet)
T-scores for junior and senior high school boys

			Grade		
T-score	*7*	*8*	*9*	*10*	*11*
80	43 and over	45 + ↑	49 + ↑	50 + ↑	54 + ↑
75	38–42	43–44	46–48	47–49	51–53
70	35–37	40–42	44–45	44–46	48–50
65	33–34	37–39	41–43	42–43	46–47
60	30–32	34–36	38–40	35–41	43–45
55	27–29	31–33	35–37	37–38	40–42
50	25–26	28–30	32–34	34–36	37–39
45	22–24	25–27	29–31	32–33	34–36
40	19–21	23–24	27–28	29–31	31–33
35	17–18	20–22	24–26	27–28	28–30
30	14–16	17–19	21–23	24–26	25–27
25	12–13	14–16	18–20	22–23	22–24
20	11 and under	13 + ↓	17 + ↓	21 + ↓	21 + ↓

Source: H. M. Barrow and R. McGee, *A Practical Approach to Measurement in Physical Education* (Philadelphia: Lea & Febiger, 1971).

Emory University test[10]

Seymour used statistical techniques to reduce a test battery designed to classify freshman male students into homogeneous groups for physical education classes from eight to four items. A correlation coefficient of over .98 was obtained between the shortened battery (consisting of softball throw for distance, vertical jump, sixty-yard dash, and basketball dribble) and the previously used eight-item battery (which also included a chinning test, a football throw, a volleyball serve, and a soccer dribble). Complete directions for administering

the test items are given in reference 10. However, procedures for combining the resulting scores, specific methods of classification on the basis of the test battery, and normative data are not presented.

Humiston motor ability test[11]

Through an examination of pertinent literature, Humiston determined the basic factors underlying general motor ability and selected twenty-two test items to measure these factors. After seven tests were eliminated due to low objectivity and/or reliability, the remaining fifteen were used as the criterion measure. These fifteen tests were administered to 181 college women and a final battery of seven tests (consisting of Alden dodge test; roll over on mat; run and climb over a box; run, turn in circle and continue between barriers; climb ladder; throw ball; catch it; and run twenty yards) was found to correlate highly with the criterion measure. Although no directions for these test items are given in the article, the location of references containing the directions is given. Humiston also states that norms were developed for a large number of women (over 2,000) at Iowa State Teachers College, but these norms are not presented in the reference.

Larson motor ability tests[12]

After factor analyzing twenty-seven test items and six test batteries and gathering further statistical evidence on several other test batteries related to the measurement of motor ability, Larson constructed two motor ability tests. One of these is designed for indoor use and the other for outdoor use. The multiple correlation obtained between the indoor test battery (consisting of dodge run, bar snap, chinning, dipping, and vertical jump) and the criterion measure (score on twenty-four items) was over .96. The multiple correlation between the outdoor test (consisting of the baseball throw for distance, chinning, bar snap, and vertical jump) and the criterion was over .98. The reliability coefficients of the individual test items selected were all above .86. Directions for administering each of the test items, procedures for scoring and classifying on the basis of the results obtained, and suggestions for the application of the tests are given in the reference.

Latchaw motor ability test[13]

Through an examination of the physical education activities of fourth-, fifth-, and sixth-grade boys and girls, Latchaw determined the fundamental skills of running, jumping, throwing, catching, striking, and kicking to be basic to these activities. After examination and revision of several tests used to measure these skills, a battery of seven tests (consisting of basketball wall pass, volleyball wall volley, vertical jump, standing long jump, shuttle run, soccer wall volley, and softball repeated throws) was established and administered to fourth-, fifth-, and sixth-grade children in twenty-one elementary schools in Iowa. Complete directions for administering these items, an investigation of the effects of age, height, and weight on the performance of these tests, and normative data are presented in the reference.

McCloy general motor achievement tests[14]

McCloy developed a General Motor Ability Test for boys and girls that involves pull-ups and a battery of track and field events. Although the track and field events must consist of a dash, a long jump, and a throw, options are permitted within each of these categories. The scores on the track and field events and on the pull-up test are converted to standard scores through the use of tables. Substitution of the sum of the converted scores into a special formula results in the general motor ability score. Different formulas are given for boys and girls. McCloy also developed a test to measure general motor capacity, an assessment of innate capacity indicating what a student could achieve if adequate experience and training are provided. This test is further described later in the chapter. Dividing the general motor ability score by the general motor capacity score (and multiplying the quotient obtained by 100) results in McCloy's General Motor Quotient. This quotient thus represents the percentage of a student's capacity that has been achieved. The tables necessary for conversion of raw scores to standard scores, an example of how the scores can be recorded and converted efficiently, and suggestions for interpretation of the obtained general motor ability scores and general motor quotient values are given in the reference.

Newton motor ability test[15]

A series of studies done in Newton, Massachusetts, to investigate motor ability tests utilized three criteria measures: a score based on performance in six sports skills, a score based on eighteen tests designed to measure various fundamental skills, and a score based on a subjective rating by a jury of fourteen competent judges who watched the students run an obstacle course. Several test items were correlated, with the three criteria resulting in a final battery of tests consisting of standing long jump, hurdles, and scramble tests. Directions for administering the tests, achievement scales, and an illustration of the use of the achievement scales for classification purposes are given in the references.

Scott motor ability tests[16]

Two batteries were devised by Scott to measure the general motor ability of females from junior high age to college age. A multiple correlation coefficient of .91 was obtained between the criterion (a composite of judges' ratings, scores on sports skills test, and scores on tests designed to measure fundamental skills) and the first battery (consisting of the four-second dash, the basketball throw for distance, the standing long jump, and the wall pass test). A second battery (consisting of an obstacle course, the standing long jump, and the basketball throw for distance) was found to correlate .87 with the same criterion. The slight loss of validity of this second battery is compensated for by the savings in time and the reduction in administrative procedures. Reliability for the five test items (calculated in various ways and on different samples of women) ranged from a low of .62 for the four-second dash to a high of .91 for the obstacle race. Directions for administering each test item, tables for converting the general motor ability scores into T-scores for junior and senior high school girls and college females, and two procedures (averaging T-scores or using a multiple regression equation) for obtaining the general motor ability scores are given in the reference.[17]

Other motor ability tests

Several other test batteries have been devised to measure general motor ability, but space does not permit a description of each of them. Many of these tests are unpublished. The names, applicability, and references for a few others are Cowan-Pratt Motor Coordination Test[18] (males and females—three to twelve years), Oberlin College Test[19] (males—college), Olympic Motor Ability Test[20] (females—high school), Peacock Achievement Scales[21] (males and females—seven to fifteen years), and Sigma Delta Psi Tests[22] (males—college).

Classification by motor educability tests
Motor educability tests

One further general method of classification is through the use of tests designed to measure motor educability, sometimes called general motor capacity. The purpose underlying a motor educability test is analogous to that of an intelligence test. The intent of both is to measure potential. Most of the research is not of recent origin and there is little agreement among physical educators as to the validity of the concept of motor educability. In general, studies[23] have found moderate positive correlations between tests of motor educability and other devices supposedly measuring much the same construct (such as sports intelligence, ratings of experts, rates of learning various skills), but seldom have these correlations been high enough to indicate a great deal of predictive value of motor educability tests. Low intercorrelations exist among the various motor educability tests, suggesting that the concept may be easier to define than to measure and that possibly different types of motor educability exist. However, motor educability tests or general motor capacity tests can be used for classification purposes and probably represent an improvement over the use of no classification methods at all. An annotated list of several tests designed to measure motor educability or similar qualities is presented below.

Iowa-Brace test[24]

In 1927 David Brace[25] reported a test designed to measure motor ability. The test involved twenty stunts, each scored on a pass-fail basis. McCloy later used the Brace Test as a starting point in an attempt to design a test of motor educability. For this revision (the Iowa-Brace Test), McCloy investigated forty stunts and selected twenty-one of them. Selection of each stunt was based on:

1. An increase in the percentage of students performing it correctly correlating with an increase in age
2. Its lack of dependence on strength, size and maturity, or power
3. High correlation with track and field events.

A total of six different combinations of ten stunts each were selected from among the stunts to measure motor educability of the following categories of students:

1. Upper elementary school boys
2. Upper elementary school girls
3. Junior high school boys
4. Junior high school girls
5. Senior high school boys
6. Senior high school girls.

Descriptions of the stunts, administration and scoring procedures, and normative data are presented in the reference 25.

Adams sports motor educability test[26]

From a review of pertinent literature, Adams proposes that two types of motor educability exist, stunt and sports. A battery of four sports-type tests (consisting of a wall volley test with a volleyball, throwing and catching a tennis ball while lying on the back, bouncing a volleyball on top of a baseball bat while confined to a circle six feet in diameter, and shooting basketball free throws) was selected from a list of forty-nine such tests. The battery was found to have a multiple correlation of nearly .80 with the entire group of tests. A regression equation for combining the scores, directions for each of the form tests, and norms for college men are given in the reference.

Carpenter tests of motor capacity[27]

Two forms of motor educability tests for use at the primary level are reported by Carpenter. The first contains a vertical jump test, a squat thrust test, six Brace-type stunts, and McCloy's Classification Index. The second form substitutes five Johnson-type tests (described later) examined in an earlier study by Carpenter[28] for the six Brace-type stunts in the first form. Carpenter used a T-score total for eight basic activities as the criterion measure and a total of 217 boys and girls for validating the motor educability batteries. Regression equations for combining the test scores, directions for administering the necessary tests, tables to aid in computing the necessary values, and normative data are provided in the reference.

Harvard modification of the Brace Test[29]

The directions and scoring system of the Brace Test were modified for use with children ages five to nine. The vocabulary used in the directions was changed to be suitable to children of this age, and the scoring system was changed from a pass-fail to a six-point scale rating the adequacy of the attempt. For example, a zero indicated an inability to start the stunt, a three indicated a good try, and a five indicated a pass by Brace's standards. The authors report using the results to classify children and to investigate the relationships between motor ability and several other variables, such as weight and intelligence. Although no normative data are presented, the modified directions are presented in the references.

Hill test[30]

McCloy reports a motor educability test designed by Hill for use with junior high school boys. McCloy suggests the test may also be applicable for upper elementary and senior high school boys. The test has two halves, with each half involving six specific tests from the Brace and the Iowa-Brace test. The test is administered and scored in the same manner as the Iowa-Brace test. Normative data for junior high school boys are given in the reference.

Johnson mat test[31]

One of the earliest attempts to measure "native neuro-muscular skill capacity"[32] is reported by Johnson. Ten exercises, all performed on a tumbling mat, were selected from an original list of one hundred. All tests selected had a minimal involvement of strength, speed, or endurance and a novelness so that the chance of previous practice was minimized. For scoring purposes a piece of ten-ounce canvas, marked with lines 3/4-inch wide (as shown in Figure 15.2), is placed over two standard 6×10 tumbling mats placed end to end. The scoring procedure consists mainly of noticing whether or not the students' feet touch the canvas at the proper locations specified for each stunt. Each of the ten stunts counts 10 points if performed correctly, resulting in a maximum score of 100 points for the entire test. Points for each stunt may be deducted for failure to stay within specified areas, failure to maintain a steady rhythm, and other infractions listed in the reference. Also included in the reference is a method of classifying students on the basis of the scores resulting from this test.

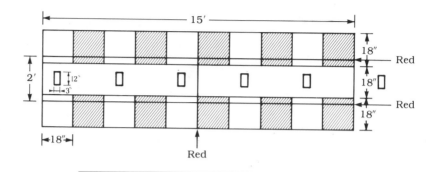

**Figure 15.2   Canvas markings for Johnson mat test
(All lines black except three marked red)**

Metheny modification of the Johnson mat test[33]

In 1938 Metheny determined that for junior high school males a battery of four of the ten items of the Johnson test correlated almost .98 with the total test. She further found that for senior high school females, scores on only three of these four tests correlated over .86 with the total Johnson score. The elimination of six items also allowed simplification of the canvas markings (Figure 15.3).

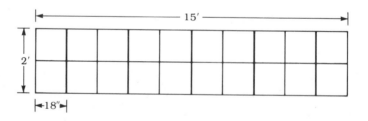

**Figure 15.3   Canvas markings for Metheny revision of the Johnson mat test
(Light lines are ¾"; dark lines are 3")**

Except for the changes due to the different canvas marking and the reduction in the number of stunts, the testing procedure, scoring, and directions for the Metheny modification remain the same as for the Johnson Test. No normative data are provided, but a description of the four stunts used and directions for administering and scoring the test are given in the reference.

Johnson general sports skills test[34]

Using a criterion of twenty-five measures of skills fundamental to basketball, soccer, softball, touch football, and volleyball, Johnson devised a test battery to measure general sports skills of college males. The final test battery of five tests (consisting of basketball dribbles, football pass for distance, soccer wall volley, volleyball wall volley, and softball throw for distance) correlated .91 with the criterion. Directions for administering each of the five test items, a regression equation for determining final scores, and norms for rating general sports skills are presented in the reference.

McCloy general motor capacity test[35]

In an effort to assess a student's potential (in contrast to achievement), McCloy devised a General Motor Capacity Test. Basically, the test battery includes the McCloy Classification Index as a measure of size and maturity, a vertical jump as a measure of power, a ten-second squat thrust test to measure agility, and the Iowa-Brace Test to measure motor educability. Various multiple regression equations are given in the reference for combining the scores from all or some of the tests depending on the sex and school level involved. The battery correlated very closely (.97 for boys, .92 for girls) with a criterion measure derived from the sum of the T-scores for several items (although these correlations are spuriously high since some of the same tests were included in both the General Motor Capacity Test and the criterion). Conversion tables for determining final general motor capacity scores, suggestions for the administration of the test, and the relationship existing between the general motor capacity scores and several variables are found in the reference. The general motor capacity score can also be used in conjunction with McCloy's general motor achievement score to obtain a general motor achievement quotient score (in theory, a representation of the degree to which a student is meeting his or her potential).

CLASSIFICATION CONSIDERATIONS

The physical educator must remember that, in practice, no method of classification is quite what it seems on paper. In theory these systems produce neat, homogeneous groups, but in reality there is almost always overlap among groups and apparent misclassifications of some students. However, even with the "roughness" of the classification procedures described in this chapter, several benefits, such as the facilitation of teaching, an increased interest and chance for success on the part of the student brought about by competing against "equals," and obvious safety advantages, should be apparent.

REFERENCES CITED

[1]Charles H. McCloy, and Norma D. Young. *Tests and Measurements in Health and Physical Education,* 3rd ed. (New York: Appleton-Century-Crofts Inc., 1954), p. 61.

[2]N.P. Neilson, and Frederick W. Cozens, *Achievement Scales in Physical Education Activities for Boys and Girls in Elementary and Junior High Schools* (New York: A. S. Barnes and Company Inc., 1934), 171 pp.

[3]McCloy and Young, *Tests and Measurements in Health and Physical Education*, 3rd ed.

[4]Joy W. Kistler, "A Comparative Study of Methods of Classifying Pupils into Homogeneous Groups for Physical Education," *Research Quarterly* (March 1934), 42– 48; and H. D. Schrock, and C. H. McCloy, "A Study of the Best Combination of Age, Height, and Weight for Basketball Classification," *Journal of Physical Education* (October 1929).

[5]Eleonore G. Adams, "The Study of Age, Height, Weight, and Power as Classification Factors for Junior High School Girls," *Research Quarterly* (May 1934) 95– 100; Karl W. Bookwalter, "An Assessment of the Validity of Height-Weight Class Divisions for High School Girls," *Research Quarterly* (May 1944), 145– 49; and Mary Delanery, "Age, Height, Weight, and Pubescence Standards for the Athletic Handicapping of Girls," *American Physical Education Review* (October 1928), 507– 09.

[6]H, Harrison Clarke, and Harold A. Bonesteel, "Equalizing the Abilities of Intramurals Teams in a Small High School," *Research Quarterly Supplement* (March 1935), 193– 96; McCloy and Young, *Tests and Measurements in Health and Physical Education*, 3rd ed., pp. 405– 06; and Harry G. Oesterich, "Strength Testing Program Applied to Y.M.C.A. Organization and Administration," *Research Quarterly Supplement* (March 1935) 197– 201.

[7]Franklin M. Henry, "Specificity vs. Generality in Learning Motor Skills," *61st Annual Proceedings* (College Physical Education Association, 1958) 126– 28.

[8]Harold M. Barrow and Rosemary McGee, *A Practical Approach to Measurement in Physical Education* (Philadelphia: Lea and Febiger 1964, 560 pp.

[9]Aileen Carpenter, "The Measurement of General Motor Capacity and General Motor Ability in the First Three Grades," *Research Quarterly* (December 1942) 444– 65.

[10]Emery W. Seymour, "Classification of Emory University Male Freshmen in Physical Education Classes," *Research Quarterly* (December 1953), 459– 62.

[11]Dorothy A. Humiston, "A Measurement of Motor Ability in College Women," *Research Quarterly* (May 1937), 181– 85.

[12]Leonard A. Larson, "A Factor Analysis of Motor Ability Variables and Tests, with Tests for College Men," *Research Quarterly (October 1941)*, 499– 517.

[13]Majorie Latchaw, "Measuring Selected Motor Skills in Fourth, Fifth, and Sixth Grades," *Research Quarterly* (December 1954), 439– 49.

[14]McCloy and Young, *Tests and Measurements in Health and Physical Education*, 3rd ed., p. 208– 14.

[15]Elizabeth Powell and Eugene C. Howe, "Motor Ability Tests for High School Girls," *Research Quarterly* (December 1939) 81– 88.

[16]M. Gladys Scott, "Motor Ability Tests for College Women," *Research Quarterly* (December 1943), 402– 05; M. Gladys Scott, "The Assessment of Motor Abilities of College Women Through Objective Tests," *Research Quarterly* (October 1939), 63– 83; and M. Gladys Scott and Ester French, *Measurement and Evaluation in Physical Education* (Dubuque, Iowa: Wm. C. Brown Co. Publishers, 1959), 493 pp.

[17]Scott and French, *Measurement and Evaluation in Physical Education.*

[18]E. A. Cowan, and B. M. Pratt, "The Hurdle Jump as a Developmental and Diagnostic Test of Motor Coordination for Children from Three to Twelve Years of Age," *Child Development* (June 1934) 107– 21.

[19]Department of Physical Education for Men—Oberlin College, "Qualifying Test for Elective Program in Physical Education," *Journal of Health and Physical Education* (October 1936) 512.

[20]Shirley J. Kammeyer, "Reliability and Validity of a Motor Ability Test for High School Girls," *Research Quarterly* (October 1956), 310– 15.

[21]William H. Peacock, *Achievement Scales in Physical Education Activities for Boys and Girls* (Chapel Hill: University of North Carolina, University Research Council).

[22]Sigma Delta Psi, School of Health and Physical Education, Indiana University, Bloomington, Indiana.

[23]Theresa Anderson and C. H. McCloy, "The Measurement of Sports Ability in High School Girls," *Research Quarterly* (March 1947), 2–11; David K. Brace, "Studies in Motor Learning of Gross Bodily Motor Skills," *Research Quarterly* (December 1946) 242–53; David K. Brace, "Studies in the Rate of Learning Gross Bodily Motor Skills," *Research Quarterly* (May 1941), 181–85; Aileen Carpenter, "Tests of Motor Educability for the First Three Grades," *Child Development* (December 1940) 293–99; Eugenia Gire and Anna Espenschade, "The Relationship between Measures of Motor Educability and the Learning of Specific Motor Skills," *Research Quarterly* (March 1942), 43–56; Clarance G. Koob, "A Study of the Johnson Skills Test as a Measure of Motor Educability," Masters Thesis, University of Iowa, 1937; and C. H. McCloy, "An Analytical Study of the Stunt Type Test as a Measure of Motor Educability," *Research Quarterly* (October 1937), 46–55.

[24]McCloy and Young, *Tests and Measurements in Health and Physical Education*, 3rd ed., pp. 85–91.

[25]David K. Brace, *Measuring Motor Ability* (New York: A. S. Barnes and Company Inc., 1927), 138 pp.

[26]Arthur R. Adams, "A Test Construction Study of Sport-Type Motor Educability Test for College Men," Microcarded Doctoral Dissertation, Louisiana State University 1954.

[27]Carpenter, "The Measurement of General Motor Capacity and General Motor Ability in the First Three Grades," 444.

[28]Peacock, *Achievement Scales in Physical Education Activities for Boys and Girls.*

[29]Vernette S. Vickers, Lillian Poyntz, and Mabel Baum. "The Brace Scale Used With Young Children," *Research Quarterly* (October 1942) 299–308.

[30]McCloy and Young, *Tests and Measurements in Health and Physical Education*, 3rd ed., p. 91.

[31]Granville B. Johnson, "Physical Skills Tests for Sectioning Classes into Homogeneous Units," *Research Quarterly* (March 1932), 128–36.

[32]Johnson, "Physical Skills Tests for Sectioning Classes into Homogeneous Units," p. 128.

[33]Eleanor Metheny, "Studies of the Johnson Test as a Test of Motor Educability," *Research Quarterly* (December 1938), 105–14.

[34]Kenneth P. Johnson, "A Measure of General Sports Skills of College Men," Microcarded Doctoral Dissertation, Indiana University, 1956.

[35]McCloy and Young, *Tests and Measurements in Health and Physical Education* 3rd ed. pp. 115–26.

Chapter 16
Physical Stature

Some of the earliest types of measurements made and recorded by physical educators may be classified under the general heading of physical stature. Originally interest centered on various anthropometric measurements such as limb lengths and widths. Great numbers of people were measured in an attempt to obtain the "ideal" proportions. The alignment of the body or posture measurement was a natural outgrowth of the interest in individual body parts. More recently, interest has shifted to the growth and development and actual composition of the human body.

Knowledge about the measurement of physical stature is essential to the physical educator for several reasons. For example, it is important to be able to assess how growth and development factors affect performance, to notice or identify abnormal growth problems, or to know at what ages various physical activities are consistent with various developmental patterns. With this in mind, we will look at body dimensions, relationships between growth and nutrition, body composition, somatotyping, and body alignment.

BODY DIMENSIONS

As mentioned, among the early measurements recorded in physical education were those describing lengths, widths, and weights of the human body and its parts. A natural result was the publication of many charts involving all or various combinations of the factors of height, weight, age, and sex. Among the earliest of these was the Wood-Baldwin[1] Age-Height-Weight Tables. Unfortunately most of these tables do not account for such factors as body build in terms of skeletal structure, or actual body composition in terms of bone, fat, and muscle. A further weakness of age-height-weight tables stems from the method of their construction. Generally a large number of people of each height, sex, and age to be represented are weighed and the average weight determined. The implication is that the average weight of the persons measured in each category is the "ideal." However, the average is only the most representative weight of the particular group and may or may not reflect the most desirable health or nutritional status. As a result, age-height-weight tables alone are generally regarded as screening devices, at best used to help identify cases that may require closer examination, perhaps by a physician. Usually people ten to fifteen percent above or below their norm value should be considered candidates for further evaluation.

Several insurance companies still compile age-height-weight tables (used in determining relationships between morbidity and various body builds). In most cases, however, these tables now incorporate some method of accounting for skeletal configuration.

RELATIONSHIPS BETWEEN GROWTH AND NUTRITION

Improper nutritional habits logically should lead to impairment of normal growth and development patterns. Using this reasoning, several attempts have been made to establish age-height-weight tables to assess nutritional status.

Instruments used to assess growth and nutritional status

Generally, the instruments used to assess growth and nutritional status are tables constructed to display "normal" growth patterns in terms of weight and height as age increases. By plotting the required values (usually over a continuous period of time), irregularities in the growth pattern, if they exist, become evident, and in most cases further examination is recommended. An annotated list of such tables follows.

Meredith height-weight charts[2]

Growth curves have been constructed by Meredith for the purpose of describing "normal" growth patterns of boys and girls from ages four to eighteen. A large number of children of the ages included were measured and the results plotted. For both height and weight, five zones are identified. For height the zones are tall, moderately tall, average, moderately short, and short. The comparable zones for weight are heavy, moderately heavy, average, moderately light, and light. A child's height and weight should fall into comparable zones, such as short and light or moderately heavy and moderately tall. Also, a child's measurements should remain in the same zones for height and weight over time. If at one measurement period dissimilar zones are recorded for height and weight or if over time a shifting of zones is noted, further observation is warranted to determine the reasons for these differences.

Wetzel grid[3]

Although the Wetzel Grid was used as early as 1937, measurement continued and the current grids are based on assessments made on over four million children from several parts of the world. Two different grids have been established, one for infants (birth to three years of age) and one for children from five to eighteen. Semiannual measurements of height and weight are recommended unless deviations from normal are identified, in which case the frequency of measurement should be increased. The grid can be used to identify children tending toward obesity and screen possible malnutrition cases.

A child's height and weight are measured and the point on the grid where the two values meet is plotted. Two pieces of information are obtained from the location of this junction: body type and body size. Body type is identified through the use of channels superimposed on the grid. Body size is specified by isodevelopmental level lines. The body type is classified as stocky (channels A3, A2); average (A1, M, B1); fair (B2); and borderline (B3). Obese children are classified as A4 and poor builds from the point of view of being too slender as B4.

A second portion of the grid is used to monitor the speed of growth. This is monitored by plotting the level (body size indicator obtained from the first part of the grid) against age. This part of the grid also indicates how a child's growth pattern relates to the general population. Five standard lines are located on the second portion of the grid indicating age schedules of development. One line, for example, indicates the ages at which a highly advanced child would reach the various isodevelopmental levels. As with other charts of this kind the purpose for using the Wetzel grid is to identify possible nutritional deviations early. Success in doing so is dependent on regular periodic measurement.

Fels composite sheet[4]

Through the use of the Fels Composite Sheet based on approximately 250 children, comparisons can be made among various measures of growth such as bone ossification, height, weight, and age at eruption of deciduous teeth. Because the plotting is done in standard scores it is possible to assess a child in relation to the population and to compare the relative position of each of the measurements recorded for a child.

Bayley growth charts[5]

As with other instruments presented in this category, the Bayley Growth Charts were derived from a large number of data and are to be used to monitor growth as indicated by periodic height and weight measurements. One graph is provided for plotting age versus weight and another for plotting age versus height. Growth curves representing the "average" weight and height are superimposed on the appropriate graph. In addition, four other growth curves representing early maturers of normally large and average builds and late maturers of average and normally small builds are superimposed. The areas between these growth curves constitute channels. Disparity in channels with regard to height and weight or the shifting of channels over periodic measurement warrant investigation.

Included in the Bayley charts are tables listing the percentage of mature height and weight of the average, accelerated, and retarded (growth patterns) child from birth to maturity. As an example of the information provided by these tables, the "average" boy is 28.6%, 49.5%, 75.0%, and 100% of his mature height at birth, age two, age nine, and age 18½ respectively.

In addition to the use of various combinations of age, height, and weight charts to assess growth patterns, the relationship between growth and nutrition is examined through the use of various anthropometric measurements. In general, several lengths, widths, and/or girths are measured and sometimes combined with measures of height and/or weight. The resulting information is used to screen nutritional problems or identify children requiring closer inspection. Three such procedures are described below.

ACH index[6]

Using data from over 10,000 children of varied social and economic backgrounds, the authors of this index selected seven measurements (consisting of chest depth, hip width, arm girth, chest width, height, weight, and subcutaneous tissue over the biceps muscle) to assess the amount and quality of soft tissue in relation to skeletal build of boys and girls from seven to twelve years of age. Due to the time-consuming nature of obtaining all seven measurements, a shortened battery consisting of the first three measurements listed has been proposed by the authors. This shortened battery can be used to screen out a fourth of the children, who then can be given the complete seven-item battery. Franzen and Palmer suggest that by using the short battery, better than 90 percent of the children who would have been screened out using the longer battery will be identified and a considerable saving of time will be achieved. The three necessary measurements are made as follows:

> Chest depth—Using a caliper, chest depth is recorded twice; after normal inspiration and after normal expiration. The chest depth is measured to the nearest tenth of a centimeter by placing the caliper firmly against the chest just above the nipple line and against the back just below the angle of the scapula.

> Hip width—Using a caliper, hip width is obtained by recording to the nearest tenth of a centimeter the distance between the widest part of the hips at the greater trochanters.

> Arm girth—A skin pencil is used to mark the highest point on the biceps as the child flexes the dominant arm. With the child then flexing the arm so that the finger tips touch the shoulder of the arm being measured, a Gulick tape is used to measure the arm girth at the point previously

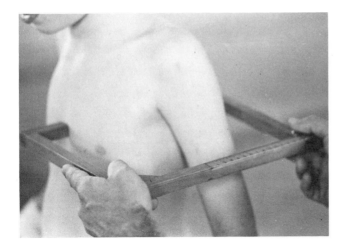

marked. The arm is measured a second time (in the same place), in the relaxed state obtained by having the child lower the arm along the side.

The three measurements are then used to determine whether or not the child should receive further examination. The sum of the two arm girth measurements is subtracted from the sum of the two chest depth measurements. By referring to Table 16.1, the difference permissible for the particular hip width of the child being measured is located. If the difference obtained from the subtraction of the two sums is less than or equal to the value obtained from the table, further examination is indicated.

Pryor width weight tables[7]

In an attempt to overcome the failure of age-height-weight tables to account for skeletal structure, Pryor devised a method to screen possible nutritional problems involving measurements of body width. Two measurements, the bi-iliac diameter (width of the pelvic crest) and the thoracic width, are combined with a measurement of height to locate a child's appropriate weight on the tables prepared by Pryor. Possible nutritional deficiencies are identified by comparing actual weight to the tabled appropriate weight.

Pelidisi formula[8]

To deal with nutritional problems resulting from wartime activities during World War I a relatively simple method of identification was sought. Pirquet and his coworkers determined that for the normal person ten times the weight (in grams) is approximately equal to the cube of sitting height (in centimeters). This relationship is expressed in the following formula:

$$\text{Pelidisi} = \frac{\sqrt[3]{10 \times \text{weight (gm)}}}{\text{sitting height (cm)}} = 100 \text{ percent}$$

Table 16.1 The ACH index of nutritional status (ages 7–12)

Width of hips	Minimum difference between arm girth and chest depth	
	Boys	Girls
Below 20.0	0.0	0.5
20.0–20.4	0.0	1.0
20.5–20.9	0.4	1.6
21.0–21.4	1.0	2.1
21.5–21.9	1.6	2.6
22.0–22.4	2.2	3.0
22.5–22.9	2.7	3.4
23.0–23.4	3.3	3.8
23.5–23.9	3.8	4.2
24.0–24.4	4.2	4.5
24.5–24.9	4.7	4.8
25.0–25.4	5.1	5.1
25.5–25.9	5.6	5.4
26.0–26.4	6.0	5.6
26.5–26.9	6.3	5.8
27.0–27.4	6.7	6.0
27.5–27.9	7.0	6.1
28.0–28.4	7.3	6.2
28.5–28.9	7.6	6.3
Over 28.9	7.9	6.4

Source: Raymond Franzen and George Palmer, *The ACH Index of Nutritional Status* (New York: American Child Health Association, 1934).

The pelidisi for children can be obtained without computation by referring to a table provided in the reference. In addition, information regarding the interpretation of the pelidisi values obtained is provided.

BODY COMPOSITION

The human body is composed of four major components: water, bone, muscle and organs, and fat. Although it is true that bone density changes with age, and fluid levels of the body can be rather drastically altered (water loss from strenuous exercise, for example), in general, these components can be accounted for and the measurement of body composition reduces to an assessment of the percentages of body weight composed of muscle and fat. Several methods have been devised and investigated[9] to accomplish this, including chemical analysis and the use of ultrasonics to estimate the amount of fat under the skin.

The most accurate methods generally used for research purposes are underwater weighing and X-ray analysis of absorption of radioactive materials. Although impractical for the teacher due to equipment demands, underwater weighing has been used to validate several of the techniques described later for determining body composition. Basically, underwater weighing involves the determination of a person's density, which is in turn used to determine the specific gravity of the body. Once this is known, the percentage of fat can be obtained by means of a formula that accounts for the differences in densities of the various body components (fat being the least dense).

In general, two categories of practical procedures for assessing body composition may be identified. Although stated in various ways, the basic method in both of these categories is to predict ideal weight from certain measurements and compare this to actual weight. For one group of procedures, measures of various circumferences and diameters are used; for the other group, skinfold measures are used.

Measures of diameters and circumferences to assess body composition

As previously mentioned, weight tables based only on height, age, and sex caused confusion between proper weight and average weight due to the lack of control for various skeletal configurations. This fact did not go unnoticed and consequently several investigators[10] have proposed solutions to rectify the omission. An annotated list of some further investigations is presented below.

Willoughby's optimal proportions method[11]

Fifty-two adult males and twenty adult females visually rated good to excellent in general status of physique were measured to gather initial data on twenty-six ratios obtained by dividing the dimension of a selected body part by the dimension of another selected body part. For example, ratios of 4.26 for men and 4.54 for women were obtained for the girth of the hips divided by the ankle girth. Refinement of the data resulted in the use of six measurements (ankle girth, mean wrist girth, mean knee girth, biacromial diameter, bi-iliac diameter, and bitrochanteric diameter) and a series of tables to determine optimal weight per inch of height. Multiplication of this value by height yields optimal body weight.

Quimby weight analysis[12]

From data gathered on 2,500 males aged 16 to 22, Quimby selected five measurements (height, shoulder width, chest width, chest depth, and hip width) for predicting actual body weight. Eight regression equations (one each for the ages 16¼, 16¾, 17½, 18½, 19½, 20½, 21½, and 22½) are presented in the references, as are directions for taking the measurements and tables for multiplying the obtained measurements by the regression constants. The author suggests the regression equation for 22-year-olds may be suitable for adults, as skeletal changes diminish above this age.

Cureton-Nordstrom skeletal index[13]

A regression equation requiring measurements of chest breadth, ankle girth, chest depth, hip width, and height is given in the reference as well as tables for obtaining the products of the measurements and the regression equation constants.

McCloy weight prediction method[14]

Measurements include height, knee width, hip width, and chest circumference, the latter two measurements are for fat measured through skinfold techniques. Fifteen regression equations (one for each age, four through eighteen) for girls and fifteen for boys are given in the reference, along with directions for obtaining the measurements, tables for converting the measurements, and sample worksheets for recording and computing predicted weights.

Wellesley weight prediction table[15]

Data were gathered from 1,780 females aged 16–20 from nineteen colleges throughout the United States. Measurements of height, weight, chest depth, hip width, and age were used from 1,580 of the subjects. Refinements of the data lead to a regression equation:

Weight = 2.65 × height (inches)+ 2.56 × chest depth (centimeters) + 2.59 × chest depth (centimeters) − 154.3

which was further simplified to
Weight = 2.6 × sum of the three measurements − 154.3.

Directions for obtaining the measurements and a table that is actually a series of solutions for various sums substituted in the simplified equation are given in the reference.

Turner's optimal weight method[16]

Through measurement of 1,612 females, Turner suggests a modification of Willoughby's system for predicting weight. Turner's modification involves eliminating the knee girth measurement, substituting a measurement of chest width for that of biacromial width, and the introduction of a regression equation rather than the multiplication of height by a constant representing the optimal weight per inch of height. With all measurements made to the nearest tenth of an inch, Turner's equation is:

Weight = .25 height + 6.29 × chest width + 3.14 × bi-iliac width + 4.89 bitrochanteric width + 7.25 × mean wrist girth + 11.85 × mean ankle girth − 179.02.

Hector's weight prediction, method[17]

Through the use of measurements made by previous investigators on thirty-one males, Hector calculated regression equations to predict total body weight and lean body weight. The equations and their method of derivation are presented in the reference.

Behnke's assessment of body build[18]

Behnke also originated a procedure for determining lean body weight. The steps necessary for assessing body weight, taking into account skeletal size, follow (all measurements are in centimeters):

1. Chest width—distance between calipers when placed under each arm at the level of the fifth to sixth rib (nipple level for males) during course of normal breathing.

2. Hip width—distance between the most widely separated parts of the iliac crests; compress soft tissue firmly.

3. Elbow width—distance between the condyles of the humerus, forearm flexed, sum of both elbows required.

4. Knee width—distance from lateral to medial condyles of the tibia, knees flexed as in sitting position, sum of both knees required.

5. Biachromial diameter—distance between the most lateral projections of the biacromial projections, sitting, elbows in contact with body, hands on thighs.

6. Bitrochanteric diameter—greatest distance between the lateral projections of the trochanters, standing; compress soft tissue firmly.

7. Wrist width—distance between the styloid processes of the radius and ulna, sum of both wrists required.

8. Ankle width—distance between the malleoli of the tibia and fibula, standing, feet parallel, about six inches apart, sum of both ankles required.

After recording these measurements the lean body weight is calculated in the following manner:

Step 1. Divide each measurement by the appropriate constant from Table 16.2

Step 2. Sum the eight quotients obtained in step 1 and divide this sum by 8 to find the mean.

Step 3. Square the mean obtained in step 2 and multiply this value by height in decimeters (centimeters/10).

Step 4. Multiply the value obtained in step 3 by 2.2 to convert kilograms to pounds.

The value obtained in step 4 is lean body weight or the amount of the body weight composed of all the components of the body except fat. To determine the percentage of fat use the following equation:

$$\% \text{ fat} = \frac{\text{actual weight} - \text{lean body weight}}{\text{actual body weight}}$$

Although various authorities disagree as to the exact percentage of fat desirable, most values suggested are in the proximity of 16 percent for men and 20 percent for women

Table 16.2   Constants for Behnke's body build assessment

Measurement	Constant	
	Males	*Females*
Chest width	15.9	14.8
Hip width	15.6	16.7
Elbows	7.4	6.9
Knees	9.8	10.3
Biacromium	21.6	20.4
Bitrochanter	17.4	18.6
Wrists	5.9	5.6
Ankles	7.4	7.4

Skinfold measures to assess body composition

Although some investigators were experimenting with skinfold measurements several years ago, relatively recent refinements in the instruments used have contributed to the increased use in this procedure for assessing body composition. With proper equipment, sufficient skill at locating certain anatomical landmarks, and some practice with the technique of using skinfold calipers, the measurement of subcutaneous fat has been found to be a fairly valid method for determining total body fat. The skinfold technique, although not difficult, does require practice to obtain reliable measures. The technique in-

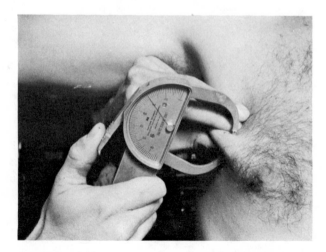

volves grasping a pinch of skin between the thumb and index finger and placing the caliper about one centimeter above the thumb and finger. The resulting measurement represents two layers of skin and the layer of fat at the site.

As with measures of circumferences and diameters, investigators have proposed a number of different combinations of skinfold measurements and regression equations for the determination of the percentage of fat and/or lean body weight of the human body. Probably the four most common sites used to measure fat with the skinfold technique are the back of the upper arm over the triceps muscle, the inferior angle of the scapula, the side of the abdomen above the hip at the umbilicus level, and the front of the thigh. An annotated list of some of the skinfold procedures recommended for assessing body composition follows.

Brozek and Keys equations[19]
Using measurements from 159 college-age men and 223 men between forty-five and fifty-five years of age, the authors constructed norms giving the values at the 20th, 40th, 50th, 60th, and 80th percentiles for specific gravity, percentage of body fat, various skinfold measures, and chest circumference for both groups of subjects involved. Several regression equations for predicting specific gravity from one or more variables are given in the reference.

Pascale, Grossman, Sloane, and Frankel equation[20]
Three skinfold measurements from the chest, five from the abdomen, one from the arm, and one from the back were secured from eighty-eight males between the ages of seventeen and twenty-five. The directions for obtaining the measurements are given in the reference. The following regression equation was found to have a multiple correlation of .85 with body density as determined by underwater weighing (measurements are in centimeters):

$$\text{Body density} = 1.088468 - .007123X_1 - .004834X_2 - .005513X_3$$

where X_1 = skinfold on chest in the midaxillary line at the level of the xyphoid

X_2 = skinfold on chest in the juxtanipple position

X_3 = skinfold on the back of the arm at the point midway between the tip of the acromium and the tip of the olecranon.

Young, Martin, Tensuan, and Blondin equations[21]
The authors made skinfold measurements at twelve sites and determined the specific gravity by underwater weighing ninety-four college women between the ages of seventeen and twenty-seven. Along with directions for locating the twelve sites, ten regression equations involving various combinations of from one to twelve skinfold measurements are given in the reference. Also presented is a table for converting specific gravity values to percentage of fat of body weight.

Sloan equations[22]

Using data secured from fifty white males aged eighteen to twenty-six, Sloan presents various regression equations for predicting body density. Of the seven skinfold measurements taken, the one at the thigh had the highest correlation with an underwater weighing assessment of body density (.80). By adding the scapula skinfold measurement, this correlation was increased to .845. The corresponding regression equation (measurements in millimeters) is as follows:

$$\text{Body density (g/ml)} = 1.1043 - .001327X_1 - .001310X_2$$

where X_1 = thigh skinfold: vertical fold in anterior midline of thigh halfway from inguinal fold to top of patella.

X_2 = scapula skinfold: fold running downward and laterally at approximately 30° to vertical from inferior angle of scapula.

Incidentally, Sloan found the less expensive, less cumbersome skinfold technique to be as accurate as the use of ultrasonic measurement for predicting body density.

Combinations of skinfold, circumference, and diameter measures to assess body composition

As would seem logical, investigators have begun to combine measurements of circumferences and diameters with skinfold measurements and to propose regression equations to predict the related parameters of body density, specific gravity, and/or lean body weight from these combined measurements. Two of the most exhaustive studies conducted to date, one on college-age males and another on college-age females, are discussed below.

Wilmore and Behnke equations[23] (College-age males)

Seven skinfold measurements and measurements of twenty-five and twenty various circumferences and diameters, respectively, were obtained from 133 college men. Using underwater weighing procedures for establishing criterion values, twelve regression equations are presented, six to predict body density, and six to predict lean body weight. For each of these two parameters a regression equation is presented using two or five skinfold measurements, two or five measurements of circumferences and/or diameters, and two or five combinations of both types of measurements. The most accurate prediction for both body density and lean body weight is the equation involving a combination of five circumference, diameter, and skinfold measurements. A multiple correlation of .958 is reported for the following combination:

$$\text{Lean body weight} = 10.14 + .93X_1 - .19X_2 + .64X_3 + .49X_4 - .59X_5$$

where X_1 = weight (kg)

X_2 = thigh skinfold (mm)

X_3 = bi-iliac diameter (cm)

X_4 = neck circumference (cm)

X_5 = abdomen circumference (cm)

Wilmore and Behnke equations[24] *(College-age females)*

In a study similar to the one described above, Wilmore and Behnke determined regression equations for predicting the density and lean body weight of college-age women. Three regression equations, one involving skinfold measurements only, one involving measurements of circumferences and diameters only, and one combining both types of measurements, are presented to predict density. Three other equations following the same format are presented for predicting lean body weight. Underwater weighing was used to obtain the criterion values and data from 128 college-age women were involved. The highest multiple correlation was obtained between the lean body weight assessed from underwater weighing and the variables included in the following regression equation:

$$\text{Lean body weight} = 1.661 + .668X_1 - .158X_2 - .081X_3 + .555X_4 - .141X_5$$

where

X_1 = weight (kg)
X_2 = scapula skinfold (mm)
X_3 = triceps skinfold (mm)
X_4 = neck circumference (cm)
X_5 = maximum abdomen circumference (cm)

From an additional part of their studies these authors report finding evidence that the various regression equations proposed over the years produce maximum predictive accuracy only when applied to samples similar to those from which the original equations were derived.

SOMATOTYPING

In an investigation of the long-held belief that human characteristics such as personality are related to body build, Sheldon and others[25] originated a method of classifying body types. The first step in the system is identifying the predominant component of body type as belonging to one of three categories. The categories are endomorphy (dominated by soft-roundness of the body), mesomorphy (dominated by muscle, bone, and connective tissue), and ectomorphy (dominated by linearity and fragility). Each individual is classified as possessing varying amounts of all three components. Scoring was originally done by assigning a value of 1 to 7 for each component. Later the use of half points was introduced. The three components are always listed in the order given above. For example, an extreme endomorph, an extreme mesomorph, and an extreme ectomorph would be identified by 711, 171, and 117 respectively. Using the whole numbers only, 343 combinations of the ratings are possible. In Atlas of Man[26] Sheldon describes and illustrates 88 of these combinations and details the procedures for somatotyping.

Due to the necessity for expensive photographic equipment and the amount of time required to become proficient with the Sheldon somatotyping technique, other investigators[27] have proposed simplified variations of the body-type classification. These systems range from the use of a subjective visual appraisal of a child to the use of regression equations requiring the ponderal index (height in inches divided by cube root of weight in pounds) and

In somatotyping, each individual is classified as possessing varying degrees of endomorphic, mesomorphic, and ectomorphic characteristics

a measurement of leg length. The directions for the application of these simplified versions of body-type classifications are found in the references.

BODY ALIGNMENT

The measurement of body alignment, or posture, is made difficult by the fact that there is little agreement on what specifically constitutes good posture. Some of the earliest attempts to assess posture by Bancroft[28] and others[29] relied on the subjective judgment of the examiner in determining deviations from normal and used a pole or a plumb line to decide whether or not the body segments were aligned properly. Since the definition of proper alignment of the body segments was not necessarily consistent among examiners, these tests were not very objective.

In an effort to improve on posture measurement, several attempts were made in the late 1920s and throughout the 1930s to construct common standards against which posture could be judged. These standards usually took the form of silhouettes or photographs. Brownell,[30] for example, had judges rate silhouettes of ninth-grade boys and from these data developed a scale of thirteen silhouettes, each having a numerical score ranging from 20 to 120. To use the scale the examiner compared a silhouette of the student being evaluated with each of the thirteen standards, starting at one end of the scale. The procedure was repeated starting at the other end, and the posture grade was obtained by averaging the scores for the two standards thus selected. Christenson[31] in 1933 reported a technique for superimposing a photograph of the student on the standards devised by Brownell and provided evidence that this procedure increased evaluation consistency.

Using methods similar to those of Brownell, Crook[32] devised a series of thirteen silhouettes to be used to evaluate the posture of preschool children. Other techniques, such as Hubbard's[33] use of shadow-silhouettes and Korb's[34] Comparograph, were introduced in the late 1930s to improve the objectivity and reliability of the use of silhouettes. The shadow-silhouettes, which range between photographs and silhouettes, were proposed as an improvement because they depict some characteristics, such as muscular development, the direction of the spine, and the difference in the height of the shoulder blades, not visible in the silhouettes. Korb's Comparograph involves photographing the subject in front of a curtain on which has been painted the outline of a normative posture developed from 2,200 subjects.

Objective posture tests

Even with the introduction of silhouettes and the attempts to improve on their use, several investigators were disturbed by the lack of consistency in posture evaluation. The result of this uneasiness was the development of several relatively objective posture tests generally involving photographing subjects to obtain measurements of angles and distances and converting these measurements to a posture grade.

Wellesley posture test[35]

Eleven aluminum pointers are placed on specific anatomical landmarks prior to photographing students. From the resulting print three measurements are obtained:

1. the amount of anteroposterior curvature in the dorsal and lumbar spine

2. the amount of segmental angulation and body tilt

3. the position of the head and neck. These measurements are weighted and summed, finally resulting in a posture grade from one of the fifteen categories encompassed by the labels from A+ to E−. Eight judges and photographs of 858 college-age women were used to establish the norm values. The norms, directions for preparing the student for the photograph, directions for obtaining the required information from the photograph, and explanations of how the validity, objectivity, and reliability of the test were examined are explained in the reference.

Cureton-Gunby conformateur[36]

In a study investigating the precision of various methods of measuring posture, Cureton and others found the use of two devices, the spinograph and the conformateur, to be more accurate than the use of silhouettes. The spinograph is an instrument that yields a tracing of the curvature of the spine. The conformateur is basically a vertical post through which movable rods extend horizontally. With the back of the subject facing the post, the rods are moved so that each one contacts a vertebra. When all the rods are so located they are locked in place.

Yale posture test[37]

Six anatomical landmarks are marked with a flesh pencil and six aluminum markers are placed on the subject prior to being photographed. On the resulting print several lines are drawn and various angles are examined to obtain measurements of the head and neck, kyphosis, lordosis, the chest, the abdomen, the shoulders, the trunk, the hips, and the knees. Complete directions for measuring these angles and considerations of the validity of the method are given in the reference.

This test was later modified[38] to include a procedure of photography using mirrors, making it possible to obtain front, back, side, and top views of the student simultaneously.

Massey posture test[39]

Massey obtained fifty anthropometric measurements and used the conformateur to obtain a silhouette on each of 200 males between the ages of seventeen and twenty-five. Through a process involving scaling and measuring forty angles and indices and using three experts to establish a criterion, Massey calculated a regression equation requiring four angles: head and neck-trunk alignment; trunk-hip alignment; hip-thigh alignment; and thigh-leg alignment. Although the value resulting from substitution in the regression equation correlated .985 with the criterion score, the equation is seldom used since it was found that the sum of the four angles correlated .97 with the criterion score. Complete directions for preparing the photographs and measuring the required angles, as well as comparisons of other posture tests, are found in the reference.

Howland alignometer[40]

The alignometer was developed by Howland as an instrument for both teaching and measuring posture. It consists of two horizontal calibrated pointers attached to a vertical pole. The top adjustable pointer is placed at the center of the sternum, and the lower pointer is located at the superior border of the symphysis pubis. When these two landmarks line up vertically, the student is in a position of balanced trunk alignment. In this position the distance of both pointers from the vertical pole will be equal. If the two pointers are not extended the same distance to touch the two landmarks, improper alignment is indicated.

Functional posture tests

One of the obvious criticisms of most of the posture tests described thus far is that a student's true posture may not be revealed when he or she is standing to be evaluated or photographed. In an attempt to overcome this weakness, some tests have been devised to evaluate posture while the student is engaged in various activities such as walking, sitting, stooping down, and others. These tests, although usually involving much subjective judgment, generally utilize some type of a rating sheet to increase objectivity.

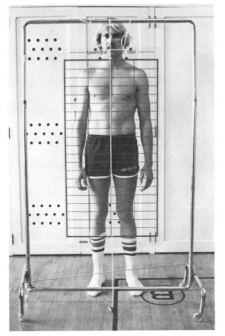

Objective posture tests consist of measuring angles and distances to arrive at a posture grade

Iowa posture test[41]

With this test, ten to twelve students can be measured as a group on foot mechanics (heel-toe walking, absence of pronation, and feet parallel) and on posture while standing, walking, sitting, stooping, and ascending and descending stairs. The various aspects are rated by the examiner as good, fair, or poor by assigning a 3, 2, or 1, respectively. The criteria for each of these ratings as well as a suggested score sheet format are given in the reference.

Washington State College test[42]

Devised as a posture screening exam to select those who require further examination, this test includes a subjective evaluation of the anteroposterior and lateral balance, the alignment of the feet and legs while the subject is standing, and the efficiency of the gait as viewed from the front, back, and side. Directions for administering and scoring the test are given in the reference.

Functional body mechanics appraisal[43]

In a manner similar to that employed in the Iowa Posture Test, a checklist is used to evaluate posture while the child is standing and while performing some everyday activities. A score of excellent, good, fair, or poor is recorded for various aspects of standing posture, lateral balance, sitting mechanics, walk-

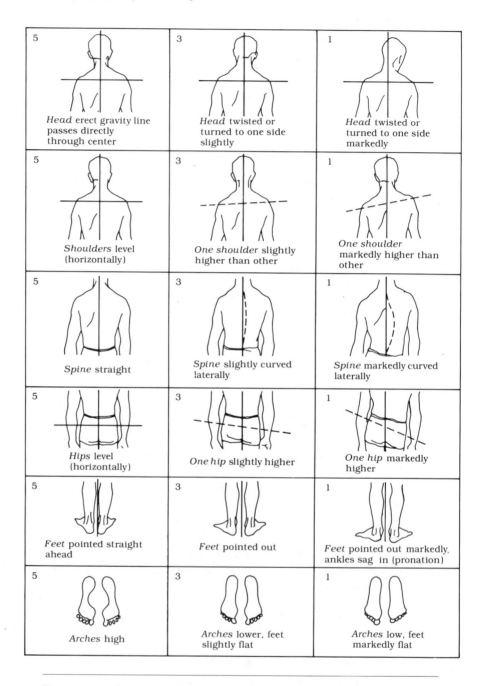

Figure 16.1   Illustrations of good, fair, and poor posture for thirteen aspects of body alignment: New York posture test

5	Neck erect, chin in, head in balance directly above shoulders	3	Neck slightly forward, chin slightly out	1	Neck markedly forward, chin markedly out
5	Chest elevated breastbone furthest forward part of body	3	Chest slightly depressed	1	Chest markedly depressed (flat)
5	Shoulders centered	3	Shoulders slightly forward	1	Shoulders markedly forward (shoulder blades protruding in rear)
5	Upper back normally rounded	3	Upper back slightly more rounded	1	Upper back markedly rounded
5	Trunk erect	3	Trunk inclined to rear slightly	1	Trunk inclined to rear markedly
5	Abdomen flat	3	Abdomen protruding	1	Abdomen protruding and sagging
5	Lower back normally curved	3	Lower back slightly hollow	1	Lower back markedly hollow

Source: Division of Physical Education and Recreation, New York State Education Department.

ing posture, reaching mechanics, climbing and descending stairs, lifting mechanics, and skipping rope. Directions are given in the reference for administering and scoring the test. A floor diagram showing a possible room arrangement for administering the test efficiently and a sample score card are also supplied.

Posture test considerations

As mentioned, part of the difficulty in evaluating body alignment is due to the lack of a definition of good posture. The early "straight line" tests may be criticized because they do not allow for individual differences and are so dependent on the standards of the examiner. To generate standards, several investigators, through the use of "experts" and various types of photographic methods, produced silhouettes, photographs, and the like. Other investigators, disturbed by the lack of reliability even when external standards were applied, reacted by devising "exact" posture tests generally involving the use of photographs and protractors to measure specific angles, and determining methods to convert these measurements into a posture grade. For such a nebulous concept as good posture, this measurement overkill is somewhat analogous to measuring height to the .001th of an inch. Functional posture tests characterized by rating posture while the student is engaged in everyday activities in some ways reverts back to the problems of imposing the examiners' subjective standards on the measurement. Rating sheets offer some improvement in objectivity, but one wonders why it is necessary to set up a particular testing situation to measure posture during everyday activities when students normally engage in these types of movements anyway. In other words, if the physical educator is well trained in recognizing posture defects, there seems to be little reason to set up an artificial, structured testing situation in which to evaluate body alignment.

One possible reason to set aside time for the measurement of posture might be to make sure that every student is assessed at periodic intervals, although it should be recognized that if students are aware that posture is being measured the poses assumed may be other than normal. Probably the best reason for taking class time to measure posture is to draw the students' attention to proper body alignment. To accomplish this objective, a test that is short, simple, and easy to score and perhaps can be administered by the students themselves would be useful. The New York Posture Test meets these criteria.

New York posture test[44]

The score sheet used to obtain a posture score for this test contains illustrations of good, fair, and poor posture for thirteen aspects of body alignment (see Figure 16.1). The student being evaluated is compared to these illustrations and assigned a score of 5, 3, or 1, respectively, on each of the thirteen items. To aid in the comparison, a plumb bob and screen are used and set up as illustrated in Figure 16.2.

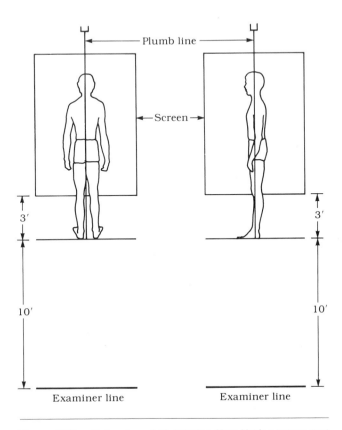

Figure 16.2   Setup for administering New York posture test

For the initial part of the test, the student stands between the plumb bob and the screen, facing the screen. The examiner stands ten feet directly behind the student. The student is told to stand in a comfortable and natural position. The examiner, by comparing what is seen with the illustrations on the score sheet, rates the student on the first five items. The sixth item on the sheet is scored by having the student step on a wet towel and then on a surface that will reveal the condition of the arches. The remaining seven items are similarly evaluated by having the student stand with the left side facing the examiner, in such a position that the left ankle bone is in line with the plumb bob. The thirteen scores are summed to obtain the final posture score, which may be compared to the norms established on over 12,500 students. These norms appear in Table 16.3

Table 16.3   Percentile ranks for posture scores for the New York posture test

Percentile rank	Posture score
99	65
98	65
93	63
84	61
69	59
50	55–57
31	49–53
16	45–47
7	39–43
2	35–37
1	13–33

REFERENCES CITED

[1]B. T. Baldwin, *The Physical Growth of Children From Birth to Maturity.* Iowa City: University of Iowa, Studies in Child Welfare, Vol. 1, 1921, pp. 149–50.

[2]Howard V. Meridith, "A Physical Growth Record for Use in Elementary and High Schools," *American Journal of Public Health,* Vol. 39 (July 1949), pp. 878–85.

[3]Norman C. Wetzel, *The Treatment of Growth Failure in Children* (Cleveland: National Education Association Service, Inc., 1948).

[4]Lester W. Sontag and E. L. Reynolds, "A Practical Method for Analyzing Growth Progress," *Journal of Pediatrics,* Vol. 26 (1945), 327–35.

[5]Nancy Bayley, "Growth Curves of Height and Weight by Age for Boys and Girls, Scaled According to Physical Maturity," *Journal of Pediatrics,* Vol. 48 (1956), 87.

[6]Raymond Franzen and George Palmer, *The ACH Index of Nutritional Status* (New York: American Child Health Association, 1934).

[7]Helen B. Pryor, *Width-Weight Tables* (Stanford, Ca.: Stanford University Press, 1940).

[8]William E. Carter, "The Pirquet System of Nutrition and Its Applicability to American Conditions," *Journal of the American Medical Association,* Vol. 77 (Nov. 1921), 1541.

[9]J. Brozek and A. Keys, "Evaluation of Leanness-Fatness in Man: A Survey of Methods," *Nutrition Abstracts and Reviews,* Vol. 20 (Oct. 1950), 247–56; and *Human Body Composition: Approaches and Applications,* J. Brozek, ed. (London: Pergaman Press, Symposium Publications Division, 1965), 311 pp.

[10]M. L. Boillin, "Determination of the Interrelations, Partial and Multiple, between Various Anthropometric Measures of College Women," *Contributions to Education,* No. 450 (New York: Bureau of Publications Teachers College, Columbia University, 1930); H. Gray and D. C. Parmenter, "Chest Depth as an Indicator of Body Weight," *Journal of the American Medical Association,* Vol. 81 (Dec. 1923), 2183; J. A. Highsmith and D. Sorenson, "A Tentative Weight Prediction Formula," *American Physical Education Review,* Vol. 33 (Sept. 1928), 448–50; M. M.

Johnson, "A Study of Certain Skeletal Dimensions Related to Body Weight in 1030 Women of College Age," Unpublished Master's Thesis, Wellesley College, 1924, 71 pp; and W. Van Dobeln, "Anthropometric Determinations of Fat Free Body Weight," *Acta. Med. Scand.*, Vol. 165 (1959), 37.

[11]David P. Willoughby, "An Anthropometric Method for Arriving at the Optimal Proportions of the Body in Any Adult Individual," *Research Quarterly*, Vol. 3 (March 1932), 48–77.

[12]Rexford C. Quimby, "What a Man Should Weigh," *Research Quarterly*, Vol. 5 (March 1934), 91–109.

[13]Thomas K. Cureton, "Weight and Tissue Symmetry Analysis," *Supplement to Research Quarterly*, Vol. 12 (May 1941), 331–47; and A. Nordstrom, "An Analysis of Body Weight," Unpublished Master's Thesis, Springfield College, 1936, 97 pp.

[14]C. H. McCloy and N. D. Young, *Tests and Measurements in Health and Physical Education*, 3rd ed. (New York: Appleton-Century-Crofts Inc. 1954), pp. 363–72.

[15]F. E. Ludlum and E. Powell, "Chest-Height-Weight Tables for College Women," *Research Quarterly*, Vol. 11 (Oct. 1930), 55–57.

[16]Abby H. Turner, "Body Weights Optimal for Young Adult Women," *Research Quarterly*, Vol. 14 (Oct. 1943), 255–76.

[17]H. Hecter, "The Relationship between Weight and Some Anthropometric Measurements in Adult Males," *Human Biology*, Vol. 31 (Feb. 1959), 235–43.

[18]A. R. Behnke, "Quantitative Assessment of Body Build," *Journal of Applied Physiology*, Vol. 16 (1961), 960–68.

[19]J. Brozek and A. Keys, "The Evaluation of Leanness-Fatness in Man: Norms and Interrelationships," *The British Journal of Nutrition*, Vol. 5 (1951), 194–206.

[20]Lake Pascale, M. Grossman, H. Sloane, and T. Frankel. "Skinfolds and Body Density in 88 Soldiers," *Human Biology*, Vol. 28 (1956), 165–76.

[21]C. Young, M. Martin, R. Tensuan, and J. Blondin, "Predicting Specific Gravity and Body Fatness in Young Women," *Journal of American Dietetic Association*, Vol. 40 (1962), 102–07.

[22]A. W. Sloan, "Estimation of Body Fat in Young Men," *Journal of Applied Physiology*, Vol. 33, No. 3 (1967), 311–15.

[23]J. Wilmore and A. R. Behnke, "An Anthropometric Estimation of Body Density and Lean Body Weight in Young Men," *Journal of Applied Physiology*, Vol. 27, No. 1 (1969), 25–31.

[24]J. Wilmore and A. R. Behnke, "An Anthropometric Estimation of Body Density and Lean Body Weight in Young Women," *The American Journal of Clinical Nutrition*, Vol. 23 (March 1970), 267–74.

[25]W. H. Sheldon, S. S. Stevens, and W. B. Tucker, *The Varieties of Human Physique* (New York: Harper and Row Publishers, 1940).

[26]William H. Sheldon, *Atlas of Man* (New York: Harper and Brothers, 1954).

[27]Cureton, "Weight and Tissue Symmetry Analysis"; Richard Munroe, "Relationships between Somatotype Components and Maturity, Structural Strength, Muscular Endurance and Motor Ability Measures of Twelve Year Old Boys," Doctoral Dissertation, University of Oregon, Dec. 1964; and C. E. Willgoose, *Evaluation in Health Education and Physical Education* (New York: McGraw-Hill Book Co., 1961), p. 303.

[28]Jessie H. Bancroft, *The Posture of School Children* (New York: The MacMillan Co., 1913), 327 pp.

[29]C. W. Crampton, "Work-a-Day Tests of Good Posture," *American Physical Education Review*, Vol. 30 (November 1925); and Charles L. Lowman, C. Colestock, and H. Cooper. *Corrective Physical Education for Groups* (New York: A. S. Barnes and Co. 1928).

[30]Clifford L. Brownell, *A Scale for Measuring Antero-Posterior Posture of Ninth Grade Boys* (New York: Bureau of Publications, Teachers College, Columbia University, 1928).

[31]Cornell H. Christenson, "An Improvement in Technique for Measuring Antero-Posterior Posture," *Research Quarterly*, Vol. 4 (Dec. 1933), 89–96.

[32]Billie L. Crook, "A Scale for Measuring the Antero-Posterior Posture of the Preschool Child," *Research Quarterly*, Vol. 7 (Dec. 1936), 96–101.

[33]C. H. Hubbard, "Advantages of a New Shadow-Silhouettograph over the Original," *Supplement to Research Quarterly*, Vol. 6 (March 1935), 50–53.

[34]Edwin M. Korb, "A Method to Increase the Validity of Measuring Posture," *Research Quarterly*, Vol. 10 (March 1939), 142–49.

[35]Charlotte MacEwan and E. C. Howe, "An Objective Method of Grading Posture," *Research Quarterly*, Vol. 3 (Oct. 1932), 144–57.

[36]T. K. Cureton, J. S. Wickens, and H. P. Elder. "Reliability and Objectivity of the Springfield Postural Measurements," *Supplement to Research Quarterly*, Vol. 6 (May 1935), 81–92.

[37]J. S. Wickens and O. W. Kiphuth, "Body Mechanics Analysis of Yale University Freshmen," *Research Quarterly*, Vol. 8 (Dec. 1937), 38–48.

[38]Carlton R. Meyers and T. E. Blesh, *Measurement in Physical Education* (New York: The Ronald Press Co. 1962), pp. 279–84.

[39]W. W. Massey, "A Critical Study of Objective Methods for Measuring Anterior Posterior Posture with a Simplified Technique," *Research Quarterly*, Vol. 14 (March 1943), 3–22.

[40]I. S. Howland, *Body Alignment in Fundamental Motor Skills* (New York: Exposition Press, 1953), 78–80.

[41]McCloy and Young, *Tests and Measurements in Health and Physical Education*, 3rd ed., pp. 257–61.

[42]Donald K. Mathews, *Measurement in Physical Education*, 4th ed. (Philadelphia: W. B. Saunders Co., 1973), pp. 312–14.

[43]Mathews, *Measurement in Physical Education*, 4th ed.

[44]*State of New York Physical Fitness Test: A Manual for Teachers of Physical Education* (Albany, N.Y.: Division of Health, Physical Education and Recreation, New York State Education Department, 1958).

Chapter 17
Physical Condition

Teaching about and developing physical condition are certainly two of the major objectives unique to physical education. Although differences of opinion exist among physical educators as to what factors are primary components of physical condition, and conflicts can be found in the literature regarding the optimum methods of developing and maintaining these factors, most would agree on the importance of sound physical conditioning practices.

This chapter will not debate what is or should be considered a factor of physical condition, the definition of physical fitness, or the activities important for developing any of the several possible factors. It will identify and expose the reader to measurements that might be adopted or modified to assess physical condition or particular aspects of it. The four main topics are cardiovascular fitness, muscular endurance, muscular strength, and motor fitness.

CARDIOVASCULAR FITNESS TESTS

Measurement of the fitness of the cardiovascular system centers around the efficiency of the body to take in, transport, and utilize oxygen. In the laboratory setting relatively sophisticated techniques have been developed to measure what is called "maximum oxygen uptake." However, these techniques require equipment, such as treadmills and bicycle ergometers, not generally available to the typical physical educator. Several practical methods, some more successful than others, have been suggested to measure the efficiency of the pulmonary and cardiovascular systems.

At the beginning of the twentieth century several tests[1] were devised involving various combinations of such measurements as pulse rate, systolic, and diastolic pressures. These tests often require determining changes in these parameters with changes in position (lying, sitting, standing). The measurements obtained are substituted into formulas, and the resulting values are purported to be an indication of the efficiency of the heart. An example of this type of test is presented below.

Barach energy index[2]

The person to be tested sits until a constant heart rate is achieved. Then the systolic pressure, diastolic pressure, and the per minute heart rate are substituted in the following formula:

$$\text{Energy index} = \frac{\text{pulse rate (systolic pressure + diastolic pressure)}}{100}$$

Values between 110 and 160 are considered good. Scoring above 200 or below 90, however, is cause for alarm according to Barach.

Around 1920 the first tests[3] using an assessment of heart rate recovery time were reported. In general these tests involve taking a resting heart rate (and in some cases pulse pressure measures), running in place or lifting dumbbells for a specified time, measuring pulse and/or pressures again at specified intervals, and comparing the recovery time to scoring tables to obtain an estimate of cardiovascular efficiency.

These early recovery rate tests led to the development between 1920 and 1945 of several similar tests,[4] some of which are still in use. Although the tests devised during this period are more sophisticated than the earlier tests in regard to standardized procedures, carefully specified exercise durations, reported reliability data, and normative information, they generally involve the same basic format of obtaining baseline measurements, exercising, obtaining recovery measurements at specified intervals, and calculating an index to indicate cardiovascular efficiency.

Initial measurements include reclining, sitting, and standing pulse rate and systolic and diastolic pressures. In some of the tests no initial measures are required. The exercise involved in most of these tests requires stepping up and down on a bench at a prescribed rate. However, many differences exist among these tests in the height of the bench, the rate of stepping, and the length of time the exercise is continued. For example, the Tuttle Pulse-Ratio Test uses a thirteen-inch bench whereas the Harvard Step Test requires a twenty-inch bench. The rate of exercise varies from twenty steps per minute in the Schneider test to forty steps per minute in the Taylor Pack Test. The duration of exercise varies from fifteen seconds in the Schneider Test to five minutes in the Harvard Step Test to exhaustion in the Taylor Pack Test.

The recovery measure is almost always heart rate. Some tests measure heart rate immediately after cessation of exercise; others specify various time intervals between pulse counts. The Schneider Test differs in this respect by measuring the time required for the heart to return to the normal standing rate.

A great variety of methods of interpreting the obtained measures are presented by the test constructors and others. Generally, the values are substituted into a formula resulting in an index of some sort. Often normative data are presented for the purpose of interpreting the numerical index into such categories as excellent, fair, and poor. In one test, the McCloy Cardiovascular Rating of Present Health, regression formulas are used to obtain the rating.

Another approach to devising a test for measuring cardiovascular efficiency was taken by McCurdy and Larson.[5] Using measures on 286 college male freshmen as the "average" criterion, 77 infirmary cases as the "poor" criterion, and 49 varsity swimmers as the "good" criterion, a list of twenty-six initial test items was reduced to five (consisting of sitting diastolic pressure, breath holding for twenty seconds after a standard exercise, difference between standing normal pulse rate and pulse rate two minutes after exercise, sitting pulse rate, and standing pulse rate). Methods of scoring, evidence of reliability, and T-score norms are provided in the reference.

To illustrate the general nature of these types of tests, the Harvard Step Test is described below.

Harvard step test[6]

No initial measurements are required. The test begins with the exercise portion, which consists of stepping up and down on a twenty-inch bench at the rate of thirty steps per minute. (Since each step consists of four beats—one foot up, other foot up, first foot down, other foot down—a metronome is set at 120 beats per minute and the students keep pace.) The exercise is continued for a maximum of five minutes. At the end of five minutes (or less if the student cannot maintain the pace) the student sits down and at one, two, and three minutes after cessation of exercise the pulse is taken for thirty seconds by a partner. The various measures are substituted into the following formula to obtain an index of physical condition:

$$\text{Index} = \frac{\text{Seconds of exercise completed} \times 100}{\text{Sum of three pulse counts} \times 2}$$

This index is then compared to the following chart for interpretation.

Above 90	excellent
80–90	high average
65–79	low average
55–64	good
Below 55′	poor

Several modifications and revisions[7] of this test have been presented in the literature. The modifications generally involve changing the bench height, altering the duration of the exercise, and providing normative data for several categories of students in addition to college males.

Since 1945 several additional revisions[8] of the basic format of the Harvard Step Test have been proposed and some different approaches to measuring cardiovascular efficiency have been suggested. Several of the newer approaches require modern equipment not usually available to the public school physical educator. For example, the Balke Treadmill Test[9] involves determining the number of minutes of walking on a treadmill at a specified rate and angle required to raise the heart rate to 180 beats per minute. However, some recent practical tests have also been devised for assessing cardiovascular fitness. An example is the Carlson Fatigue Curve Test.[10] In this test a student alternately runs in place as fast as possible for ten seconds and rests for ten seconds until ten bouts of running have been completed. The total number of times the right foot hits the ground during the ten bouts represents the "production" or work done by the student. Five pulse counts taken for ten seconds each time (prior to the activity, ten seconds and two, four, and six minutes after the cessation of the activity) are added together and the sum is multiplied by 6 to represent the "cost" of the activity to the individual. The production and cost values can be plotted in various ways over time to determine changes in cardiovascular fitness levels. This test, which is described fully in the reference, along with minimal normative data obtained from a study using 200 soldiers as subjects, has several advantages. It requires a minimum of equipment, permitting a large group of students to be tested at one time, and it is suitable as a conditioner as well as a measurement device. To aid in the counting of the number of times the right foot contacts the floor, it is suggested that the student being tested remove the left shoe.

Another example of a practical test to measure cardiovascular fitness is the twelve-minute run for distance developed and later modified by Cooper[11] to be used in conjunction with his Aerobics program. This simple test merely involves recording the distance a student can negotiate in twelve minutes. The distance is then compared to one of various tables presented by Cooper to determine the fitness level. This test, for which Cooper reports a correlation coefficient of .90 with treadmill measurements of maximum oxygen consumption, and one he subsequently developed involving a measurement of the time required to run 1.5 miles have the same advantages as the Carlson Fatigue Curve Test.

Tests of cardiovascular fitness require close attention to safety considerations and proper administration techniques. Due to the strenuous nature of these tests the teacher would be wise to ensure proper medical clearance before administration.

MUSCULAR ENDURANCE

Muscular endurance is the physiological capacity for a muscle or sometimes a set of muscles to continue functioning at a prescribed level. Some tests used to measure muscular endurance are among the most familiar in physical education. Examples include sit-ups, the flexed-arm hang, and curls, to name a few. Muscular endurance tests are often classified as either dynamic or static. Both of these categories may be further divided into repetitive or timed exercises. Examples of tests in each of the four possible categories are presented below.

Dynamic repetitive

In this category are many of the familiar, traditional physical education tests, including sit-ups, chins, dips, and squat thrusts. Usually each student performs as many repetitions of the exercise as possible until the muscle or muscles involved are unable to repeat the correct movement.

Dynamic timed

Again many familiar endurance exercises are included in this category but a time limit is set during which the student is to complete as many repetitions as possible. An example is the two-minute sit-up test.

Static repetitive

The obvious distinction between dynamic and static tests of muscular endurance is the presence of movement in the former and the lack of it in the latter. An example of a static repetitive test of muscular endurance is a grip strength test in which the student is required to exert a particular force at prescribed intervals. Usually a metronome is used to indicate the required cadence.

Static timed

The classical example of a static timed test of muscular endurance is the flexed arm hang in which the student, after assuming a position identical to that at the top of a chin-up, holds this position as long as possible. The score is the length of time the position is maintained until the chin drops below the level of the bar.

One of the major reasons the tests mentioned in this section are so popular is the fact that little or no equipment is required for their administration. Also, at least on the surface, they appear to be simple to administer since they seem to involve relatively uncomplicated directions. Unfortunately this is not necessarily the case. These tests often suffer from low objectivity—that is, the scores resulting from the administration of these tests are often contaminated by the lack of consistency among test administrators.

In the chin-up test, for example, consider how differences in the following procedures might alter a student's score. Which grasp is used, the forward or the reverse? Is a full extension required at the bottom of each repetition? Is resting permitted? Is kipping or swinging allowed? Where does the administrator stand to accurately determine if the chin is higher than the bar at the top of the movement?

In the common sit-up it is now recommended that the knees be bent. How far should they be bent? Should the student rotate to touch the opposite elbow to the knee? In the lying portion of the movement what part of the body must touch the floor; the shoulder blades, the elbows, or the head? Must the hands remain clasped behind the head? If so, what determines when they are not? These questions and others must be answered and the decisions enforced if these seemingly simple tests are to be objective and useful for measuring and comparing students in muscular endurance.

MUSCULAR STRENGTH TESTS

As with the assessment of muscular endurance, measures of muscular strength may be classified as static or dynamic depending on whether or not completion of the test requires movement. Often the words isometric and isotonic are substituted for static and dynamic, respectively. Isometric exercises and tests are characterized by muscle contraction with little or no overt movement. Isotonic activities, on the other hand, involve a body part moving through some range of motion while exerting a force. Unlike muscular endurance measurement, where duration (in the form of either time or number of repetitions) is a factor, strength measurement usually is concerned with a single maximal effort.

Current practical muscular strength tests most commonly involve either the measurement of the amount of force exerted during an isometric contraction or the amount of resistance that can be overcome during one complete specific movement. They can be divided into strength indexes, isometric tests, and isotonic tests. Recent developments have added a new category—isokinetic tests in which strength is assessed throughout the range of movement of a muscle or muscle group. Unfortunately the expensive mechanical equipment required is not commonly available to the typical public school educator.

Strength indexes

Near the turn of the century, D. A. Sargent devised the Intercollegiate Strength Test.[12] This battery of tests involving measures of the strength of the expiratory muscles, grip, back, legs, and arms served as the basis of strength measurement for almost fifty years. During this time some investigators[13] concerned themselves with revisions of the Intercollegiate Strength Test. The remaining strength test research reported during this period might be categorized into two areas. Many investigators, working from the premise that strength is basic to most any physical characteristic, devised strength tests to predict such traits as general motor ability and athletic ability. Studies by Anderson[14] and McCloy[15] are examples of these types of strength tests. Other researchers[16] attempted to devise short and practical test batteries to accurately predict total body strength.

In many cases, norms and relatively elaborate scoring procedures were devised for combining the values obtained on various parts of the test batteries. The references cited include these norms, directions for administering the several test items, and in many cases statistical evidence of the quality of the test items and batteries.

Isometric strength tests

The primary task in measuring muscular strength isometrically is quantifying the amount of force exerted during the muscular contraction. This is accomplished through the use of various types of meters consisting basically of a spring arrangement connected to a dial. Generally, on the dial is registered the amount of spring deflection or stretch, and this is usually calibrated to convert the force to pounds or kilograms. Hand grip dynamometers, back and leg lift dynamometers, and tensiometers are examples of such devices.

One of the earliest reported isometric strength tests was devised by Martin.[17] A spring scale with a handle attached to one end and a leather loop to the other is used to measure the force it takes to "break" the position of contraction of a set of muscles. For example, to test the muscles that extend the forearm, the student lies on the back on a table and holds the forearm to be tested perpendicular to the table. The leather loop is placed around the wrist. The tester stands at the head of the table. At a command the student attempts to extend the forearm while the tester pulls in the opposite direction. When the forearm "breaks" by crossing an imaginary vertical line, the test is over. The maximum force recorded before the "break" is the strength score for the particular muscles involved. Various tests for measuring several different muscles are presented in the reference. Unfortunately, the physical effort required on the part of the administrator is considerable, making the test somewhat impractical. The cable-tension strength tests developed by Clarke solved this problem.

Clarke and others originally used tensiometers for assessing the strength of muscles weakened through orthopedic disabilities. In 1964 a study was initiated by Clarke and Munroe[18] in which the tensiometer was used to devise short batteries of tests to measure overall strength of both males and females from fourth grade through college. In all, eight batteries were established, four for males and four for females. For each sex a separate battery was devised for upper elementary school, junior high school, senior high school, and college. Although the researchers started with twenty-five separate test items (using the average score on all twenty-five as the criterion measure), each of the resulting eight batteries consist of some combination of three of the following eight test items: shoulder extension, shoulder flexion, trunk extension, trunk flexion, hip extension, hip flexion, knee extension, and ankle plantar flexion. The multiple correlations between the eight batteries and the criterion range between .928 and .965. Procedures for administering the tests, descriptions of the necessary equipment, and ten sets of norms are presented in the reference.

Isotonic strength tests

Many of the test items in the early strength index test batteries, such as dips and pull-ups, are currently used to measure muscular strength isotonically, but with a very important change. Instead of substituting the number of rep-

etitions into a strength index formula, the present method involves determining the total amount of weight the student can lift in one execution of the exercise and relating this amount to body weight. Through an initial trial and error estimation procedure, an amount of weight is decided on and added to the body by means of belts or ropes and weight plates or dumbbells. The amount of weight is lessened or increased, depending on the result, until the maximum weight lifted during one execution of the exercise is determined. The usual method of accounting for initial body weight differences among students is to form a ratio of total weight lifted to body weight. For example, if, following the above procedure while doing dips on the parallel bars, it is determined that a student weighing 125 pounds can do one correct dip with a 15-pound weight attached, the total weight lifted is 140 pounds (125 + 15). The strength score for this test item would be 1.12, obtained by dividing 140 by 125. In this way strength scores for individuals of differing body weights can be compared meaningfully.

MOTOR FITNESS TESTS

Probably a majority of physical educators would include the measurements discussed thus far in this chapter—cardiovascular fitness, muscular endurance, and muscular strength—under a general heading of physical fitness.

Some would include additional measures (flexibility, for example). For the most part, however, when assessments of flexibility, power, balance, speed, or agility, or combinations of these characteristics, are added to measures of cardiovascular fitness, muscular endurance, and muscular strength, the resulting battery is classified as a motor fitness test. In general, the term *motor fitness* is taken to be more inclusive than *physical fitness*. Further, the terms *athletic ability* or *general motor ability* are usually considered even more inclusive than *motor fitness* since they include elements of skill and coordination. Although complete agreement will not be likely among all physical educators, one fairly common interpretation of the relationship among these terms is shown in Figure 17.1.

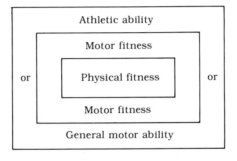

Figure 17.1   Relationships among some common fitness terms

A great number of tests can be found in the literature that might serve to measure motor fitness (although the names of the tests do not always suggest this as their purpose.) The AAHPERD Youth Fitness Test will be described in some detail as an example of this type of battery; several others will be listed and in some cases annotated.

AAHPERD youth fitness test[19]
In the mid and late 1950s a significant concern for the fitness levels of the youth of America developed as a result of several factors, including the large number of young men rejected during military physical examinations and the finding by Kraus[20] and others that American children did not compare well to children of other countries on very basic tests of fitness. One result of this growing concern was the creation of several national committees to investigate the problem. Some members of the AAHPERD Research Council constituted one such committee and, although several other individuals and organizations were to be involved, it was this group that initiated what is now termed the AAHPERD Youth Fitness Test. From its inception in 1957, the test has undergone two major revisions and updating of normative data, the latest occurring

in 1975. Currently a new revision is being contemplated that would separate the health-related items from the motor performance items. The health-related items will involve assessment of abdominal strength, flexibility, cardiovascular endurance, and body composition. This battery would be classified more as a physical fitness test than a motor fitness test.

The AAHPERD Youth Fitness Test consists of six items and is designed to measure overall general fitness of both boys and girls in grades five through twelve. The six items are pull-ups (boys), flexed arm hang (girls), flexed leg sit-ups for one minute, shuttle run, standing long jump, 50-yard dash, and 600-yard run-walk (or optional runs of one mile or nine minutes for age ten to twelve or one and one-half miles or twelve minutes for ages thirteen and over). In the AAHPERD Youth Fitness Test Manual, the equipment, description, rules, and scoring method associated with each of the six test items are given along with several illustrations. In addition, a history of the development of the test battery, methods for recording test scores, various charts and forms useful in administering the battery and reporting the results, and percentile norms (one set based on sex and age and another based on a classification index involving sex, age, height, and weight) are presented. A set of percentile norms for college-age men and women is also included.

Motor fitness tests for elementary school

Very few motor fitness tests are reported that are specifically for elementary school children. Those available usually are constructed for the upper elementary grades or are part of quite general tests designed for use by a wide age range (children six to eighteen years of age, for example). With few exceptions, motor fitness tests for this age group are designed for use by both boys and girls.

Glover physical fitness items for primary children[21]

As the name implies, the seven items (chosen from an initial list of eighteen) are not combined into a particular battery. The scores on each item are compared to percentile norms to determine the status and spot any weaknesses of primary-age children. Directions for administering the test items, percentile norms, and statistical evidence of the reliability and validity of the items are given in the reference.

Kirchner elementary school physical fitness test[22]

Using 150 elementary school boys and an initial list of seventeen items, Kirchner devised a five-item final battery (consisting of five-second run, standing long jump, sit-ups, chest raising, and squat thrust) to measure motor fitness. Illustrated directions for administering the test items and statistical evidence supporting the selections of items for the final battery are given in the reference.

Other motor fitness tests constructed for use totally or partially by elementary school children are as follows:

AAU Physical Fitness and Proficiency Test[24]

California Physical Performance Tests[25]

Indiana Physical Fitness Tests for the Elementary Level[26]

New York State Physical Fitness Test[27]

Oregon Motor Fitness Tests[28]

President's Council on Physical Fitness Screening Test[29]

Motor fitness tests for junior and/or senior high school

Although most motor fitness tests for junior and senior high school children are constructed to accommodate both sexes, some are reported for males and some for females only.

California physical fitness pentathlon[30]

The test battery consists of five events with one event chosen from each of five groups. The events and groups are as follows:

Group	Events
I	Standing long jump, standing hop, step and hop
II	Pull-up, rope climb, push-up
III	150-, 220-, 300-yard run
IV	Bar snap for distance, bar vault for height
V	Frog stand for time, sit-up, squat thrust

Directions for the events and their administration, tables and descriptions for using classification indexes, a sample score sheet, scale score norms, and recommended minimum standards are given in the reference.

The Elder Motor Fitness Test[31] is also designed for use with junior high school males.

Division of girl's and women's sports physical performance test[32]
Illustrated directions, T-score norms, and a discussion of the uses of the test battery are presented in the reference. The eight-item battery consists of the standing long jump, basketball throw, potato race, push-ups, pull-ups, 10-second squat thrust, thirty-second squat thrust, and sit-ups.

Two other motor fitness tests designed for girls only are the Purdue University Motor Fitness Test[33] and the Shaffer Motor Fitness Test.[34]

The New York State physical fitness test[35]
This is an example of the several motor fitness tests devised for use by both sexes at the junior and senior high school level. The components measured to obtain the total score are: posture, accuracy, strength, agility, speed, balance, and endurance. Sample score sheets and a booklet containing a description of the test, general directions, specific test item directions, how to interpret the test scores, how to use the test results, how the test was developed, and norms may be secured by contacting the New York State Education Department.

Other motor fitness tests applicable to these students are as follows:

AAU Physical Fitness and Proficiency Tests[36]

The California Physical Performance Tests[37]

The North Carolina Fitness Test[38]

The Oregon Motor Fitness Test[39]

President's Council on Physical Fitness Screening Test[40]

Motor fitness tests for adults
Several tests of motor fitness for adults have been developed. Most of these are associated with one of the various branches of the military or with a particular university.

United States Air Force tests[41]

Fifteen initial test items were reduced to three from data gathered on over 15,000 subjects. The indoor version of the battery includes sit-ups, pull-ups, and a 250-yard (ten laps of 25 yards each) shuttle run. The outdoor version involves the same events except the shuttle run is 300 yards (five laps of 60 yards each). The reference contains the information on the need for a physical conditioning program, how to plan the program, activities that can be used, techniques of instruction, and organization and administration of the program. The evaluation appears in an appendix of the manual and includes directions, sample score sheets, and norms, as well as descriptions of the test items.

United States Army tests—women[42]

This is a five-item test battery that allows the person being tested to select one event from each of five pairs of exercise type events. Illustrated directions are provided in the reference. The test appears as an appendix, the body of the manual devoted to a discussion of the need for exercise and a specific program for developing physical fitness.

Indiana motor fitness test[43]

The T-score for the chin test is added to the T-score for the push-up test and the resulting sum is multiplied by the T-score for the vertical jump to obtain the final score on this motor fitness test. Included in the reference are T-score norms, directions for administering the test, a sample score card, and data relating to the reliability and validity of the test battery.

Iowa physical fitness battery[44]

T-score norms for six items (bounce, sit-ups, chair stepping, obstacle race, dynamometer pull, and spring scale pull) are listed, and any combination may be used. The multiple correlation coefficients between nine combinations and a measure of work output are listed. The directions for administering each of the six items are given in the reference.

Several other test batteries, such as the University of Illinois Physical Fitness Appraisal[45] and the Yale Physical Fitness Test,[46] are available for use with adults. The JCR Test,[47] the McCloy Home Tests of Physical Condition,[48] and the previously cited California Physical Fitness Pentathlon[49] are examples of other adult motor fitness tests that are not associated with the military or a particular university.

REFERENCES CITED

[1] J. H. Barach, "The Energy Index," *Journal of the American Medical Association,* Vol. 62 (Feb. 1914), 525–27; C. Ward Crampton, "A Test of Condition," *Medical News,* Vol. 87 (Sept. 1905), 529–35; J. H. McCurdy and L. A. Larson, *The Physiology of Exercise,* 3rd ed. (Philadelphia: Lea and Febiger, 1939), pp. 337–39; and W. J. Stone, "The Clinical Significance of High and Low Pulse Pressures with Special Reference to Cardiac Load and Overload," *Journal of the American Medical Association,* Vol. 61 (Oct. 1913), 1256–59.

[2] Barach, "The Energy Index."

[3] T. B. Barringer, Jr., "Studies in the Heart's Functional Capacity as Estimated by the Circulatory Reaction to Graduated Work," *Archives of Internal Medicine,* Vol. 17 (May 1916), 670–76; W. L. Foster, "A Test of Physical Efficiency, *American Physical Education Review,* Vol. 19 (Dec. 1914), 623–36; and "Physical Education in the State of Michigan," *American Physical Education Review,* Vol. 25 (April 1920), 138–39.

[4] Lucien Brouha, "The Step Test: A Simple Method of Measuring Physical Fitness for Muscular Work in Young Men," *Research Quarterly,* Vol. 14 (March 1943), 31–36; J. Gallager, Roswell and Lucien Brouha, "A Simple Method of Testing the Physical Fitness of Boys," *Research Quarterly,* Vol. 14 (March 1943), 23–30; Darwin A. Hindman, "Nomographs for Interpolating Scores on the Schneider Test," *Research Quarterly,* Vol. 1 (Dec. 1930), 26–33; Charles McCloy and Norma Young, *Tests and Measurements in Health and Physical Education,* 3rd ed. (New York: Appleton-Century-Crofts, 1954), pp. 294–95; E. C. Schneider, "A Cardiovascular Rating as a Measure of Physical Fitness and Efficiency," *Journal of the American Medical Association,* Vol. 74 (May 1920), 1507–10; Craig Taylor, "A Maximal Pack Test of Exercise Tolerance," *Research Quarterly,* Vol. 15 (Dec. 1944), 291–302; and W. W. Tuttle, "The Use of the Pulse-Ratio Test for Rating Physical Efficiency," *Research Quarterly,* Vol. 2 (May 1931), 5–17.

[5] J. H. McCurdy and L. A. Larson, "Measurements of Organic Efficiency for the Prediction of Physical Condition," *Supplement to Research Quarterly,* Vol. 6 (May 1935), 11–41.

[6] Brouha, "The Step Test."

[7] Lucien Brouha and J. Roswell Gallager, "A Functional Fitness Test for High School Girls," *Journal of Health and Physical Education,* Vol. 14 (Dec. 1943), 517; L. Brouha and M. V. Ball, *Canadian Red Cross Society's School Meal Study* (Toronto: University of Toronto Press, 1952), p. 55; Harriet L. Clarke, "A Functional Physical Fitness Test for College Women," *Journal of Health and Physical Education,* Vol. 14 (Sept. 1943), 358–59; Doyice J. Cotten, "A Modified Step Test for Group Cardiovascular Testing," *Research Quarterly,* 42 (March 1971), 91–95; Gallager and Brouha, "A Simple Method of Testing the Physical Fitness of Boys"; Jean Hodgkins and Vera Skubic, "Cardiovascular Efficiency Scores for College Women, in the United States," *Research Quarterly,* Vol. 34 (Dec. 1963), 454–461; P. V. Karpovich, Merritt P. Starr, Robert Kimbro, Charles Stoll, and Raymond Weiss. "Physical Reconditioning After Rheumatic Fever," *Journal of the American Medical Association,* Vol. 130 (April 27, 1946), 1198–1203; Ernest D. Michael and Arthur Gallon, "Periodic Changes in the Circulation during Athletic Training as Reflected by a Step Test," *Research Quarterly* (Oct. 1959), 303–11; John L. Patterson, Ashton Graybiel, Harry Flenhardt, and M. Jones Madsen, "Evaluation

and Prediction of Physical Fitness Utilizing Modified Apparatus of the Harvard Step Test," *American Journal of Cardiology,* Vol. 14 (Dec. 1964), 811–27; Vera Skubic and Jean Hodgkins, "Cardiovascular Efficiency Test for Girls and Women," *Research Quarterly,* Vol. 34 (May 1963), 191–98; and Vera Skubic and Jean Hodgkins, "Cardiovascular Efficiency Test Scores for Junior and Senior High School Girls in the United States," *Research Quarterly,* Vol. 35 (May 1964), 184–92.

[8]P. O. Astrand and Irma Ryhming, "A Nomograph for Calculation of Aerobic Capacity (Physical Fitness) from Pulse Rate during Submaximal Work," *Journal of Applied Physiology,* Vol. 7 (Sept. 1954), 218–21; Charles Billings, J. Tomashifski, E. T. Carter, and William Ashe, "Measurement of Human Capacity for Aerobic Muscular Work," *Journal of Applied Physiology,* Vol. 15 (Nov. 1960), 1001–06; and A. W. Sloan, "A Modified Harvard Step Test For Women," *Journal of Applied Physiology,* Vol. 14 (Nov. 1959), 985–86.

[9]B. Balke, G. P. Grillo, E. B. Konecci, and U. C. Luft, "Work Capacity after Blood Donation," *Journal of Applied Physiology,* Vol. 7 (Nov. 1954), 231–38.

[10]H. C. Carlson, "Fatigue Curve Test," *Research Quarterly,* Vol. 16 (Oct. 1945), 169–75.

[11]Kenneth Cooper, *Aerobics* (New York: Bantam Books, 1968), 182 pp.; and Kenneth Cooper, *The New Aerobics* (New York: Bantam Books, 1970), 191 pp.

[12]D. A. Sargent, "Intercollegiate Strength Tests," *American Physical Education Review,* Vol. 2 (Dec. 1897), 216.

[13]Charles McCloy and Norma Young, *Tests and Measurements in Health and Physical Education* (New York: Appleton-Century-Crofts, 1954), p. 129; and Frederick Rogers, *Physical Capacity Tests in the Administration of Physical Education* (New York: Bureau of Publications Teachers College, Columbia University, 1925), 93 pp.

[14]Theresa W. Anderson, "Weighted Strength Tests for the Prediction of Athletic Ability in High School Girls," *Research Quarterly,* Vol. 7 (March 1936), 136–42.

[15]Charles McCloy and Norma Young, *Tests and Measurements in Health and Physical Education* (New York: Appleton-Century-Crofts, 1954), p. 141.

[16]Leonard Larson, "A Factor and Validity Analysis of Strength Variables and Tests with a Test Combination of Chinning, Dipping and Vertical Jump," *Research Quarterly,* Vol. 11 (Dec. 1940), 82–96; and Arthur J. Wendler, "An Analytical Study of Strength Tests Using the Universal Dynamometer," *Supplement to Research Quarterly,* Vol. 6 (Oct. 1935), 81–85.

[17]E. G. Martin, "Tests of Muscular Efficiency," *Physiological Reviews,* Vol. 1 (July 1921), 454–75.

[18]H. H. Clarke and Richard Munroe, *Test Manual: Oregon Cable-Tension Strength Test Batteries For Boys and Girls From Fourth Grade Through College* (Eugene Or.: Microcard Publications in Health, Physical Education, and Recreation, 1970), 65 pp.

[19]*AAHPER Youth Fitness Test: Rev. Ed.* (Washington, D.C.: American Alliance for Health, Physical Education, and Recreation, 1975), 74 pp.

[20]Hans Kraus and Ruth P. Hirschland, "Minimum Muscular Fitness Tests in School Children," *Research Quarterly,* Vol. 25 (May 1954), 178–88.

[21]Elizabeth G. Glover, "Physical Fitness Test Items for Boys and Girls in the First, Second, and Third Grades," Microcard Masters Thesis, The Womens College, University of North Carolina, 1962, 125 pp.

[22]Glenn Kirchner, "The Construction of a Battery of Tests Designed to Measure Strength, Endurance, Power and Speed among Elementary School-Age Boys," Microcard Masters Thesis, University of Oregon, 1959, 106 pp.

[24]*Amateur Athletic Union Physical Fitness Test* (New York: Amateur Athletic Union).

[25]*California Physical Performance Tests,* rev. ed. (Sacramento, Ca.: Bureau of Physical Education, Health Education and Recreation, Ca. State Dept. of Education, 1971), 70 pp.

[26]C. C. Franklin and N. G. Lehsten, "Indiana Physical Fitness Tests for the Elementary Level (Grades 4–8)," *Physical Educator,* Vol. 5 (May 1948), 38–45.

[27]*The New York State Physical Fitness Test: A Manual For Teachers of Physical Education,* rev. ed. (Albany, N.Y.: Physical Education Bureau, State Education Department, 1966), 64 pp.

[28]H. Harrison Clarke, *Application of Measurement to Health and Physical Education,* 4th ed. (Englewood Cliffs, N.J.: Prentice Hall, Inc., 1967), pp. 203–08 and 436–37.

[29]*Youth Physical Fitness: Suggested Elements of a School Centered Program —Parts One and Two* (Washington, D.C.: U.S. Government Printing Office, 1961), 19 pp.

[30]"The California Physical Fitness Pentathlon," *Bulletin of the California State Department of Education,* 11 (Nov. 1942), 25 pp.

[31]Haskell P. Elder, "Appraising the Motor Fitness of Junior High School Boys," Microcard Dissertation, Springfield College, 1956, 174 pp.

[32]Eleanor Metheny, "Physical Performance Levels for High School Girls," *Journal of Health and Physical Education,* Vol. 16 (June 1945), 308–11 and 354–57.

[33]Chappelle Arnett, "The Purdue Motor Fitness Test Batteries for Senior High School Girls," *Research Quarterly,* Vol. 33 (Oct. 1962), 323–28.

[34]Gertrude Shaffer, "A Practical Physical Fitness Test for Junior and Senior High School Girls," *Physical Fitness News Letter* (Eugene: University of Oregon, February 1962).

[35]*The New York State Physical Fitness Test.*

[36]*Amateur Athletic Union Physical Fitness Test.*

[37]*California Physical Performance Tests,* rev. ed.

[38]Harold Barrow and Rosemary McGee, *A Practical Approach to Measurement in Physical Education,* 2nd ed. (Philadelphia: Lea and Febiger, 1971), pp. 249–55.

[39]Clarke, *Application of Measurement to Health and Physical Education,* 4th ed.

[40]*Youth Physical Fitness: Suggested Elements of a School Centered Program —Parts One and Two.*

[41]*Physical Condition: Air Force Manual 160–26* (Washington, D.C.: Government Printing Office, April 1956), 163 pp.

[42]*Physical Fitness Program for Women in the Army: Department of the Army Pamphlet 21–2* (Washington, D.C.: Government Printing Office, Feb. 1965), 37 pp.

[43]Karl Bookwalter, "Further Studies of the Indiana University Motor Fitness Index," *Bulletin of the School of Education,* Indiana University, Vol. 19 (Sept. 1943), 1–22.

[44]M. Gladys Scott and Esther French, *Measurement and Evaluation in Physical Education* (Dubuque, Iowa: WM. C. Brown Publishers, 1959), pp. 307–10.

[45]Thomas Cureton, *Physical Fitness Appraisal and Guidance* (St. Louis: The C.V. Mosby Company, 1947), 390–423.

[46]Erwin Blech and Alfred Scholz, "Ten Year Survey of Physical Fitness Tests at Yale University," *Research Quarterly,* Vol. 28 (Dec. 1957), 321–26.

[47]B. E. Phillips, "The J C R Test," *Research Quarterly,* Vol. 18 (March 1947), 12–29.

[48]Charles McCloy and Norma Young, *Tests and Measurements in Health and Physical Education,* 3rd ed. (New York: Appleton-Century-Crofts, 1954), pp. 224–25.

[49]"The California Physical Fitness Pentathlon."

Chapter 18
Sports Skills

Generally, a large portion of the physical education curriculum is devoted to teaching various sports skills. It naturally follows that a significant portion of the time spent in testing would deal with measuring student achievement in these sports skills and that many tests have been devised for use at various age levels for a great variety of sports.

INDIVIDUAL SPORTS

As a general rule sports in which the participant competes individually, such as archery, bowling, golf, springboard diving, and swimming, are best measured by simply performing the activity and scoring it in the normal manner. The score thus obtained is usually compared to scores made by classmates or to some appropriate set of norms. There are some tests reported, however, that have been designed to measure specific portions of some of these activities (putting in golf, for example). Sample tests for measuring skills in the five previously mentioned sports are presented below.

Archery
For the most part archery tests differ only in the number of arrows shot and/ or the distances from which they are released. Almost all archery tests use a standard archery target set up as illustrated in Figure 18.1

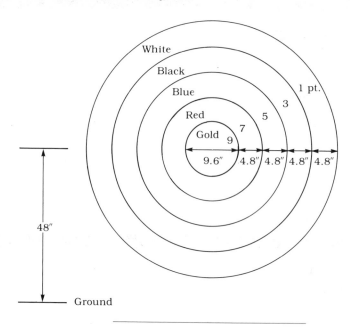

White
Black
Blue
Red
Gold

Ground

48″

Figure 18.1   Standard archery target

AAHPERD archery skill test[1]

Girls shoot two ends (for this test one end equals twelve arrows) from ten yards and twenty yards. Boys shoot two ends from ten, twenty, and thirty yards. A standard archery target and normal scoring procedures are utilized. In the reference, information about equipment and the rules and the procedures to follow are presented along with percentile norms based on sex, five age classifications (12– 13, 14, 15, 16, 17– 18), and distance from the target.

Bohn archery test[2]

Thirty arrows are shot from thirty yards at a standard archery target on each of two test days. Reliability coefficients and validity coefficients are presented in the reference.

Hyde archery achievement tests[3]

The Columbia Round, a standard event used in archery competitions (consisting of twenty-four arrows shot from fifty yards, twenty-four arrows shot from forty yards, and twenty-four arrows shot from thirty yards), is the basis for the scales presented by Hyde. The total of seventy-two arrows is shot in ends of six arrows each, and standard scoring procedures are used. Scales are presented in the reference for the first Columbia Round shot by a student (after a specified minimum of practice) and for the final Columbia Round (at the end of a unit of archery instruction). The second scale is presented in four parts—one part for total score and one part for each of the three specified distances. The procedures used to establish the scales are also described in the reference.

Reichart school archery standards[4]

Reichart suggests that, due to differences in equipment, time, and leadership, variation in standards are necessary to provide motivation for disparate ability groups. The Scholastic Round (twenty-four arrows shot from forty and from thirty yards), the Junior Scholastic Round (twenty-four arrows shot from thirty and from twenty yards), the Range Round (sixty arrows shot from a single distance of either fifty, forty, thirty, or twenty yards), and the Miniature Round (sixty arrows shot from fifteen yards at a modified target) are discussed in the reference.

Bowling

Probably the best assessment of bowling ability is obtained by averaging three to five bowling scores for an individual. However, it is helpful to have norms with which the obtained average can be compared. Two sets of norms for college students are described below. In addition, a test for quantifying an evaluation of spot bowling and a test for measuring bowling form are presented.

Phillips and Summers bowling norms[5]

Scores were obtained from over 3,600 college-age women bowlers. The scores required to classify students into categories of superior, good, average, poor, and inferior are presented for each of eight ability levels.

Martin and Keogh bowling norms[6]

Bowling scores were obtained from over 300 college males and females classified as inexperienced (previously bowled less than ten games and had no formal instruction) and experienced bowlers. Descriptive data regarding the subjects, the procedures used, and norms with categories of superior, good, average, poor, and inferior for both experienced and inexperienced are presented in the reference.

Liba and Olson spot bowling test[7]

Using thirty-three college women who were straight ball bowlers and had completed an eight-week bowling course, Liba and Olson devised a procedure involving two observers using a checklist to objectively rate release point and point of aim accuracy. The procedures and statistical evidence of the worth of the method are presented in the reference.

Vondreau bowling form test[8]

Vondreau devised a rating sheet to evaluate bowling form. Four areas are rated from 1 to 5: shoulders during delivery; path of the ball; backswing, delivery, follow through; and total pinfall for the first three balls. A rating is made in each area for three balls rolled at a full ten-pin set-up. The criteria for each rating, sample evaluation card, and a method for obtaining a quotient and bowling grades using the system are presented in the reference.

Golf

Several tests of specific golf skills have been developed. For the most part they are concerned with the measurement of the two major considerations in golf — distance and accuracy. A partial list of golf tests is presented below. Most of these tests are designed for males and females.

Benson golf test[9]

After five practice shots the student is given twenty trials of hitting a golf ball with a five iron on a test area marked as shown in Figure 18.2.

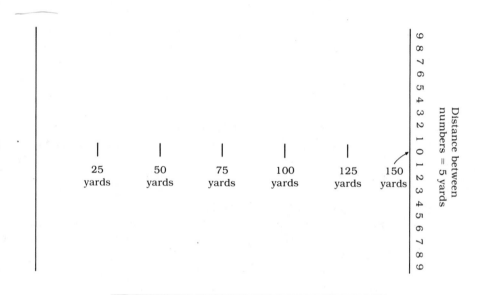

Figure 18.2   Test area markings for Benson golf test

The scorer, standing behind the student being tested, estimates the distance and the amount of deflection for each trial. The two scores that result are the mean of the twenty distance estimates and the mean of the twenty deflection estimates.

Bowen putting test[10]

Bowen devised a test to help determine if differences in points of aim affect success in putting. The test involves twenty-five trials from each of three different distances over four types of terrain. Although no normative data are presented, directions for setting up and administering the test are given in the reference.

Chui golf test[11]

Chui devised two tests to help investigate the effectiveness of an electronic golf device as a teaching aid. One uses a four iron, one uses a seven iron. Both tests involve a target of concentric circles around a pin and a scoring system reflecting the accuracy of the shots and the flight of the ball. Specific distances, scoring procedures, and testing directions are given in the reference.

Clevett golf test[12]

Clevett devised a golf test consisting of hitting a golf ball with various clubs at targets. Three separate tests and targets are described—one for long-distance clubs, one for approach shots, and one for putting. The scoring procedures, target sizes and markings, and test administration procedures are given in the reference.

McKee golf test[13]

The golf test designed by McKee consists of measuring the distance and deflection from a straight line of a golf ball's flight after being hit by a five iron. Each student is given twenty trials, although a ball rolling along the ground or remaining airborne for less than 0.6 seconds is not counted as a trial. Specific directions for laying out the test, methods for calculating range, velocity, angle of impact, and angle of deflection, as well as evidence to suggest that cotton golf balls can be used satisfactorily for this test, are presented in the reference.

Nelson golf pitching test[14]

Nelson's test was constructed to measure a student's ability to pitch close to the pin. It allows three practice trials followed by ten shots at a target consisting of a series of concentric circles with the pin in the center of the smallest circle. Directions for efficiently administering the test to two students at a time and the specific distances and target dimensions are given in the reference.

Vanderhoof golf tests[15]

Vanderhoof devised several batteries of golf tests utilizing various combinations of and scoring procedures for a driving test, a full-swing five-iron test, and a short-swing seven-iron test. In addition to scoring the tests on the basis of where the ball lands, the three test items involve arranging ropes horizontally at specified heights and distances from the tee to assess the vertical component of the flight of the golf ball. As the tests are designed to be performed indoors, plastic golf balls are used. Specific test directions, reliability, validity, and intercorrelational data, and regression equations based on measurements from 110 college females are presented in the reference.

West and Thorpe golf approach shot test[16]

This test was designed to measure the ability to perform an eight-iron approach shot from twelve feet from the pin. A target (see Figure 18.3) consisting of six concentric circles with the pin placed in the center is constructed on a

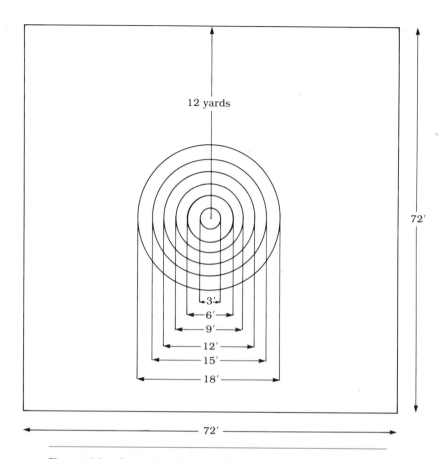

Figure 18.3   Target for West and Thorpe eight-iron approach test

level, closely mown, grassy area. Each student is scored on twelve trials on each of two days. Two practice trials are allowed. Scoring for each trial consists of multiplying the value of the circle in which the ball comes to rest by 1 (if the ball is topped); 2 (if the ball is hit at an angle of projection 29° or lower as measured subjectively by the test administrator); or 3 (if the ball is hit at an angle of 30° or higher). The target specifications, discussion of the test development, and statistical data concerning the reliability of the test are presented in the reference.

Many other tests of golfing ability appear in the literature, often in studies investigating differences in various styles or teaching techniques. For example, in studies by Kelliher[17] and by Neale and Anderson,[18] the merits of conventional and croquet styles of putting are examined. In the Kelliher study two tests are described. One is devised to measure alignment ability, and the other to assess alignment ability plus distance judgment. In the Neale and Anderson study a special measuring device using a light projector and a mirror is described for assessing accuracy of aim.

Springboard diving

To provide for the possibility of competition in individual sports, it is necessary to somehow arrive at a score for a performance. In the individual sports listed thus far the scores are obtained in some objective manner (e.g., number of bowling pins knocked down or number of strokes to get the golf ball into the cup). In several individual sports, such as gymnastics, ice skating, and ski jumping, the scores, or at least some portion of the scores, are determined in a subjective manner involving the rating of a performance. The rating is usually done by "expert" judges, often using set criteria. The NCAA procedures used to determine scores in springboard diving competitions are explained below as an example of a subjective scoring system utilized in an individual sport.

NCAA springboard diving scoring system[19]

Various numbers of diving judges are used depending on the level of competition. It is most common to have three judges, although five or more are often used in championship meets. When more than three judges are used, such procedures as eliminating the highest and lowest awards and/or multiplying by a mathematical constant are employed to adjust each diver's final score in such a way that it reflects what the score would have been with three judges. This is done, of course, to permit comparisons of scores from situations in which differing numbers of judges are present.

After each dive, each judge gives a numerical award that may range from 0 to 10 (including values of ½). This numerical score is used to quantify the verbal description of the dive according to the following criteria:

0	completely failed
½ – 2	unsatisfactory
2½ – 4½	deficient
5 – 6	satisfactory
6½ – 8	good
8½ – 10	very good

Each judge takes into account the diver's performance on the approach to the end of the board, the take-off, the technique and grace of the dive during the passage through the air, and the entry into the water. The award given by each judge is to reflect the overall assessment of success on these stages of the dive. The difficulty of the dive is not to be considered by the judge. Each dive listed in the rule book is assigned a degree of difficulty rating (ranging from 1.0 to 3.0). The total award for a dive is obtained by multiplying the sum of the judges' awards by the degree of difficulty for the dive completed.

Finally the total awards for each dive are summed to determine each diver's final score. The diver achieving the highest final score is declared the winner of the competition.

Bennett diving test[20]

To overcome the fact that the normal scoring procedure for springboard diving is too difficult for beginning divers, Bennett devised a test composed of fifty items ranging from simple stunts to difficult dives. An individual's score is simply the number of items passed (according to specified criteria). A student may attempt each item as many times as desired. The complete list of test items and the criteria for passing each satisfactorily, along with some evidence of the validity, reliability, and objectivity of the test, are presented in the reference. Although the test was devised for college-age women, it appears to be applicable to males and females of all ages with little or no modification.

Swimming

In competitive settings, swimming ability is assessed by measuring the amount of time required to cover a specified distance using a particular stroke. In other situations, however, time is not the only criterion used. The references listed below contain examples of some of the types of measurements that have been developed in this area.

Connor swimming test[21]

In a study designed to compare objective (timing and counting the number of strokes required to cover a distance) and subjective (ratings made by judges) scoring methods, Connor used a fifty-yard swim in the prone position and a combined test consisting of a twenty-five-yard swim while prone followed by a twenty-five-yard swim while on the back. Girls and boys aged five to twelve were used as subjects and several tables of correlations are given in the reference.

Cureton swimming endurance test[22]

Cureton developed a regression equation utilizing a 20-yard sprint time and a sum of drop-off times (time differences between successive laps) for the 100-yard swim to determine the endurance of speed swimmers. The equation and directions for its use are given in the reference.

Rosentsweig revision of the power swimming test[23]

In 1957 Fox[24] published a test that measured the power of various swimming strokes by recording the distance swum with five complete strokes. A rope suspended under water was used as a starting point to eliminate the push off from the wall as a factor in the distance covered. In 1968 Rosentsweig published a revision of this test. Changes include using another swimmer rather than a rope to assist in the start, measuring the distance covered at the shoulders rather than the ankles of the swimmer, and using twelve strokes rather than five to allow more variation in the resulting scores. Rosentsweig suggests that a subjective rating and the best distance score from two trials be combined to obtain each swimmer's final score. The reference contains test directions and statistical data obtained from 184 college females for the front crawl, side, elementary back, back crawl, and breast strokes.

Hewitt achievement scores for swimming[25]

Hewitt compiled scaled scores for high school males and females and for college males. The high school data, collected on a total of 647 females and 446 males enrolled in six different high schools, is converted into percentage norms for the following events: twenty-five-yard flutter kick (timed); fifty-yard front crawl (timed); twenty-five-yard elementary back, side, and breast strokes (number of strokes); and ten-minute endurance swim (number of yards covered).

The college data, collected over a period of six years and representing over 6,000 college males (twenty-five-yard pool), are converted to scale score norms for the following events: twenty-and twenty-five-yard underwater swim (number of yards covered); twenty-five-yard front crawl, breast, and back strokes (timed); fifty-yard front crawl, breast, and back strokes (timed); fifty-yard elementary back, side, and breast strokes (number of strokes); and fifteen-minute endurance swim (number of yards covered).

In both references reliability and validity data are presented along with descriptions of administrative procedures for each event.

Pennington swim test[26]

Pennington devised two swimming test batteries for college females in beginning swimming classes. The first was designed to identify swimmers too advanced to be in a beginning swimming class. This battery consists of submersion, prone flotation, and propulsions through the water. Each student is rated in the three categories by two judges using a checklist specifying the number of points for various proficiencies demonstrated by the prospective beginning swimmers. The second test battery was constructed for use at the conclusion of a beginning swimming unit. The battery consists of the following ten items, scored as indicated: treading water (timed with a maximum of five minutes); prone glide with push-off (distance covered); breath holding (timed); bobbing (number performed with maximum of thirty); underwater swimming (distance covered); elementary backstroke (number of strokes to travel twenty-five yards); side stroke (number of strokes to cover twenty-five yards); front crawl (number of yards covered); surface dive (subjectively scored by judges according to a ten-point scale with specific criteria given); and front dive (scored in same manner as surface dive). Specific test directions, reliabilities, and raw data used to establish the test batteries are given in the reference.

DUAL SPORTS

Badminton

Some badminton tests are designed to measure specific skills, such as serving, clearing, or smashing; others attempt to measure overall badminton playing ability. Both types are listed and annotated below.

French and Stalter badminton test[27]

French and Stalter devised six tests to measure badminton playing ability. The six tests (serve, clear, smash, wrist volley, and two footwork tests labeled diagonal and shuttle) were given to fifty-nine players of varying abilities. From the data collected the authors present five regression equations utilizing various combinations of the tests. Specific test directions and reliability and validity data can be found in the reference.

Badminton smash test[28]

Through the use of a mechanical device, badminton shuttlecocks are dropped from overhead to a student located thirteen feet from the net. After seven practice trials each student is given ten tries to smash the shuttlecock into one of two target areas located on the sides of the court on the opposite side of the net. In the reference an illustration of the mechanical device and directions for marking the target areas and scoring the test are provided. In addition, percentile norms based on fifty college males and fifty-two college females are given.

Lockhart and McPherson badminton wall volley[29]

After a fifteen-second practice trial, three trials of thirty seconds each are given with rest between the trials. The student serves toward a wall from behind a starting line located 6½ feet from the wall. On the wall is a line five feet above and parallel to the floor. The object following the serve is to volley the shuttlecock off the wall above the line as many times as possible in the thirty seconds. During the volleying the student may advance toward the wall as far as a restraining line located three feet from the wall. If control of the shuttlecock is lost during the trial it may be restarted with another serve. Statistical data regarding the reliability and validity, along with T-Score norms based on scores from 529 college sophomore females, are found in the reference.

Miller wall volley test[30]

Through film analysis, Miller determined that 7½ feet is the minimum ideal height for a driven clear shot to cross the net and go over the extended racket of an average-sized opponent. After one minute of practice and a period of rest the student taking Miller's wall volley test serves the shuttlecock from a re-straining line ten feet from a wall marked with a line 7½ feet above and parallel to the floor. The serve, if it hits above the line, and every other time the student can hit a sponge-tipped shuttlecock above the line in the thirty-second trial, counts one point. The final score is the total number of legal hits made during three trials. In the reference Miller traces the development of badminton skills tests up to 1951, gives specific directions for the wall volley test, presents re-liability and validity data, and provides normative information based on 100 females and 115 males.

Scott serve and clear tests[31]
For the short-serve test a rope is suspended twenty inches above and parallel to the net. The student serves twenty short serves, attempting to place the shuttlecock between the rope and the top of the net and make it land in a target area having the highest value at the intersection of the short and center lines. (See Figure 18.4.) A rope fourteen feet from the net and eight feet high is used in the clear test to ensure the shuttlecock is hit high and deep. The student must hit the shuttlecock from deep in the court opposite the rope arrangement, attempting to make the shuttlecock go over the rope and land in a target area near the back of the court. For both the short serve and the clear tests twenty trials are given and scored.

Scott and Fox long-serve test[32]
This test uses the same rope arrangement as that used with the Scott clear test but the target area resembles that used in the Scott short-serve test ex-cept, of course, it is located near the intersection of the side boundary and the long service line rather than the short service line. The sum of points awarded for twenty trials constitutes a student's score for this test.

Fencing
Measurements reported for the sport of fencing generally center around de-terminations of reaction time, response time, movement time, and accuracy. Usually mechanical devices involving targets and chronometers are devised for measuring these variables. Sanger[33] describes such a device used in a study to determine the relationships of these characteristics to foil fencing success as established on the basis of a round-robin tournament. Busch[34] describes the construction of a moving fencing target for similar purposes. Interestingly, both authors conclude there is minimal correlation between these variables and fencing success.

Handball
Cornish handball test[35]
Using 134 students and the net score (points scored minus points given up) in a twenty-three-game tournament as the criterion measure, Cornish inves-tigated the efficiency of five handball tests for measuring handball ability. In

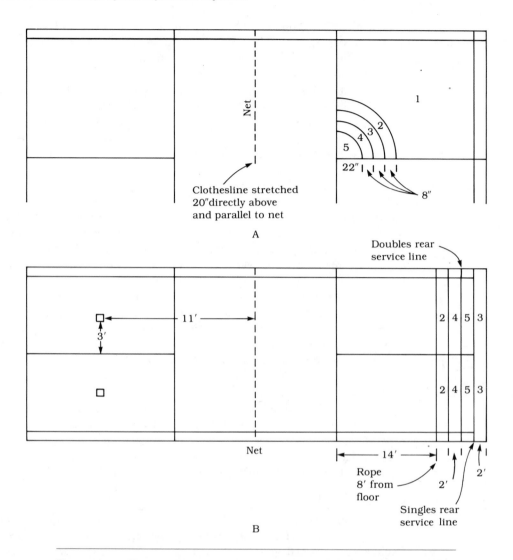

Figure 18.4   Floor markings for Scott badminton serve (A) and clear (B) tests

the reference Cornish describes and illustrates the court markings (see Figure 18.5) for the thirty-second volley, front wall placement, back wall placement, service placement, and power tests. Based on reliability and validity data, Cornish selects the power test as the best single test and the combination of the thirty-second volley and the service placement tests as the best battery to measure handball ability.

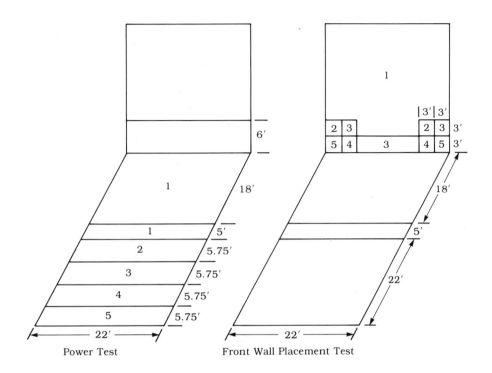

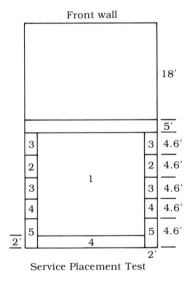

Figure 18.5   Floor and wall markings for Cornish handball test

Pennington handball test[36]

Pennington and three other investigators selected and administered seventeen strength, motor ability, and handball test items to thirty-seven male undergraduate college students. Using average score per game in a partial round-robin tournament as a criterion measure, the authors conclude that the best single test item is the service placement test; the best combination of two items, the service placement and the total wall volley tests; and the best combination of three items, the service placement, the total wall volley, and the back wall placement tests. The test descriptions, one correlation matrix, and the regression equation for the three-item battery are given in the reference.

Railey handball serving tests[37]

Railey devised tests for measuring the velocity of the handball serve and its accuracy. The velocity test requires relatively sophisticated electronic equipment; the accuracy test requires a target painted on the front wall of the handball court. Specific explanations of equipment, target dimensions, and administration procedures for the two tests are given in the reference.

Table tennis
Mott-Lockhart table tennis test[38]

Using a wall volley approach with one side of the table tennis table moved into a vertical position to serve as the wall, Mott and Lockhart developed a table tennis test. A line six inches above the surface of the horizontal portion of the table is chalked on the vertical section of the table to serve as a net reference. Each student is given three nonconsecutive trials of thirty seconds each in which to hit the ball as many times as possible against the vertical portion of the table in a normal table tennis manner. The best of the three trials is taken as the final score. Reliability and validity coefficients are given in the reference, although there is no explanation of how they were obtained. Specific directions, equipment requirements, and T-score norms are also provided in the reference.

Tennis

Many tests to measure tennis ability are reported in the literature. They have progressed from using only a wall volley task, to combining measures of various tennis skills into a test battery, to developing tests as much like the game itself as possible. Brief examples of some of the most commonly used tests and their modifications are presented below.

Dyer backboard test[39]

Among the first of the published tennis tests is the Dyer Backboard Test. In its original form this test required the student to rally a tennis ball against a backboard as many times as possible in thirty seconds. A net line three feet high was drawn on the backboard. The score for the trial was the number of hits on or above the net line minus a number one less than the number of tennis balls used by the student during the thirty-second trial. The score for the test was the sum of the scores for the three trials. A revision of this test was published by Dyer[40] three years after the initial test was reported. In the revision Dyer added a restraining line five feet from the backboard to eliminate the possibility of standing next to the wall and volleying with very short strokes. She also changed the method of obtaining another tennis ball when one went out of control during a trial. Instead of having the new ball tossed or handed to the student by an assistant, a box of tennis balls is placed near the starting point on the court and the person taking the test must secure a new ball when necessary. The scoring procedure was also revised by eliminating the subtraction of the number of extra tennis balls used during a trial. The score for the revision is simply the number of hits on or above the net line within the thirty-second time limit. In the reference containing the revision Dyer presents some normative data.

Two subsequent revisions of the Dyer test have appeared in print. In Hewitt's[41] revision the restraining line is twenty feet from the backboard, and the students initiate the test with a serve rather than a courtesy stroke. Hewitt also presents reliability and validity data. Scott and French[42] move the restraining line back to 27.5 feet from the backboard, and present reliability and validity data and T-score norms based on scores on their revision from 583 college women in beginning tennis classes.

Broer-Miller tennis test[43]

Assessment of how accurately a tennis player can hit a forehand and backhand drive is obtained with the Broer-Miller Test. One side of the tennis court is marked off into four zones, and the area beyond the baseline is sectioned into three more zones (see Figure 18.6). Each zone is assigned a score value; the

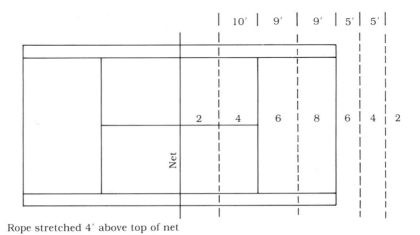

Rope stretched 4′ above top of net

Figure 18.6   Court markings for Broer-Miller tennis forehand-backhand drive test

values are highest near the baseline. From behind the baseline on the side of the tennis court not zoned the student is allowed fourteen forehand drives and fourteen backhand drives. To ensure that the stroke used is truly a drive, the tennis ball must pass between the net and a rope stretched parallel to and four feet above the net. If the tennis ball goes over the rope the student is given a score of one-half the value indicated by the zone in which the ball bounces. Complete directions, scoring procedures, zone dimensions and associated values, a sample score card, and statistical data relating to the test's reliability and validity are given in the reference.

Like the Dyer test the Broer-Miller Test has been modified by others. Surburg,[44] in a study investigating the effectiveness of various teaching methods on the development of the forehand tennis drive, added a second rope one foot over the net and revised the scoring procedures so that tennis balls passing between the net and the one-foot rope are scored according to the original Broer-Miller directions and those passing between the two ropes are given one-half values. In Sheppard's[45] revision the zone dimensions are altered slightly and the tennis ball to be hit is thrown to a certain area by the tester rather than bounced by the student.

DiGennaro tennis test[46]

A test battery measuring the forehand drive, backhand drive, and serve was developed by DiGennaro. For both of the drive tests the student attempts to hit the tennis ball over the net but below a rope located three feet above the top of the net into the center circle of a target of concentric circles. Each trial is initiated by the tester bouncing the ball in a designated area. After five practice trials, twenty test trials for both the forehand and the backhand are given. The service test also involves a concentric circle target. This target is located in a corner of the service area. Target sizes and placement on the tennis court, scoring procedures, reliability and validity data, and percentile norms based on sixty-four college male beginning tennis players are presented in the reference.

Kemp-Vincent rally test[47]

In an attempt to overcome some of the criticisms of commonly used tennis skills tests (such as failure to measure skills under game conditions, need for special equipment, line markings, and extensive amounts of time), Kemp and Vincent devised a tennis rally test involving two players. For this test two players of similar ability rally for three minutes. The ball is put into play initially and whenever necessary during the three minutes with a courtesy stroke. The total number of times both players hit the ball and the number of errors (e.g., failure to get the ball over the net, failure to keep the ball within the boundaries) each player makes are recorded. Each player's score is obtained by subtracting the number of errors from the total number of hits. Further directions, a list of errors, and a statistical analysis are presented in the reference.

Everett-Dumas tennis self-tests[48]

The skill portion of the self-test is composed of nonstroking and stroking sections. The nonstroking items are mostly bouncing tasks. The stroking section employs several activities involving various tennis strokes and serves. Standards such as "be successful on fifteen out of twenty tries" are suggested. Examples of scoring charts, rating scales, and checklists are also given in the reference.

Hewitt tennis achievement tests[49]

A test battery consisting of measures of the serve and forehand and backhand drive was developed by Hewitt to measure tennis achievement. For both drive tests one side of the tennis court is marked off in zones and a rope is stretched seven feet above and parallel to the top of the net (see Figure 18.7). After a warm-up, each student is given ten trials on the forehand side and ten trials on the backhand side. The tennis ball is to be hit between the rope and the top of the net into the target area. The use of a tennis ball machine to start each trial is preferred if one is available. Otherwise the tester initiates the action by hitting the ball to the student.

For the service test the target area is located in the service area, and, after a warm-up, ten trials of this test are given. In addition to noting where the tennis ball hits in the target area, the distance the ball bounces is recorded and used as an indicator of the speed of the serve. Complete directions, scoring procedures, target specifications, reliability and validity data, and scale score norms based on sixteen junior varsity and varsity, thirty-six advanced, and ninety-one beginning tennis players are given in the reference.

Tennis classification tests

Tennis classes often have large enrollments and the ability to group students increases teaching efficiency. Some relatively quick and easily administered tests have been proposed for classification purposes. Hewitt[50] devised two thirty-second classification tennis tests that do not require the use of a tennis backboard. One test involves using a tennis racket to bounce a tennis ball on the court to a height of hip level or above as many times as possible in the thirty-second time limit. The second test requires the students to hit a tennis ball above shoulder height as many times as possible in thirty seconds while alternating the racket face between hits. Norms, directions, and reliability and validity data are given in the reference.

Murphy[51] also suggests a two-item classification battery. One item is a one-minute wall rally against a tennis backboard from a restraining line twenty feet from the backboard. The second item involves bouncing a tennis ball up off a racket which is held about waist high and turned alternately to the forehand and backhand side between hits. The score on this item is the highest number of successive hits during a one-minute time period.

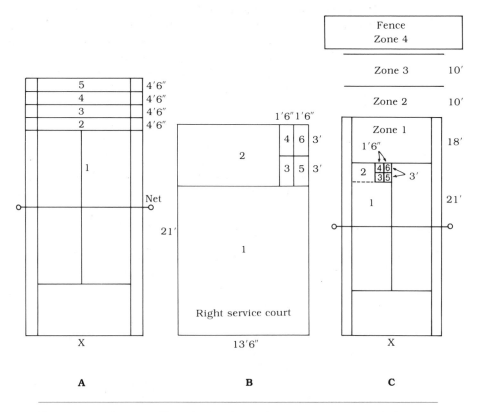

Figure 18.7   Court markings for Hewitt tennis achievement tests; A, forehand and backhand drives; B, service test; C, speed of service

TEAM SPORTS

Baseball and softball

Tests for measuring baseball and softball skills have been devised for various reasons and for several categories of students. Some tests have been constructed for assessing overall playing ability, others for examining specific skills. Additionally tests have been devised for predicting and classifying baseball and softball playing ability. Examples of tests to accomplish some of these purposes are presented below.

Rodgers and Heath playground baseball tests[52]

One of the earliest published batteries in this area was devised by Rodgers and Heath and involves items such as the baseball throw for accuracy, catching fly balls, batting, catching ground balls, and a hit and run test. In the reference directions for each item, T-score norms for fifth- and sixth-grade boys, reliability and validity data, and a one-hundred-item true-false test are presented.

Everett test to predict baseball playing ability[53]

In an attempt to devise a battery of screening tests to increase the accuracy of selecting baseball team members, Everett initially selected test items to measure motor ability (running speed and agility) and the ability to throw for distance, visualize spatial relationships, and make quick decisions. Items assessing these traits and a criterion measure consisting of coaches' ratings of hitting, fielding, base running, and basic execution were administered to thirty college varsity baseball players. The best single item Everett found for predicting baseball ability was the Sargent jump. Test directions, statistical data, and a regression equation for combining three test items are presented in the reference.

Kelson baseball classification plan[54]

Using eight-to twelve-year-old boys and a combination of judges' ratings and batting averages as the criterion measure, Kelson found the baseball throw for distance to be as adequate for classification purposes as combinations of other common tests involving baseball skills.

Wendler softball tests[55]

Three softball tests (fielding ground balls, throwing, and catching fly balls) devised by Wendler are described in the reference. Some correlation coefficients between these items and general ability test items are given.

McCloy pendulum test for batting[56]

A complete description of this test, including a diagram depicting the instrument required for its administration, is given in the reference.

Fox and Young test for softball batting ability[57]

The authors describe the equipment, field markings, administration and scoring procedures for a softball batting test involving the use of a batting tee. Reliability and validity data are also provided.

Scott and French softball skills tests[58]

The authors present the directions and other pertinent information for a series of test items measuring several specific softball skills. No particular battery of the items is recommended. The measurements described include a repeated throws test, a distance throw test, a fielding test, and two batting tests involving the use of a batting tee.

Shick softball tests[59]

Shick developed a battery consisting of three test items (repeated throws test, a fielding test, and a target test) for measuring the defensive softball skills of college women. The test directions, a diagram of required wall and floor markings, and statistical information are given in the reference.

Basketball

During the 1930s several physical educators, both men and women, reported various basketball skills test batteries and rating systems. From the 1940s on, the literature on basketball skills tests deals more with modification of earlier test items, factor analysis studies, and the establishment of norms for the test batteries and individual test items already devised. Many of the early basketball skills test developers proceeded in a similar manner. A relatively large number of possible test items were gathered, administered to a group of subjects, and rejected or accepted as part of the final battery on the basis of reliability, validity, objectivity, and practicality. Sometimes regression equations for combining the battery items, and occasionally norms, were also developed.

Early basketball tests

Edgren basketball test[60]

Eight basketball skills tests, four tests of general athletic ability, and a motor ability test were administered to sixty college men. The students were then divided into two groups of thirty, with one group receiving basketball instruction and the other serving as a control group. The total battery of tests was again administered to all sixty students. From the data gathered, Edgren concluded that five of the eight basketball skills tests were the most efficient measures of basketball ability. The items selected were speed pass, accuracy pass, speed dribble, dribble and shoot, and ball handling. A synopsis of previous experimentation in basketball skills measurement and directions for the test items used by Edgren are given in the reference.

Young-Moser basketball test[61]

Starting with eighteen tests and reducing to five on the basis of validity, reliability, objectivity, and practicality, Young and Moser selected the wall speed pass, moving target, bounce and shot, free jump, and Edgren ball handling test as their battery to measure playing ability in women's basketball.

Friermood basketball test[62]

A sample score card, percentage norms, and a diagram of a possible arrangement of testing stations for administering the four-item battery are presented in the reference. The battery consists of passing accuracy (throw a basketball through a four foot × three foot frame); pivoting for efficiency and form (subjective scores given for four specific pivots); dribbling for speed and control (timed dribble through a prescribed figure-eight path); and shooting accuracy (five free throws and six lay-ups).

Howard basketball rating system[63]

In a book published in 1937 Howard presents a rating system to evaluate basketball players by observing them and recording certain aspects of their performances during two and one-half minutes of play. Each player is observed and rated six times. A literature review, validity and reliability data, and regression equations for various methods of converting the observational data are presented in the book.

Schwartz basketball test[64]

Five trials of the jump and reach test, two thirty-second trials of a pass and catch for speed test, five trials of a test requiring a basketball to be bounced over a six-foot area, ten trials of a shooting accuracy test, and ten trials of a pivot, bounce, and shoot test make up the Schwartz battery for measuring senior high school girls' basketball achievement levels. In the reference, administrative and scoring directions, scale score norms, and suggestions if weaknesses are found in certain areas are given.

Glassow, Colvin, and Schwarz basketball test[65]

In an attempt to improve on already published basketball batteries, the authors offer several combinations of test items and regression equations for combining resulting scores. The authors conclude that the most efficient battery is a combination of the bounce and shoot, zone toss, and wall speed pass tests. Test directions, reliability and validity data, and norms are given.

Dyer, Schurig, and Apgar basketball test[66]

Starting with ten items and choosing four on the basis of statistical data from 517 girls ranging from seventh graders to college senior physical education majors, the authors propose a battery for measuring girls' basketball playing ability. The four items are moving target, Edgren ball handling, bounce and shoot, and free jump and reach. Test directions, a floor plan for efficient administration, T-score norms, and scoring procedures appear in an appendix in the reference.

Voltmer and Watts basketball rating scale[67]

Voltmer and Watts present an example of a rating scale that can be used to assess the performance of basketball players during scrimmage or competition. Sample score sheets and directions for their use, a rationale for the specific items scored, and data regarding the validity of the system are presented in the reference.

Basketball tests since 1940

Lehsten basketball test[68]

In an attempt to build a practical test battery for measuring basketball skills of high school boys, Lehsten began with eight basketball skills tests. Using the sum of five judges' ratings as a criterion (each judge's rating was a mean score for three observations) and eighty-six students as subjects, Lehsten devised a five-item battery consisting of the dodging run, baskets per minute, forty-foot dash, wall bounce, and vertical jump tests. Directions for all eight items, scale score norms for each of the eight items as well as for the eight-and five-item batteries, and other statistical data are presented in the reference.

Leilich basketball study[69]

A total of twenty-eight tests (fourteen involving basketball skills and twelve others involving assessment of strength, motor ability, flexibility, speed, coordination, agility, and kinesthesis) were administered to 110 college women students. Through factor analysis, six factors were identified. Some statistical data (not including reliability figures), directions for administering the test items, and a summary score card are given in the reference.

Miller basketball test[70]

Although no specific test directions are given by Miller, norms are presented for college women physical education majors for a one-half minute shooting test (N = 1,812), a bounce and shoot for time test (N = 1,645), a bounce and shoot for accuracy test (N = 1,645), and a push pass for accuracy test (N = 1,646). Suggestions for categories of superior, good, average, fair, and poor for each test are also given.

Blake and Sikkema dribble and shoot test[71]

Specific directions are presented for a sixty-second dribble and shoot test which is actually a modification of the bounce and shoot test described by Glassow, Colvin, and Schwarz.

AAHPERD Basketball Test for boys and girls[72]

In two separate booklets, one for boys and one for girls, the purpose, equipment required, description, rules, scoring, and diagram of nine basketball skills tests are presented. The nine tests include the front shot, side shot, foul shot, under-the-basket shot, speed pass, jump and reach test, overarm pass for accuracy, push pass for accuracy, and dribble test. The items are identical for boys and girls except shorter distances are used for girls on tests 2, 7, and 8. Each of the booklets also contains general directions for administering the entire battery, a diagram for locating the testing stations, sample score sheets, a personal data record, a personal profile record, and percentile norms based on age.

LSU long and short basketball test[73]

Developed by Nelson, this test measures the ability to shoot long and short basketball shots and to handle the basketball. A restraining line in the form of an arc having a radius equal to the distance from directly under the basket to the top of the free throw circle and its center directly under the basket is marked on the gym floor (see Figure 18.8). The student starts behind the restraining line and on the command "Go" shoots a long shot. The student must then rebound the ball and take a short shot (from anywhere inside the restraining arc), remembering to dribble properly if it is necessary to move with

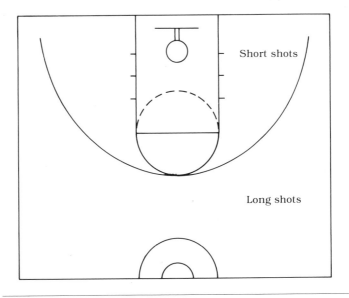

Figure 18.8   Floor markings for LSU long and short basketball test

the ball. After the short shot attempt the student rebounds, moves to any position behind the restraining line, and takes another long shot. The alternating of long and short shots continues for a one-minute period. The score for the trial is the total number of long shots made multiplied by 2 plus the total number of short shots made. Two trials are given, with the sum of the two taken as the score for the test. Complete directions and a scoring scale based on 100 college men are given in the reference.

Field hockey
Cozens, Cubberley, and Neilson field hockey scales[74]

Directions, diagrams, and scoring procedures for six field hockey tests are presented in the reference. The six tests are dribble twenty-five yards for speed, dribble and push pass for speed and accuracy, obstacle dribble and goal shot, penalty corner hit, penalty hit, and corner hit for accuracy and speed. In separate sections of the reference, norms are given for high school girls and college women.

Schmithals and French field hockey tests[75]

Based on an examination of tests from seven sources published between 1928 and 1938 and on the subjective judgment of three nationally rated umpires, the author devised six tests to measure field hockey skills. Using fifty-one subjects and a subjective rating from three experts as a criterion score, the six tests were analyzed statistically. The best single measure for classification purposes was found to be a test that involved dribbling, dodging, tackling, and driving. A description of each of the six tests, directions for their administration including diagrams for field markings, and the statistical data obtained are presented in the reference.

Strait field hockey skills test[76]

Criticizing earlier tests on the basis of low validity or being too unlike the game, Strait devised a single-item field hockey skills test using a backboard for rebounding a driven ball and involving the skills of dribbling, driving, fielding, and dodging. The test was constructed and evaluated through the use of 109 subjects from three different ability levels, a criterion score was obtained from three experts, and statistical examination of the data was made. In the reference the specific pattern and sequence of skills in the test, directions for administering the test and marking the field, and reliability and validity data are given.

Friedel field hockey test[77]

Friedel devised the Pass Receiving, Field and Drive While Moving Test to assess the field hockey skills of high school girls. Sixty-eight high school girls served as subjects in the test construction; the Schmithals-French test was used as a criterion measure. On a field marked as shown in Figure 18.9 each student is given twenty trials, ten from the right and ten from the left. As the ball is thrown from one side by the tester toward the target area, the student, starting from the start line, runs to contact the ball. The ball is then dribbled to the end line, where the student turns and drives the ball over the start line. The student may follow the ball if a second drive is necessary. Time is started when the ball is thrown. The score is the total time required for twenty trials.

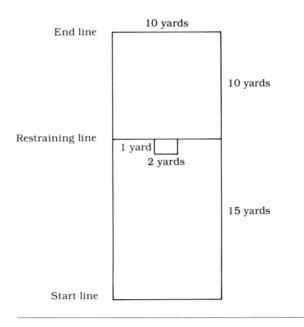

Figure 18.9   Field markings for Friedel field hockey test

Stewart field hockey test[78]

Two thirty-six-inch-square targets are marked twelve inches apart on a smooth hard wall, with the bottom of the targets at floor level. A restraining line eleven feet long is placed eight feet from and parallel to the wall. Each student is given six trials of hitting a field hockey ball at the targets alternately (left, right, left, etc. — starting with either target) from behind the restraining line. A trial lasts thirty seconds. The score for one trial is the number of good hits (must be struck from behind the line and *inside* the target lines — on the line does not count as good) in thirty seconds; the total score for the test is the sum of the best three trials. The author suggests having two extra balls placed behind the student (twenty feet from wall) and that four students be tested at each station having all four perform trial one, then all four perform trial two, and so forth to avoid fatigue and facilitate scoring.

The test was given to 228 college women enrolled in field hockey classes or on field hockey teams at three midwestern institutions. A mean score of 26 was obtained. A mean score of 35 was obtained when the test was administered to participants in a national tournament.

Football

Borleske touch football test[79]

Eighteen preliminary tests measuring touch football skills were selected after forty-six physical education instructors suggested the elements of the game to be measured. Using eighty-seven college male students as subjects and a rating score derived from fifteen judges as a criterion, Borleske devised a five-item battery and a three-item battery of tests for measuring overall touch football ability. The five-item battery correlates .925 with the criterion and involves forward pass for distance, running fifty yards with football, punting for distance, catching forward pass, and pass defense-zone tests. The three-item battery contains the first three tests listed above and correlates .88 with the judges' ratings. No norms or statistical data (other than validity coefficients) are presented in the reference cited but directions, diagrams, and suggestions for administering and scoring the tests are given.

McCloy football potential tests[80]
McCloy reports the work of Brechler, Cormack, and Hatley, who devised regression equations involving various physical performance tests, such as shot put, dash, and long jump measures. Using coaches' ratings as the criterion, the scores resulting from use of the regression equations indicate potential for various of the positions on a football team.

Brace tests of football ability[81]
In an investigation of validity of football achievement tests, Brace examined eight individual measures and the total score resulting from their administration to sixty-five college football team candidates. The tests were forward pass at a target, fifty-yard dash with a football, forward pass for distance, pull-out (an agility and short dash test), blocking, punting for distance, dodge and run, and charging (a leg power test). Of the individual items, Brace found that the fifty-yard dash correlated highest with the total score from all eight measures. Brace also correlated the total score with coaches' ratings (.33), players ratings of each other (.48), and various indices involving quarters played, letters earned, and games played. Directions and complete statistical data are presented in the reference.

AAHPERD football skills test[82]
As part of a development of standardized skills tests, AAHPERD has published a football skills test manual. The booklet contains directions and norms for administering, scoring, and interpreting the following ten football tests: forward pass for distance, fifty-yard dash with football, blocking, forward pass for accuracy, punt for distance, zigzag run with football, catching, pull-out (an agility and dash test), kickoff, and dodging run with football.

Ice hockey
Brown ice hockey tests[83]
Along with twelve lesson plans for teaching ice hockey to girls and an eighteen-item knowledge test, Brown presents a three-item skills test. The items are a dribbling and dodging test, a goal shooting test, and a speed skating while dribbling test. Test directions are given in the reference.

Merrifield and Walford ice hockey tests[84]

These two investigators devised six tests to measure ice hockey ability. The tests, for which general and specific directions, diagrams, and statistical data are presented in the reference, are forward speed skating, backward speed skating, skating agility, puck carrying, shooting, and passing. Using fifteen hockey club male college students as subjects and a rating of overall ability from a hockey coach as the criterion measures, the authors determined that the puck carrying test is the best single measure and recommended that the forward skating, puck carry, and either the backward skating or the skating agility test be used in combination for the most valid measure of ice hockey ability.

Soccer

Since the 1930s a great number of people have reported the construction of tests for measuring soccer playing ability. Many of the early tests contain similar items. Slight differences, such as the number of trials allowed or a change in the distance between objects around which the student must dribble the soccer ball, are usually present. The trend in recent tests is to devise a single test item to encompass many soccer skills, rather than a battery of separate items.

The descriptions below indicate the types of items most common in early soccer tests.

Dribble test

Probably the most common element in all the early tests is some form of a dribbling test. Typically the student stands behind a starting line and, on the signal "Go," dribbles the soccer ball alternately to the left and to the right of a series of objects placed in a line. Upon reaching the final object the student dribbles around it and returns to the starting line, again by dribbling through the objects. Variations among the different tests include the distances between the objects, the number of objects, the number of trials permitted, and the choice of the final score (best of three times, sum of time for two trials, and so forth).

Kick test

Another very common item found in several of the early soccer tests is a kick for distance, accuracy, or both. The distance a soccer ball can be kicked is measured by a place kick, by kicking a ball rolled by the investigator, or by kicking a ball that has bounced once after being thrown up in the air by the student. An element of accuracy is added to some of the distance kicks by using pie-shaped markings on the field. The ball must land within the pie-shaped area (kick made from the point) to count.

Accuracy of kicking is generally assessed using some sort of target. Very often the soccer goal, or at least its dimensions, forms the target. Various numbers of kicks are given from various distances and different points are awarded depending on the target area hit by the ball.

Volleying

Several early soccer tests included some form of a test in which the student attempts to volley a ball against a wall as many times as possible within a given time period, using only legal soccer techniques. Different test constructors altered the length of the time period, the number of trials, the distance of a restraining line from the wall, the placement and duties of helpers, and the location or use of spare soccer balls. This test item serves as the basis for many of the single item tests devised in later years.

Other tests

Tests designed to measure trapping, the throw in, tackling, and goal keeping are also found in several of the early tests. These tests often were less than satisfactory, however, because the scores resulting from their application usually reflected the ability of the tester or helper as well as the ability of the student being tested. The annotated list of soccer tests presented below indicates the large number and variety of tests developed for this sport.

Vanderhoof soccer skill test[85]

In one of the earliest soccer test batteries published, Vanderhoof describes ten separate items including tests to measure dribbling, trapping, the throw in, place kicking for accuracy, drop ball kicking, volleying, the throw down, tackling, the corner kick, and goal-keeping ability. Vanderhoof describes each test, suggests scoring procedures, and gives one example of a profile score card.

Heath and Rodgers soccer tests[86]

Using fifth- and sixth-grade boys as subjects, the authors examined the use of a 100-item true-false knowledge test and a 4-item skills test (dribble, throw in, kicking goals-place kick, kicking goals-rolling ball). Reliability coefficients, intercorrelations, various validity coefficients, and local T-score norms are presented in the reference.

Cozens, Cubberley, and Neilson soccer scales[87]

Dribbling, dribbling for speed and left foot pass for accuracy, dribbling for speed and right foot pass for accuracy, place kick for accuracy, place kick for distance, punt for distance, and throw in for distance are the seven test items described by the authors. Score scales for the seven items for high school girls and college women and for four of the items for junior high school girls are given in the reference.

Shaufele soccer test[88]

Shaufele examined six test items including dribbling, goal shooting, passing judgment, kicking for distance, passing and volley kicking, and wall volleying. Using eighty-four ninth- and tenth-grade girls as subjects and the subjective ratings of three instructors and two students, Shaufele determined that the wall volley is the best single measure of soccer ability. Because Shaufele's wall volley test serves as the basis of several similar soccer test items developed by later experimenters, it is described fully below.

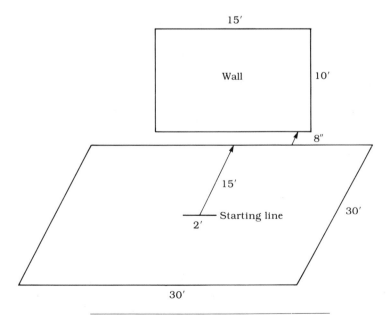

Figure 18.10   Shaufele soccer wall volley test

Using floor and wall markings as shown in Figure 18.10, the student is given two trials (on separate days) of one minute each to see how many times the ball can be kicked and rebounded against the target. The student starts each trial behind the starting line but after the initial kick is only restricted to staying in the thirty feet square area. Six assistants are placed around the thirty feet square area and are instructed to retrieve an errant ball and place it as quickly as possible on the line where it went out. The score is the highest number of hits on either trial.

Bontz soccer test[89]

The test devised by Bontz was one of the earliest attempts to construct a single item to measure several soccer skills at once. Bontz used 124 fifth- and sixth-grade children and a subjective rating by seven judges to examine the reliability and validity of her test. Each student was required to successfully complete four trials of the test with each foot. The total time for the eight trials constituted the final test score. The test consists of dribbling along a seventy-five-foot line, kicking the ball against a twelve-foot wall parallel to the dribbling line, recovering the resulting rebound, and continuing to dribble until a shot can be taken at a goal placed ninety feet from the rebound wall. The shot must be taken before crossing a line eighteen feet in front of the goal.

McDonald soccer test[90]

The McDonald Soccer Test is another example of a one-item test. It consists of a wall volley using a target 30 feet wide and 11½ feet high. A stationary ball is placed behind a restraining line nine feet from the wall and on the command "Go" the student kicks the ball as many times as possible in thirty seconds. Four trials are given; the sum of the best three is taken as the test score. To count, the ball must be kicked from behind the restraining line and hit within the target area. If a ball goes out of control the student has the option of chasing it, picking it up with the hands, returning to the restraining line, and continuing, or letting the errant ball go and getting one of two spare balls (again using the hands) placed nine feet behind the restraining line. McDonald used fifty-three college players classified into three ability levels and three coaches' ratings to examine the worth of the test. Statistical data are presented in the reference.

Mitchell[91] modified the McDonald Test for use by upper elementary school boys by changing the target size, moving the restraining line closer to the wall, settling on three twenty-second trials, and adding a forecourt area similar to that used by Shaufele. Mitchell also outlawed the use of hands by the student being tested to conform to the rules of soccer. Statistical data based on the use of 192 fifth- and sixth-grade boys for subjects and both an experimenter rating and a teacher-coach rating as criteria are presented in the reference. The wall and floor markings for Mitchell's test are shown in Figure 18.11.

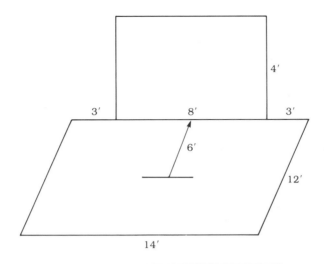

Figure 18.11   Mitchell soccer wall volley test

Crawford soccer test[92]

After polling ten experts to determine what skills should be tested, Crawford devised tests for dribbling, foot passing and receiving, trapping, volleying, and place kicking. A criterion measure consisting of a subjective rating by three judges and thirty female physical education majors at the University of Oregon was used to evaluate the five test items. Diagrams and instructions as well as statistical data, including a regression equation, are presented in the reference.

Wiley soccer test[93]

Wiley suggests a battery of four tests, including a dribble test, a heading test, a place kick for distance test, and the McDonald soccer test for assessing soccer students. The administration and scoring procedures are presented in the reference. In addition, some normative suggestions are given.

Johnson soccer test[94]

Basically, Johnson's soccer test is a modification of McDonald's kicking test. It is a wall volley using a 24 foot by 8 foot target, a 15-foot restraining line, and three thirty-second trials. Each trial is started by having the student drop a ball behind the restraining line. To count as a hit the ball must be kicked against the target and rebound past the restraining line. Spare balls are available fifteen feet behind the restraining line. The only time the student may touch the soccer ball with the hands is at the beginning of the test or in obtaining a spare ball. Statistical data involving the scores of seventy-five students classified into three different ability levels and relating to reliability and validity of the test are presented in the reference.

Tomlinson soccer test[95]

In an attempt to include several soccer skills in one test, Tomlinson devised a test requiring the student to dribble through an obstacle course before shooting for a goal. The test is started by the tester rolling the ball to the student, who then traps the ball, dribbles it along a prescribed zigzag course, and kicks for a goal from a line twelve feet in front of the goal. The goal kick is given various points depending on where it goes through the goal. Field markings and complete directions are given in the reference.

Saurer soccer norms[96]

Saurer suggests a need for developing local T-score norms and provides an example of how this might be accomplished for the place kick for distance. Using data from twenty-nine college women physical education majors, Saurer presents a table to convert distance kicked into T-scores. She obtained a mean distance of sixty-two feet, a standard deviation of 14, and a range of 32– 109.

Speedball

Speedball test batteries often contain tests found in soccer batteries, although occasionally tests for measuring kicking the ball up to oneself or to another player and tests involving the use of the hands are included. Drop kicking and punting are also assessed in some speedball batteries.

Cozens, Cubberley, and Neilson speedball scales[97]

The test items are identical to those described for soccer. Scales are presented for junior high school, senior high school and college women.

Buchanan speedball tests[98]

Buchanan devised a three-item battery and two two-item batteries for measuring speedball proficiency of high school girls. She used high school girls for subjects, a subjective rating of three teachers as a criterion, and nine experimental test items in developing the batteries. The items included lift to others, throwing and catching against a wall while standing, throwing and catching while moving, kick up to self of bounced ball, dribbling around objects and passing to goal, passing, dribbling, drop kick, and punting. The three-item battery, which correlated .946 with the criterion measure, contains items 2, 6, and 8. The two-item batteries, each correlating .93 with the criterion, contain tests 1 and 8 and tests 2 and 6.

Crawford speedball tests[99]

Starting with six experimental test items, two of which were from her soccer test battery, Crawford devised a three-item battery for measuring speedball ability. The six original items were kick up to self, foot passing and receiving (same as soccer test), passing with hands, dribbling (same as soccer test), lifting to teammates, and punting. The best combination resulted in the following regression equation: $1.5 \times$ dribble $+ 1.3 \times$ foot passing and receiving $+ 1.0 \times$ kick to teammate $- 123$. The lifting to teammate test did not include the use of another student but rather used a target on a wall to determine the accuracy of the kick up. Directions for marking walls and fields, administering and scoring the tests, as well as statistical considerations, are provided in the reference.

Miller speedball skill tests[100]

Although no statistical data or criterion measure are given, Miller presents the markings and directions for five speedball tests and recommends various combinations of them for use in assessing speedball ability. The tests are dribble and pass, speed toss, kick up to self, foot pass to wall, and wall zone pass. In addition Miller presents a twenty-six-item checklist for judging speedball players in a game.

Cozens and Cubberley speedball tests for men[101]

Except for the elimination of the throw-in test and the addition of an advanced version of the soccer dribble for speed and left foot (and right foot) pass for accuracy, this battery is the same advocated by Cozens, Cubberley, and Neilson. The two dribbling and passing tests are made more difficult by requiring the students to kick for a goal from eighteen yards rather than six yards.

Volleyball

A great number of volleyball skills tests have been published in a variety of sources. Although some appeared before the mid 1930s, it was not until about this time that statistical data regarding the consistency and worth of the tests

began to be included in the articles. In general, the tests range from a single item to batteries containing up to five separate measures. By far the most common single test item is the wall volley or repeated volley test. Typically the student stands in front of a wall on which a line is marked and is given a period of time to repeatedly volley the ball as many times as possible using correct volleyball form. Several different types of restrictions are imposed depending on the specific wall volley test being used (usually a function of the age, sex, and ability level of the group being tested). Examples of these restrictions follow.

1. **Restraining line** Although the directions for some wall volley tests do not specify that a restraining line be marked on the floor parallel to the wall, most do impose this condition and the most common distance from the wall is three feet. In most of the tests the student must volley the ball while standing behind the restraining line in order for the volley to count. However, a few tests require the student to be behind the line only to start the trial and when control of the ball is lost and it is necessary to start again.

2. **Height of volley** Several different heights have been used for the line marked on the wall above which the volley must hit. The normal range is seven and one-half feet to eleven and one-half feet.

3. **Length of volley line** Some test directions do not specify how long the line marked on the wall should be but others indicate a length. Most commonly, ten feet is suggested but a line only five feet long is used in one test. In addition, some test directions specify vertical lines be marked at the ends of the horizontal line.

4. **Start of test** Almost all the tests are started by having the subject toss the ball with an underhand motion against the wall above the horizontal line and then volley the rebound using proper volleyball techniques. Occasionally a "set to self" or toss from the tester or an assistant is utilized.

5. **Number and duration of trials** Several combinations of these two elements are used. In general, the number of trials varies between one and ten and the duration of a trial between fifteen seconds and one minute.

6. **Final score** The best single trial of several, the sum of all trials, the sum of the best two trials, and the sum of the best five trials are some examples of how the final score is derived for the wall volley portion of the tests. In one test the students are instructed to continue until ten legal volleys are made and the number of fouls committed is subtracted from 10 for the final score.

Wall volley tests for volleyball are so common that in 1963 West[102] published an article comparing eight different examples. She presents reported reliability and validity coefficients and the specific administrative procedures for each one. In addition West gives suggestions for administering, scoring, and using the results from wall volley tests for volleyball.

The second most common test included in volleyball batteries is the serving test. These tests range in complexity from counting the number of legal serves made out of so many tries to rather elaborate scoring systems involving different numbers of points for hitting targets of various sizes and placements. Additionally, some tests use a rope stretched above the net at a specified distance to include a measure of velocity as well as accuracy of the serve.

Volleyball test batteries also include items designed to measure passing, retrieving from the net, setting up, and ball handling skills. Very few batteries include tests for spiking or blocking and those that do generally advocate a subjective rating of these skills. The lack of objective tests in these areas stems primarily from the fact that other players' abilities are often an integral part of the scores achieved by a student.

One additional point should be considered when examining a volleyball test battery for possible use. Until 1957 women's volleyball rules permitted the players to set the ball up to themselves (i.e., one girl could hit the ball twice in succession). Tests devised before this rule change thus generally permitted this technique as well.

French and Cooper volleyball tests[103]

Voicing a dissatisfaction with previously designed volleyball measures primarily due to a lack of inclusion of statistical evidence of the worth of the tests, the authors used an activity analysis to determine what skills should be measured. They settled on the serve, set up to self, pass, volley, and recovery from the net. Using 227 high school girls as subjects and the subjective ratings of four trained judges as a criterion measure, French and Cooper devised four test items to measure these skills. The specific court markings and administrative directions, along with some statistical data regarding validity, are reported in the reference. The authors suggest that the most efficient combination for assessing volleyball activity is the serving test and the repeated volley test.

Bassett, Glassow, and Locke volleyball tests[104]

After performing a survey of the volleyball testing literature and finding seventeen serving tests, five setting up tests, three receiving and passing tests, three recovering the ball from the net tests, seven receiving and returning the ball across the net tests, one killing the ball test, and one repeated volley test, the authors selected two items, serving and volleying, for further study. They examined the reliability and validity of the two tests, using the scores obtained from ninety-nine women students enrolled in volleyball classes at two universities and from twenty physical education majors. Directions for administering and scoring the two tests as well as pertinent correlation coefficients are given in the reference.

Russell and Lange volleyball tests [105]

The French and Cooper volleyball tests were constructed for high school girls. Russell and Lange modified the serving and repeated volley items of the French and Cooper tests for use by junior high school girls. The modification of the wall volley test consisted of using three trials of thirty seconds each rather than ten trials of fifteen seconds each, and the modification of the serving test involved using two trials of ten serves each rather than only one trial of ten serves. The authors investigated the reliability and validity using various combinations of trials or best scores and various criterion measures. These data along with scales for both tests are presented in the reference.

Crogen volleyball classification test [106]

Crogen selected the members for sixteen volleyball teams based on the scores achieved in a wall volley test using a line twelve feet long and 7½ feet above the floor, a restraining line six feet from the wall (used only for the initial volley or for starting over), and a scoring system requiring the student to continue until ten legal hits are made and then subtracting from 10 the number of fouls committed. A round-robin tournament was then conducted with the assumption that if the wall volley test was valid for classification purposes, the teams composed of players achieving the higher scores on the test would win more games than teams composed of players achieving lower scores. The data affirming this assumption to some degree are presented in the reference, along with the author's suggestion that the length of the test should be at least doubled.

Brady volleyball test [107]

Suggesting that no volleyball test with statistical data available for men could be found in the literature, Brady examined several experimental test items. Through the use of scores from 282 freshmen college men enrolled in beginning volleyball class, 240 sophomores enrolled in intermediate classes, and 15 members of a nationally prominent YMCA volleyball team, and a criterion measure obtained from subjective ratings of experienced teachers, Brady eliminated all experimental items except a wall volley. The test involves a line five feet long located on a smooth wall 11½ feet above the floor. No restraining line is used and one trial lasting one minute is given. The reference contains some discussion of the reliability and validity of the test.

Lamp volleyball tests [108]

In a study designed to investigate the relationship between chronological age, physiological age, height, weight, grip strength, and volleyball playing ability, Lamp devised a battery of four volleyball tests. The tests were selected on the basis of a pilot study involving correlating the test scores with the subjective ratings obtained from two "experts." Tests to measure the serve, set-up, pass, and volley were administered to 429 girls and 377 boys in seventh, eighth, and ninth grades. Data pertinent to reliability, objectivity, and validity of the items, as well as diagrams and descriptions for administering the tests, are presented in the reference.

Snavely volleyball tests[109]

Tests to measure the serve, spike, pass placement, and net recovery are described in the reference. Although directions for administering the tests are given, no scoring procedures or statistical data are presented.

Mohr and Haverstick volleyball test[110]

The purpose of this study was to examine the influence of the restraining line in the repeated volley test for volleyball. Using 100 freshman and sophomore college women for subjects and the subjective ratings of three experienced judges employing a specific rating form, the authors determined the reliability of the repeated volleys test to be virtually unchanged when a restraining line of three, five, or seven feet is used. However, their results indicate that the validity of the test is best with a seven foot restraining line.

Laveaga volleyball tests[111]

Several suggestions given more in the nature of teaching devices and drill activities than structured tests are presented in the two references listed. Ideas for assessing the serve, ball handling, setting, and attacking are described. The use of court markings, ropes parallel to the net, and wall markings are suggested although specific scoring procedures and statistical evidence regarding the reliability and validity of the tests are not.

Brumbach volleyball serve test[112]

Ten trials are given to serve the volleyball, using proper techniques, over the net but below a rope stretched four feet above the net. The court into which the ball is served is marked off with lines parallel to the net, fifteen feet, twenty-five feet, thirty feet (end line), and thirty-two feet from the net. Scores of 2, 4, 6, and 4, respectively, are given for each ball landing in the area bounded by these lines, provided the ball passes between the rope and the net. If the ball travels over the rope the point values are halved. Serves hitting the rope are taken over with no penalty.

Odeneal and Wilson Volleyball self-tests[113]

In a chapter devoted to self-testing and evaluation, the authors describe tests for the service, pass, set-up, volley, and spike. The first four involve wall and floor markings similar to most volleyball tests. The spiking test consists of a tester setting the ball up to be spiked by the student being tested and subjectively rating the performance using the ideal form provided by the authors as a criterion.

Clifton volley test[114]

To accommodate the 1957 rule change in women's volleyball disallowing two successive hits by a single player, Clifton devised a single hit wall volley test for women. A test employing a line ten feet long and 7½ feet above the floor, a restraining line ten feet long and seven feet from the wall, and two thirty-second trials with two minutes of rest between trials was validated using forty-five freshman and sophomore girls enrolled in general college volleyball classes. The subjective rating of five experienced judges using a set scale was used as a criterion measure. Complete directions and statistical data are provided in the reference.

Liba and Stauff volleyball pass test[115]

Reliability, validity, and logical data for the establishment of the dimensions for the volleyball chest pass are given in the reference, as are test administration and scoring directions. For college women, the test involves ten trials, each initiated with a toss to self, using an area as shown in Figure 18.12. Each trial is scored for height and for distance. The score is three points if the ball goes over the thirteen foot high rope, two points if the ball goes between the two ropes, one point if the ball goes under the eleven foot high rope, and no points if the ball does not reach the ropes. The distance score is obtained from the floor markings (higher value given if the ball hits on a line). The height score is multiplied by the distance score to obtain the trial score, and the ten trial scores are summed to obtain the test score.

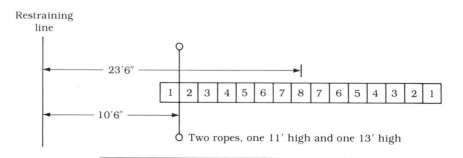

Figure 18.12   Top view of markings for Liba-Stauff volleyball pass test for college women

Liba and Stauff modified the test dimensions for use by junior high school girls. The specifications for this test are shown in Figure 18.13.

Bell volleyball tests[116]

Bell suggests several self-testing activities using ropes and floor markings. Some diagrams and discussion of administrative techniques are presented in the reference but scoring procedures or statistical evidence are not.

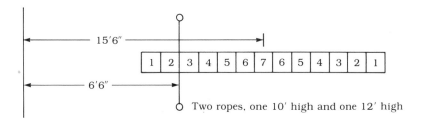

**Figure 18.13   Top view of Liba-Stauff volleyball pass test
for junior high school girls**

Trotter volleyball tests[117]

In a chapter devoted to volleyball evaluation techniques, Trotter presents a description of several of the volleyball tests published in previous literature. In addition, she describes the Trotter self-volley, Trotter wall target volley, and the Trotter service tests. The wall target volley and the service tests are similar to others in the literature, with Trotter's suggestions for markings and scoring procedures. However, the self-volley test is unique. An area ten feet by fifteen feet (one-sixth of one side of a volleyball court) is marked off on the floor. The student is given three thirty-second trials to see how many legal volleys (to self) can be made in the time allowed. The volleys must be higher than the net, which is set at varying heights depending on the age of the students being tested.

Kronqvist and Brumbach volleyball test[118]

The authors used the scores from seventy-one tenth- and eleventh-grade boys to modify the Brady wall volley test (which was designed for college men). The authors' version of the wall volley uses a line five feet long and eleven feet high on a smooth wall, no restraining line, and three twenty-second trials. As a criterion measure to assess the validity of the test, the subjective ratings from three experienced teachers employing a rating scale suggested by Laveaga was used. Administrative and scoring procedures and discussion of reliability and validity of the test and objectivity of the judges are given in the reference.

Cunningham and Garrison volleyball test[119]

The authors devised a wall volley test with a line three feet long located ten feet above the floor, no restraining line, and two thirty-second nonconsecutive trials. The wall volley test and the Liba-Stauff volleyball pass test were administered to 111 freshman and sophomore women students enrolled in general volleyball classes. Three experienced judges were used to obtain a criterion measure. Complete directions for administering and scoring the wall volley test, as well as statistical data regarding reliability, validity, scoring procedures, and comparisons of the two tests are given in the reference.

AAHPERD volleyball skills test[120]

Complete directions for four volleyball tests (volleying, serving, passing, and setting up) are given in this manual. The rationale behind the tests, information about reliability and validity, diagrams for required court and wall markings, score cards, and percentile norms for boys and girls from ages ten to eighteen are also presented.

Slaymaker and Brown volleyball tests[121]

One chapter of this book is devoted to evaluation, and tests for serving, passing, setting, bumping, net retrieving, and spiking are presented. The passing test is a wall volley, and the bumping test is a wall volley requiring the student to use a legal bump in volleying the ball to the wall. The spiking test is a subjective evaluation using a five-point checklist as a criterion. For all six tests directions are given, and for three some normative data are presented, but the source of the normative information and statistical data are not found in the reference.

Helman volleyball skill tests[122]

Thirty-one experts were asked to rate the most important volleyball skills that should be measured. The forearm pass, the face pass, and the spike were identified. Helman devised three experimental test items for each of the three skills identified and administered them to seventy-six college women enrolled in general volleyball classes. The resulting final battery contains an overhead volley test (face pass), a bump to self test (forearm pass), and a wall spike test.

For the overhead volley test the student is given two nonconsecutive thirty-second trials. The ball is tossed up and volleyed above the head with two hands as many times as possible in the time allowed. The student must remain in a fifteen by fifteen foot area and the ball must reach or go above a mark twelve feet high on the wall. Loss of control (dropping the ball, catching the ball, using one hand, bumping, or hitting the ball underhanded) results in starting the count over again at zero. Balls not over the twelve-foot mark, hit while the student is outside the required area, or hitting the wall do not count but do not result in starting over. The sum of both trials is used as the final score. The bump to self test uses the same area and rules as the overhead volley test except the forearm pass, rather than the face pass, is used.

For the wall spike test the student starts and remains behind a restraining line fifteen feet long and located thirteen feet from a wall. Starting with a toss to self, the student spikes the ball to the floor in such a way that it rebounds off the wall and rebounds to her. As many spikes as possible are executed during three nonconsecutive twenty-second trials. The sum of the best two trials is taken as the test score.

The test items were validated with the ratings from three experimental volleyball players using a nine-point scale. Reliability was measured using a test-retest procedure. Diagrams, an organizational floor plan, test directions, and statistical data are presented in the reference.

REFERENCES CITED

[1]*Archery Skills Manual* (Washington, D.C.: American Alliance for Health, Physical Education, and Recreation (AAHPER)).

[2]Robert W. Bohn, "An Achievement Test in Archery," Microcard Master's Thesis, University of Wisconsin, 1962, 81 pp.

[3]Edith I. Hyde, "National Research Study in Archery," *Research Quarterly*, 7 (Dec. 1936), 64–73.

[4]Natalie Reichart, "School Archery Standards," *Journal of Health and Physical Education*, 14 (Feb. 1943), 81.

[5]Marjorie Phillips and Dean Summers, "Bowling Norms and Learning Curves for College Women," *Research Quarterly*, 21 (Dec. 1950), 377–85.

[6]Joan Martin and Jack Keogh, "Bowling Norms for College Students in Elective Physical Education Classes," *Research Quarterly*, 35 (Oct. 1964), Part 1, 324–27.

[7]Marie Liba and Janice Olson, "A Device for Evaluating Spot Bowling Ability," *Research Quarterly*, 38 (May 1967), 193–201.

[8]Kathryn Vondreau, "Objectively Evaluating Bowling Form," *Bowling-Fencing-Golf Guide* (Washington, D.C.: The Division of Girl's and Women's Sports (DGWS), AAHPER, 1971), pp. 31–32.

[9]H. Harrison Clarke, *Applications of Measurement to Health and Physical Education*, 5th ed. (Englewood Cliffs, N.J.: Prentice-Hall, 1967), p. 317.

[10]Robert T. Bowen, "Putting Errors of Beginning Golfers Using Different Points of Aim," *Research Quarterly*, 39 (March 1968), 31–35.

[11]Edward F. Chui, "A Study of Golf-O-Tron Utilization as a Teaching Aid in Relation to Improvement and Transfer," *Research Quarterly*, 36 (May 1965), 147–52.

[12]Melvin Clevett, "An Experiment in Teaching Methods of Golf," *Research Quarterly*, 2 (Dec. 1931), 104–12.

[13]Mary Ellen McKee, "A Test for the Full Swinging Shot in Golf," *Research Quarterly*, 21 (March 1950), 40–46.

[14]Barry Johnson and Jack Nelson, *Practical Measurements for Evaluation in Physical Education*, 2nd ed. (Minneapolis, Minn.: Burgess Publishing Company, 1974), pp. 251–52.

[15]Ellen R. Vanderhoof, "Beginning Golf Achievement Tests," M.S. Thesis, State University of Iowa, 1956, 44 pp.

[16]Charlotte West and Joanne Thorpe, "Construction and Validation of an Eight-Iron Approach Test," *Research Quarterly*, 39 (Dec. 1968), 1115–20.

[17]M. S. Kelliher, "Analysis of Two Styles of Putting," *Research Quarterly*, 34 (Oct. 1963), 344–49.

[18]Daniel C. Neale and Bruce D. Anderson, "Accuracy of Aim with Conventional and Croquet-Style Golf Putters," *Research Quarterly*, 37 (March 1966), 89–94.

[19]*The Official NCAA Swimming Guide 1976* (Shawnee Mission, Kansas: NCAA Publishing Service, SW–49–50).

[20]LaVerne M. Bennett, "A Test of Diving for Use in Beginning Classes," *Research Quarterly*, 13 (March 1942), 109–15.

[21]Donald J. Connor, "A Comparison of Objective and Subjective Testing Methods in Selecting Swimming Skills for Elementary School Children," M.S. Thesis, Washington State University, 1962, 72 pp.

[22]Thomas K. Cureton, "A Test for Endurance in Speed Swimming," *Research Quarterly*, 6 (May 1935), 106–12.

[23]Joel Rosentsweig, "A Revision of the Power Swimming Test," *Research Quarterly*, 39 (Oct. 1968), 818–19.

[24]Margaret G. Fox, "Swimming Power Test," *Research Quarterly*, 28 (Oct. 1957), 233–37.

[25]Jack E. Hewitt, "Achievement Scale Scores for High School Swimming," *Research Quarterly*, 20 (May 1949), 170–79; and Jack E. Hewitt, "Swimming Achievement Scale Scores for College Men," *Research Quarterly*, 19 (Dec. 1948), 282–89.

[26]Cheryl L. Pennington, "The Effect of Two Types of Swimming Progressions on the Acquisition of Basic Swimming Skills by the Female, College Non-Swimmer," M.S. Thesis, University of Colorado, 1969, 90 pp.

[27]Esther French and Evelyn Stalter, "Study of Skill Tests in Badminton for College Women," *Research Quarterly*, 20 (Oct. 1949), 257–72.

[28]Johnson and Nelson, *Practical Measurements for Evaluation in Physical Education*, 2nd ed., pp. 260–61.

[29]Aileen Lockhart and Frances A. McPherson, "The Development of a Test of Badminton Playing Ability," *Research Quarterly*, 20 (Dec. 1949), 402–05.

[30]Frances A. Miller, "A Badminton Wall Volley Test," *Research Quarterly*, 22 (May 1951), 208–13.

[31]M. Gladys Scott, "Achievement Examinations in Badminton," *Research Quarterly*, 12 (May 1941), 242–53.

[32]M. Gladys Scott and Esther French, *Measurement and Evaluation in Physical Education* (Dubuque, Iowa: Wm. C. Brown Company Publishers, 1959), pp. 222–25.

[33]Robert N. Singer, "Speed and Accuracy of Movement as Related to Fencing Success," *Research Quarterly*, 39 (Dec. 1968), 1080–83.

[34]Roxanne E. Busch, "The Construction of a Fencing Skill Test Using a Moving Target," M.Ed. Thesis, University of North Carolina, 1966, 50 pp.

[35]Clayton Cornish, "A Study of Measurement of Ability in Handball," *Research Quarterly*, 20 (May 1949), 215–22.

[36]Gary Pennington, James Day, John Crowatzky, and John Hansan, "A Measure of Handball Ability," *Research Quarterly*, 38 (May 1967), 247–53.

[37]Jimmey H. Railey, "Effects of Imitative Resistance Exercise and Direct Practice on Handball Serving Skill," *Research Quarterly*, 41 (Dec. 1970), 523–27.

[38]Jane A. Mott and Aileen Lockhart, "Table Tennis Backboard Test," *Journal of Health and Physical Education*, 17 (Nov. 1946), 550–52.

[39]Joanna Dyer, "The Backboard Test of Tennis Ability," *Supplement to Research Quarterly*, 6 (March 1935), 63–74.

[40]Joanna Dyer, "Revision of the Backboard Test of Tennis Ability," *Research Quarterly*, 9 (March 1938), 25–31.

[41]Jack Hewitt, "Revision of the Dyer Backboard Tennis Test," *Research Quarterly*, 36 (May 1965), 153–57.

[42]M. Gladys Scott and Esther French, *Evaluation in Physical Education* (Dubuque, Iowa: Wm. C. Brown Company Publishers, 1959), pp. 144–48.

[43]Marion R. Broer and Donna Mae Miller, "Achievement Tests for Beginning and Intermediate Tennis," *Research Quarterly*, 21 (Oct. 1950), 303–21.

[44]Paul R. Surburg, "Audio, Visual, and Audio-Visual Instruction with Mental Practice in Developing the Forehand Tennis Drive," *Research Quarterly*, 39 (Oct. 1968), 728–34.

[45]Geralyn Shepard, "The Tennis Drive Skill Test," *Tennis-Badminton Squash Guide June 1972–74* (Washington, D.C.: DGWS, AAHPER, 1972), pp. 39–42.

[46]Joseph DiGennaro, "Construction of Forehand Drive, Backhand Drive, and Service Tennis Tests," *Research Quarterly*, 40 (Oct. 1969), 496–501.

[47]Joann Kemp and Marilyn F. Vincent, "Kemp-Vincent Rally Test of Tennis Skill," *Research Quarterly*, 39 (Dec. 1968), 1000–04.

[48]Peter Everett and Virginia Dumas, *Beginning Tennis* (Belmont, Ca.: Wadsworth Publishing Company, 1962), 62 pp.

[49]Jack E. Hewitt, "Hewitt's Tennis Achievement Test," *Research Quarterly*, 37 (May 1966), 231–40.

[50]Jack E. Hewitt, "Classification Tests in Tennis," *Research Quarterly*, 39 (Oct. 1968), 552–55.

[51]Chet Murphy, "Too Many Players and Too Few Courts? Here's an Answer," *Journal of Health, Physical Education and Recreation*, 45 (May 1974), 28–31.

[52]Elizabeth G. Rodgers, and Marjorie L. Heath, "An Experiment in the Use of Knowledge and Skill Tests in Playground Baseball," *Research Quarterly* (Dec. 1931), 113–31.

[53]Peter Everett, "The Prediction of Baseball Ability," *Research Quarterly* (March 1952), 15–19.

[54]Robert Kelson, "Baseball Classification Plan for Boys," *Research Quarterly* (Oct. 1953), 304–07.

[55]Arthur J. Wendler, "A Critical Analysis of Test Elements Used in Physical Education," *Research Quarterly*, (March 1938), 64–76.

[56]C. H. McCloy and Norma D. Young, *Tests and Measurements in Health and Physical Education*, 3rd ed. (New York: Appleton-Century-Crofts, Inc., 1954), pp. 322–24.

[57]Margaret G. Fox and Olive G. Young, "A Test of Softball Batting Ability," *Research Quarterly* (March 1954), 26–27.

[58]Scott and French, *Evaluation in Physical Education*.

[59]Jacqueline Shick, "Battery of Defensive Softball Skills Tests for College Women," *Research Quarterly* (March 1970), 82–87.

[60]H. D. Edgren, "An Experiment in the Testing of Ability and Progress in Basketball," *Research Quarterly*, 3 (March 1932), 159–71.

[61]Genevieve Young and Helen Moser, "A Short Battery of Tests to Measure Playing Ability in Women's Basketball," *Research Quarterly*, 5 (May 1934), 3–23.

[62]H. T. Friermood, "Basketball Progress Tests Adaptable to Class Use," *Journal of Health and Physical Education*, 5 (Jan. 1934), 45–47.

[63]Glenn W. Howard, *A Measurement of the Achievement in Motor Skills of College Men in the Game Situation of Basketball* (New York: Bureau of Publications, Teachers College, Columbia University, 1937), 109 pp.

[64]Helen Schwartz, "Knowledge and Achievement Tests in Girls Basketball on the Senior High School Level," *Research Quarterly*, 8 (March 1937), 143–56.

[65]Ruth Glassow, Valarie Colvin, and Marguerite Schwarz, "Studies in Measuring Basketball Playing Ability of College Women," *Research Quarterly*, 9 (Dec. 1938), 60–68.

[66]Joanna Dyer, Jennee Schurig, and Sara Apgar, "A Basketball Motor Ability Test for College Women and Secondary School Girls," *Research Quarterly*, 10 (Oct. 1939), 128–47.

[67]E. F. Voltmer and Ted Watts, "A Rating Scale of Players Performance in Basketball," *The Journal of Health and Physical Education*, 11 (Feb. 1940), 94–95, 123–25.

[68]Nelson Lehsten, "A Measure of Basketball Skills in High School Boys," *The Physical Educator*, 5 (Dec. 1948), 103–09.

[69]Avis Leilich, "The Primary Components of Selected Basketball Tests for College Women," Doctoral Dissertation, University of Indiana, 1952, 102 pp.

[70]Wilma Miller, "Achievement Levels in Basketball Skills for Women Physical Education Majors," *Research Quarterly*, 25 (Dec. 1954), 450–55.

[71]Pat Blake and Geraldine Sikkema, "Sixty Second Dribble and Shoot," *DGWS Guide 1963–1964*, Barbara Drinkwater, ed. (Washington, D.C.: AAHPER), pp. 46–48.

[72]*AAHPER Skills Test Manual: Basketball for Boys* (Washington, D.C.: AAHPER, 1966), 47 pp; and *AAHPER Skills Test Manual: Basketball for Girls* (Washington, D.C.: AAHPER, 1966), 47 pp.

[73]Johnson and Nelson, *Practical Measurements for Evaluation in Physical Education*, 2nd ed., pp. 233–34.

[74]F. W. Cozens, H. J. Cubberley, and H. P. Neilson, *Achievement Scales in Physical Education Activities for Secondary School Girls and College Women* (New York: A. S. Barnes & Co., 1937), pp. 27–32, 66–68, 88–89.

[75]Margaret Schmithals and Esther French, "Achievement Tests in Field Hockey for College Women," *Research Quarterly* (Oct. 1940), 84–92.

[76]Clara J. Strait, "The Construction and Evaluation of a Field Hockey Skills Test," M.S. Thesis, Smith College, 1960, 74 pp.

[77]Jean Friedel, "The Development of a Field Hockey Skill Test for High School Girls," M.S. Thesis, Illinois State Normal University, 1956, 34 pp.

[78]Harriet Stewart, "Field Hockey Backboard Test," *Field Hockey-Lacrosse Guide August 1966–68* (Washington, D.C.: DGWS, AAHPER, 1968), pp. 44–46.

[79]Stanley Borleske, "A Study of the Achievement of College Men in Touch Football," *Research Quarterly* (May 1937), 73–75.

[80]McCloy and Young, *Tests and Measurements in Health and Physical Education*, 3rd ed., pp. 327–28.

[81]D. K. Brace, "Validity of Football Achievement Tests as Measures of Motor Learning and as a Partial Basis for the Selection of Players," *Research Quarterly* (Dec. 1943), 372–77.

[82]*Skills Test Manual: Football*, David Brace, consultant (Washington, D.C.: AAHPER, 1965), 48 pp.

[83]Harriet Brown, "The Game of Ice Hockey," *The Journal of Health and Physical Education* (Jan. 1935), 28–30, 54–55.

[84]H. H. Merrifield and Gerald Walford, "Battery of Ice Hockey Skill Tests," *Research Quarterly* 40 (March 1969), 146–52.

[85]Mildred Vanderhoof, "Soccer Skill Tests," *Journal of Health and Physical Education* (Oct. 1932), 42, 54–56.

[86]M. L. Heath and Elizabeth Rodgers, "A Study in the Use of Knowledge and Skill Tests in Soccer," *Research Quarterly* (Dec. 1932), 33–53.

[87]Cozens, Cubberley, and Neilson, *Achievement Scales in Physical Education Activities for Secondary School Girls and College Women*, pp. 36–43, 68, 92, 118.

[88]Evelyn F. Schaufele, "The Establishment of Objective Tests for Girls of the Ninth and Tenth Grades to Determine Soccer Ability," Master's Thesis, State University of Iowa, 1940.

[89]Jean Bontz, "An Experiment in the Construction of a Test for Measuring Ability in Some of the Fundamental Skills Used by Fifth and Sixth Grade Children in Soccer," Master's Thesis, State University of Iowa, 1942.

[90]Lloyd G. McDonald, "The Construction of a Kicking Skill Test as an Index of General Soccer Ability," Master's Thesis, Springfield College, 1951.

[91]J. R. Mitchell, "The Modification of the McDonald Soccer Skill Test for Upper Elementary School Boys," Master's Thesis, University of Oregon, 1963, 67 pp.

[92]Elinor A. Crawford, "The Development of Skill Test Batteries for Evaluating the Ability of Women Physical Education Major Students in Soccer and Speedball," Doctoral Dissertation, University of Oregon, 1958, 79 pp.

[93]Roger Wiley, *Soccer: A Syllabus for Teachers* (Ann Arbor, Mich.: Edwards Brothers, Inc., 1962), 64 pp.

[94]Joseph R. Johnson, "The Development of a Single-Item Test as a Measure of Soccer Skill," Master's Thesis, The University of British Columbia, 1963, 65 pp.

[95]Rebecca Tomlinson, "Soccer Skill Test," *Soccer-Speedball Guide, July 1964–1966* (Washington, D.C.: DGWS, AAHPER), pp. 16–20.

[96]Judith Saurer, "Skill Testing in Soccer," *Soccer-Speedball-Flag Football Guide* (Washington, D.C.: NAGWS, AAHPER, June 1974–76), 27–28.

[97]Cozens, Cubberley, and Neilson, *Achievement Scales in Physical Education Activities for Secondary School Girls and College Women*, pp. 36–42, 68, 92, 118.

[98]Ruth E. Buchanan, "A Study of Achievement Tests in Speedball for High School Girls," Master's Thesis, State University of Iowa, 1942.

[99]Crawford, "The Development of Skill Test Batteries for Evaluating the Ability of Women Physical Education Major Students in Soccer and Speedball."

[100]Shirley B. Miller, "Speedball Skill Tests," *Soccer-Speedball Guide* (Washington, D.C.: DGWS, AAHPER, July 1962–64), pp. 83–90.

[101]F. W. Cozens and Hazel Cubberley, "Achievement Tests in Soccer and Speedball," *Speedball for Men* (Washington, D.C.: AAHPER, 1967), 38–43.

[102]Charlotte West, "Wall Volley Skills Test," *Volleyball Guide* (Washington, D.C.: The Division of Girl's and Women's Sports, AAHPER, July 1963–1965), 33–37.

[103]Esther L. French and Bernice Cooper, "Achievement Tests in Volleyball for High School Girls," *Research Quarterly* (May 1937), 150–57.

[104]Gladys Bassett, Ruth Glassow, and Mable Locke, "Studies in Testing Volleyball Skills," *Research Quarterly* (Dec. 1937), 60–72.

[105]Naomi Russell and Elizebeth Lange, "Achievement Tests in Volleyball for Junior High School Girls," *Research Quarterly* (Dec. 1940), 33–41.

[106]Corrine Crogen, "A Simple Volleyball Classification Test for High School Girls," *The Physical Educator* (Oct. 1943), 34–37.

[107]George F. Brady, "Preliminary Investigations of Volleyball Playing Ability," *Research Quarterly* (March 1945), 14–17.

[108]Nancy A. Lamp,."Volleyball Skills of Junior High School Students as a Function of Physical Size and Maturity," *Research Quarterly* (May 1954), 189–200.

[109]Marie Snavely, "Volley Ball Skill Tests for Girls," *Selected Volleyball Articles* (Washington, D.C.: National Section for Girls and Women's Sports, AAHPER, 1955), 59–60.

[110]Dorothy R. Mohr and Martha J. Haverstick, "Repeated Volleys Tests for Women's Volleyball," *Research Quarterly* (May 1955), 179–84.

[111]Robert Laveaga, *Volleyball Instructor's Guide* (Chicago: The Athletic Institute, 1958), 63 pp; and Robert Laveaga, *Volleyball*, 2nd ed. (New York: The Ronald Press, 1960), 128 pp.

[112]Wayne Brumbach, *Beginning Volleyball: A Syllabus for Teachers* (Ann Arbor, Mich.: Edward Brothers, 1961), 69 pp.

[113]William Odeneal and Harry Wilson, *Beginning Volleyball* (Belmont, Ca.: Wadsworth Publishing Co., 1962), 57 pp.

[114]Marguerite Clifton, "Single Hit Volley Test for Women's Volleyball," *Research Quarterly*, (May 1962), 208–11.

[115]Marie Liba and Marilyn Stauff, "A Test for the Volleyball Pass," *Research Quarterly* (March 1963), 56–63.

[116]Virginia Bell, "Self Testing with Rope and String," *Volleyball Guide* (Washington, D.C.: DGWS, AAHPER, July 1963–65), pp. 24–28.

[117]Betty Jane Trotter, *Volleyball for Girls and Women* (New York: The Ronald Press, 1965), 227 pp.

[118]Roger A. Kronqvist and Wayne Brumbach, "A Modification of the Brady Volleyball Skill Test for High School Boys," *Research Quarterly* (March 1968), 116–20.

[119]Phyllis Cunningham and Joan Garrison, "High Wall Volley Test for Women's Volleyball," *Research Quarterly* (Oct. 1968), 486–90.

[120]*Skills Test Manual: Volleyball*, Clayton Shay, consultant (Washington, D.C.: AAHPER, 1969), 36 pp.

[121]Thomas Slaymaker and Virginia H. Brown, *Power Volleyball* (Philadelphia: W. B. Saunders Company, 1970), 115 pp.

[122]Rute Helmen, "Development of Volleyball Skill Tests for College Women," *Volleyball Guide* (Washington, D.C.: DGWS, AAHPER, July 1971–73), pp. 47–53.

Chapter 19
Dance and Rhythm

Dance performances traditionally are evaluated subjectively by one or more "experts." Sometimes, in an attempt to increase the objectivity of the judgment, a rating scale, such as one suggested by Lockhart and Pease[1] or one developed by Dvorack,[2] is used.

The lack of objective measures in dance stems from three interrelated reasons. First, a large element in dance is interpretation. By its very nature this is an area where there is no "correct" or "incorrect" response. Therefore, criteria against which to judge interpretation do not exist. Second, as pointed out by Shelly[3] in the 1930s, a whole dance performance is equal to more than the sum of its parts. Because elements such as expression and interpretation, again having no absolutely correct translation, are interwoven into the performance, it becomes impossible to separate dance into specific elements, measure these, and combine the results into a "dance score." However, as will be presented later, one of the most important elements of dance, that of rhythm, has been singled out and several different approaches for its measurement have been devised. Third, there is a lack of universally recognized definitions of many of the elements of dance. Although it was pointed out in Chapter 1 that if something exists it exists in some amount and therefore can be measured, if there is disagreement as to the form of that something, objective measurement is difficult. Even for rhythm, which is probably the most often measured element of dance, the definitions range from " . . . measured energy"[4] to " . . . ordered movement which runs through all beauty"[5] to " . . . the periodic succession or regular recurrence of events in time which constitute the organization of temporal relationships."[6]

Since the early 1900s a great deal of dance literature has appeared and much research has been conducted. Much of the literature centers on the worth of the activity, teaching techniques, and opinion articles written by leaders in the field. As can be noted by scanning the *Compilation of Dance Research 1901–1964*[7] and *Research in Dance I*[8], a large portion of the research in dance has been done at the master's thesis level. In the process of doing research it is often necessary to develop measuring instruments and techniques. These, along with other dance and rhythm tests, will be presented under the following headings in the remainder of this chapter:

Tests of musical ability that have been developed and applied in various ways to investigate elements associated with dance and rhythm.

Tests involving mechanical devices, mostly for the assessment of rhythm, practical (in terms of equipment) tests, and tests devised to predict dance ability through the measurement of other skills.

Tests involving a relatively new trend in the assessment of rhythm based on a precise definition involving time and space.

TESTS OF MUSICAL ABILITY

Several investigators[9] over the years have devised tests intended to measure musical ability. In general, these tests are made up of several parts designed to measure separate elements of musical ability. Although the number and names of these elements differ from test to test, some common categories are pitch discrimination, intensity discrimination, consonance discrimination, tonal memory, and rhythms. The usual strategy for assessing these attributes involves presenting a series of recorded sounds to the student and asking if the pitch, intensity, tone, and rhythm of the first is the same as or different from the second. Generally, a large number of such exercises are used to determine the score for each element tested. The subscores are then combined in various ways to obtain the desired measures. Researchers[10] have examined the validity of these instruments and have generally found it to be questionable.

In addition to investigations concerning validity, research has been done to determine the relationship that exists between these tests and various physical parameters.

Musical rhythmic ability versus motor rhythm
Annett[11] compared scores on part of the Seashore test[12] to an assessment of motor rhythm obtained from the subjective judgments of three raters who scored 122 physical education majors on precision, grace, and spontaneous movement while performing a triple step-hop movement. A questionnaire and school marks in physical education were also utilized, and the various correlation coefficients and questionnaire results are presented in the reference. Briggs[13] devised a Motor Rhythmic Performance Test for girls in grades nine through twelve, consisting of walking and skipping to different rhythms using

the Musical Aptitude Profile by Gordon as the criterion measure. She reports a correlation of .657 between the two.

Musical rhythmic ability versus motor performance

Using a revised version of the Seashore test of rhythm and scores on the Sargent jump, sixty-yard dash, basketball throw for distance, lie-sit-stand, Brace motor educability, and the Mott-Lockhard table tennis tests, as well as measures of intelligence, reading ability, and sight, Bond[14] compared rhythmic perception and gross motor performance. The revision of the Seashore test involved measuring rhythm through presentation of visual, tactile, and auditory senses. Bond concludes that rhythmic perception and gross motor performance as she measured them are not significantly related. Reliabilities and intercorrelations among all the variables are presented in the reference.

Musical rhythmic ability versus dancing ability

McCristal[15] and Blake,[16] in separate studies, investigated the relationship between musical rhythmic ability and tap dancing and square dancing, respectively. McCristal modified the Seashore rhythm test so that a foot pedal rather than the hands were used, and constructed a mechanical device for measuring the ability to tap the feet in time with a beat given by a bell connected to a metronome. In the reference a correlation matrix showing the relationships between the foot rhythm test, the Seashore test, a reaction time test, and a questionnaire score is given.

Blake, using three raters, obtained an initial and a final level of square dancing skill score for seventy men and women enrolled in beginning square dancing classes. She also obtained a pre and post score for each student on the Seashore test of audio-perceptual rhythm. Blake indicates a correlation of .39 was obtained between the pre and post square dance scores while a correlation of .47 was obtained between the pre and post Seashore scores.

Musical rhythmic ability tests as discriminatory devices

Sanderson[17] used two tests of musical ability (Seashore and Kwalwasser-Dykema), a questionnaire, and 102 Black, 113 Jewish, 72 German, 138 Italian, and 125 Polish children to determine if differences exist in musical ability among children of different national and racial origin. Her conclusions and reliability and intercorrelation coefficients are presented in the reference.

Brennan,[18] in an attempt to distinguish between gymnasts and dancers and between skilled and unskilled, measured seventy-two girls on thirteen selected characteristics. Among the tests were two parts of the Drake Musical Aptitude Test used to measure rhythm. In part one the student and a recording count together up to four with the recording providing the tempo. After a silent interval, the student is instructed to continue counting (starting with five) until told to stop. The final number reached is compared to the number that should have been obtained if the correct tempo was used. Fifty exercises of this type were used. Part two is exactly the same except during the interval between four and five a distraction is presented. Brennan found no difference between gymnasts and dancers or between "skilled" and "unskilled" on this particular rhythm test.

Dance and rhythm tests
Tests involving mechanical measuring devices
Several investigators[19] have devised mechanical devices designed to assess the ability of a student to match a particular beat or tempo, usually supplied by a recording or a metronome. In general, these devices allow the investigator to compare the musical tempo to the attempted reproduction of it by the subject by recording these two occurrences simultaneously on moving paper. For example, in Heinlein's[20] study, eight preschool children were instructed to march in time with a song while being observed by psychology students trained in observation techniques. Several of the observers had fairly extensive musical backgrounds. On the mechanical device described in the reference, Heinlein was able to record on four separate horizontal lines the time in seconds, the actual musical beat, the actual time of a child's foot contact with the ground, and the instant the observer surmised the child's foot contacted the floor. The last item was recorded by having the observers depress a telegraph key when the child's foot contacted the floor. Interestingly, Heinlein found the pattern produced by the observers matched more closely the music tempo than it did the pattern produced by the children's foot contacts with the floor.

Practical dance and rhythm tests
Lemon and Sherbon tempo test[21]
In a study to examine the relationships between rhythmic ability and motor ability, the authors administered Carl Seashore's test of perception of rhythm,[22] Robert Seashore's test of motor rhythm,[23] and an original rhythm test consisting of two parts. In part one, by beating on a drum or by stepping, the student expresses four different rhythm patterns. First, the test administrator beats a certain rhythm on a drum and the student repeats it in the same fashion. Four tempos are tested. Next, the four tempos (in a different order) are tested by the tester beating them on a drum but the student repeating them by stepping. Finally, the tester presents the four tempos (again in a different order) one at a time by stepping, and the student repeats them on the drum. In part two of the test a metronome is set at a certain tempo (sixty-four beats per minute) and turned on for the student to perceive the beat. The metronome is stopped and the student told to step at the same rate. The number of steps taken in ten seconds is compared to twelve, which is the correct number of beats in this time at the indicated tempo. The same procedure is followed twice more, but with the metronome changed to 120 beats per minute and 184 beats per minute. The correct number of steps is twenty-two for the second setting and thirty-two for the third. The score for the test is the total number of deviations from the appropriate number of steps. Several conclusions and various correlation coefficients of interest are presented in the reference.

Waglow social dance test[24]

A melody was recorded in six different rhythms (waltz, tango, slow fox trot, jitterbug, rumba, and samba), with a known number of measures of each rhythm. Students are arranged in pairs, one to take the test and the other to score. The student taking the test begins at a specified mark on the floor. The scorer records the number of times the student returns to the marked spot during the execution of the proper dance step. This number is compared to the appropriate number obtained from knowing the number of measures of each rhythm, and any difference is recorded as a deviation. The absolute values of the six deviations are summed for the final score. Complete directions and coefficients of objectivity, reliability, and validity are presented in the reference.

Ashton motor rhythm test[25]

Through input from a research class and from experienced dance instructors, a rating scale of from zero to four was devised. For each point on the scale, specific criteria relating to beat, rhythm pattern, ability to maintain and vary movement, ability to change direction, and style of movement were developed. This rating scale is used to evaluate students as they perform to selected musical excerpts. The specific musical selections, their order, number of measures, and duration are listed in the reference for two parallel forms of the test. Each form consists of three parts. In part one the walk, skip, and run are evaluated. In part two the skip, run, fast walk, slow walk, and skip and run are tested. In part three the schottische, slow waltz, moderate waltz, and polka are examined. The possible range of scores is 0–156. In the reference are the complete directions for constructing the musical recording, the rating scale used for scoring, and descriptive statistical information derived from administration of the test to a large number of college women.

McCulloch rhythmic response test[26]

To develop a test for first-grade children of ability to make a rhythmic response through movement, McCulloch administered sixty-five items to 196 first graders. Through the use of judges' ratings the list of items was eventually reduced to seven, but then augmented to fourteen to increase reliability. The final battery contains items to measure pulse beat, accent, rhythmic patterns, and musical phrasing. Reliability and validity and the directions for administering and scoring the test are presented in the reference.

Lang test of rhythmic response[27]

The purpose of Lang's study was to develop a test to measure the level of development in selected rhythmic tasks of girls ages nine to thirteen. A review of the literature resulted in the development of a series of tests in the following five areas: tempo continuation, metrical discrimination, rhythmic pattern repetition, musical phrase recognition, and basic step performance. Two separate pilot studies were done to refine the items in each test. The final tests (described in the reference) were administered to 230 girls aged nine to thirteen, and the resulting data were used to establish reliability, objectivity, and age level norms. Scoring directions, a sample score sheet, administrative directions, and a list of materials required are also presented in the reference.

Bentley rhythmic memory test[28]

A short, ten-item test, in which the student must determine if the second half of each item is the same as the first half and, if it is different, on which pulse the change is made, is described by Bentley in the reference listed. The scoring procedure is also detailed.

Coppock test of rhythmic response[29]

Coppock devised a test of rhythmic response using twenty-three musical patterns, each of which is played three times. The student listens the first two times and then attempts to walk in time to the tempo the third time. Both meter and tempo are rated using a five-point scale. Coppock recorded scores on this test, the Gordon measures of musical perception, and the Scott and French motor ability test and obtained other information from 111 college women. Several correlation coefficients between the various measures and descriptive statistics regarding the test of rhythmic response are presented in the reference.

Johnson and Nelson dance tests[30]

The authors present descriptions and normative data for a dance leap test for determining the power of the legs for horizontal leaping, a rhythm run dance test to measure a dancer's coordination and control in running a given distance at one level, and a fall and recovery test to assess the agility of a dancer in falling and recovering in dance movement.

Prediction of dance ability

Benton,[31] Frial,[32] and Bushey[33] are examples of investigators who have studied the relationship between dance ability and measures on other attributes such as agility, balance, strength, power, kinesthetic sense, flexibility, and motor educability. In general, these investigators determined dance ability through subjective ratings by experts, administered batteries of tests assessing the characteristics mentioned above, and applied correlational statistical techniques to examine the relationship of interest. Benton and Frial present regression equations. All three investigators present correlation coefficients and test directions in their respective references.

Recent rhythmic ability tests

Schwanda[34] presents a study to investigate a rather specific interpretation of rhythm, defining rhythmic accuracy as, "the ability to be in a specific point in space at a specific point in time." The Drake Musical Aptitude Tests were administered to forty-one university freshmen women. Those ten scoring the highest and the ten scoring the lowest were selected as subjects. Each subject was then filmed while performing a forward lunge in which the arm was swung forward and upward to a target. The arm was supposed to stop on every other beat and recover (back to the side of the body) on every alternate beat with the tempo set at sixty-six beats per minute. Through analysis of the film it is possible to determine the deviation from the target in both time and space. No

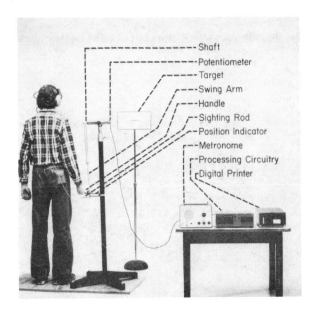

Motor Rhythm Analysis System

Frank L. Smoll, Dept. of Kinesiology, University of Washington, Seattle difference was found between the two groups of students. Complete test directions appear in the reference.

A similar study, accomplished without filming, was done by Smoll.[35] Using a metronome, a target, and a series of electrical-mechanical components, Smoll recorded on moving paper the actual tempo provided by the metronome and the anterior-posterior movements of the arm attempting to simulate the tempo. Although no wiring schematic is given, the method of scoring, an example readout, and a picture of the apparatus set up are presented in the reference. Smoll and Palmatier[36] later refined the motor rhythm analysis system to reduce the amount of time required to collect data.

REFERENCES CITED

[1]Aileene Lockhart and Esther Pease, *Modern Dance: Building and Teaching Lessons,* 3rd ed. (Dubuque, Iowa: Wm. C. Brown Co. Publishers, 1966), 189 pp.

[2]Sandra E. Dvorack, "A Subjective Evaluation of Fundamental Locomotor Movement in Modern Dance Using a Five-Point Rating Scale," M.S. Thesis, South Dakota State University, 1967, 84 pp.

[3]Mary Jo Shelly, "Some Aspects of the Case for and against Objective Testing of Dance in Education," *Research Quarterly* (Oct. 1930), 119–24.

[4]Dorothy M. Muzzey, "Group Progress of White and Colored Children in Learning a Rhythm Pattern," *Research Quarterly* (Oct. 1933), 62–70.

[5]Betty Lynd Thompson, *Fundamentals of Rhythm and Dance* (New York: A.S. Barnes and Company, 1933), p. 3.

[6]Frank Smoll, "A Rhythmic Ability Analysis System," *Research Quarterly* (May 1973), 232–36.

[7]Esther E. Pease, *Compilation of Dance Research 1901–1964* (Washington, D.C., AAHPER, 1964), 53 pp.

[8]*Research in Dance I* (Washington, D.C., AAHPER, 1968), 45 pp.

[9]Raleigh M. Drake, *Drake Musical Aptitudes Test* (Chicago: Science Research Associates, 1957), Edwin Gordon, "A Three-Year Longitudinal Predictive Validity Study of the Musical Aptitude Profile" (Iowa City: University of Iowa Press, 1967), 78 pp.; Jacob Kwalwasser, *Tests and Measurement in Music* (Boston: C. C. Birchard, 1927), 146 pp.; Carl E. Seashore, *The Psychology of Musical Talent* (New York: Silver Burdette, 1919), 288 pp.; and Robert H. Seashore, "Stanford Motor Skills Unit," *Psychological Monographs* 39 (1928), 223 pp.

[10]Flora M. Brennan, "The Relation between Musical Capacity and Performance," *Psychological Monographs* (1927), 190–248; Andrew W. Brown, "The Reliability and Validity of the Seashore Tests of Musical Ability," *Journal of Applied Psychology* (1928), 468–76; and Vernon V. Tarrell, "An Investigation of the Validity of the Musical Aptitude Profile," *Journal of Research in Music Education* (Winter 1965), 195–206.

[11]Thomas Annett, "A study of Rhythmical Capacity and Performance in Motor Rhythm in Physical Education," *Research Quarterly* (May 1932), 183–91.

[12]Carl E. Seashore, *The Psychology of Musical Talent.*

[13]Ruth Arlene Briggs, "The Development of an Instrument for Assessment of Motor Rhythmic Performance," M.A. Thesis, University of Missouri, 1968, 54 pp.

[14]Marjorie H. Bond, "Rhythmic Perceptions and Gross Motor Performance," *Research Quarterly* (Oct. 1959), 259–65.

[15]K. J. McCristal, "Experimental Study of Rhythm in Gymnastics and Square Dancing," *Research Quarterly* (May 1933), 63–75.

[16]Patricia Ann Blake, "Relationship between Audio-Perceptual Rhythm and Skill in Square Dance," *Research Quarterly* (May 1960), 229–31.

[17]Helen E. Sanderson, "Differences in Musical Ability in Children of Different National and Racial Origin," *Journal of Genetic Psychology* (1933), 100–19.

[18]Mary Alice Brennan, "A Comparative Study of Skilled Gymnasts and Dancers on Thirteen Selected Characteristics," M.S. Thesis, University of Wisconsin, 1967, 133 pp.

[19]Nadine Buck, "A Comparison of Two Methods of Testing Response to Auditory Rhythms," *Research Quarterly* (Oct. 1936), 36–45; Edith C. Haight, "Individual Differences in Motor Adaptations to Rhythmic Stimuli," *Research Quarterly* (March 1944) 38–43; Margaret N. H'Doubler, *Rhythm Form and Analysis* (Madison, Wisc.: Kramer Business Service, 1932), p. 3; Christian Paul Heinlein, "A New Method of Studying the Rhythmic Responses of Children Togetl.er with an Evaluation of the Method of Simple Observation," *Journal of Genetic Psychology*, 1929), 205–28; Mary E. Shambaugh Muzzey, "Group Progress of White and Colored Children in Learning a Rhythm Pattern"; "The Objective Measurement of Success in the Teaching of Folk Dancing to University Women," *Research Quarterly* (March 1935), 33–58; and Shirley E. Simpson, "Development and Validation of an Objective Measure of Locomotor Response to Auditory Rhythmic Stimuli," *Research Quarterly* (Oct. 1958), 342–48.

[20]Heinlein, "A New Method of Studying the Rhythmic Responses of Children Together with an Evaluation of the Method of Simple Observations."

[21]Eloise Lemon and Elizabeth Sherbon, "A Study of the Relationships of Certain Measures of Rhythmic Ability and Motor Ability in Girls and Women," *Research Quarterly* (March 1934), 82–85.

[22]Carl E. Seashore, *The Psychology of Musical Talent.*

[23]Robert H. Seashore, "Stanford Motor Skills Unit."

[24]I. F. Waglow, "An Experiment in Social Dance Testing," *Research Quarterly* (March 1953), 97–101.

[25]Dudley Ashton, "A Gross Motor Rhythm Test," *Research Quarterly* (Oct. 1953), 253–60.

[26]Margaret L. McCulloch, "The Development of a Test of Rhythmic Response through Movement of First-Grade Children," Doctoral Dissertation, University of Oregon, 1955, 99 pp.

[27]Lucile M. Lang, "The Development of a Test of Rhythmic Response at the Elementary Level," M.Ed. Thesis, University of Texas, 1966, 128 pp.

[28]Arnold Bentley, *Musical Ability in Children and Its Measurement* (New York: October House Inc., 1966), 151 pp.

[29]Doris E. Coppock, "Development of an Objective Measure of Rhythmic Motor Response," *Research Quarterly*, (Dec. 1968), 915–21.

[30]Barry Johnson and Jack Nelson, *Practical Measurements for Evaluation in Physical Education*, 2nd ed. (Minneapolis, Minn.: Burgess Publishing Co., 1974), pp. 303–07.

[31]Rachel J. Benton, "The Measurement of Capacities for Learning Dance Movement Techniques," *Research Quarterly* (May 1944), 137–44.

[32]Paula I. S. Frial, "Prediction of Modern Dance Ability through Kinesthetic Tests," Thesis, State University of Iowa, 1965, 89 pp.

[33]Suzanne R. Bushey, "Relationship of Modern Dance Performance to Agility, Balance, Flexibility, Power and Strength," *Research Quarterly* (Oct. 1966), 313–16.

[34]Nancy A. Schwanda, "A Study of Rhythmic Ability and Movement Performance," *Research Quarterly* (Oct. 1969), 567–74.

[35]Smoll, "A Rhythmic Ability and Analysis System."

[36]Frank Smoll and Ronald Palmatier, "A Second-generation Motor Rhythm Analysis System," *Behavior Research Methods and Instrumentation* (1977), 508–10.

SECTION 6

GRADING

INTRODUCTION TO SECTION 6

Although the philosophy and rationale underlying various grading procedures differ greatly among educators, prospective physical education teachers should be aware of certain considerations in determining what marking system to use and the mechanical aspects of converting sets of scores into marks. The complexities of grading, some suggestions for minimizing the shortcomings of marks, and the mechanical aspects of determining marks are presented in this section.

Chapter 20
Grading Complexities

The difficulties and complexities involved in grading have been a part of the educational process for a long time. In fact, almost regularly, articles appear in magazines and professional literature either condemning some current grading practice or suggesting some new approach. This difference of opinion is partially explained by the fact that many different philosophies of education exist. Further dissatisfaction results from the fact that determining what mark should be assigned to each student is a very complex task, made so by the lack of precise units in which to measure, the lack of valid and reliable instruments and tests with which to measure, the difficulties involved in constructing precise measuring instruments, and the innate unpleasantness caused by passing judgment when the natural instinct of most teachers is to help and to teach.

The difficulties involved in arriving at marks and the belief that marks are a deterrent to learning (because students worry more about their grades than about learning) have led some educational leaders to advocate the total abolition of marks and measurement. Unfortunately, the suggestion that this practice would lead to improved achievement is virtually impossible to verify, since measurements of achievement would be required to compare this system to any other.

A great number of reasons for the existence of marks are espoused by other educational leaders. Usually lists of the uses of marks include some or all of the following:

1. Motivation and guidance of the learning, educational, and vocational plans, and personal development of the student

2. Communication to the parents of the student's progress

3. Condensation of information for use in college admissions and scholarship determinations

4. Communication to possible employers of the student's strengths and limitations

5. Appraisal of the student for use by the school itself in tailoring education to the needs and interests of the student and in evaluating the effectiveness of teaching methods.

Just as the complete abolition of marks can be questioned, some of the claims made to justify them require inspection. For example, because a single mark at the end of a unit is removed in time from the actual learning process and because it has little diagnostic value, the use of marks to direct learning is much less efficient than everyday indications of success or failure. A student who for some reason does not perform as well as his or her peers throughout some unit of instruction should not have to wait until the end of the unit to find this out.

In spite of the controversy concerning all the positive and negative aspects that can be listed concerning grades, most educators would probably agree that some type of a system is necessary to communicate a student's achievement level to those interested, for whatever reason. Perhaps instead of abolishing marks or trying to discover some way around their use, educators should attempt to improve the validity and reliability of the marks they assign and to use marks correctly. It is probably the misuse rather than the use of marks that causes much of the dissatisfaction with grading practices used today.

Although many minor difficulties arise, two major shortcomings are involved in marking. The first concerns the fact that marks, which are judgments of one person by another, are based on subjective evidence. In some instances the amount of subjectivity included in a set of marks is great. Marks based on an evaluation of a student's answers to an essay examination, participation in class discussions, and effort put forth in class are examples of situations where subjective judgment is involved to a great extent. Even marks arrived at through seemingly precise and objective methods involve more subjectivity than might initially be apparent. The use of objective tests (e.g., true-false, multiple-choice) still requires somewhat subjective decisions, such as determining which items should be included on the test and what response is most correct for each item. Often a precise formula is devised for combining certain achievements of the students, but in fact this formula is generally based on a subjective weighting of the importance of the course objectives. Thus, although it is true that some marks involve a greater amount of subjectivity than others, it is also true that all marks involve some degree of subjectivity.

Generally, the greater the degree of subjectivity involved in the marking system the greater the unreliability. A subjective system, if repeated, would probably not assign the same marks to the same students. This lack of objectivity and consequent lowering of reliability leads to the second, more serious, shortcoming of marks, the lack of a common understanding of what a particular mark represents.

Marks are relative to the type of marking system used, the particular instructor who assigns them, the makeup of the class, the institution where they were earned, and many other related factors. For example, an E might stand for excellent in one marking system but for failing in another; a mark of B from an instructor who rarely gives them has a different meaning from a B from an instructor who seldom gives anything lower; an A obtained in a class of superior students may represent a more significant achievement than an A received in an average class; and the same performance rated as an A at one institution might be rated lower at another institution.

While the use of insufficient objective evidence reduces the reliability of marks, the lack of a clear and generally accepted definition of what a particular mark represents affects their validity. Marks, which should reflect the degree to which a student has achieved the course objectives, are often contaminated by many other factors.

No specific rules can be firmly established because every situation in which marks are assigned is different in some respects. Differences exist in such areas as teaching techniques, course objectives, equipment and facilities available, type of students in class, and many others. However, some general guidelines can be established through which some of the discontent with marking systems can be reduced. In the following paragraphs the effects of various grading practices on the reliability and validity of marks are examined.

GRADING PRACTICES

Absolute or relative?

Absolute marking systems are characterized by set standards. These standards are usually established by the teacher (or the department) and are explained to the students at the beginning of the course. Typically, each course assignment and test is worth a certain number of points. Marks are assigned at the end of the course by comparing the total number of points accumulated by each student to the number of points necessary to achieve each mark.

The use of absolute marking systems is often advocated for several reasons: The final computation of marks is relatively simple; students are evaluated on the basis of their achievement of course objectives; marks are not influenced by the performances of other students; motivation is increased because students know exactly what is expected of them and they can trace their progress; and the course can be evaluated since the degree to which the students are meeting the course objectives can be fairly easily determined.

Unfortunately some problems are encountered when one attempts to put an absolute marking system into practice. The level of achievement necessary to obtain a particular mark is usually established by an individual teacher and therefore is subject to his or her idiosyncrasies. The requirements may vary widely from one teacher to another. It is probable that the standards are derived at least in part from observation of prior student performances, causing these standards to be somewhat relative. Further, unless all measurements are quite objective, the process used by the teacher to award points (on an essay examination, for example) can greatly influence the final percentage of each mark assigned.

Another serious disadvantage of absolute marking systems stems from an overreliance on classroom assignments and tests as precise measuring instruments. In effect the teacher is claiming to know what 100 percent of achievement is in the course and, further, to know quite accurately what percentage of achievement each student has reached. Typical classroom measuring devices are seldom accurate enough to allow such a conclusion.

Relative marking systems grade students in respect to the achievement of their peers. Grading "on the curve" is one example of such a system. A teacher using relative marking practices ranks the students based on their performances on various assignments and tests completed throughout the course. The percentages of the different marks to be given (A's, B's, C's, or whatever) are estimated partly on the basis of determining the overall level of the class compared with previous classes. If, for example, the teacher concludes that the present class, in general, performed better than an average class of this type, the percentage of high marks awarded is increased over that assigned in the average class. Once the percentages are determined, the marks are assigned. For example, if the teacher decided to award fifteen percent A's to a class of forty students, the top six students would receive the A marks.

Relative marking procedures take into account disparity of instruction that exists and can tolerate less than perfect measuring devices. However, problems exist. A student's grade is dependent on the performance of classmates rather than on his or her own achievement in mastering the course objectives. It is claimed that the system dictates that a certain number of students receive high marks (and low marks) even though their levels of achievement may not warrant it. Finally, the criteria for grades are established by the students rather than the teacher.

These criticisms of relative marking systems all stem from the same problem. All classes to which marks are to be assigned are not normally distributed in respect to the achievement of the course objectives. Notice that if a class is, in fact, "normal," there would be little difference resulting from the use of either absolute or relative standards. However, some classes as a whole may be above or below average due to self-selection (students with special talents electing certain courses) or ability grouping. Variations in ability and achievement from one class to another do not necessarily rule out using relative marking systems. Allowances can be made by not insisting on rigorous adherence to a previously established ideal distribution of marks in each small, probably atypical class, but only in the composite distribution of marks for many similar classes. Further, although it may be true that students tend to set the standards in the relative systems, it does not follow that the standards will be set lower than the teacher would set them. It is not, for example, reasonable to assume that the students in a class about to run the 100-yard dash would previously agree among themselves to run slowly.

In summary, both absolute and relative marking systems have advantages and disadvantages. In situations where course objectives can be very clearly defined, measurement techniques are relatively accurate, and the teacher has sufficient data accumulated over time, absolute systems are to be favored. When these conditions do not prevail, relative systems offer more satisfactory results. In real life most awards are determined on relative terms. For example, the first runner to reach the 100-yard mark is declared the winner in the 100-yard dash, not the runner who achieves some previously established time. However, one would be hesitant to be operated on by the best of a poor group of future surgeons or to fly in an airplane piloted by the best of a sad lot of pilot applicants. In many cases the marking system finally adopted is a combination of the two methods, as when set standards based on previous student performances determined over a period of years are used.

Achievement or other factors?

Factors other than the degree of achievement of the course objectives are often included in the determination of a student's grade. Such practice transforms the grade from a report of the student's achievement of the course objectives to a weapon used to control and direct various behaviors. Unfortunately this causes one of the previously mentioned shortcomings, the lack of clearly defined standards as to what various marks mean. The inclusion of such factors as attendance, purchase and care of a specified uniform, appropriate shower-taking procedures, and the like in the determination of a student's grade for a volleyball unit, for example, reduces the communication value of the grade. How, for instance, would a future teacher become aware that even though Bill learned the volleyball skills and knowledges exceptionally well, he received a C because of failure to wash his uniform once a week?

To base a grade or some part of a grade on judgments of such factors as character, citizenship, effort, attitude, and sportsmanship is even less defensible because such judgments are often very subjective and low in validity and reliability. Only if these factors are among the specified course objectives is it appropriate to consider them in the assignment of marks. The teacher should be able to defend these factors as valid objectives of the physical education course and make every effort to secure objective, reliable, and valid measures of these factors.

Most of the factors listed here are concerns of the entire curriculum, not just physical education. Certainly an awareness and assessment of students' efforts, attitudes, and character should be among the responsibilities of school teachers and administrators. However, for the most part, evaluations of the students' progress in these areas should be made through checklists, reports, conferences, counselors, and other similar techniques rather than through marks.

Status or improvement?

Obviously all students are not equally talented mentally or physically. In an effort to account for this fact some teachers base marks on the amout of improvement rather than on the level of achievement attained. Most often the amount of improvement is determined through the difference between scores made on a test given early in the course and one given at or near the end of the course. Besides balancing initial differences in ability, two other advantages of grading on improvement are often cited. Motivation might be increased if students know relative class level will not be the major factor in determining their marks, and the results of the initial testing can be used to place students into homogeneous groups to increase teaching efficiency.

Unfortunately there are many disadvantages to grading on improvement. As previously mentioned, any test contains some measurement error. Therefore when a test is given prior to and at the completion of a course in an effort to assess the amount of improvement, two error terms exist. It is only possible to compare the actual scores on the two tests. There is no way of determining how much of the gain (or lack of it) may be due to errors of measurement.

In some physical education courses only very crude initial tests can be given. For example, it is not very practical to determine a student's initial ability in swimming or trampolining (except verbally). Thus some activities preclude the use of grading on improvement. Also, it is difficult to assure that each student exerts maximum effort on the initial test.

Yet another disadvantage of grading on improvement involves the fact that it is usually much more difficult to improve when already at a high level of achievement than when starting at a low level. This fact may result, if grading is done on the basis of improvement only, in unfairness to those students in the class who are initially more talented than their classmates. For example, who improves more, a student who decreases a 100-yard dash time from 10.0 seconds to 9.7 seconds or a student who reduces the time from 14.0 seconds to 12.0 seconds?

Finally, for most educational purposes it is more useful to know whether a student is good, poor, or average compared to peers than it is to know that the student changed more or less rapidly than they did during the instructional period. It is the actual level of achievement that matters most in real-life situations as well.

As previously stated, one of the main reasons that educators, and especially physical educators, prefer to mark on improvement is the fact that this practice gives all students a more nearly equal chance to earn high marks. A great number of educators, again especially physical educators, are averse to giving low marks because they feel they discourage effort, which in turn increases the probability of low marks, and the cycle continues until the student dislikes the subject area. The concern to physical educators is that when this stage is reached the student is less apt to continue in physical activity during his or her lifetime. Besides the fact that little, if any, evidence exists to support this contention, it is illogical. It seems dubious that students feel rewarded when given high marks for improvement when actual performance level is less than most of their peers. For example, poor swimmers know they are poor swimmers and so do their peers; an honest student knows that in the long run it is actual level of achievement that is important, not the rate of improvement.

Suppose for the moment the contention that low marks cause a student to dislike school or more specifically that low physical education marks destroy incentive and reduce the possibility of a student engaging in physical activity is true. The obvious and simple solution of not giving low marks is a little like a physician treating the symptoms rather than the cause of the illness. Perhaps an investigation should be made to determine why a student is receiving low marks rather than rectifying the situation by eliminating low marks. Three other approaches should be investigated.

First, the number of opportunities for achieving success should be increased. Fortunately, people differ in what they can do well. Providing varied opportunities in which to excel should increase the number of different students capable of achieving success. The ramification of this suggestion for physical educators is to broaden the curriculum from, for example, offering touch football, basketball, and softball every year to offering as many different and varied activities as possible. Due to the fact that the skills required to succeed in physical education are relatively heterogeneous in comparison to those required in other subjects, varying the physical education curriculum probably will result in a higher percentage of different students achieving success than in the other areas. For example, learning how to swim a particular stroke is not nearly as dependent on knowing how to do a forward roll as, say, learning to derive a square root is on knowing how to divide. Fortunately there is currently a trend in physical education toward offering increasingly varied curricula.

A second alternative to meddling with the grading procedures to provide success lies in ability grouping and enrolling students in courses suitable to their skill levels. If differences in initial ability are small, grading on improvement becomes unimportant. Other subject areas, such as mathematics, English, and the sciences, are ahead in regard to ability grouping, although some progress in this area is now being seen in physical education with the advent of modular and computer scheduling. To adopt this suggestion physical educators need to develop valid and reliable measuring devices to use in classifying students by ability.

The third suggestion involves educating students (and others) to the fact that a mark is simply an expression of the level of achievement of the course objectives attained by the student. It is not meant as a reward or a punishment. Further, it needs to be stressed that not every student can be expected to excel in every course. In short, the worth of physical education must be conveyed to the students through the teaching procedures and the curriculum, not through the awarding of high grades regardless of the level of proficiency.

What symbols?

As pointed out at the beginning of this chapter, new systems for reporting student achievement are constantly being developed and promoted. A relatively recent trend, although it seems to be lessening now, is the increase in the use of the pass-fail system, particularly in colleges and universities across the United States. The particular symbols that are selected will to some extent depend on the decisions made on the previous considerations mentioned. For example, in the absolute system of grading the marks given are usually in the form of percentages, whereas in the relative system marks of A, B, C, D, and F are commonly employed.

The most common formats for symbolically representing the level of achievement are probably percentages, pass-fail, and A, B, C, D, F. Others sometimes used are pass-no record; descriptive grading, in which written comments describing student achievement are used; and various types of rating sheets, in which specified portions of student performance are rated using a previously established scale. Although the other decisions influence what symbols to use, two further considerations should be noted.

The first consideration involves a paradox. If a format is selected in which there are only a few categories, the information that is conveyed is minimal. On the other hand, the chances of misclassifying a student are reduced. For example, in the extreme case of the pass-fail format, the top student in class and the student who just barely passed are given the same symbol and yet their achievements might have differed tremendously. However, using this format there are only two possible misclassifications that can be made: a student who should have received an F may be given a P or a student who should have received a P may be given an F.

On the other end of the spectrum, if a format is selected in which there are a great many categories (such as percentages), the information given to the student and others is maximized but the opportunities for misclassification also increase. Thus, when determining which format to use, a general rule to remember is the higher the number of categories, the more reliable measuring procedures are required.

The second consideration in selecting a marking format is communication. In reality this is probably the most important consideration for any marking system, regardless of particular philosophy or circumstances. Some educators have suggested that the entire procedure of somehow magically arriving at some symbol to represent a student's achievement be dropped in favor of simply writing down on paper sentences to indicate "exactly" where the student stands in respect to mastery of the course objectives. The rationale is that this procedure would eliminate one of the major shortcomings of grades, that of the lack of a clear, universal understanding of what a symbol stands for. In fact, there currently seems to be a trend in elementary schools to adopt this procedure.

One immediate result of the "descriptive approach" is the lack of reducability of these written statements, which would pose problems to a student's future teachers, college admissions personnel, and employment directors. However, even if this result could be eliminated in some manner, descriptive grading does not necessarily communicate any more efficiently than other formats. Words, just as symbols, have different meanings to different people. Consequently, interpretation of a particular word, sentence, or paragraph used in descriptive grading may or may not result in the reader obtaining the teacher's message any more correctly than if some symbol had been used. In any event, the decision as to which format should be adopted for reporting grades should be based on the determination of which format will provide the clearest communication to those reading the grades.

Measurement or evaluation?

In Chapter 2 a differentiation between the meanings of the words *measurement* and *evaluation* was made. In respect to marking procedures, a measurement is some type of quantitative description of a student's achievement, whereas an evaluation is concerned with a qualitative judgment of a student's achievement. In other words, if a mark is considered a measurement, it should simply represent the degree to which the student has achieved the course objectives. If a mark is considered an evaluation, it should indicate to some degree how adequate the level of achievement attained is for a particular student.

There are several advantages in treating marks as measurements rather than evaluations. Judgments of how adequate a student's achievement has been depend not only on how much was achieved but on the opportunity for achievement and effort. This fact makes it very difficult to report evaluations precisely in some standard marking system. Finally, it is probably of more value to a future teacher or employer to know that a student was outstanding, mediocre, or poor in a particular aspect of education than to know that the student did as well as could be expected or that the student failed to live up to the expectations of a teacher. Given valid and reliable measurements of a student's achievement in various areas, the future teacher or employer can make his or her own evaluations in light of current circumstances, which would probably be more valid than having on hand evaluations made by others under totally different conditions.

GRADING CONSIDERATIONS

Adoption of the following ten suggestions would help to eliminate or at least reduce the undesirable characteristics of marks and make them a functioning and useful part of the educational process.

1. Carefully determine defendable objectives for each course before it begins.

2. Group students according to ability in the physical skills necessary for the course.

3. Construct tests and measurements as objectively as possible, realizing that all tests are subjective to some degree.

4. Remember that no matter how well constructed, no test is perfectly reliable.

5. Realize that the distribution of grades for any one class does not necessarily fit any particular curve but that over the long run physical skills are probably fairly normally distributed.

6. Determine marks that reflect only the level of achievement in meeting the course objectives and not other miscellaneous factors.

7. Establish grades on the basis of status, not improvement.

8. Avoid using grades to reward the good effort of a low achiever or to punish the poor effort of a high achiever.

9. Choose a grading format that maximizes communication for each particular situation in which grades are given.

10. Consider grades as measurements, not evaluations.

Chapter 21
Grading Mechanics

Four steps are involved in the mechanical process of arriving at a symbol to represent each student's level of achievement regarding the course objectives. Although each may be accomplished in a variety of ways due to differing situations and philosophies, the four steps basic to any grading practice involve determining and weighing the course objectives, measuring the amount of achievement toward the course objectives, combining measurements to obtain for each student a composite score, and converting the composite scores to the particular grading format chosen.

STEP 1—DETERMINE COURSE OBJECTIVES AND THEIR RELATIVE IMPORTANCE

Without question this is the most important of the four steps. In fact it is basic to every aspect of teaching a course, not just grading. A considerable amount of thought should go into the determination of what the students are to gain from a particular course. Important aspects of teaching, such as sequence of material presentations, necessary equipment, teaching procedures, assignments, and grading procedures, cannot be considered until the course objectives are established. Obviously this decision must precede the teaching of the course and should be based on as much knowledge regarding the abilities of the prospective students as can be obtained. Other factors that will influence this decision involve the general objectives of physical education and practical considerations such as the number of students, the facility limitations, the length of the course or unit, the number and length of the meeting times, and so forth.

The objectives finally decided on for a physical education course can generally be classified into three broad categories of physical, mental, and social. It should be noticed that if the objectives are stated in behavioral, rather than vague terms, the second step (measuring achievement) will be made easier. In other words, a list of the specific knowledges, the actual performance levels, and the social conduct expected to be achieved by each student should be prepared.

The weighting of the importance of the course objectives will vary greatly from one situation to another depending on such factors as the philosophy of the teacher and the age and ability of the students. For example, more emphasis would logically be placed on the physical and mental objectives for a physical fitness unit for tenth-grade boys than for a coeducational volleyball unit at the same grade level. The actual weight given to the importance of each course objective is a decision to be made by the teacher and should result in a balanced and defensible list of goals to be achieved by each class member.

Two major advantages accrue from carefully going through this procedure before a course begins. The planning of student experiences, teaching methods, and grading procedures is facilitated, and student anxiety can be reduced if the students are informed prior to the start of the course what is expected of them.

STEP 2—MEASURE THE DEGREE OF ATTAINMENT OF COURSE OBJECTIVES

Recall that in Chapter 2 measurement was defined as the procedure of assigning a number to each member of a group based on some characteristic. In this case the characteristic involved is the degree of achievement of each course objective. Unlike step one, step two (and three and four) occur after the teaching (and supposedly the learning) has taken place. This is not to imply that all measuring should be done at the end of a unit or course. To the contrary, there is much merit in obtaining measures throughout a unit, as this leads to increased awareness on the part of the student (and the teacher) as to progress toward the objectives. However, the testing or measuring used in determining the degree of achievement attained for the purpose of grading students should obviously not occur before the completion of instruction and learning.

The purpose of sections three, four, and five of this book is to aid the prospective physical educator in constructing, evaluating, selecting, and administering tests and other devices in order to arrive at the number to assign to each student that most accurately represents his or her level of achievement of the particular course objective being measured.

STEP 3—OBTAIN A COMPOSITE SCORE

Seldom does a course have a single objective. Often more than one measurement is made in an effort to determine the amount of achievement for each

objective. For these reasons it is usually necessary to combine several scores in order to arrive at a single value representing each student's overall level of achievement of the course objectives. This composite score is then normally converted into whatever symbol format (e.g., A-B-C-D-F, P-F) is being used. The correct manner used to obtain the composite score depends on several factors, the most important of which is the precision of the scores that are to be combined.

In the case of performance scores it is quite apparent why a composite score cannot be obtained by totaling the various raw scores. Usually units differ and feet cannot be added to seconds, or the number of exercise repetitions cannot be added to a distance recorded in inches. The following example illustrates why adding raw scores on two tests that have the same units (such as written tests) may not result in the desired composite score. The important fact that is often overlooked is that a score from a set of scores having a large variability will have more weight in the composite score than a score from a set of scores with little variability, regardless of the absolute values of the scores. As a simple illustration imagine that the scores from a class of twenty-five students were distributed as shown in Table 21.1 on three tests worth nine points, nine points, and twenty-seven points.

This rather extreme example was chosen to make a particular point. The variability of the scores on the first two tests is greater than the variability for test three. It would seem logical that, because the total number of points possible on test three is triple that of tests one or two, the score achieved on test

Table 21.1   Test score distributions from a class of twenty-five students

Test 1 (9 points)		Test 2 (9 points)		Test 3 (27 points)	
Score	Frequency	Score	Frequency	Score	Frequency
9	1	9	1	27	
8	2	8	2	26	
7	3	7	3	25	
6	4	6	4	24	7
5	5	5	5	23	11
4	4	4	4	22	7
3	3	3	3	21	
2	2	2	2	20	
1	1	1	1	19	

three would have the most influence on the student's composite score. Notice, however, some possibilities:

Student	Score on test one	Score on test two	Score on test three	Total raw score
A	5	5	24	34
B	8	7	22	35
C	9	5	23	37
D	3	3	24	30

Student A was one of the seven students achieving the highest score made on test three and his scores on the first two tests were "average." Student A received a composite raw score of thirty-four. The composite raw score for student B, who was above average on the first two tests but was among the lowest scorers on test three, is higher than that for student A. Student C scored at the average on two tests and above average on one test, as did student A. However, because student C's above-average performance came on test one (on which the scores were more variable than the test on which student A achieved above average, test three), student C's composite raw score was also higher than student A's. Finally, even though student D scored as high as anyone in the class on test three, the low scores made on the first two tests lowered this composite raw score below the others.

The point of the illustration is that unless two (or more) sets of scores are similar in variability (which is not necessarily an uncommon phenomenon), summing a student's raw scores to arrive at a composite score may lead to some incorrect conclusions.

One other observation can be made from this example. Assume that, instead of representing the distributions of scores on three tests, the values in Table 21.1 describe the distributions of the measures of how well the mental, social, and performance objectives were met by the students. Further, assume that the teacher decided the mental objective, the social objective, and the performance objective should represent 20%, 20%, and 60% of the final grade, respectively. To achieve this weighting the teacher simply made the number of points possible for each of the three objectives the desired percentage of the total number of possible points. However, as concluded previously, unless the variability of the three sets of scores is somewhat similar, the weighting will be different from that originally planned. The solution is to do the weighting after a score for each objective is obtained rather than to attempt to build the weighting factor into the point system unless equal or nearly equal variability among the sets of scores can be assumed to occur.

If the calculation of composite scores by combining raw scores is not feasible due to different units of measurement or a lack of equal variability among the sets of scores, how can composite scores be formed? Basically, the answer is to convert each set of scores into the same standard distribution so that a common basis is established to make comparing, contrasting, and summing of scores from several sets of scores possible. It is at this point that, for each set of scores, precision and assumptions of normality become important considerations.

In the case of precision of scores it must be determined whether the scores are ordinal (ranks) measures or more precise than ranks and belong to an interval scale. Using an ordinal scale of measurement it is only possible to say that A is larger than B; however, because an interval scale has equal-sized units, it is possible to state how much larger A is than B.

The second consideration involves determining whether the distribution of scores approximates a normal distribution. If it does not is it because the particular trait being measured is not normally distributed or is it because, although the trait is normally distributed, the sample at hand for some reason does not reflect this fact?

On the basis of these two considerations five possible situations arise. In Table 21.2 the correct method for obtaining composite scores in each situation is specified.

Only five situations exist because if the scores are ordinal measures of whatever is being measured it is quite obvious that the distribution of scores (a ranking of the students) cannot approximate a normal distribution. If the scores are interval measures, a visual inspection of the frequency distribution will serve to reveal the closeness of the approximation to the normal distribution. Statistical tests are available to determine whether a distribution is significantly different from a normal distribution. However, such tests are beyond the scope of this text. If uncertainty exists as to whether or not a score distribution approximates the normal distribution closely enough, the teacher can utilize the normalization method of converting scores to a standard distribution.

Before discussion of the procedures involved in the three methods (rank, normalizing, and standard scores), an important point should be explained. For each set of scores the end result of the rank method is simply a ranking of the students, whereas the end result of the other two methods is a set of standard scores. However, it is not possible to arrive at a composite score if some of the sets of scores are converted to ranks and some are converted to standard scores. Thus, if one of the several scores being summed to obtain a composite score must be expressed as a rank, then all the scores must be expressed as ranks. For this reason it is wise to plan in advance the type of measuring that will be used during a course.

Rank method

Probably the simplest method and the one requiring the least precise measurement is numerical ranking of the performance of each student in class on each test taken. The best performance is given a 1, the second best performance a 2, and so on until the worst performance is given a rank equal to the number of students being measured.

To obtain a composite score for each student in the numerical ranking system where 1 represents the best achievement, the ranks for each student

Table 21.2   Methods of obtaining a composite score based on shape of distribution and scale of measurement

Shape of distribution	Scale of measurement	
	Ordinal	Interval
Nonnormal	Rank method	Rank method
Nonnormal but trait is normally distributed	Normalizing method	Normalizing method
Approximately normal	—	Standard score method

are simply summed and the lowest total represents the overall best achievement. In the event that some ranks are missing for some students, a mean rank for each student may be used and is obtained by dividing the sum of the ranks by the number of rank values contributing to that sum. If it is desired to weight the various rankings, the rankings to be considered most important can be added in more than once to arrive at the total. For example, assume that three rankings were obtained, the first to count 10 percent, the second 40 percent, and the third 50 percent of the final grade. For each student a composite score would be obtained by adding to the first rank a value obtained by multiplying the second rank by 4 and a value obtained by multiplying the third rank by 5. As before, the lowest total (or mean) would represent the best overall achievement.

A variation of the numerical ranking system is to rank the students into a set number of categories. For example, the best five achievements are rated as 1, the next five as 2, and so on. Another variation goes one step further by giving the categories letter grades rather than numerals. This procedure does not require any particular number of achievements to be classified into each category and reverses the value of the ranking so that a high rank is best. The system has some merit in being more informative to the students than pure numerical rankings, but the principles underlying arriving at a composite score are the same. In fact, a composite score is obtained in this system by changing the letter grades to numerals and proceeding in a fashion similar to that described for the numerical ranking system. The following example illustrates one possible variation of this system: The categories A+, A, A−, B+, B, B−, C+, C, C−, D+, D, and D− are given the values 12, 11, 10, 9, 8, 7, 6, 5, 4, 3, 2, and 1, respectively. A student received an A+ on the social objectives (10 percent), a B− on the mental objectives (40 percent), and a C− on the performance objectives (50 percent). To arrive at a composite score for the student the letter grades are converted to their numerical equivalents, multiplied by the weight of the corresponding objective, and summed:

$$(12 \times 1) + (7 \times 4) + (4 \times 5) = 12 + 28 + 20 = 60.$$

Dividing this sum by 10 (the sum of the weights) and comparing the resulting value to the categories converts this student's performance to a C+.

Normalizing method

The normalizing method should be used when the scores obtained in measuring a trait that is known or believed to be normally distributed do not appear to result in an approximation of the normal curve. If the measurements are ranks, the normal curve will not be approximated, but through the normalizing method the ranks can be converted to standard scores. Other reasons, such as not obtaining a representative sample, may cause a distribution to be other than normal even though the trait being measured is normally distributed. The normalizing method is much like converting a set of raw scores into a distribution of some standard score such as the T-score discussed in Chapter 5. The difference, however, is that the raw scores are first converted to percentile ranks, which in turn are converted into a standard score scale (in most cases T-scores are used). A description of the procedures for converting a set of raw scores into percentile ranks appears in Chapter 5, and the resulting percentile ranks can be converted into T-scores through the use of Table 21.3. As an illustration of how this procedure converts a non-normal distribution into a normal distribution, notice that a score, regardless of its raw score standard deviation distance from the mean, that falls 34.13 percent above the mean (one standard deviation above the mean in a normal curve) is equivalent to a T-score of 60, which is one standard deviation above the mean in the T-score scale.

An example of the normalizing method resulting in a T-score corresponding to each raw score is shown in Table 21.4.

Table 21.3   Conversion of percentile ranks to T-scores

Percentile rank	T-score	Percentile rank	T-score	Percentile rank	T-score
.02	15	13.57	39	90.32	63
.03	16	15.87	40	91.92	64
.05	17	18.41	41	93.32	65
.07	18	21.19	42	94.52	66
.10	19	24.20	43	95.54	67
.13	20	27.43	44	96.41	68
.19	21	30.85	45	97.13	69
.26	22	34.46	46	97.72	70
.35	23	38.21	47	98.21	71
.47	24	42.07	48	98.61	72
.60	25	46.02	49	98.93	73
.82	26	50.00	50	99.18	74
1.07	27	53.98	51	99.38	75
1.39	28	57.93	52	99.53	76
1.79	29	61.79	53	99.65	77
2.28	30	65.54	54	99.74	78
2.87	31	69.15	55	99.81	79
3.59	32	72.57	56	99.87	80
4.46	33	75.80	57	99.90	81
5.48	34	78.81	58	99.93	82
6.68	35	81.59	59	99.95	83
8.08	36	84.13	60	99.97	84
9.68	37	86.43	61	99.98	85
11.51	38	88.49	62		

Note: Although the T-score scale theoretically extends from 0 to 100, in actual practice T-scores lower than 15 or higher than 85 are rare and thus are not included in the table.

Table 21.4   Example of normalizing method

Raw score	f	cf	cfm	pr	T-score (from Table 21.3)
85	1	6	5.5	91.7	64
74	1	5	4.5	75.0	57
63	1	4	3.5	58.4	52
59	1	3	2.5	41.7	48
53	1	2	1.5	25.0	43
47	1	1	0.5	8.4	36
	6				

The determination of percentile ranks is dependent only on frequency of occurence. Therefore, if the ranks of 1, 2, 3, 4, 5, and 6 are substituted in Table 21.4 for the raw scores of 85, 74, 63, 59, 53, and 47, respectively, the resulting T-scores would not be changed.

Standard score method

If the raw score distribution can be assumed to closely approximate a normal distribution, conversion of the raw scores to a standard score scale such as the T-score scale can be accomplished as described in Chapter 5. The net result of this procedure is, as in the normalizing method, a T-score corresponding to each raw score.

If all sets of scores are converted to T-scores or some other standard scale, a common basis exists for comparing scores made on two different tests even though the two raw scores are expressed in different units. More important to the present discussion, it becomes possible to add T-scores representing various achievements to obtain meaningful composite scores that can be used in determining final grades. Weighting of the various objectives can be accomplished as in the ranking system by simply multiplying the T-score by the appropriate constants determined by the teacher.

Once a composite score is obtained for each student, the final step is to change this score to the appropriate symbol of the particular format being used. As in each of the other three steps, various factors will affect how this is done. The decision of what procedures to follow is based on the form of the composite score, policies of the school system or department, and the preference of the individual teacher.

STEP 4—CONVERT COMPOSITE SCORES TO THE SYMBOL FORMAT CHOSEN

If one of the methods in step three is followed, the composite scores will be in one of two forms. Each student will have a total or average ranking or a total or average standard score. In effect both of these forms are actually an ordering of the students, although in the ranking method usually the lowest total (or lowest average) represents the best achievement while in the standard score method the highest total (or highest average) represents the best achievement. The procedures for converting the set of composite scores to grades are similar regardless of the form and involve answering two related questions. Is the class to be graded below, at, or above average in achievement of the course objectives in comparison to other similar classes? What percentage of the students should receive each particular symbol of the chosen format?

If tests and measuring devices were absolutely reliable and valid and if course objectives remained constant over time, these questions would not need to be answered prior to converting composite scores to grades. However, measurements are not perfect, objectives change, unexpected or events unplanned occur, facilities and equipment change over time, and several other factors make it impossible to compare the achievement of the current class to previous classes on a strictly objective basis. Grading is especially difficult for new teachers because of the lack of experience on which to base the answers to these questions. After arriving at some subjective answers several methods can be used to convert the composite scores to symbols. Two of these methods and some common variations of them are presented below.

Percentage method

The percentage method may be used with composite scores in the form of rankings or standard scores since it is not the value of the score that matters but its position in the distribution. Once the teacher makes the decision as to the percentage of each symbol to be assigned it remains only to multiply these various percentage values by the number of students in the class. The resulting products are the actual numbers of each symbol to be assigned. For example, for a class of forty-five students, which on the basis of test scores and other evidence has achieved substantially above the average of other similar classes, a teacher decides to allot 15 percent A's, 25 percent B's, 45 percent C's, 10 percent D's, and 5 percent F's. Multiplying (and rounding) each percentage by 45 would result in the seven highest-ranking students being assigned A's; the next eleven, B's; the next twenty, C's; the next five, D's; and the two lowest ranking students, F's.

If the composite scores are in the form of standard scores or the sum (or average) of several rankings (but not if the composite scores are a single rank in which the best student has a rank of 1, the second best student has a rank of 2, and so on), it is possible to modify the percentage method slightly by noticing natural breaks in the distribution of the composite scores. If in the above illustration, for example, the composite scores of the seventh and eighth best students differed by very little, it would be difficult to justify assigning an A to the student ranking seventh and a B to the student ranking eighth. Depending on the value of the composite scores of the students who ranked sixth and ninth, it may be that the students who ranked seventh and eighth should both be assigned A's or, perhaps, B's. In other words, natural breaks occurring in the composite score distribution should be considered, especially around the areas where a change occurs in the grade to be assigned. Knowing that virtually all measurements made in physical education contain some unreliability, a teacher is on safer ground stating that a difference exists between the achievement levels of two students whose composite scores differ by five points rather than by one point.

Curve method

Although "grading on the curve" is a phrase often heard in educational settings, it is not well understood. Actually, grading on the curve is a variation of the percentage method in which the assumption is made that the differences in student ability in a class are normally or at least approximately normally distributed and thus the percentages of each symbol assigned are determined through use of the normal curve.

Some of the confusion about grading on the curve stems from the fact that it is possible to approach the problem from two directions. The practical limits of the normal curve (±3 standard deviations) can be equally divided into the number of different symbols to be assigned, or certain standard deviation distances from the mean may simply be selected as the limits for each symbol assigned.

To illustrate each approach the data presented in Table 3.1 will be used and it will be assumed that the sixty-five scores represent the composite scores for a class of sixty-five students. Situation: The composite scores for sixty-five students have been compiled, and the teacher desires to use the normal curve to determine the cutting points for assigning the grades of A, B, C, D, and F.

The mean and standard deviation of the composite scores are determined. For the sixty-five scores these values are 63.4 and 14.9, respectively.

For practical purposes the normal curve may be considered to extend ± 3 standard deviation units above and below the mean. (Recall that 99.73 percent of the area under the normal curve occurs between these two points.) This total distance of six standard deviation units is divided equally into the same number of parts as different symbols are to be assigned. In the illustration this number is 5. This results in each of the five symbols encompassing 1.2 standard deviation units of the normal curve ($6 \div 5 = 1.2$).

Since the grading format chosen in this illustration has an uneven number of symbols, one-half of the middle symbol (C) falls on either side of the mean. Thus a grade of C will be assigned to those students who composite scores lie between .6 standard deviation units above and .6 standard deviation units below the mean. Notice that the total distance encompassing C grades is .6 + .6, or 1.2 standard deviation units.

Grades of B will be assigned to students whose composite scores are between .6 and 1.8 standard deviation units above the mean; grades of D will be assigned to those whose composite scores lie between .6 and 1.8 standard deviation units below the mean. The 1.8 value is obtained by adding the standard deviation distance each grade is to encompass, 1.2, to .6.

If this process is continued, it will result in the limits of 1.8 and 3.0 standard deviation units above the mean for grades of A and 1.8 and 3.0 standard deviation units below the mean for grades of F. One can simply specify, however, that composite scores more than 1.8 standard deviations above the mean correspond to A's and composite scores more than 1.8 standard deviations below the mean correspond to F's.

The final procedure involves expressing the standard deviation units in terms of the composite score values. Since one standard deviation is equivalent to 14.9 composite score units, the cutting point between C's and B's and between C's and D's must lie 8.94 composite score units above and below the mean, respectively. The value of 8.94 results from multiplying 14.9 by .6. The two cutting points are 72.3 and 54.4 (63.4 ± 8.94). The cutting points between B's and A's and between D's and F's are obtained by adding to and subtracting from the mean the product of 14.9 × 1.8. The resulting product is 26.82, and the cutting points are 90.2 and 36.6.

In Figure 21.2 the relationship among the standard deviation units, composite score units, and grades are shown. For simplification the teacher would probably round off the cutting points and establish a conversion chart for assigning grades to the composite scores. Such a conversion chart is shown in Table 21.5.

By using Table 5.1 in Chapter 5, it is possible to determine the percentage of the area of the normal curve that lies between the various standard deviation units obtained in Figure 21.1. If a grading format involving five symbols is used in conjunction with the normal curve the teacher is in effect de-

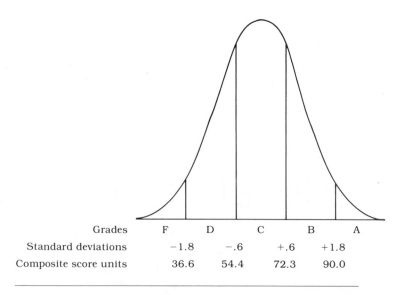

Grades	F	D	C	B	A
Standard deviations	−1.8	−.6	+.6	+1.8	
Composite score units	36.6	54.4	72.3	90.0	

Figure 21.1   Relationship among grades, standard deviation units, and composite score units

Table 21.5 Conversion of composite scores to grades: first approach

Composite score	Grade
91 or over	A
73–90	B
55–72	C
38–54	D
37 or below	F

ciding to assign approximately 3.5 percent A's, 24 percent B's, 45 percent C's, 24 percent D's, and 3.5 percent F's.

Applying the conversion chart displayed in Table 21.5 to the 65 composite scores results in the assignment of three A's (4.6 percent), fifteen B's (23.1 percent), thirty C's (46.1 percent), fourteen D's (21.6 percent), and three F's (4.6 percent). Slight differences occur between the normal curve percentages and the actual percentages due to rounding in establishing the conversion chart and the fact that the set of sixty-five scores is not exactly normally distributed.

The second approach to grading on the curve, that of selecting certain standard deviation distances from the mean as the limits for each symbol, is also based on the assumption that the differences in student ability in a class are, at least, approximately normally distributed. In this approach, instead of dividing the six standard deviations (the practical limit of the normal curve) into equal units for each symbol, distances are selected that conform to the teacher's notion of the percentage of each symbol to be assigned. As one of an infinite number of possibilities, a teacher may decide on the limits depicted in Table 21.6.

The selection of these particular standard deviation distances would result in assigning approximately 7 percent A's, 25 percent B's, 36 percent C's, 25 percent D's, and 7 percent F's to a set of normally distributed scores. As in the first approach, these standard deviations must be converted to the units

Table 21.6 Curve grading by selecting standard deviation distances

Standard deviation distance	Grade
above +1.48	A
+.47 to +1.48	B
−.47 to +.47	C
−1.48 to −.47	D
below −1.48	F

of the composite scores by multiplying the selected constants by the standard deviation of the composite scores. For the data used in the previous example (mean = 63.4 and standard deviation = 14.9), the resulting cutting points are displayed in Table 21.7.

Table 21.7   Conversion of composite scores to grades: Second approach

Composite score	Grade
86 and above	A
71 – 85	B
57 – 70	C
41 – 56	D
40 and below	F

Application of this conversion chart to the sixty-five composite scores results in the assignment of five A's (7.7 percent), sixteen B's (24.6 percent), twenty-three C's (35.3 percent), sixteen D's (24.6 percent), and five F's (7.7 percent). As before, slight differences between the normal curve percentages and the actual percentages occur due to rounding and the fact that the sixty-five scores are not exactly normally distributed.

Although any set of standard deviation distances may be chosen, if the assumption regarding normality is assumed true, the selected values will necessarily result in a symmetrical assignment of grades. If a nonsymmetrical distribution of grades is desired, the second approach to curve grading actually becomes the percentage method described previously.

Glossary

Ability grouping   Placing students into groups that are homogeneous in respect to some trait, such as scholastic ability or physical skills.

Abscissa   The horizontal or X-axis in the Cartesian coordinate system.

Absolute marking system   The procedure of determining grades on the basis of previously set criteria of performance.

Achievement test   A test designed to measure the extent to which a student has grasped some body of knowledge.

Adjective checklist   A measurement technique used primarily in the affective domain. Adjectives reflecting one's current state are selected from a large number of possibilities.

Affective domain   Area concerned with objectives of interests, attitudes, values, and the development of appreciations.

Age norm   The average score achieved by students of a particular age group. Age norms usually present average scores for several different ages.

Alignometer   A device consisting of two horizontal calibrated pointers attached to a vertical pole used for teaching and measuring posture.

Analytic scoring   A method of scoring responses to essay questions that involves identifying specific facts, points, or ideas in the answer and awarding credit for each one located.

Anecdotal record   A written account made by a teacher to record the details of an event involving one or more students.

Anthropometry   The study of human body measurements.

Aptitude test   A test designed to measure potential in a particular area.

Attitude   An emotion or feeling toward some fact or state.

Average   A term designating any of several measures of central tendency, such as the median, mean, or mode.

Battery   A group of tests usually administered together for measuring some characteristic.

Bimodal distribution   A set of data having two distinct points at which scores tend to concentrate.

Bipolar adjectives   A set of two descriptive words opposite in meaning, such as fast-slow or good-bad, used in some types of attitudinal measurement instruments.

Body image   The perceptions one has about his or her body and its parts.

Calipers   A measuring instrument having two adjustable jaws for assessing thickness, diameter, and distance between surfaces.

Cardiovascular fitness   The ability of the heart and circulatory system to respond (particularly to the stress of exercise).

Central tendency   A point in a distribution of scores chosen to represent all of the scores due to its central location. The median, mean, and mode are examples of measures of central tendency.

Checklist   A list of items to be looked for when measurement is made using observation techniques.

Classification questions   A written test question format in which the same set of responses is used for several stem questions.

Cognitive domain   Area concerned with objectives that deal with the recall or recognition of knowledge and the development of intellectual skills and abilities.

Completion question   A written test question format requiring the student to correctly fill in or finish an incomplete statement, sentence, or pattern.

Composite score   A single value used to express the result of combining several scores.

Concurrent validity   The degree to which a test correlates with a criterion measure obtained at nearly the same time as the test scores.

Construct validity   The degree to which a test measures an intangible quality or attribute (such as sportsmanship or creativity).

Content validity   The extent to which the items on a test adequately sample the subject matter and abilities that the test was designed to measure.

Continuous data   Data that may take any value within a defined range of values—that is, data that are capable of any amount of subdivision, such as weight or distance.

Correlation   The degree of relationship between two or more sets of measurements obtained from the same individuals.

Correlation coefficient   A statistical calculation procedure resulting in a coefficient expressing the relationship between two variables.

Criterion score   A measurement used as a standard by which one or more other measures of the same trait can be evaluated.

Cumulative frequency   The number of scores that lie below a given point in a frequency distribution.

Cumulative frequency of the midpoint   The number of scores that lie below the midpoint of a given interval in a frequency distribution.

Curve method   A technique for assigning grades based on the assumption that student abilities are approximately normally distributed.

Data   Factual information used for reasoning or computation.

Descriptive statistics   A branch of statistics that describes the properties of a set of data.

Deviation   The distance a score lies from some specific reference point.

Diastolic pressure   The pressure exerted by the blood in the vascular system during the diastole or resting portion of the heart beat.

Dichotomous data   Data capable of being subdivided into only two categories, such as pass-fail.

Difficulty index   A numerical expression of the proportion of individuals answering a written question correctly.

Discrete data   Data that can only take specific values and are not capable of indefinite subdivision. The number of people in a room is an example of a discrete variable.

Discrimination index   A numerical expression reflecting the extent to which students who are judged to be good in terms of some criterion succeed on a written test item and those who are judged to be poor by the same criterion fail on the item.

Dispersion   The variability or spread of a distribution of scores around some measure of central tendency.

Distractor   Any of the incorrect options in a multiple-chioce or matching test item.

Dynamic repetitive exercise   A method of measuring muscular endurance that requires a student to perform as many repetitions of a specified movement as possible.

Dynamic timed exercise   A method of measuring muscular endurance that requires a student to perform as many repetitions of a specified movement as possible within a given time period.

Ectomorphy   A body type typified by fragility, slenderness, and angularity.

Endomorphy   A body type typified by heaviness, roundness, and softness.

Endurance   The ability to sustain movement over time.

Equivalent forms   Two or more tests designed for measuring the same characteristics or attributes.

Error score   The difference between an observed score and its corresponding true score.

Essay question   A type of question that requires a student to compose a written response.

Evaluation   A judgment of merit based on a comparison of various measurements, impressions, and other evidence to some standard.

Frequency distribution   An arrangement of data where the frequency of scores similar in value is tabulated by placing like scores into groups called intervals.

Frequency polygon   A graphing technique to display the characteristics of a set of data. The graph is constructed by (1) plotting on the X-axis the midpoints of each of the intervals from a frequency distribution; (2) plotting above each of these points the corresponding frequency on the Y-axis; and (3) connecting the resulting points.

Global scoring   A method of assessing responses to essay questions that involves converting the general impression obtained from reading the answer into a score.

Grade norm   The average score achieved by students in a particular grade in school. Grade norms usually present average scores for several different grades.

Grouped data   Data that have been arranged in such a manner that scores similar in value are grouped together as in a frequency distribution.

Grouping error   The error introduced when scores are grouped in a frequency distribution which results from each score in an interval being represented by the midpoint of the interval.

Halo effect   The tendency of a scorer or rater to be biased in the evaluation of some specific ability because of a general attitude toward the student being measured.

Heterogeneity   The condition of being unlike. This description is often applied to the abilities of students and to individual test items.

Histogram   A graphing technique to display the characteristics of a set of data in which the frequency of scores occurring in each interval of a frequency distribution is represented by a vertical bar.

Homogeneity   The condition of being similar. This description is often applied to the abilities of students and to individual test items.

Interlocking items   A condition that sometimes exists on written tests where statements in the stem of one question either answer or give clues to the correct answer of another question.

Internal consistency   The result of a test being composed of items which all measure nearly the same thing. This is a type of reliability.

Interval measurement   A level of measurement resulting in values that permit the making of statements of equality of intervals in addition to statements of sameness or difference (nominal) or greater than or less than (ordinal).

Interval size   The range of score values in an interval in a frequency distribution.

Interview   A meeting at which information is obtained orally from an individual.

Inventory   A written set of questions or tasks constructed to elicit a description rather than a measurement of some aspect of an individual's characteristics.

Isokinetic exercise   An exercise in which a muscle contracts and shortens against an accommodating load or resistance that varies according to the force generated by the muscle.

Isometric exercise   An exercise in which a muscle contracts but does not shorten.

Isotonic exercise   An exercise in which a muscle contracts and shortens against a set load or resistance.

Item analysis   A process involving the examination of the functioning of individual items on a test.

Keyed response   The one response in a multiple-choice question that is the best answer and thus regareded as the correct response.

Kuder-Richardson formulas   Formulas for estimating the reliability of a written test from a single administration of the test.

Lean body weight   The amount of an individual's body weight that is not fat. Generally this is estimated through the substitution of various anthropometric measurements in appropriate formulas.

Level of significance   The probability of determining that a significant difference exists between two statistics when it actually does not.

Mark   Symbol used to indicate level of achievement; a grade.

Mastery test   A test designed to measure whether or not a student has achieved enough to satisfy a prescribed standard or criterion.

Matching questions   A test format that requires a student to select an item from one list that is most closely associated with an item from another list.

Mean   A measure of central tendency calculated by adding all of the scores and dividing the resulting sum by the number of scores.

Mean deviation   A measure of the amount of variation in a set of scores calculated by dividing the sum of the absolute values of the deviations from the mean by the number of scores.

Measurement   The process of assigning numerical or symbolic values to members of a group for the purpose of distinguishing among the members on the basis of the degree to which they possess the characteristic being assessed.

Measures of central tendency   Statistics such as the median, mean, and mode that reflect the center of a distribution of scores.

Median   The point in a set of scores above and below which fifty percent of the scores fall.

Mesomorphy   A body type typified by huskiness and muscularity.

Midpoint   The point halfway between the limits of an interval in a frequency distribution.

Mode   The most frequently occurring score in a distribution.

Motor ability   The innate and learned ability to perform fundamental motor tasks.

Motor capacity   The innate ability to learn motor tasks.

Motor educability   The ability to quickly learn unfamiliar complex motor tasks.

Motor fitness   The ability to perform efficiently large muscle motor activities involving agility, balance, power, and speed.

Multiple-choice questions   A written test format requiring a student to select the best of two or more responses to a direct question or incomplete statement.

Multiple correlation   The degree of relationship between a criterion variable and the weighted sum of two or more other variables.

Muscular endurance   The ability of a muscle or muscle group to sustain movement and/ or contraction for a period of time.

Muscular strength   The ability of a muscle or muscle group to exert force.

Musical rhythmic ability   The ability to recognize an ordered recurrent alternation of strong and weak elements in the flow of sound.

Net D   An index of discrimination for written test items that indicates the proportion of good discriminations remaining after neutral and bad discriminations are removed.

Nominal measurement   A level of measurement that permits only the making of statements of sameness or difference.

Norm   The average or typical score or measure for individuals of a specific group. Norms are usually compiled into tables displaying the average score value for a series of varying homogeneous groups.

Normal curve   A theoretically defined distribution that is bell shaped and characterized by a large concentration of scores near the middle and a gradually declining number of scores toward the extremes.

Normalizing method   A statistical procedure for transforming any distribution of scores into one whose characteristics approximate the normal distribution.

Objective questions   Questions that can be scored by comparison to predetermined correct answers thus eliminating subjectivity in the scoring procedure.

Objectivity   The aspect of test reliability that is concerned with effect of variability in scores resulting from different people administering and scoring a test.

Observed score   The score, which may or may not contain error, that is obtained with the application of any measurement process.

Open book test   A test format permitting a student to consult notes and books during the test.

Ordinal measurement   A level of measurement that permits the ordering of the students measured in addition to statements of sameness or difference (nominal).

Ordinate   The vertical or *Y*-axis in the Cartesian coordinate system.

Pass-fail system   A system of grading where a previously set criterion is used to determine whether a student passes or fails a test, course, or whatever is being graded.

Pearson Product-Moment Correlation Coefficient   A numerical expression of the degree of relationship between two sets of scores. The value ranges between plus 1 and minus 1 and is symbolized by the letter *r*.

Percentage method   A method of converting composite scores into marks or grades by multiplying the percentage of each symbol decided on by the number of students to be graded.

Percentile   The point in a distribution below which a given percentage of the scores lies.

Percentile norms   A table displaying the percentile ranks for various score values in a distribution.

Percentile rank   A number representing the percentage of scores in a distribution lying below a given score.

Predictive validity   The degree to which a test makes accurate forecasts concerning the future behavior it is designed to measure.

Profile   A graphic technique for displaying the results of several measures expressed in the same units.

Psychomotor domain   Area concerned with objectives that deal with movement and factors that influence movement.

Q-sort technique   A technique for standardizing the measurement of the applicability of various statements to a specific student.

Questionnaire   A measuring instrument composed of written questions pertaining to a specific topic and generally used in the gathering of descriptive and attitudinal information.

Quotient   The result when one number is divided by another. Often used to allow comparison of initially unlike students by dividing a performance score by an appropriate norm value.

Range   The number of possible score values between two specified extremes. The range is calculated by adding 1 to the difference between the highest and lowest score.

Rank difference correlation coefficient   A statistical technique for calculating a correlation coefficient for measurements made at the ordinal level.

Rank method   A method of combining various measures for each individual into a composite score based on assigning ranks to performances and summing the ranks.

Rating scale   A scale used to increase consistency among judges when rating a quality, trait, or attribute.

Ratio measurement   A level of measurement that permits the making of statements of equality of ratios, such as one variable is twice another, in addition to statements of sameness or difference (nominal), greater or less than (ordinal), and equality of intervals (interval).

Raw score   The measurement first obtained in the scoring of a test before any transformation of the data occurs.

Regression equation   An equation derived through statistical procedures used to predict one variable based upon knowledge of scores on one or more other variables.

Relative marking system   A grading system in which students are graded in respect to the achievement of their peers rather than in accordance to a previously determined criterion.

Relative scoring   A method of scoring responses to essay questions that involves reading all the answers to one question and arranging the papers in order according to their adequacy.

Reliability   The extent to which a test consistently yields the same results when repeated under the same conditions.

Reliability coefficient   A mathematical expression of the degree of association between or among variables.

Responses   The choices listed under the stem for a multiple-choice question; includes the keyed response and the distractors.

Round-robin tournament   A tournament format structured in such a way that every player or team plays every other player or team.

Scale   A sequential gradation of scores used to indicate various degrees of some characteristic.

Scatter   The amount of heterogeneity among scores in a distribution; variability.

Scatter diagram   A graphic device for depicting the degree of association between two sets of scores. Scores on one variable are located on the abscissa, the corresponding score is located on the ordinate, and a dot is made at the junction. The resulting dots display the association present.

Score   A symbol, usually numerical, assigned to describe the quality or quantity of performance.

Self-report   A process for obtaining an individual's own appraisal of himself or herself. Usually requests a person's personal evaluation of abilities, characteristics, or performances.

Semantic differential   A measurement technique to assess an individual's perception of various concepts. A student is required to rate the concept of interest on several scales (usually five- or seven-point scales) with bipolar adjectives such as "weak" and "strong" located at each end.

Semi-interquartile range   One-half of the range between the 25th percentile and the 75th percentile.

Semiobjective question   A question format, such as short answer, completion, or mathematical problems, that may require some subjective judgment on the part of the scorer.

Short answer question   A question format that requires the individual to compose an answer as for an essay question, but constraints are placed on the length of the response.

Significant difference   A large enough difference between two statistics that the probability that the difference can be attributed to chance is less than some defined limit.

Skewness   A property of a distribution that occurs when there is a relatively high frequency of scores above the mean (negative skew) or below the mean (positive skew).

Skinfold measurement   An anthropometric measurement procedure for determining body composition. Calipers are used to assess the amount of subcutaneous and fat tissue.

Social distance scale   A sociometric device used to determine the degree to which an individual accepts or rejects each of the members of a specified group.

Sociogram   A sociometric device for obtaining preferences among individuals in a group in order to assess the social structure of the group.

Sociometric device   Any of several techniques requiring individuals in a group to rate one another in various ways for the purpose of gathering personal-social information.

Somatotype   A body structure classification system.

Spearman-Brown Prophecy Formula   A formula used to estimate the reliability of a lengthened test provided the material added to the test is similar in nature to that already on the test.

Specific determiner   A word or phrase in a true-false test item that provides an unintended clue to the correct answer.

Spinograph   An instrument that through the use of a pointer traces the contour of the spine onto a blackboard for posture assessment.

Split-half reliability coefficient   A numerical expression of reliability based on the correlation between the scores on two halves (generally the odd-numbered items versus the even-numbered items) of the test.

Standard deviation   A unit of measure of the variability or dispersion of a set of scores around their mean. Mathematically the standard deviation equals the square root of the mean of the squared deviations of the scores from the mean of the distribution of scores.

Standard error   The standard deviation of the sampling distribution of a statistic.

Standard norms   Norms in which standard scores corresponding to various levels of performance are presented for members of homogeneous groups.

Standard score   A score transformed in some way from a raw score for simplification of comparison or interpretation.

Standard score method   A method of combining various measures for each individual into a composite score based on summing appropriately weighted standard scores.

Static repetitive exercise   A method of measuring muscular endurance requiring a student to exert a specified force at prescribed intervals until the pace cannot be maintained.

Static timed exercise   A method of measuring muscular endurance requiring a student to maintain a specific position involving muscular contraction for as long as possible.

Statistic   A numerical fact about a set of data.

Stem   The incomplete statement or question portion of a multiple-choice question.

Synthesis   The putting together of elements and parts to form a whole.

Systolic pressure   The pressure exerted by the blood in the vascular system during the systolic or contracting portion of the heart beat.

Table of specifications   A test blueprint specifying the proportion of the test items dealing with each aspect of content and educational objectives.

Take-home test   A test format allowing students to complete the test outside of the school environment.

Test-retest method   A method of examining the reliability of a test by correlating scores for the same individuals on two administrations of the same test.

t-ratio   A statistical procedure used in testing various hypotheses such as whether or not the difference between two means is significant or can be reasonably attributed to chance.

True-false questions   A test question format involving a statement which the student is required to judge as true or false.

True score   A theoretical error-free score for each individual measured.

T-score   A standardized score belonging to a distribution having a mean of 50 and a standard deviation of 10.

Ungrouped data   Data in raw score form. Usually ungrouped data are put in order from low to high or high to low, but like scores are not grouped into intervals.

Validity   The degree to which a test measures what it is intended to measure.

Validity coefficient   A numerical expression of the degree to which a test measures what it is intended to measure.

Variable   A property whereby the members of a group differ from one another.

Variance   A unit of measure of the dispersion of scores about their mean. Mathematically, the variance equals the mean of the squared deviations of the scores from their mean.

z-score   A standard score belonging to a distribution having a mean of 0 and a standard deviation of 1.

Index